FOURTH EDITION

Managing Conflict through Communication

Ruth Anna Abigail
Azusa Pacific University

Dudley D. Cahn
State University of New York, New Paltz

Allyn & Bacon

Boston   Columbus   Indianapolis   New York   San Francisco   Upper Saddle River
Amsterdam   Cape Town   Dubai   London   Madrid   Milan   Munich
Paris   Montreal   Toronto   Delhi   Mexico City   Sao Paulo   Sydney
Hong Kong   Seoul   Singapore   Taipei   Tokyo

Acquisitions Editor: Jeanne Zalesky
Assistant Editor: Megan Lentz
Marketing Manager: Wendy Gordon
Editorial Production Service:
Production Manager: Fran Russello
Manager, Visual Research: Beth Brenzel
Manager, Rights and Permissions: Zina Arabia
Image Permission Coordinator: Kathy Gavilanes
Manager, Cover Visual Research & Permissions: Karen Sanatar
Full-Service Project Management: Shiji Sashi/Integra Software Services Pvt Ltd
Art Director: Jayne Conte
Cover Designer: Bruce Kenselaar
Printer/Binder: Courier Companies, Inc.

Credits and acknowledgments borrowed from other sources and reproduced, with permission, in this textbook appear on appropriate page within text

---

Copyright © 2011 Pearson Education, Inc., publishing as Allyn & Bacon, 75 Arlington Street, Suite 300, Boston, MA 02116. All rights reserved. Manufactured in the United States of America. This publication is protected by Copyright, and permission should be obtained from the publisher prior to any prohibited reproduction, storage in a retrieval system, or transmission in any form or by any means, electronic, mechanical, photocopying, recording, or likewise. To obtain permission(s) to use material from this work, please submit a written request to Pearson Higher Education, Rights and Contracts Department, 501 Boylston Street, Suite 900, Boston, MA 02116, or fax your request to 617-671-3447.

Many of the designations by manufacturers and seller to distinguish their products are claimed as trademarks. Where those designations appear in this book, and the publisher was aware of a trademark claim, the designations have been printed in initial caps or all caps.

Library of Congress Cataloging-in-Publication Data

Abigail, Ruth Anna.
 Managing conflict through communication/Ruth Anna Abigail, Dudley D. Cahn.—4th ed.
   p. cm.
 Rev. ed. of: Managing conflict through communication/Dudley D. Cahn,
Ruth Anna Abigail. 3rd ed.
 Includes bibliographical references and index.
 ISBN-13: 978-0-205-68556-1 (alk. paper)
 ISBN-10: 0-205-68556-0 (alk. paper)
 1. Conflict (Psychology) 2. Interpersonal conflict. 3. Conflict management.
I. Cahn, Dudley D. Managing conflict through communication. II. Title.
BF637.I48L85 2011
303.6—dc22
                                                                    2009048323

10 9 8 7 6 5 4 3 2 1 - CRS - 13 12 11 10 09

Allyn & Bacon
is an imprint of

ISBN-10:   0-205-68556-0
ISBN-13: 978-0-205-68556-1

www.pearsonhighered.com

Contents

Preface   xi

PART I   Managing the Conflict Process   1

1   Introduction to the Study of Conflict   1

Objectives   1

Key Terms   1

Defining Interpersonal Conflict   3

The Inevitability of Conflict   6
  Conflict Is a Fact of Life   6
  Interpersonal Violence Is Not a Fact of Life   7

Defining Conflict Management and Skills   8

Communication Processes in Conflict   9

Conflict Communication as Productive or Destructive   11

Negative View of Conflict   13

Manage It   15

Notes   18

2   A Process View of Conflict   20

Objectives   20

Key Terms   20

Processes in General   21

Patterns and Cycles in Constructive Conflict Processes   22

Patterns and Cycles in Destructive Conflict Processes   26
  The Confrontation Avoidance Cycle and the "Chilling Effect"   27
  The Competitive Escalation and Violence Cycles   30

The Confrontation Process: Six Steps to Successful Interpersonal Conflict Resolution   34
  Preparation: Identify Your Problem/Needs/Issues   35
  Tell the Person "We Need to Talk"   36

Interpersonal Confrontation: Talk to the Other about
Your Problem   36

Consider Your Partner's Point of View   37

Manage the Problem: Come to a Mutual Understanding and Reach
an Agreement   38

Follow Up on the Solution: Set a Time Limit
for Reevaluation   39

Manage It   39

Notes   42

3 Communication Options in Conflict   44

Objectives   44

Key Terms   44

The Other-Centered Orientation: Nonasssertive Communication Behavior as an Option   45

Avoiding as an Option   48

Accommodating as an Option   49

The Self-Centered Orientation: Passive Aggressive and Aggressive Communication as Options   49

Passive-Aggressive Communication as an Option   49

Aggressive Communication Behavior as an Option   51

The Relationship-Centered Orientation: Assertive Communication Behavior as an Option   53

Compromise as an Option   56

Collaboration as an Option   56

Collaboration: The Preferred Approach   57

Low Personal and Relationship Stress   57

High Personal and Relationship Growth and Satisfaction   58

Enacting Collaboration   58

Communication Considerations: Choosing the Appropriate Communication Option   62

The Occasion (Including Time and Location)   62

The Other Person   63

Your Needs   63

Manage It   64

Notes   66

CONTENTS v

4 Responding to Conflict: The S-TLC System 68

Objectives 68

Key Terms 68

Communication in Conflict Situations 69

The S-TLC System 69
- Stopping: Taking Time Out 70
- Thinking about the Conflict: Analyzing Conflict Situations 70
- Listening in Conflict Situations 73
- Communicating in Conflict Situations: I-Statements 74

Manage It 79

Notes 83

5 Managing Win–Lose Conflicts through Negotiation 84

Objectives 84

Key Terms 84

Intangible Issues 85

Tangible Issues 86

Negotiation Basics 88
- Competitive Negotiation 90
- Cooperative Negotiation 90

Manage It 97

Notes 100

PART II Breaking the Cycle of Escalation 102

6 Managing the Conflict Climate 102

Objectives 102

Key Terms 102

The Threat of Power Abuse 103
- Sharing Power 107

The Threat of Competition 109

The Threat of Distrust 111

The Threat of Defensive Behavior 113

Manage It 115

Notes 118

7 Managing Stress 120

Objectives 120

Key Terms 120

Types of Stress 122
- Eustress and Hypostress 122
- Hyperstress 122
- Distress 125

Changing How We Look at Life's Challenges 129
- The First Solution 129
- The Second Solution 130
- The Third Solution 130

Sources of Hyperstress and Distress 131

Constructive and Positive Thoughts/Beliefs as Responses to Hyperstress and Distress 131

Manage It 135

Notes 137

8 Managing Anger 139

Objectives 139

Key Terms 139

Experiencing Anger 142

Managing Anger: Three Different Ways of Expressing or Not Expressing One's Anger 143
- Before Expressing Anger 147
- Expressing Anger Effectively: Dos and Don'ts of Anger Management 149
- Responding to Another's Anger 151

Manage It 152

Notes 154

CONTENTS   vii

9 Managing Face   156

Objectives   156

Key Terms   156

Understanding the Demands of Face   158

Two Types of Face: Positive and Autonomous Face   159

Facework   161
- Preventive Facework   161
- Supportive Facework   163
- Corrective Facework   164
- Repair Rituals   164

Responding to Others   168

Conflict and Impression Management in Cyberspace   169

Manage It   170

Notes   172

10 Managing Conflict through Forgiveness   174

Objectives   174

Key Terms   174

Relational Transgressions   175

Why Study Forgiveness and Reconciliation?   176

Defining Forgiveness and Reconciliation   176

Advantages of Forgiveness   178
- Forgiveness Benefits Our Mental Health   178
- Forgiveness Benefits Our Physical Health   178
- Why Don't People Forgive?   179

Working through Forgiveness   180
- Learning to Forgive   180
- Levels of Forgiveness   180

Working through Reconciliation   182
- Levels of Reconciliation   182
- Steps toward Reconciliation   182

Moving beyond Victimization   187

Seeking Forgiveness   188

Manage It   188

Notes   191

11 Managing Others' Disputes through Mediation   194

Objectives   194

Key Terms   194

Alternatives to Dispute Resolution   195

Formal versus Informal Mediation   196

The Role of the Mediator   197
- Mediators as Communication Rules Enforcers   199

The Mediation Process: Step by Step   200
- Intake   200
- Opening Statement   201
- Describing the Dispute   202
- Common Ground   203
- Final Agreement   205
- Ending the Mediation   206

Manage It   207

Notes   210

PART III   Deeping Our Understanding of Conflict Management   211

12 Managing Conflict from a Theoretical Perspective   211

Objectives   211

Key Terms   211

Intrapersonal Theories of Conflict   212
- Psychodynamic Theory   213
- Attribution Theory   216
- Uncertainty Theory   218

Relationship Theories of Conflict   220
- Social Exchange Theory   220
- Systems Theory   224

Manage It   225

Notes   228

13 Managing Group Conflict 229

Objectives 229

Key Terms 229

The Nature of Conflict in Groups 230
Types of Conflict 231
Conflict as Group Developer 234

When Conflict Creates Poor Outcomes 236
Role Conflict 236
Groupthink 237
The "Abilene Paradox" 238
The "Lucifer Effect" 239

Strategies to Resolve Conflict 240

Manage It 241

Notes 243

14 Managing Organizational Conflict 245

Objectives 245

Key Terms 245

Organizational Diversity and Conflict 246
Civility as a Response 247

Work–Life Conflict 249

Workplace Bullying 251
From the Playground to the Boardroom 251
Managing Bullies 253

Manage It 255

Notes 257

15 Managing Social Conflict 260

Objectives 260

Key Terms 260

Understanding Intractable Issues 261
Patriotism and Nationalism 264

Theories of Social Conflict   266
  Critical Theory   266
  Ripeness Theory   267

Ways of Approaching "The Other"   268

Managing Conflict through Nonviolent Communication   270

Understanding Your Worldview   270
  Components of a Worldview   271
  The Importance of a Worldview   271

Manage It   272

Notes   276

16 Creativity and the Ideal Conflict Manager   277

Objectives   277

Key Terms   277

Creativity as It Relates to Conflict   278
  Traits of Creative People   278
  Why Is Creativity Important?   279
  Misassumptions Preventing Creativity   280

Can We Learn to Be Creative?   280

Barriers to Creativity   280

Creativity as Thinking Differently   282

Creativity as Seeing Differently   284
  Mind Mapping   284
  Visual Journaling   286

Principles of Effective Conflict Management   288

Manage It   299

Notes   302

Index   303

Preface

WHY STUDY CONFLICT?

People tend to feel negatively about conflict, and they do not handle confrontations well. We believe that the common mismanagement of conflict explains the bad name given to the subject. We intend to help you learn more constructive attitudes and more positive conflict management and resolution skills, so that you feel less apprehensive about engaging in interpersonal conflict and better able to manage and resolve it.

Conflict is one of the "grand challenges" of our time, occurring because of deep divisions in our society that carry over into our interpersonal relationships. There are cultural divides between ethnic, racial, and religious groups. There are political and value barriers that separate conservatives and liberals. There are gender gaps between the sexes. There are economic and power divides between upper and lower economic and social classes. There are age barriers between our younger and older citizens. When these divides carry over into interpersonal relations, even people of similar backgrounds find differences difficult to overcome.

Where there is a divide, we look for bridges. An effective bridge in interpersonal relations is communication. As a first step the conflicting parties must meet to deal with the issues that divide them. They must take time out of their busy schedules, allocate resources they may find limited, pay attention to matters they may consider unimportant, and listen in order to create or repair channels of communication that lay a foundation for bridging the gap that separates them. Meeting together and paying attention to the issues and each other is an important first step, but more is needed. In this next step, the conflicting parties must communicate. How do they do that? What do they say? How do they say it? Because they have thoroughly researched the communication processes in conflict situations, communication scholars have a great deal to offer students interested in studying conflict.

First, communication as a discipline offers a wide variety of pedagogical tools for successfully managing conflict situations. Communication textbooks provide general principles and skills that are applicable to conflict situations. Many, like this one, analyze common problems and issues to teach you how to manage conflicts in your everyday life. Our goal is to add to your communication competence. After learning what is effective or "what works," students are often amazed at how a change in their behavior produces such different results.

Second, communication scholars are sensitive to ethical concerns as they create solutions to challenges such as conflict. We are not only interested in "what works" in conflict situations, but what is appropriate. We want everyone to have an equal say in the decisions that affect them, to create mutually satisfying solutions to their problems, and nonviolent solutions that they can live with and support. This may require a moral change along with behavioral changes, so that conflicting parties learn to respect each other and work together in ethical ways to produce morally sound agreements.

Third, many communication scholars view communication, conflict, anger, mediation, and negotiation as processes. A process is dynamic, ongoing, and ever changing. It evolves through steps or stages. Taking a process view of conflict helps students like you to better understand the way conflict changes over time, often escalates, and sometimes gets out of hand, so that you can take concrete steps to change the direction of your own conflicts and intervene in the conflicts of others.

Fourth, communication researchers study the role of stress and negative attitudes as key contributors to conflict—anger as an escalator of conflict, and emotional residues as barriers to reconciliation. These psychological factors are as important as the social and physical behavior of the conflicting parties.

Because of these contributions by the communication discipline, the purpose of this textbook is to apply a communication approach to the study of conflict. While the challenge of conflict initially appears enormous, the subject is divisible into more manageable parts or learning modules. Moreover, as a discipline, communication has identified many principles and techniques that prevent conflicts from resulting in serious damage to the parties involved. Some of these principles and techniques are preventive in nature; others repair channels of communication and restore relations.

WHAT IS NEW IN THIS EDITION?

As we finish this fourth edition of *Managing Conflict through Communication*, we are struck by the fact that our students continue to come to us with little previous conflict training. We have kept that in mind during this revision, making sure that we provide practical advice concerning conflict before delving into more theoretical notions about it. While we do not want to reduce the subject of conflict to mere behavioral techniques, we do wish to help our students learn how to better manage conflict in their everyday lives. We view each chapter as a learning module, beginning with specific objectives, followed by instruction including a summary clearly tied to the opening objectives, and finally ending with practical exercises or rubrics that apply key ideas in the chapter to learners' lives and case studies. Our thinking is that successfully doing the rubrics is an indication that our students have mastered the content.

The new edition is updated to reflect advances in the communication study of conflict. New chapters on Group Conflict, Organizational Conflict, Intractable (social) Conflicts, and Creativity have been included as a result. In addition, following use of the text in class, we have made many changes in the content to increase readability, clarity, and reader interest. Students like to know exactly how to confront someone they know personally and how to better manage their present conflicts. They want to know specifically what to say and exactly how to say it. Introducing the S-TLC system for responding to conflict and six steps to successful confrontation, the first portion of the text responds to the students' need to learn immediately how to effectively deal with problems and issues when they arise.

While preferred ways to manage conflicts are described in the early chapters, in the middle chapters, we hone in on a number of factors that may escalate the conflict and require more advanced management techniques. There we explain these more advanced concepts and techniques that further your skills at managing and resolving interpersonal conflicts in light of the potentially escalating factors. In addition to introducing you to the process nature of conflict and the role emotion plays in escalating conflict, the middle part of the textbook tackles difficult management skills and techniques for dealing with stress and anger, face saving, regulating the conflict climate, forgiving/reconciling, and mediating the conflicts of others.

We include new material in the final set of chapters in an attempt to deepen learners' conflict management understanding and skills. There we focus on relevant communication and conflict theories, group dynamics, organizational behavior, and moral issues. The textbook concludes with a chapter on the creative management of conflicts and "ideal conflict manager," which summarizes the key techniques and principles described in earlier chapters.

As you use this book, remember that conflict often results in personal change. Expect to question thoughts, feelings, and behaviors that you have taken for granted in the past and to add new ideas and actions to your ways of thinking and behaving.

ACKNOWLEDGMENTS

The most important people for us to thank are the students who have used the first three editions of the book and have given us great feedback about its utility. We also want to thank all the students who permitted us to use their stories in illustrating the concepts in this book.

RUTH ANNA'S ACKNOWLEDGMENTS

First, I'd like to thank the many students who used this book in my classes and offered suggestions for revisions, as well as letting me use their stories to illustrate important points. I'd also like to thank Barbara Baker and Shelley Lane. We all met at USC in 1979 and it would be hard for me to estimate the impact both have had on my life. Thanks, my good friends!

I would also like to thank the members of my department, the Center for Adult and Professional Studies at Azusa Pacific University, and especially Fred Garlett (EJ), my dean, who have all been a great support to me in my scholarly endeavors. Thanks especially to the "hall people" who help me maintain sanity and perspective: Frank Berry, Stephanie Fenwick, Brent Wood, and Sarah Visser. Special thanks also to the circle of friends: Trish Hanes, Joyce Kirk-Moore, Leah Klingseis, Rebecca Knippelmeyer, Caron Rand, Gillian Symonds, Julia Underwood and Melanie Weaver—you all know why.

On a personal note, I thank my husband, Bogdan Mulka, for laughter, conversation, and wonderful times. Thank you for encouraging my creative endeavors, whether writing or making art. My adult children, Kathy and David Lulofs, continue to bring me joy and fill me with pride.

LEE'S ACKNOWLEDGMENTS

In the previous revision, I felt strongly that it was time to respond to the assessment movement in American colleges by adding more practical and applied material to the text and writing with an eye on outcomes, hence the "management" orientation to the previous edition. However, this time around, I have my coauthor Ruth Anna Abigail to thank for taking the reins on this edition and adding theoretical and intellectually challenging set of chapters, which we added as Part 3.

As in previous editions, I have my students to thank for their help and input. This is probably due to the fact that I also teach this course entirely online, which is quite a different experience from teaching face to face. Students seem more open to express themselves online, revealing what they don't know as much as what they do. From their comments, I am able to determine their needs and problems reading the text, doing the assignments, and discussing the key ideas. Because I found myself explaining more and revising parts of our early edition of this textbook, I feel that there is a better way to organize the chapters and explain some of the key concepts and principles. Thanks to my students for their input and encouragement, the end result is a clearer work with a broader perspective than our earlier editions.

As I have done in earlier works, I would like to express my appreciation to the many scholars who have shared with me their ideas, criticisms, and suggestions on the books I have written on conflict. Among them (in alphabetical order) are William Benoit, Charles Brown, Nancy Burrell, Daniel Canary, Donald Cushman, Clare Danielsson, Steve Duck, Sally Lloyd, Loreen Olson, Michael Roloff, Teresa Sabourin, Stella Ting-Toomey, Steve Wilson, and Dolf Zillmann. I have been most fortunate to know them all and work with them on the subject of conflict or family violence.

Like many other authors, I have my spouse to thank for her patience, understanding, and willingness to put up with my mood swings and occasional fuzziness she could see in my eyes as I would swing from attention to inattention, which occurred as I reflected on what I had recently written or realized that I should have written instead. Sharon has strongly encouraged my writing efforts and allowed me a lot of time and the necessary space to accomplish this project like she did for the ones before. I appreciate the fact that, while we have learned how to collaborate as our marriage evolved, she did not see this project as an issue for a family conflict.

CHAPTER 1

Introduction to the Study of Conflict

OBJECTIVES

At the end of this chapter, you should be able to:

- Define interpersonal conflict and give examples of conflict situations.
- Explain why conflict is a fact of life.
- Explain why violence is not a fact of life.
- Define conflict management and give examples.
- Explain how conflict management has the potential to convert potentially destructive interpersonal conflicts into productive ones.
- Explain why many people view conflict negatively.
- Explain how people could view conflict positively.

KEY TERMS

communication: linear vs. transactional
conflict management
conflict metaphor
conflict resolution
destructive conflict
emotional residues
incompatible goals
incompatible means
inevitability of conflict principle
interdependence
interpersonal conflict
interpersonal violence
meta-conflict perspective
negative view of conflict
outcomes
positive view of conflict
problematic situation
productive conflict
sense of urgency
situation

For the longest time, I thought conflict was like having a big wave come at me on the beach. If I moved fast enough, I might be able to dive under it. Sometimes I could just stand my ground against it. And other times, it knocked me on my rear. But until recently, I didn't really think I could ride that wave, to turn it into something useful. I'm not sure I can do that with all my conflicts—I am better off diving under some, but they don't knock me down as often as they used to.

If you are like most people, you probably would rather not have conflict knock you down or cause you to go diving to avoid it. On the contrary, you probably want to know how to confront someone you know personally and how to better handle your present conflicts. You want to know what you can say and how you can say it. To meet this need, we designed this textbook to help you use effective communication behavior to manage your everyday conflicts. We believe that if you learn how to apply basic conflict management principles in conflicts while in college, you may continue to use these ideas and techniques after you graduate in your future partnerships, family, work, and other important interpersonal relationships.

In this chapter, we introduce you to the study of a subject that is as common as getting up in the morning: dealing with conflict in our everyday lives. Most of us are able to recognize when we are in a conflict. If a friend says, "We need to talk," we know a different situation exists than "I need to talk to you." If a friend needs to talk *to* us, we can act as a sounding board or a source of advice, but when a friend says, "*we* need to talk," we usually know there's a problem, and the problem includes us.

Conflict is one of the grand challenges of our time. It occurs because there are deep divisions in our society that carry over into our interpersonal relationships. There are cultural divides between ethnic, racial, and religious groups. There are political and value barriers that separate conservatives and liberals, gender gaps between the sexes, economic and power divides between upper and lower economic and social classes, and age barriers between younger and older citizens. While we typically think of these divides as the source of conflict in interpersonal relations, even people of similar backgrounds find it difficult to overcome differences.

Where there is a divide, we must look for bridges. A common bridge for barriers in interpersonal relations is communication. As a first step in communicating, the conflicting parties must meet to deal with the issues that divide them. They must take time out of their busy schedules, pay attention to matters they consider unimportant, perhaps spend money and allocate often-limited resources, and listen to people they would like to ignore. In so doing, the conflicting parties create or repair channels of communication and thus lay a foundation for bridging the gap that separates them. Sometimes it takes outside intervention to bring the conflicting parties together.

Meeting together and paying attention to the issues and to each other is an important first step, but more initiatives are needed to put an end to the conflict. In the next step, the conflicting parties must communicate. How do they communicate? What do they say? How do they say it? Communication scholars have thoroughly researched the communication processes in conflict situations and thus have a great deal to offer students interested in studying conflict.

First, communication as a discipline offers a wide variety of pedagogical tools for successfully managing conflict situations. Communication textbooks provide general principles and skills that are applicable to conflict situations. Many, like this one, analyze specific common problems and issues to teach you how to manage conflicts in your everyday life. Our goal is to add to your communication competence. After learning what is effective, students are often amazed at how a change in behavior can produce such dramatic results. They are pleased to discover that they can learn something useful and desirable in a communication course that studies conflict management.

Second, communication scholars are sensitive to ethical concerns as they create solutions to challenges such as conflict. They are interested not only in what works in conflict situations but also in what is appropriate. They want everyone to have input, to have an equal say in the decisions that affect them, and to create mutually satisfying solutions to their problems—nonviolent solutions that they can live with and continue to support. This may require a moral change in addition to behavioral changes, so that conflicting parties learn to respect each other and work together in ethical ways to produce morally sound agreements.

Taking into consideration the communication discipline's contributions, the purpose of this textbook is to apply a communication approach to the study of conflict. Although the challenge of conflict initially appears enormous, the subject is divisible into manageable parts. Moreover, as a discipline, communication has identified many principles and techniques that prevent conflicts from resulting in serious damage to the parties involved. Some of these principles and techniques are preventive in nature; others repair channels of communication and restore relations.

Our approach to managing conflict is to provide solid information at the outset that prepares you to start dealing with your conflicts immediately, followed by information that deepens your understanding of conflict. In Part I, we define conflict, illustrate conflict as a process, and provide an overview to the different means of communicating in a conflict situation. In addition, we demonstrate useful techniques for communicating in conflict situations: steps to effectively confront conflicts, the stop-think-listen-and-communicate (S-TLC) system, and negotiation. We close Part I with a discussion of the ways in which people's communication behaviors contribute to the climate of the conflict. In Part II, we demonstrate how to better manage your handling of various factors that contribute to conflict escalation and containment—namely, stress, anger, loss of face, and emotional residues. In Part III, we discuss various ideas that deepen your theoretical knowledge of conflict, such as social-psychological theories of conflict, problem solving, mediation, and viewing conflict on a larger scale.

To start the learning process, then, in this chapter we define interpersonal conflict and discuss some of the different ways people view it. We believe that conflict is not simply a part of life; *conflict is life as usual*. People regularly experience times when their wants and desires are contradictory to the wants and desires of people important to them. Equally important, we can see no reason for conflicts to ever evolve into violent behavior. Conflicts exist as a fact of life, but we believe violence does not. In addition to defining interpersonal conflict, we also define conflict management and explain how to convert destructive conflicts into productive ones. These ideas make it worth your time and effort to learn how to more effectively manage your interpersonal conflicts.

DEFINING INTERPERSONAL CONFLICT

English-speaking people use many different terms as synonyms for interpersonal conflict or their experience of it: *confrontation, verbal argument, disagreement, differences of opinion, avoidance of confrontation, avoiding others, changing the topic, problem-solving discussion, interpersonal violence, physical abuse, sexual abuse, verbal abuse, silent treatment, stonewalling, glaring at one another, making obscene gestures, expressions of anger, hostile reactions, ignoring the other, unhappy relationships, simply giving in, accommodating, going along reluctantly, not making waves, competition, negotiation, bargaining, mediation, disputing, quarreling, threatening,* and *insulting*. Even though this is a long list, you can probably add to it. Because there are so many events people refer to as conflict, we think it is important that we have a common reference point in the form of a definition for interpersonal conflict as we begin this text.

We define **interpersonal conflict** as a problematic situation with the following four unique characteristics:

1. the conflicting parties are interdependent,
2. they have the perception that they seek incompatible goals or outcomes or they favor incompatible means to the same ends,
3. the perceived incompatibility has the potential to adversely affect the relationship leaving emotional residues if not addressed, and
4. there is a sense of urgency about the need to resolve the difference.

If you are like a lot of us, when you first read a definition of a key term, you don't realize all that the definition entails. So, let's consider what is interesting, unique, and useful about the way we define interpersonal conflict. First, our definition focuses on the idea of a **situation,** which exists where there are people who play out particular roles in a given context that consists of a familiar setting at a particular time. Many situations tend to recur, so we experience a déjà vu feeling like "we were here before." Buying lunch at a fast-food restaurant is a situation on a small scale; interviewing for a job is a situation on a larger scale. Conflicts are situations that generally exist somewhere between these two examples. **Problematic situations** arise when partners perceive that they seek different outcomes or they favor different means to the same ends. We view conflict as two or more competing responses to a single event, differences between and among individuals, mutual hostility between individuals or groups, or a problem needing resolution.

Instead of focusing on the situation, many other conflict textbook authors define interpersonal conflict as an expressed struggle or conflict interaction, suggesting that it consists of visible interaction or a verbal exchange.[1] However, we recognize that some conflicts are not overt, apparent, or open. Just as one can claim that "we cannot not communicate," a conflict may exist even when people are not arguing or even talking to each other. We can recognize that we are experiencing a conflict long before we actually say or do anything about it. By emphasizing the notion of a conflict situation, we can include people who are not speaking to each other, purposively avoiding contact, giving each other the silent treatment, using nonverbal displays to indicate conflict, or who are sending mixed messages to each other. For example, one study found that when people experienced negative emotions, they became more evasive and equivocal.[2] Thus, it is likely that when people are first thinking about a conflict, they may not even say anything about it; rather, they may evade the topic or communicate about it in ambivalent terms.

Second, by emphasizing the interdependence between or among the conflicting parties, we focus on conflict in interpersonal relationships. **Interdependence** occurs when those involved in a relationship characterize it as important and worth the effort to maintain. We want to underscore the fact that *interpersonal conflicts occur with people who are important to us.* We may argue with a stranger, have a difficult time returning a defective product to a store, or endure the bad driving habits of another on the road, but these are not examples of interpersonal conflict because the conflicting parties are not interdependent; they have no interpersonal relationship. Some of the skills involved with arguments with strangers overlap the skills taught in this book. If you have to return a product to a store, for example, and you expect resistance or difficulty, explaining the situation carefully using the skills outlined in later chapters should boost your chances of success. However, we don't befriend, love, or intend to live with everyone we meet. While this doesn't give us permission to act irresponsibly, simply because treating people respectfully generally decreases the probability of conflict, it does free us from thinking that we have to worry about our relationship with a person we don't know.

In addition to the perception of a problematic situation experienced by interdependent people, a third characteristic—the idea of incompatible goals or means—is central to definitions of conflict. **Incompatible goals** occur when we are seeking different outcomes; for example, we each want to buy a different car but we can only afford to buy one. **Incompatible means** occur when we want to achieve the same goal but differ in how we should do so; for example, we agree on the same car, but not on whether to finance it or pay cash. Incompatible goals and means can create the perception that the other is frustrating one's attempts to achieve something, or they may create a perception of relationship violation. Simons argued that in conflict people believe another threatens their interests.[3] What we want to emphasize is this: Whether or not people's perceptions of the conflict situation are accurate, *until they are able to confirm or change those perceptions, they act as though their perceptions are real*. Our perceptions drive our view of reality, and, sometimes, they drive us quite poorly! Thus, it is vital that we learn to assess our perceptions for their truthfulness, checking them against the facts and then choosing our actions wisely.

Fourth, the conflicts that interest us most are those that could adversely affect relationships because they create emotional residues. **Emotional residues** are like carpet stains—they are noticeable, make people feel uncomfortable and dissatisfied with the relationship, and lead people to desire change. If people dominate their partners and always win their arguments, the partners may feel unhappy and look for more satisfying relationships elsewhere. If conflicts leave people feeling dissatisfied, they may refuse to forgive, seek revenge, or become abusive. If people feel helpless in a relationship, they may grow apathetic, uncaring, or uninterested in it. If people avoid dealing with issues, their relationship may stagnate because problems are not getting resolved. The point is that our relationships generally deteriorate when we manage them poorly. Most people in a relationship would rather look for opportunities to make their partners feel better and cause the relationship to grow. But if they perceive that they cannot do that, they may look elsewhere for relationship satisfaction.

Fifth, our definition emphasizes that the issue or problem underlying the conflict has reached a point where it needs effective management sooner rather than later. Although letting problems mount up is usually not a good idea, people often let unresolved issues fester and grow until they can't take it any longer and explode. The interpersonal conflicts that interest us most are those that have this **sense of urgency** because they are approaching the point where they must receive attention or else. We can relate this idea to the previous one where we draw attention to the potential for adverse effects on the relationship, if the issues are not addressed.

THE INEVITABILITY OF CONFLICT

Conflict Is a Fact of Life

Simons wrote over 30 years ago that at one end, conflict is seen as a disruption of the normal workings of a system; at the other, conflict is seen as a part of all relationships.[4] A number of recent studies have demonstrated that conflict is a "common and inevitable feature" in close social relationships.[5] We encounter it at home, at school, and at work.

> I never thought that I would have "roommate" problems after graduating from college. Actually, the problems are with my new husband, but they remind me of stuff I went through in college—when to do the dishes, how to sort the mail, who should take messages, when does the trash go out, who picks up after his(!) dog, who does the housework. I am amazed at the number of issues that arise when living with another person.

Think over years past and recall the conflicts, complaints, or grievances you had with these three types of people: (1) neighbors living a few houses away, (2) next-door neighbors, and (3) family members (or teammate, close friend, roommate, or romantic partner). With the more distant neighbors, the appearance of their home and yard, noise, or their pets and children trespassing on your property may have upset you, but when the same problems happen with a next-door neighbor it becomes more serious. Things like disagreements over property lines, dropping in on you too often, borrowing tools and not returning them, unsightly fences, invasions of privacy, making noises far into the night, blinding lights, talking to you every time you go out into your yard (especially when sunbathing) become onerous when we feel as though we can't escape them. What about your family members? Here you could probably write a book. You may have had disagreements over study habits, sleeping habits, smoking, snoring, messiness, household chores, use of a car, friends who are noisy or sleep over, paying bills, buying furniture, TV, tools, and borrowing clothes. If you substitute teammate, close friend, or romantic partner, you have likely accumulated a list of disagreements.

Undoubtedly, you can add many examples to these lists. The question is this: What happens to conflicts as relationships become closer, more personal, and more interdependent? If you compare the lists you created for the three types of relationships above, you probably found that as the relationship becomes closer and more interdependent (from a distant neighbor to a next-door neighbor and from a next-door neighbor to a roommate, teammate, close friend, or romantic partner),

- the more conflicts occur,
- the more trivial (minor) complaints become significant ones, and
- the more intense your feelings are.

As we go from our relationship with a distant neighbor to that of a roommate, we are not only becoming physically closer, but we also feel emotionally closer. In addition, the behavior of someone close to us usually has more consequences for us than the behavior of those more physically and emotionally distant. This interdependence means that the individuals involved can become problematic by interfering with each other's goal achievement whether the goals are emotional, psychological, or material.

Researchers have identified seven types of emotional, psychological, and material resources that produce satisfaction in long-term romantic relationships.[6] As you might have guessed, those aspects that provide satisfaction in relationships have the potential to create conflict when people perceive they are lacking. In order of importance, they are:

- love—nonverbal expressions of positive regard, warmth, or comfort
- status—verbal expressions of high or low prestige or esteem
- service—labor of one for another
- information—advice, opinions, instructions, or enlightenment
- goods—contributions of material goods
- money—financial contributions
- shared time—time spent together

In the best kind of long-term romantic relationship, partners believe that they get what they deserve. Although this research focuses on romantic partners, many of these seven resources are relevant to other types of interpersonal relationships, including roommates, neighbors, friends, coworkers, and family.

Since we do become closer to and more interdependent with some people than with others, we can expect more conflict. No wonder Stamp found that conflict plays a role in the creation and maintenance of interpersonal relationships.[7] The **inevitability of conflict principle** runs contrary to the idea that, if we look long and hard, we can find people with whom we can share conflict-free lives. It means that we should cease our efforts to find perfect people and learn how to manage the conflicts we are sure to have with those closest to us. We need to learn how to deal with minor as well as major conflicts, how to maintain our objectivity when engaged in conflict, and how to keep our self-control. The narrative below illustrates these ideas:

> Before I started keeping track of my conflicts, I didn't think that I was involved in many conflicts. Now, I see that I have a lot of conflicts, and that I could have handled them differently. Acquaintances, outsiders, and strangers make me angry, but I choose not to get into a verbal conflict with them. It just isn't worth the time or effort. Basically, I just walk away or change the topic.
>
> I also noted that I deal with my conflicts differently with people closest to me. I have the greatest difficulty reaching an agreement usually with the people that I care most about. It frustrates me when the people closest to me cannot understand how I feel. Such is the case with my father. He is home alone all day and does nothing to keep himself busy. In my opinion I think he enjoys getting into conflicts with me just to have something to do and to make me communicate with him.

Although conflict is inevitable, we argue that it need not always turn violent. Unfortunately, too many people see violence as a necessary way to deal with conflict, but other options exist.

Interpersonal Violence Is Not a Fact of Life

Because of its ubiquitous nature, violence in interpersonal conflict has received a significant amount of attention from social scientists in communication and other disciplines.[8]

Interpersonal violence is not difficult to recognize; it occurs when a partner imposes his or her will on another through verbal or physical intimidation. The term *violence* refers to medium to severe acts, such as physical violence and verbal abuse.[9] It is a violation of what many people consider to be socially acceptable. Abusive behavior ranges from less intense, such as verbal attack, to more intense, such as physical attack. People may plan their attacks, or they may think they act spontaneously with violence or abuse.[10] According to our view, interpersonal violence, physical aggression, and abusive relationships are a type of interpersonal conflict, albeit an extreme and unhealthy type.

We take this opportunity to introduce the concept of interpersonal violence because every interpersonal conflict carries with it the seeds of abuse. Not only is this so, but frequently people expect their conflicts to turn violent.[11] Violence is becoming increasingly prevalent in American social life, making interpersonal conflict management an essential social skill. A recent study revealed that as many as 35 percent of high-school students experience a physical altercation in a year's time.[12]

The idea that conflicts need not turn violent implies that we have options when handling our differences with others. The notion of choice applies to interpersonal violence in two ways. First, when we turn violent or others use violence against us, people are using force to prevent others' freedom of choice. Second, the notion of choice should help us realize that we need not turn violent in the first place. We always have choices in conflict situations, we are all responsible for our own actions, and we can make a difference in our lives and others. Although conflict is inevitable, it need not, and should not, harm our relationships with others, get out of hand, and turn violent.

By teaching nonviolent solutions to problems, setting an example in our daily lives, and raising our children to resolve interpersonal conflicts peacefully, we are helping to reduce a serious social problem. Thus, learning to avoid escalation (i.e., learning de-escalation) is an important goal of this textbook. We next turn our attention to the idea of managing our conflicts.

DEFINING CONFLICT MANAGEMENT AND SKILLS

Everyday language reflects the variety of ways in which we regard conflict: We talk about handling conflict, dealing with it, avoiding it, or resolving it. We define **conflict management** as the communication behavior a person employs based on his or her analysis of a conflict situation. Another concept, **conflict resolution,** refers to only one alternative in which parties solve a problem or issue and expect that it will not arise again. Conflict management involves alternative ways of dealing with conflict, including resolution or avoiding it altogether.[13] Effective conflict management occurs when our communication behavior produces desirable results for all the parties concerned.

Note that we define conflict management as communication behavior because behaviors can become skills. In recent years, communication scholars have focused on the idea of "communication competence," describing communication skills that are useful in conflict situations. A communication skill may be viewed as "the successful performance of a communicative behavior…[and] the ability to repeat such a behavior."[14]

One way to understand this is to refer to a recently televised, *So you think you can dance?* competition, where one of the judges made a distinction between *moving* and *dancing*. He accused one contestant of merely moving around the stage. Dancing, he said, requires experience, good training, and practice. When one dances, the person engages in a performance. Those who simply move about do not express any feeling or engage others. We can use this analogy to compare communication behaviors to communication skills.

Skills are not innate; they are learned. We develop them through experience. The only way you learn how to handle conflict situations more competently is to work through the conflicts you encounter—that is, learning from this textbook and trying to practice your new skills. Due to the complexity of the task, few successfully ride a bicycle the first time. Most fall off. Sometimes they are lucky and stop before hurting themselves. Soon, with a great deal of concentration, riding a bike is manageable, and then it becomes something that is almost second nature. The problem is that most of us are more willing to learn how to ride bicycles than we are to learn conflict management skills. Communication competence takes knowledge about the way conflict works, knowledge of the skills that are used in conflict situations, and practice. This textbook discusses the skills associated with framing messages in conflict situations—specific message behaviors that have proven effective in various kinds of conflicts. The goal is to connect thinking about conflicts with acting in conflicts so as to choose the most effective behaviors possible.

In addition to focusing on behaviors that can become skills, our definition of conflict management has two important implications. First, our definition implies that you have communicative choices to make when in a conflict situation. You can choose among various options to deal with conflicts. You may avoid or confront conflicts. You may react peacefully or violently. You may treat others with respect and civility or verbally abuse others. You may simply give in or insist on "having everything your way."

Second, our view suggests that, in order to effectively manage conflict, you must analyze it by taking a meta-conflict perspective. You may recall that one of the fundamentals of interpersonal communication is the idea of *meta-communication*, where one tries to objectively look at interaction between people and talk about it intelligently. We might sit back, observe a couple of friends interact, and then describe their interaction pattern to them. Perhaps we observe that one person dominated the conversation, that is, talked the most and controlled the topic of discussion. In conflict, the ability to take a **meta-conflict perspective** means that you can look back on the conflicts you have experienced, analyze what you did well and what you did poorly, and learn from your mistakes. Eventually, you may even monitor your present interpersonal conflicts, realize what is going on, alter your behavior, and better manage the conflicts.

COMMUNICATION PROCESSES IN CONFLICT

In basic communication courses, you probably learned that the communication process was once viewed as one person sending a message to another person (receiver) through some channel. Such a communication model also contains a provision for noise (interference) and for receiver feedback, so that the receiver could indicate to the message sender that she or he received the message as intended. We can apply this communication process model as managers of conflict. One conflicting party (the message sender) may send any of the following messages to the other party of the conflict (the message receiver):

> I am not speaking to you.
> I don't want to talk about that.
> I disagree with you.
> I want to fight.
> I don't like you.
> I don't like what you said.
> I don't want to see you anymore.
> I want something to change.

The sender of such messages may use any of the following channels:

> Face-to-face
> Synchronous via some medium like a cell phone or instant messaging
> Asynchronous via an email, text message, or a relay person as the message carrier

Noise may consist of distractions in the face-to-face environment (such as TV, other people, or loud sounds) or technical difficulties that delete messages via the Internet or cut off contact on a cell phone.

In a conflict, feedback from others may consist of nonverbal reactions, such as facial cues (anger, hurt, sadness), body movements (standing up or walking out), gestures (making a fist, becoming more dynamic and lively), tone of voice (screaming, yelling), or verbal responses (name-calling or swearing).

While the above description of conflict and communication processes may sound familiar to many of us, these processes are a bit more complicated than the simple sending and receiving of messages. When conflicts arise, they arise because of the way both people act with respect to one another. In essence, we make our conflicts together; it is rare that a conflict is entirely the fault of one person in the relationship. Recognizing that, we would hope to create and manage a more productive conflict process—one that might begin with the words, "We need to talk," and end when people reach an agreement.

In the above paragraphs, we talked about the way people communicate that they are in conflict with one another. We described a **linear model of communication**, using the words *sender*, *receiver*, *channel*, *noise*, and *feedback*. For the most part, this model emphasizes accuracy: Is what was "received" the same meaning as what was "intended or sent"? While this approach can be helpful to our understanding, it doesn't explain the entire process of communication. When applied to conflict, the linear model suggests that interpersonal conflict is something we *do to* someone. For example, we might take a position and try to convince the other of our view.

From a linear point of view, our focus is on the end result, which means getting the other to change his or her mind or behavior to coincide with our position. In addition, using a linear model to explain conflict often results in trying to fix the "blame" of the conflict situation on one person or another, not recognizing that both people in a conflict situation contribute to the emergence of the conflict. In the extreme, this mode of thinking might lead us to go so far as to accuse the other of being stupid, making a bad decision, or doing something wrong behaviorally. We may yell and scream until the conflict tilts in our favor.

Obviously this can do damage to our relationship with others. Fortunately, there are other ways to manage conflicts. Our need for an alternative approach leads us to the "transactional" model of communication.

While the linear view emphasizes the end product of communicating (convincing, persuading, controlling, or dominating the other), the **transactional model of communication** emphasizes managing and coordinating. Such an approach recognizes that this view of communication (and by extension, conflict) isn't something we *do to* one another, but something we *do with* one another (like teamwork). A conflict is not seen as something that happens when one person "sends" a message to another indicating that he or she is unhappy with some behavior of the other. Rather, conflict is seen as the behaviors of each person, in response to one another, exchanging messages, hearing each other out, cooperating, and conjointly creating an understanding in which both people perceive themselves as being in conflict with one another, mutually sharing responsibility for the conflict situation, and working together to better deal with it. One student described it as "trying to build a sandcastle by directing someone else's hands."[15] Conflict is viewed as giving and taking, working together for a solution to a problem, discussing and arriving at mutual understandings, consensus, agreement, and resolution. Both conflicting parties have a responsibility toward empathizing with each other, avoiding judgment, keeping an open mind, welcoming feedback, and realizing that both may have to adapt to resolve the issue.

The advantage of the transactional view is that we begin to recognize the importance of both people's behavior in the conflict situation. One person acting "competently" in a conflict situation, using good communication skills, usually cannot bring the conflict to a mutually satisfying resolution. It takes two people to make a conflict, and it takes two people to manage or resolve it. The way people talk about the conflict together, the way they express messages in response to one another, and the way they "read" each other's nonverbal messages as the conflict is being enacted all create the conflict situation as well as manage it or move it to resolution. Moreover, it is not simply that the actions we choose are a result of the way we interpret situations; instead, what happens in this conflict affects how we think about conflict in the future.

The primary difference between the linear and transactional focus in communication is seen in the visual metaphors we might use to explain each. While the primary visual metaphor for the linear model is a conveyor belt (messages sent and received in a linear fashion), in the transactional model, communication (and hence conflict as a type of communication) is seen more as a dance that two people do together (messages cocreated by managing and coordinating).

CONFLICT COMMUNICATION AS PRODUCTIVE OR DESTRUCTIVE

Effective conflict management consists of acting and reacting in problematic situations in such a way as to convert potentially destructive interpersonal conflicts into productive ones. When conflict exists, you must take action to deal with the problem, either through open confrontation or through less direct, more tacit methods.

Conflict is destructive or dysfunctional when it leaves the participants dissatisfied. Perpetual conflicts can produce perpetual problems in a relationship.[16] On the other hand, conflict is productive or it serves a useful purpose when the participants are all satisfied and think that they have gained as a result of the conflict. However, feelings about the outcome are not enough to determine the productivity of a conflict. Some conflicts, although uncomfortable in the short run, may serve the needs of those in the relationship in the long run, or may even serve others outside the parties' relationship or society at large.

This makes sense, particularly for people who are uncomfortable engaging in conflict at the outset. If, for example, you have a new roommate, and you find almost immediately that your personal habits are diametrically opposed, you might feel uncomfortable as you initiate a conflict with your roommate in order to find some point of agreement on your habits. Because you do not know the other well, the conflict episode may seem strained and awkward. Afterward, you may think you did not respond verbally in the best way possible. However, if you see improved changes in behavior over time, then we can conclude that it was a productive conflict. It pays to enlarge your view of a conflict to include not only the outcomes or results but also you and your partner's feelings about one another's actual behavior within the conflict itself as measures of successful conflict management.

From these general ideas, then, we offer a more specific definition. A conflict is destructive when it harms the relationship because the partners do not manage it in a way that is mutually satisfactory. Moreover, when participants in the conflict lose sight of their original goals, when hostility becomes the norm, when mismanaged conflict becomes a regular part of the interaction between people, it is destructive. Most importantly, we characterize **destructive conflict** as a tendency to expand and escalate the conflict to the point where it often becomes separated from the initial cause and takes on a life of its own. Consider this person's account of poorly handled conflicts.

> I gave one friend, Jason, an incorrect reason why another friend, Tim, was not going to have a drink. I told Jason that Tim had a problem with alcohol, which wasn't really true. When Tim found out what I told Jason, he got upset (understandably) with me, and we had a nasty argument, which continued to the following night. I remember yelling, swearing, flaying my arms in the air, kicking a chair, and accusing him of being from an alcoholic family (which wasn't true).

According to our view, destructive conflict occurs when there is an increase in the number of issues, number of people involved, costs to the participants, and intensity of negative feelings. It includes a desire to hurt the other person and to get even for past wrongs. Destructive conflict occurs when there is escalation and parties fail to consider their options. Lastly, destructive conflict places heavy reliance on overt power and manipulative techniques.

We believe that **productive conflict** occurs when a conflict is kept to the issue and to those involved. It reduces the costs to the participants and the intensity of negative feelings. It includes helping the other person and letting go of past feelings. Productive conflict occurs when there is no escalation and no interpersonal violence. It features an awareness of options in conflict situations. Productive conflict does not rely on overt power and manipulative techniques. Along with these characteristics, we think that a productive view of conflict situations includes flexibility and a belief that all conflicting parties can achieve their important goals.

Productive conflict is distinguished from destructive on the basis of mutually favorable or unfavorable outcomes. We need to say more about the idea of **outcomes,** or the results people are seeking to achieve when they engage in conflict. Sometimes, these goals are clear at the outset, and at other times they develop as the conflict continues.

We realize that the term *outcomes* may suggest the resolution of some issue or solution of some problem. However, many people are satisfied even when these goals are not achieved. All they want from the conflict situation is for the other party to show interest in the problem; show concern for their feelings; and pay attention to their wants, needs, or interests, even if their wishes are not fulfilled. These are more personal, emotional outcomes that are associated with perceived fairness, acceptance as a person, and justice. There is a common understanding that complaints need attention from those responsible. In conflicts, both parties are anxious to tell their side of the story and want others to hear them out. If you take the time and make an effort to meet with me and show interest in my concerns, I may leave a conflict situation at least somewhat satisfied or feeling better than if you continue to ignore me or treat me badly. Better yet, you may make future decisions based on my recent input.

NEGATIVE VIEW OF CONFLICT

One of the challenges in getting people to learn more about conflict management is that people often don't even like to use the word *conflict* to describe their experiences, as this narrative demonstrates:

> I don't have conflicts, because to me, a conflict is when you have no place left to go. I'm right; you're wrong, so let's forget it. Up to that point, I bargain or argue, but I don't have conflicts.

Even when we are able to recognize one when we are in the middle of it does not mean that we have begun to think about conflict as something that is potentially helpful. Conflicting parties often experience a curious tension; that is, they expect (logically and intellectually) to experience conflict but want to settle it as soon as possible so that their lives can return to "normal."

What comes to mind when you think of interpersonal conflict? How would you complete this sentence: *To me, conflict is like...*

Would you describe conflict as like a war, battle, or fight? Would you say conflict is more like a struggle, uphill climb, or contest of wills? Is it like feeling sick to your stomach? Do you think of conflict as like being on trial, a day in court? Perhaps you see it as a game, match, or sport? Or would you describe it more as a communication breakdown, a barrier between you and another? The photo given here shows one person's view of conflict: It is something that makes her feel bound and gagged.

Conflict is almost always associated with negative feelings. We know that many people do not feel confident about handling a conflict. In a study, researchers asked people to describe past interpersonal conflicts and found that they overwhelmingly used negative terms to describe their conflicts: "It is like being in a sinking ship with no lifeboat," "like a checkbook that won't balance," or "like being in a rowboat in a hurricane."[17] The participants in the study described their conflicts almost uniformly as destructive or negative, suggesting that when they effectively managed an interpersonal conflict, respondents did not think it was a conflict at all.[18] This is typical of a **negative view of conflict:** The idea that conflicts are painful occurrences that are personally threatening and best avoided or quickly contained.

To say what conflict is like is an exercise in creating a **conflict metaphor,** where you are asked to compare one term (*conflict*) with something else (struggle, exploding bombs, being on trial). Metaphors are not only figures of speech but also a reflection of how we think.

Bound. *Amy Munive's conflict art reflects her negative perceptions of conflict as something that renders her helpless and speechless.*

How we think about something like conflict and the metaphors we may create for it create an expectation as to what can, will, or should happen, and the sort of emotions that might occur. How people think about conflict in general terms affects how they see their current situation, how they see the conflict issue, what choices they think are available to them, and how they view the other person's actions. You can know a great deal about conflict management, but if you hold a negative view of conflict your behaviors will be less competent when faced with one.

What do we learn from a collection of metaphors people give when asked what conflict is like to them? First, interestingly, we find that not everyone uses a metaphor to describe a conflict unless they are prompted to do so.[19] However, those who do so often use metaphors that are associated with the strategy used to respond to conflict: People who use negative strategies use more negative metaphors and others who are more passive use metaphors that reflect powerless feelings.

Second, we learn that not all people choose the same adjectives when describing what conflict means to them. People choose different adjectives to describe their perception of interpersonal conflict. These words reflect somewhat different views, which are themselves in conflict. Quite often a person who sees conflict as a "battlefield with relationships being the casualties" does not compare it to being on trial or a day in court, as another might. Probably, neither person thinks of conflict as like a basketball game, a tennis match, or some other sport. Although people vary in their perceptions of conflict, most seem to reject the idea that interpersonal conflict is a positive, healthy, and fortunate event—one they should welcome.

This common but negative attitude toward conflict hinders us from learning how to better manage our conflicts. Although people often think that they can learn new communication skills to improve the way they handle interpersonal conflicts, they do not realize that their attitudes, beliefs, and emotional reactions may have to undergo change as well.

Just as one can view a glass of water as half empty but another sees it as half full, so can we switch from a negative view of interpersonal conflict, where we see it as threatening, to a positive view, where we see it as an opportunity to resolve problems and improve our relationships with the people who mean the most to us. One woman reports her change in attitude toward conflict.

> The most valuable lesson I have learned is that conflict is not necessarily bad. I no longer see conflicts as a danger to relationships. My acceptance of conflicts as the result of relationships has helped minimize the discomfort I feel in conflict situations.

This is a **positive view of conflict.** It is helpful to take a more positive view of conflict because the fact of the matter is that conflict is here to stay.

MANAGE IT

Our goal in this first chapter is to introduce you to the study of interpersonal conflict. Conflict is a problematic situation that occurs between interdependent people who seek different goals or means to those goals. Two additional characteristics of conflict are that the perceived differences have the potential to adversely affect the relationship if not addressed and that there is a sense of urgency about the need to resolve the differences. Our definition broadens the study of conflict because nonverbal messages can adversely affect relationships as much as verbal ones like arguing and bickering. Problematic situations that are examples of conflicts include avoiding the other person or topic and glaring at the other person or giving the other a "silent treatment."

Although many people may not admit it, most people encounter conflict quite frequently. Conflict is inevitable—as relationships become closer, more personal, and more interdependent, more conflicts occur, trivial (minor) complaints become more significant, and feelings become more intense. Conflict holds a kind of dread for us—because we know we have often mishandled it in the past. This negative view of conflict may lead us to avoid improving situations and interpersonal relationships; thus, we urge our students to adopt a more positive view of conflict.

The rise of violence in interpersonal relationships makes interpersonal conflict management an essential social skill. Although conflict is inevitable, interpersonal violence is not because other options are usually available. We always have choices (or options) in conflict situations, and we are all responsible for our own actions.

Conflict management is the communication behavior we employ based on our analysis of a conflict situation. In addition, a productive view of conflict situations includes flexibility and the belief that all conflicting parties can achieve their important goals. We may not realize it at the time, but constructive responses to conflict situations are inherent in (all) most conflict situations. When action is called for, there are appropriate actions that can produce positive, constructive, and favorable outcomes.

The benefits of a more constructive approach, especially in cases where the interpersonal relationship is of importance, are obvious. How you convert potentially destructive conflicts into productive ones is the subject of the following chapters.

Finally, we need to recognize that communication is not simply saying what's on one's mind. Communication (and, by extension, conflict) isn't something we do to the other person, but something we do with one another (like teamwork or like a dance). We communicate in conflict situations by stopping, thinking, and listening before communicating.

The advantage of the transactional model is that we recognize the importance of both people's behavior in the conflict situation. One person acting competently in a conflict situation and using good communication skills usually cannot bring the conflict to a resolution. It takes two people to make the conflict, and it takes two people to manage or resolve it. By taking both parties' behavior into consideration, we can better determine what communication option we should exercise in a given conflict situation. We can respond by avoiding the conflict, sitting down and discussing it with the other person, or reacting with aggressive speech or violent behavior. The best of these options is communicating about the conflict. The various ways to approach a conflict are discussed in the next chapter.

Think About It

1. Describe your family. With whom in your family do you have the most conflict with? What can we conclude after hearing about family conflicts from a number of people?
2. Some argue that humans have an instinct for conflict. Do you think it is an inborn trait? Does it make us more or less human? If it is innate, is it a valuable asset?
3. Is it possible to view interpersonal conflicts positively? Can you give examples of positive outcomes from your own experience?
4. In problematic situations, how do you respond to the important people in your life? Do you deny that a problem exists, change the subject, or avoid the problematic person? What prompted you to take a class in conflict management?
5. Do you believe that if you have the right partner the two of you will live conflict free? Is it possible to find someone who presents no problems? Do you expect others to respect your property and privacy? What do you do when they don't?
6. What are the real-world implications of saying "interpersonal violence is not a fact of life"? Under what conditions would you see interpersonal violence as acceptable? Why?
7. Before reading this chapter, how did you feel about confronting others when a conflict arises? Did you feel positive or negative about it? How did that affect the way you handled past conflicts? Do you think you would be more successful if you felt more positively about conflict?

Apply It

1. Imagine representing your attitudes toward conflict visually rather than through language. What would your conflict art look like? What materials would you use? What kinds of colors would you use? What kinds of images would best represent your feelings about conflict? Write down a description of what you would do, or better yet, take some time to actually make your conflict art.
2. Ask your friends to describe their feelings about conflict. What kinds of words do they use? Do they tend to think of conflict as negative or positive?
3. Take a piece of paper and draw two columns on it. On one side, describe an unproductive conflict. On the other, describe a productive conflict. What are the differences between the two conflicts? How can you apply your learning to the next conflict you face?

Work with It

1. Read the following conflict narrative and answer the questions following it. There are three of us presently living together. The conflict is with an ex-roommate who lived with two of us last semester. She moved out with a friend because it was free room and board. Sometimes she decides she doesn't feel like driving the 12 miles home, so she stays the night with us. This went on just about every night last week. When here, she wore my clothes every day (without asking first), slept on our couch (which gave us no place to study), ate our food, and used our personal items like shampoo and makeup. I finally had enough when she walked by me after class wearing my brand new wool coat with the sleeves rolled up and said, "Hi! I'm wearing your coat!" I don't mind if people borrow my clothes, but I prefer that they ask first and that I get them back in the condition I lent them. Also, I'd like it if she would plan when she is spending the night so she could bring her own clothes, makeup, and food. As the saying goes, "I love her but I can't afford to keep her!" After a week of this I finally had it with her and really blew up! I screamed and yelled at her and she burst into tears, packed up, and left. It felt good letting off all that pent-up anger, but I somehow wish it hadn't worked out this way.
   a. How would you apply the authors' definition of interpersonal conflict to this narrative?
   b. What do you think the friends' view of conflict is (positive or negative) and why?
   c. Are conflicts like these expected among friends?
   d. Was there potential for violence here? Why or why not?
   e. How would you apply the authors' definition of conflict management to this narrative? Was it managed or mismanaged, and why?
   f. How could the friends have converted this interpersonal conflict into a more productive one?
2. This exercise asks you to write an essay describing the conflicts you encounter over at least a two-week period. Before writing, you need to keep track of your conflicts for a couple of weeks or more (see conflict records that follow). You may include recent conflicts that occurred prior to this assignment if you remember them in detail.

(Continued)

When preparing to write this essay, keep in mind our definition of a conflict situation. Some students say they cannot do the papers in this class because they have no conflicts. This means that they do not understand Chapter 1. Remember that unexpressed conflicts do exist. For example, according to the way conflict is defined in this textbook, a conflict exists any time we would prefer to do something but give in to others and do something else, or we may simply avoid confronting others, which is a type of conflict. So, we actually may have more conflicts than we may think. In your essay, address the following topics:

a. What do you think of the authors' definition of interpersonal conflict? (e.g., you might start out giving the authors' definition and explain how well it fits with the conflicts you are presently observing in your life.)
b. Would you say that it is inevitable to experience conflict with these individuals?
c. In what ways were the conflicts *productive* and in what ways *destructive*?
d. Conclude with a paragraph on *how satisfied* you are with the way you and the others handled these conflicts and *any problems* you have when attempting to manage your interpersonal conflicts.

Conflict Records
Instructions: Make 10 copies of this record. Over the next two weeks or so, observe your conflicts and fill out a record for each one. After you accumulate 10 or more, you should be ready to write your paper.

Interpersonal Conflict Record
Date: _____ Time: _____ (AM/PM) Length of argument (time): _____
Topic/Issue of conflict:
How often has this issue come up in the past?
Rarely 1 2 3 4 5 6 7 8 9 Very Often
What actually started/triggered the conflict?
Description of the conflict: verbal argument, physical abuse, silent treatment/stonewalling, changed subject/made light of conflict, etc.:
Emotions you experienced:
How did it end?
Intensity of disagreement:
Low 1 2 3 4 5 6 7 8 9 High
Degree of resolution:
Resolved 1 2 3 4 5 6 7 8 9 Unresolved

NOTES

1. See, for example, Linda L. Putnam, "Definitions and Approaches to Conflict and Communication," in John G. Oetzel and Stella Ting-Toomey (Eds.), *The Sage Handbook of Conflict Communication: Integrating Theory, Research, and Practice* (Thousand Oaks, CA: Sage Publications, 2006).
2. Joseph P. Forgas and Michelle Cromer, "On Being Sad and Evasive: Affective Influences on Verbal Communication Strategies in Conflict Situations," *Journal of Experimental Social Psychology* 40 (2004), 511–518.
3. Herbert W. Simons, "The Carrot and the Stick as Handmaidens of Persuasion in Conflict Situations," in Gerald R. Miller and Herbert W. Simons (Eds.), *Perspectives in Communication in Social Conflicts* (Englewood Cliffs, NJ: Prentice Hall, 1974), pp. 172–205.

4. Herbert W. Simons, "Persuasion in Social Conflicts: A Critique of Prevailing Conceptions and a Framework for Future Research," *Speech Monographs* 39 (1972), 227–247.
5. Fran C. Dickson, Patrick C. Hughes, Linda D. Manning, Kandi L. Walker, Tamara Bollis-Pecci, and Scott Gratson, "Conflict in Later-Life, Long-Term Marriages," *Southern Communication Journal* 67 (2002), 110–121.
6. Uriel G. Foa and Edna G. Foa, *Societal Structures of the Mind* (Springfield, IL: Thomas, 1974); Katherine D. Rettig and Margaret D. Bubolz, "Interpersonal Resource Exchanges as Indicators of Quality of Marriage," *Journal of Marriage and the Family* 45 (1983), 497–509.
7. Glen H. Stamp, "A Qualitatively Constructed Interpersonal Communication Model: A Grounded Theory Analysis," *Human Communication Research* 25 (1999), p. 543.
8. Loreen N. Olson and Dawn O. Braithwaite. "'If You Hit Me Again, I'll Hit You Back': Conflict Management Strategies of Individuals Experiencing Aggression during Conflicts," *Communication Studies* 55 (2004), 271–286.
9. Loreen N. Olson, "Exploring 'Common Couple Violence' in Heterosexual Romantic Relationships," *Western Journal of Communication* 66 (2002), p. 104.
10. Dudley D. Cahn, "Family Violence from a Communication Perspective," in Dudley D. Cahn and Sally A. Lloyd (Eds.), *Family Violence from a Communication Perspective* (Thousand Oaks, CA: Sage, 1996), p. 6.
11. Linda M. Harris, Kenneth J. Gergen, and John W. Lannamann, "Aggression Rituals," *Communication Monographs* 53 (1986), 252–265. See also Craig A. Anderson and Brad J. Bushman, "Human Aggression," *Annual Review of Psychology* 53 (2002), 27–51.
12. Monica H. Swahn, Thomas R. Simon, and Robert M. Bossarte, "Measuring Sex-Differences in Violence Victimization and Perpetration within Data and Same-Sex Peer Relationships," *Journal of Interpersonal Violence* 23 (2008), 1120–1138.
13. Dudley D. Cahn, *Intimates in Conflict* (Hillsdale, NJ: Erlbaum, 1990), p. 16.
14. Brian H. Spitzberg and Michael L. Hecht, "A Component Model of Relational Competence," *Human Communication Research* 10 (1984), 577.
15. Timothy Phillips, unpublished reflection paper (MLOS 501), Azusa Pacific University, May 22, 2008.
16. Courtney W. Miller, Michael E. Roloff, and Rachel S. Maris, "Understanding Interpersonal Conflicts that Are Difficult to Resolve: A Review of Literature and Presentation of an Integrated Model," in Christian S. Beck (Ed.), *Communication Yearbook*, Vol. 31 (Hillside, NJ: Lawrence Erlbaum, 2007), pp. 118–171.
17. Suzanne McCorkle and Janet L. Mills, "Rowboat in a Hurricane: Metaphors of Interpersonal Conflict Management," *Communication Reports* 5 (1992), 57–66.
18. Ibid., p. 63; see also Jacqueline S. Weinstock and Lynne A. Bond, "Conceptions of Conflict in Close Friendships and Ways of Knowing among Young College Women: A Developmental Framework," *Journal of Social and Personal Relationships* 17 (2000), 687–696.
19. Suzanne McCorkle and Barbara Mae Gayle, "Conflict Management Metaphors: Assessing Everyday Problem Communication," *The Social Science Journal* 40 (2003), 137–142.

CHAPTER 2

A Process View of Conflict

OBJECTIVES

At the end of this chapter, you should be able to:

- Name and explain the five stages or phases of constructive, successful conflict.
- Identify the stages in a specific conflict that you experienced.
- Explain the steps in the avoidance cycle, chilling effect, competitive escalation cycle, and violence cycle
- List and explain the six steps to effective confrontation

KEY TERMS

argument
chilling effect
competitive argument
competitive escalation cycle
confrontation
confrontation steps
confrontation avoidance cycle
cycle
differentiation phase

imagined interaction
initiation phase
informational reception apprehension
physical aggression
prelude to conflict
process
process view of conflict
resolution phase

schismogenesis
scripts
self-talk
triggering event
undesired repetitive pattern (URP)
verbal aggression/abuse
violence cycle

In Chapter 1, we defined conflict as a kind of communication process within which a problematic situation with certain characteristics arises. We defined conflict management as the behavior a person employs based on his or her analysis of a conflict situation. All communication is processual; conflict is a kind of communication situation that has particular characteristics, which, if not handled effectively, can make an interpersonal relationship problematic and even end a relationship.

Two key terms for our consideration now are *situation* and *behavior*. Both are embedded in a series of instances that follow one another (as in a video of people meeting, talking, and departing). Such a view of reality is, as Thomas argued, "concerned with the influence of each event upon the following events."[1] When we learn to take this view, we begin to see situations as phases or stages, reflecting a switch to a process orientation. If the series continues to repeat itself (like a perpetual motion machine), it becomes a **cycle.** A **process view of conflict** sees conflicts as a series of stages. In some cases, conflicts become cycles because they get bogged down in particular stages and repeat themselves. Understanding conflict as a process subject to destructive cycles helps us to identify the behaviors that make conflict destructive, and, it is hoped, choose behaviors that will keep the conflict from becoming so.

In this chapter, we explore the process model of conflict and demonstrate how choices made in different stages of the conflict may contribute to productive or destructive outcomes. Our purpose here is not only to identify the stages through which many conflicts progress but also to suggest some of the behaviors that contribute to successful resolution of conflict and other behaviors that either go nowhere or cause the conflict to turn violent.

PROCESSES IN GENERAL

What does it mean to take a process view of something? A **process** is dynamic, ongoing, and continuous (not static, at rest, or fixed). It is evolutionary in nature. Viewing objects, people, events, and social situations as processes means that we understand:

1. Processes have stages or phases of development through growth or deterioration.
2. They have a history in which a distinctive pattern emerges.
3. They consist of continual change over time.
4. They have ingredients that interact (affect one another) that may or may not lead to the next stage (depending on the ingredients).
5. At any given point in time and space, they represent some outcome, stage, or state of being (like a picture or a single frame in a film).

The way we talk about something often fails to reflect a process view—such as "the happy couple," "a divorced person," or "an ex-convict"—which suggests that people do not change, are not at one stage of a developing life cycle or relationship, or do not learn from their experiences and grow. We forget that communication is a process when we focus on simply getting our message understood by others without trying to see their point of view, adapting to it, and cocreating meaning. Failing to see a conflict as a process explains why some people are not interested in learning how to manage it. So, we don't take a process view:

- when we see something as unchanging (e.g., he was a naughty child, so he is probably a problem adult),
- when we see something as having no history (e.g., nothing in your past is important or affects you today),
- when we see something at its present age only and not as a stage in development (e.g., you will always be this way and never change), or
- when we do not consider the ingredients that make up something (e.g., you do not consider how your goals, fears, and abilities, others' expectations of you, and your deadlines or time limits interact to create how you view yourself).

A process view of conflict, on the other hand, sees the conflict situation as dynamic, changeable, and moving toward some end. We know that resolving conflict does not end conflict forever, however much we might want that to be the case. We will engage in conflict again and again, and we have a pretty good idea how these conflicts unfold.

PATTERNS AND CYCLES IN CONSTRUCTIVE CONFLICT PROCESSES

As depicted in Figure 2.1, a process view suggests that a *successfully* resolved conflict moves through a series of five recognizable stages, steps, or phases, with each stage affecting the next: the prelude to conflict (known as the frustration or latent stage in some theories), the triggering event (a behavior that at least one person in the conflict

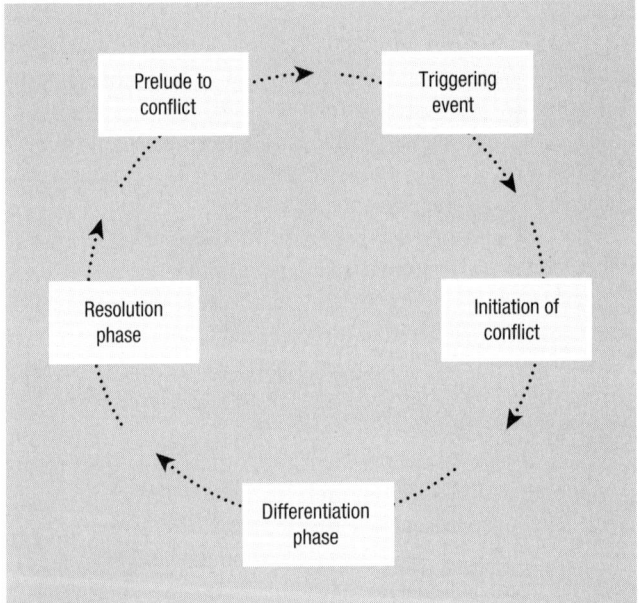

FIGURE 2.1 A Process View of Conflict. The process view of conflict assumes that all we have experienced prior to a particular conflict forms the group for the conflict we are currently experiencing. Prior experiences comprise the prelude to the conflict. A triggering event causes us to perceive that we are in a conflict with another person. After a triggering event, we (or the other person) will initiate the conflict through nonverbal means (withdrawal, silence, slamming doors, etc.) or verbal means ("we need to talk"). The differentiation phase includes working out the conflict, including the identification of the issue and feelings about it. The resolution phase includes the outcome to the conflict and becomes part of the prelude to the next conflict experienced.

points to as the "beginning" of the problem), the initiation phase (where at least one person makes known to the other the presence of a felt conflict), the differentiation phase (where the participants work out the problem using various strategies and tactics), and the resolution phase (where those involved agree to some outcome to the conflict).

The **prelude to conflict** consists of the variables that make conflict possible between those involved. The prelude comprises four variables:

- the participants in the conflict situation (number, age, sex, etc.)
- the relationship between them (which may vary in closeness and distribution of power) and their conflict history
- other interested parties to the conflict (including bystanders)
- the physical and social environment of the conflict situation.

In the prelude to conflict, the potential for manifest conflict exists because of the people involved and the other social and physical factors that define the situation. Like the first block in a line of dominoes, these variables affect the course of conflict.

The **triggering event** or conflict stimulus is a behavior that at least one person in the conflict points to as the "beginning" of the problem. Examples include saying something upsetting, doing something offensive, breaking a relationship rule, or not doing something one is expected to do by others. An important point to understand about triggering events is that the parties involved don't always point to the same behavior as the trigger for the conflict. The events that trigger a conflict for two people may be removed in time. For example, you may have experienced some long-term dissatisfaction with the way your roommate leaves his or her clothes and objects all over the house. For you the trigger of your conflict is the roommate's messiness. You finally say something to the other person and, in doing so, trigger a conflict for her or him about the other's perception of you as controlling. For that person a conflict exists in which the trigger is your attempt to influence her or his behavior. While you both are experiencing one conflict episode, the behavior that each of you see as the trigger to it is sometimes different. Having said that, we often engage in conflicts where the parties can agree on the trigger. For example, a daughter comes home after her curfew and her parents confront her about it. Both might agree in this case that she should have come home on time. So, sometimes the parties can agree that a particular event triggered the conflict.

The **initiation phase** or response occurs when the conflict becomes overt. This happens when at least one person makes known to the other that a conflict exists, such as reacting to another's upsetting comment, pointing out the offensive nature of the other's behavior, calling attention to the breaking of a relationship rule, or reminding the other that she or he is expected to do something the person is not doing.

The **differentiation phase** or ongoing interaction pattern occurs when the participants use constructive or destructive strategies and tactics, presenting both sides of the story, moving back and forth, and escalating and de-escalating. Lasting anywhere from a few minutes to days or even weeks, this is the stage where the conflict becomes quite obvious to everyone. Although parties may view the open disagreement as "the conflict," from a communication point of view, the revelation of differences is the fourth stage in the interpersonal conflict process.

This phase serves a useful purpose by allowing both parties to explain how they see the situation that gives rise to conflict and what they want to happen as a result of the conflict. Sometimes, only one participant wants to address the conflict; the other person avoids confronting the issues. The relationship, the conflict history of the participants, and their preferred styles in doing conflict all act as ingredients that affect how the conflict proceeds.

The **resolution phase** or outcome occurs when those involved agree to some outcome to the conflict. Thus, we argue that a successful conflict results in a win–win outcome, where the participants are unlikely to have to deal with the issue again. Resolution is a probable outcome when the agreement satisfies all concerned. If the conflict is resolved, then a decision has been made by the parties to end the disagreement, and they are both satisfied with the outcome. Alternatively, a win–win outcome can be a kind of issue management, where the participants have decided that the issue is settled for the time being while recognizing that it may arise again in the future.

Win–lose or lose–lose outcomes occur at earlier stages of the conflict cycle, as a result of people entering into the negative conflict cycles described in the next section. In this textbook, we argue that conflict management may result in resolution or it may not. When it results in resolution the outcome is an agreement that satisfies all concerned. In other cases, the best decision may be to accommodate or avoid confrontation for reasons discussed in previous chapters. In all of these cases, one is managing the conflict process. One manages the conflict process whether the conflict is resolved satisfactorily or not.

Regardless of the outcome reached, the way in which a conflict is managed will affect the way future conflicts are resolved or managed between the affected parties. Thus, we illustrate the conflict process as a cycle, where the resolution or management of one conflict becomes part of the prelude of the next conflict. At this point, we are focusing on a constructive conflict situation in which an incident progresses through stages until successfully resolved.

When people are able to bring their conflicts to successful resolution, it reinforces positive thinking about conflict. Each successful conflict we engage in increases the chances that future conflicts are productive, because we learn that conflict isn't dreadful and something we must avoid.

In examining the process model of conflict, you should realize that we have recast the event we call "conflict" as a process in order to examine in more detail the series of steps or stages from beginning to end. However, like fingerprints, not all conflicts are exactly alike. Some may follow the five-step sequence of events faster or slower, and there is often an uneven distribution of time within the model. For example, the prelude to conflict may occur over several months and the actual overt manifestations of conflict happen in a matter of minutes, or vice versa.

Moreover, as we show in the next section, from a process perspective, an unsuccessful conflict is one that becomes diverted at one of the stages. A conflict may begin to progress through the phases and stop, or it may return to a previous stage when new issues are introduced and added to the conflict. As in examining any communication event, the model may illuminate, but it may also distort our expectations. The model is used for explanation and analysis, not as a Procrustean bed into which all conflicts must fit exactly.[2] The following are a few examples of how successfully managed conflicts proceed through the five stages.

Example 1

Prelude. For the first time in about two weeks, my dad, brother, and I were all in the same place at the same time. We went to dinner together, giving us our first chance in weeks to talk together. We had just ordered dinner when the inevitable question came up. What am I going to do after I graduate? When the question came up this time, I had an answer. I told him about the progress I had made in job contacts and other possibilities I was considering. I especially wanted to travel during the summer with a sports team as a sports information director, but I had made no specific plans. Pop asked if I had sent in my application yet. I said that I hadn't.

Trigger. My older brother, Stuart, chimed in that I'd better do it soon. This is when the conflict started. The tone in Stuart's voice was what set me off. He was using a condescending attitude toward me, which I hate.

Initiation. I told him that it was none of his business; that he need not tell me what to do.

Differentiation. Stuart got mad, as usual, and told me that I was interpreting the situation wrong. He basically told me that I shouldn't feel the way I do because they were only showing that they care. This rubbed me the wrong way because I've had enough of people telling me how I should feel. I tried to explain how I felt but was interrupted several times with the response that I was wrong to feel that way. I told him that I thought I was being more than fair in telling my family my plans and feelings.

Resolution. At this point, my father intervened and made us both apologize to each other for making such a scene. We did and moved on to other topics that were safer to discuss.

Example 2

Prelude. Our daughter is not a morning person. My husband is one, but I am usually the one who drags her out of bed for school. The other morning I was having a hard time waking up, and I didn't worry too much about it because my husband was up and I didn't have to get up early. I finally got up just before my daughter had to leave.

Trigger. My husband remarked "I got Jenny up for you." That really irritated me, because when he says that it sounds like taking care of our daughter is a favor he does me instead of an obligation we both have.

Initiation. I remarked that it really bothered me when he said that.

Differentiation. He said that he realized that it would be easier for all concerned if he got her up this morning. I said I didn't like the way he said it.

Resolution. He apologized and said he didn't mean it the way it sounded. He appreciated that I always got her up. He was just trying to reassure me that I didn't have to worry about getting Jenny to school. I told him I appreciated being reassured but really needed to believe we were in this together. He agreed, and we dropped it.

PATTERNS AND CYCLES IN DESTRUCTIVE CONFLICT PROCESSES

Communication scholars often look for patterns of interaction, both functional and dysfunctional. Viewing conflict as a process has led to the identification of the above five stages, which represent a functional pattern of interaction because the conflicts are resolved in a mutually satisfactory way. A process view also suggests that dysfunctional conflicts are not successfully resolved. They fail to move through the same five recognizable stages, steps, or phases characteristic of successfully resolved conflicts, and they enter destructive cycles of their own. After starting with the prelude phase, they are diverted at one of the subsequent stages: the triggering event or stimulus, the initiation phase or response, the differentiation phase or ongoing interaction pattern, or the resolution phase or a constructive outcome.

As we think about conflicts as processes with recognizable phases, it's important to consider them in the context of the many routine activities we perform. For example, you probably arise about the same time each day, have a breakfast similar to the one from the day before, put on your clothes in the same order, and walk or drive to classes or work using the same route as always. Sometimes routines are nearly unconscious behaviors. Routinized events are **scripts** that we perform with little deviation each time we do them. People repeat similar behaviors each time they encounter the event. Without scripted events, it is more difficult getting through the day. Imagine having to make a new decision for each choice that confronts you! The unfortunate truth, though, is that sometimes our conflict behavior becomes scripted.

Conflicts that become scripted behavior are what Cronen and colleagues call an **undesired repetitive pattern (URP)**,[3] or the feeling of being trapped in a set of circumstances beyond one's control. Those involved in URPs can have automatic, "knee-jerk" responses to one another: Something one of them says triggers an automatic response in the other, and the episode quickly escalates out of control. It happens when those involved have a pretty good idea of what the other is going to say next, or at least they think they do. URPs recur, are unwanted, and generally occur regardless of the topic or situation. Those in the URP have a feeling that the pattern is hard, if not impossible, to avoid.

URPs sometimes have an escalation effect, in which the exchanges between those involved gets increasingly intense. **Schismogenesis** (the escalation of the cycle) occurs when the behaviors of one person intensify the behaviors of another person.[4] Schismogenesis is complementary in nature when the exchanges balance each other (e.g., as one person becomes more dominant, the other becomes more submissive; as one person shows off, the other becomes more admiring, which leads to more exhibitionism). Schismogenesis is symmetrical when each person tries to outdo the other's behavior. Seeking revenge often leads to symmetrical schismogenesis, as blood feuds escalate through retaliation after retaliation.

The belief that conflicts are cyclical has led to the identification of two common dysfunctional conflict cycles:

- the confrontation avoidance cycle (including the "chilling effect")
- the competitive conflict escalation cycle (including the violence cycle)

A key point is that issues are not resolved in either of these cycles, which stem in large part from the attitudes people have about conflict and from the way those attitudes are validated by their conflict behavior.

The Confrontation Avoidance Cycle and the "Chilling Effect"

The first of the dysfunctional conflict cycles is confrontation avoidance, which is depicted in Figure 2.2. Chapter 1 noted that the bulk of conflict management advice is slanted toward open conflict or confrontation, largely because people would rather avoid it altogether. But we now know that not every conflict requires engagement. Some issues *are* better left alone. Either they are unimportant or they may take too much time and energy to deal with constructively. However, as we begin our discussion of this dysfunctional cycle, we are saying that some people tend to avoid confrontation with most everyone and with most issues. We are not talking about a single instance of parties avoiding a conflict, but rather a pattern that an individual displays in responding to conflict.

The **confrontation avoidance cycle** is characteristic of those people whose first impulse is to avoid initiating conflict or to quickly withdraw when conflicts arise. This type of conflict management style is similar to the communication styles of shyness or reticence because it occurs across situations and people. Typically, unsuccessful conflict management becomes mired down in one of the first four stages of conflict. The confrontation avoidance cycle is typical of a conflict that doesn't progress past stage two. It is at the choice-making portion of the initiation stage that people often get stuck in an avoidance cycle. When one sees confrontation in general as something to avoid, she or he can easily decide to avoid the

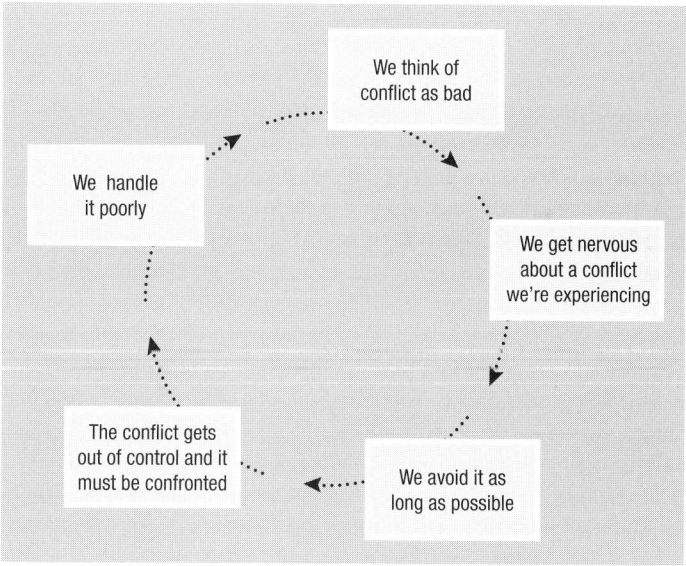

FIGURE 2.2 The Confrontation Avoidance Cycle. The cycle begins with the belief that conflict is something that we should avoid if at all possible. Because we would like to avoid conflict, experiencing one makes us nervous. Generally, something that makes us nervous is something we put off. Unfortunately, many issues worsen when left alone, so eventually we have to confront them. Our anxiety causes us to handle the conflict badly. Our negative perception of conflict is confirmed, and the cycle starts again.

current confrontation. If one cannot avoid this particular confrontation, the person who generally avoids confrontation has his or her negative perceptions reinforced when conflict is finally addressed after it has gotten beyond the stage where productive resolution is possible.

In a confrontation avoidance cycle, a conflict has a prelude stage (e.g., one or more of the participants has a past history of poorly managing conflicts), followed by a stage two triggering event (e.g., one partner forgets an important date), but instead of progressing to stage three, initiation, the offended individual does not initiate the conflict because she or he prefers to avoid most confrontations. Either the conflict isn't resolved, which hurts the relationship, or issues build up until one eventually erupts, resulting in a mismanaged conflict. This is reinforcing because the pain associated with the previous conflict discourages one or both partners from wanting to address future issues.

Probably the most widespread misassumption about conflict, and the one that has the greatest chance of creating a confrontation avoidance cycle, is the notion that conflict is abnormal. People who experience conflict want to end it as soon as possible so that their lives can "return to normal"—harmony being the norm. The truth is that both excessive conflict and excessive harmony are abnormal. Harmony and conflict are processes in life; people move back and forth between them. Harmony in a relationship is desirable, but it does not allow growth because it does not allow change. Rummel noted that "the desire to eradicate conflict, the hope for harmony and universal cooperation, is the wish for a frozen, unchanging world with all relationships fixed in their patterns—with all in balance."[5] This misassumption affects the way people approach the study of conflict management. They are motivated to learn about conflict so they can do it better, and faster; their motivation is not to gain a true understanding of the process while they are in it.

Related to the notion that conflicts are abnormal is the idea that conflicts are pathological: They are symptoms of a system that is functioning incorrectly. Some conflicts are indeed pathological. We have all had the experience of observing people who continued a conflict long after it made any sense to do so. For the most part though, conflict is a sign that a system (an interpersonal relationship, a task group, or an organization) is functioning well and testing itself to make sure the boundaries are clear and understandable to those involved.

Another misassumption, perpetuated by numerous popular writings on conflict management, focuses on reducing or avoiding confrontation. Some people avoid conflict as long as they can, and therefore the problem continues.

At the risk of oversimplification, one could identify two basic approaches to conflict interaction—confronting and avoiding—although people may do both in different relationships. When dealing with an avoider, one may have to heighten the avoider's awareness of the conflict so that it is impossible to ignore. For example, a newly married couple may have different expectations about how to account for their whereabouts to the other. The wife may frequently leave the house without indicating a destination or return time. The more conscientious husband indicates that such behavior is worrisome but gets little response from his wife. Were he to copy his wife's behavior for a few days, she might realize how inconsiderate her behavior is. Communicating one's needs to the other is not necessarily the most effective way to resolve a conflict if the other does not understand the negative aspects of the behavior involved.

Roloff and Ifert claim that confrontation avoidance can serve useful purposes, as long as it eliminates arguing and does no damage to the relationship.[6] Sometimes, avoidance in the present allows for the reintroduction of a difficult topic at a later time.[7]

However, if any participant in the conflict feels that leaving the issue unresolved is more costly than confrontation, avoidance is potentially destructive.[8]

In some cases, spouses have learned in their marriages that they are better off avoiding some conflicts. In Bill's case, presented below, avoidance is around a particular issue, but not a general habit for the couple.

> **Prelude.** This is a second marriage for both of us, and my wife brought three kids with her. Her oldest daughter seems really wacky to me.
>
> **Trigger.** Her daughter's nutty behavior is a problem. Last week, she telephoned her boyfriend who is in Europe and ran up a $300 telephone bill. However, I don't comment on it, even though it is getting worse. I feel that it is not worth creating a scene.

There was no initiation stage (or differentiation or resolution), because Bill chose to avoid confronting his wife or her daughter. Thus, the issue is unresolved and may continue for years to come. Interestingly, this avoidance behavior is more typical of husbands than of wives in marital relationships.[9]

A special case of avoidance is called the **chilling effect,** in which one person in a relationship withholds grievances from the other, usually due to fear of the other person's reaction.[10] This cycle is presented visually in Figure 2.3. People are likely to avoid conflict in low-commitment relationships, whereas in strong, committed relationships, conflict is more spontaneous and emotional.[11] Research indicates that a chilling effect is likely to occur when the other person appears to have attractive alternatives to the relationship with the withholder and when the other's commitment to the withholder seems weak. If you are

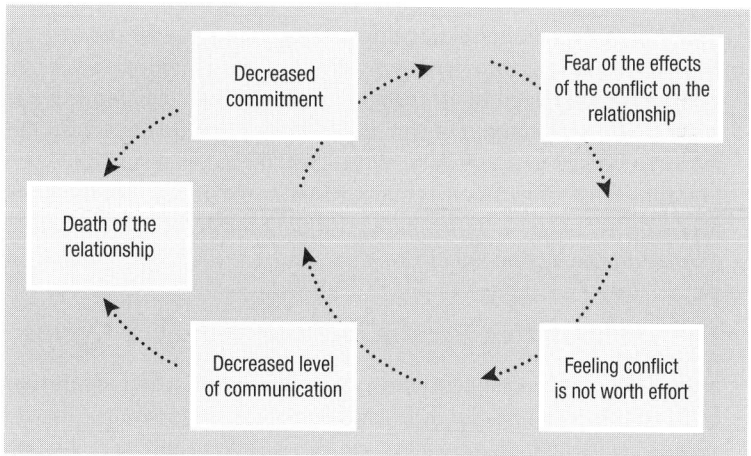

FIGURE 2.3 The Chilling Effect in Conflict. The chilling effect begins with the perception that conflict has negative effects. This fear leads us to belief that conflict is not worth the effort it would take to enact. When conflicts are avoided, however, other types of communication in the relationship decrease. A decrease in communication often leads to a decrease in commitment to the relationship. After several cycles of decreased communication and decreased commitment, we may simply cycle out of the relationship altogether.

worried that your friend does not care much about you and that your friend could easily leave the relationship, you are not likely to tell your friend when you have a grievance. Conversely, if you are not worried about my leaving because I have no alternatives and care about you, you are more likely to express your dislikes and desires. You have nothing to fear from conflict.[12]

A milder version of the chilling effect occurs when one avoids confronting another because she or he feels powerless to do so.[13] In stronger cases, even committed partners, who are sometimes trapped in abusive relationships, fear confrontation with their partners. The chilling effect is different from the avoidance cycle in that it exists only between two people rather than with everyone in general and includes an element of fear (afraid of the other or afraid of losing the other).

The chilling effect shows how unsuccessful conflict becomes mired down in one of the first four stages. In this case, the conflict has a prelude stage (e.g., one or more of the participants has reason to fear the reaction of the other person based on a past history of abuse during conflict), followed by a stage two triggering event (e.g., one partner does something that upsets the other), but instead of progressing to the stage three initiation (or later stages), the offended individual does not initiate the conflict because he or she again fears the outcome.

The chilling effect focuses on the negative aspects of the other person that irritate or anger the withholder. These negative aspects become areas of perceived incompatibility and evolve into ongoing conflicts. Sometimes the withholder describes the conflict to friends or other third parties but does not confront the irritating person; therefore the conflicts remain unexpressed. Generally, the withholder does not confront the other because of fear of damaging the relationship. However, a chilling effect is negative in desirable, ongoing relationships because it puts communication barriers between those involved, which undermines the relationship and mutual happiness for the partners.

There are two ways to respond to a threatening partner. First, in cases where one merely lacks the habit of asserting oneself, one may overcome this fear and learn to stand up to the other person, but this is not possible in cases where the partner is stronger, meaner, and better equipped to abuse. Second, people caught in controlling, abusive relationships have to seek outside help (usually the police, courts, or other authorities). The best time to counter abuse is the first time it happens, because after that it becomes more difficult to take action against it.

The Competitive Escalation and Violence Cycles

Another dysfunctional conflict cycle is the **competitive escalation cycle,** in which the conflict bogs down in the differentiation stage when competitive interests lead to divergence rather than integration. Figure 2.4 illustrates this cycle.[14]

In this cycle, the participants are so concerned with winning that they are unable to respond to integrative messages, if indeed those messages even make it into the conflict interaction. Consider this example:

> **Prelude.** I already knew where my favorite blouse was—it was in my sister's room. She seems to have this habit of borrowing whatever she wants without my permission. I went into her room and . . .

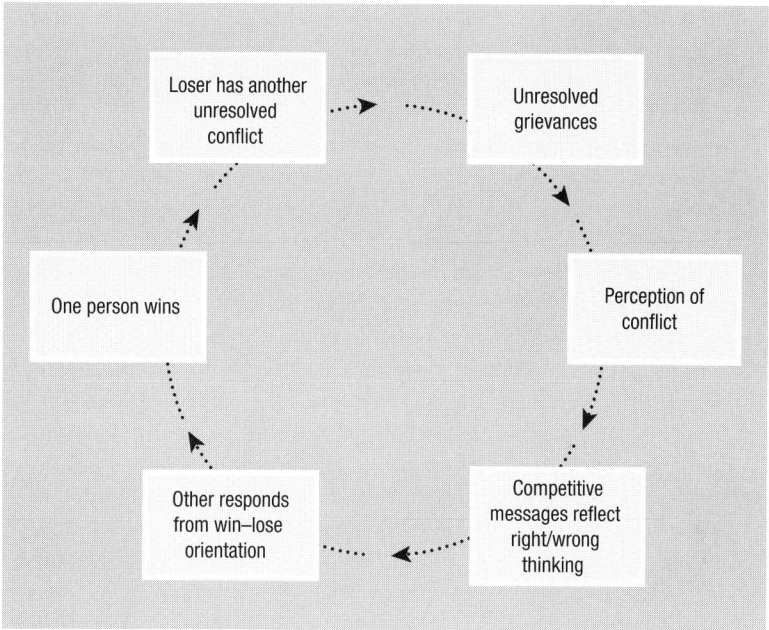

FIGURE 2.4 The Competitive Escalation Cycle. This cycle is fueled by previously unresolved grievances that color the perception of the current conflict. The conflict is initiated with competitive messages that indicate an "I'm right–you're wrong" stance on the part of the initiator. The cycle is intensified when the other responds with a win–lose orientation as well. The outcome is generally that one person wins, and the other loses. The person who has lost has another unresolved grievance that will affect future conflicts.

Trigger. Under her bed was where I found my blouse. I was so angry that I had KILL written on my forehead. I went searching for my sister throughout the house, like a lion searches for its prey. When I found her . . .

Initiation. I brought up all the past times that she had taken something from me without permission, and then I accused her of "stealing" my blouse.

Differentiation. She started screaming at me, and I called her a kleptomaniac. Neither of us was trying to de-escalate the conflict. She stormed off to her bedroom and I went to mine. We haven't spoken for two days. But like past occurrences, we will eventually get over it. At least until something like this happens again!

Resolution—there was none.

In this narrative, you can see how the cycle operates. One sister has unresolved grievances concerning the borrowing of clothes, and it affects the way she views the current emerging conflict. As she communicates her anger about having her clothes borrowed, she not only talks about this incident but all the past grievances as well, reflecting the belief that she is in the right and her sister is in the wrong. As it might be expected, the sister also takes a right/wrong position and yells back. One person has the sense that he or she has won (typically, the one who walks out first), and the other person feels as though he or she has lost, creating yet another grievance that will color the perception of future conflicts.

We need not fall into this pattern. Conflicting parties may view an **argument** either as a rational exchange of claims about some ideas or as a competition. When we take the first view, we may argue about politicians, politics, whether a movie is worth seeing, whether being a vegetarian is reasonable, and so on. Life gives us many opportunities to express our opinions by stating claims and offering reasons for making those claims. Many of us find people who are reluctant to express an opinion to be boring. On the other hand, an argument becomes competitive when one person's desire to express an opinion becomes a need to win an argument without space for anyone else's opinion to receive equal consideration. A controlling partner who always has to win arguments uses conflicts to serve his or her personal needs. **Competitive argument** occurs when one has a desire to win no matter what harm it does to a relationship. It becomes problematic when one can't take losing or "never loses" an argument. We are turned off by either type. It is no fun engaging in conflict with them. In extreme cases, competition has the potential to adversely affect the relationship, if either person finds the competition upsetting.

A special case of competitive escalation is the **violence cycle,** as illustrated in Figure 2.5. The degree of violence can range from relatively minor (verbal threats, threatening gestures) to outrageous acts of physical abuse, torture, and bodily harm. Violence involves harming another person physically, emotionally, or mentally. For example, a couple may start by disagreeing over where to place fruits and vegetables in the refrigerator ("they should go over here"; "no they should go there"), but escalate into **verbal aggression/abuse** (insults, name calling, and the like),[15] and may even wind up screaming and throwing objects. The conflict may end here unresolved and leaving a bad memory. In Figure 2.5, we illustrate this with a dotted line. In some cases, verbal abuse may escalate into **physical aggression,** when one or both parties physically attack the other as the continuation of arrows in Figure 2.5 depict. We should point out that communication scholars are quite concerned about such interpersonal behaviors.[16] Verbal abuse and physical aggression are not recommended and often characterize problematic relationships in need of help, although the partners may not think so.

Both competitive escalation and violence cycles are all too common occurrences that show how an unsuccessful conflict becomes mired down in the fourth stage—differentiation. Here, the conflict has a prelude stage (e.g., one or more of the participants has a past history of poorly managing conflicts), followed by a stage two, triggering event (e.g., one person takes something he or she shouldn't or a partner forgets an important date). The conflict moves through stage three, initiation, but gets mired down in stage four, differentiation, instead of progressing to the final stage, resolution. Like the preceding three destructive cycles, the resulting process takes on quite a form that is different from that of a successfully resolved conflict.

Pruitt and Rubin argue that competition in a conflict creates a pattern of interaction that intensifies the competition and the desire to outdo the other. Whereas the competition may start with friendly banter, later moves become more unfriendly,

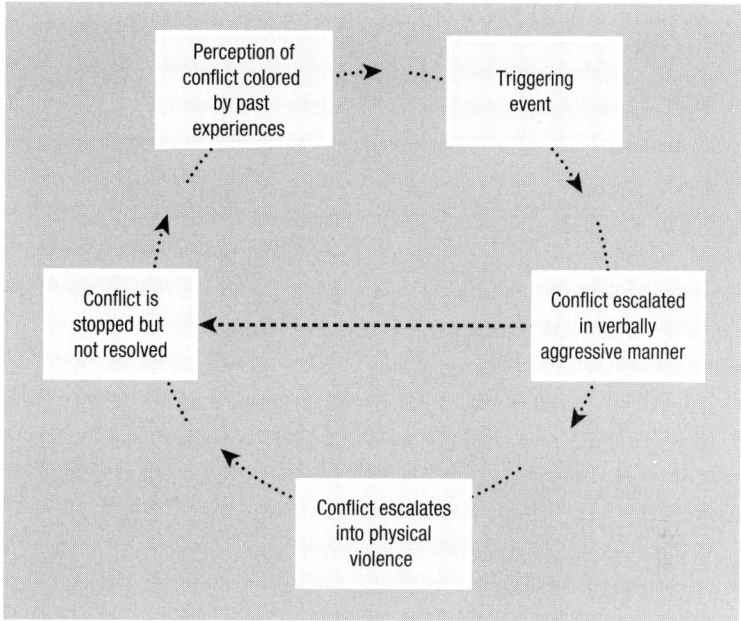

FIGURE 2.5 The Violence Cycle. A special case of competitive conflict escalation is the violence cycle. The degree of violence can range from relatively minor (verbal threats, threatening gestures) to outrageous acts of physical abuse, torture, and bodily harm. Violence cycles begin with perceptions of unresolved conflict that color the perception of a current triggering event. A cycle may begin in disagreement but escalate into verbal aggression and/or abuse. The conflict may end here, unresolved and leaving a bad memory—illustrated with a dotted line. In some cases, verbal abuse may escalate into physical aggression, when one or both parties physically attack the other as the continuation of arrows depict. At some point, the conflict is stopped, either by the participants themselves or by a third party, but such behavior results in unresolved grievances that fuel the next cycle.

increasing the number of issues in the conflict. As issues are introduced, the conflict is less likely to focus on a particular issue and is more likely to result in an irritating universal level such as "You're always bugging me." Moreover, although the conflict may have started with one person's desire to simply win, this desire is distorted into a desire to win coupled with a desire to hurt the other with the loss. More parties may become involved as the conflict escalates. The most difficult part about this process, though, is the fact that each competitive move makes it more and more difficult for those in the conflict to de-escalate because they see it as "backing down."[17] In the case of the violence cycle, one person forces his or her own decision down the throat of the other person, leaving that individual dissatisfied with the outcome. The issue will continue to fester because it was not resolved in a mutually satisfying way. If angry enough, the other will turn to vengeful acts to get even or to passive-aggressive behavior to get his or her way.

There are a number of behaviors that contribute to the escalation of a conflict, cause it to get out of hand, and perhaps lead to violence. We refer to these in Figure 2.5 as escalatory behavior:

- talking louder; yelling
- standing up
- getting into the other's face, space invasion
- making a threatening gesture (fist, finger)
- pushing/shoving/poking with finger/hitting
- swearing/cursing
- attacking the other's face with insults, name calling, putdowns, racial/ethnic slurs, etc.
- disconfirming the other
- making verbal threats
- pushing sensitive buttons (i.e., bringing up unrelated sensitive issues)
- increasing competition and encouraging rivalry
- damaging the other's possessions
- mocking the other
- shutting the other out or walking away
- being egged on by bystanders

THE CONFRONTATION PROCESS: SIX STEPS TO SUCCESSFUL INTERPERSONAL CONFLICT RESOLUTION

As you have discovered by reading about conflict processes, it is regrettably too easy for conflicts to spin off into destructive cycles. In this section, we describe a series of steps for effective confrontation, which can help you to get through your conflict without, it is hoped, diverging into a destructive cycle.

We begin by defining **confrontation** as a conflict process in which the parties call attention to problems or issues and express their feelings, beliefs, and wants to one another. So, if a neighbor's barking dog upsets you and could lead to significant deterioration in your relationship, then you are engaging in interpersonal confrontation when you consider the problem or issue, arrange to meet with the neighbor, tell him or her about the problem, observe the other's feedback, come to some sort of understanding, and reevaluate the outcome at some future date. Obviously, assertiveness plays a role in interpersonal confrontation. While assertiveness is the ability to speak up for one's interests, concerns, or rights in a way that does not violate or interfere with those of others, confrontation is viewed in this chapter as a conflict process event that involves dynamic interaction between the parties involved. Thus, confrontation involves a series of steps of which assertiveness is only one.

Because of the potential benefits, we need to know how to effectively confront others about conflicts that eat away our relationship. We handle many of our everyday conflicts with little pomp and circumstance. If you are able to address a problem as it happens, a simple, "You know, it bothers me when you do that" may draw the other person's attention to the behavior and result in an agreement to stop or modify it. When problems are more complex, we need a plan for conflict management.

There are six **confrontation steps** to move through as you manage a conflict with another person. They are:

1. Preparation: Identify your problem/needs/issues.
2. Tell the person "We need to talk."
3. Interpersonal confrontation: Talk to the other person about your problem.
4. Consider your partner's point of view: Listen, empathize, and respond with understanding.
5. Resolve the problem: Make a mutually satisfying agreement.
6. Follow up on the solution: Set a time limit for reevaluation.

Although we would like to avoid giving the impression that all conflicts, large and small, are resolved by following six easy steps, it helps to know what to do and what not to do when confronting someone with whom you disagree. Also, keep in mind that when you find yourself stopped at one step, we advise backtracking one or more steps to allow for a more thorough discussion before attempting moving forward. That being said, let's begin with the first step, preparation for confrontation.

Preparation: Identify Your Problem/Needs/Issues

The first step is preparation, where you identify your problem, needs, and the issues. "Preparation is the most extensive and, in many ways, the most important stage of the confrontation process."[18] This process is the stop and think portion of the S-TLC model that we will describe more fully in Chapter 4. At this stage, self-talk is important. **Self-talk,** as you can guess, is verbalizing, either out loud or to ourselves, that is, inner messages. People can talk themselves out of confronting others; they can talk themselves into it; or they can talk themselves into handling confrontation in negative, destructive ways. In Chapter 1, we noted that many people prefer to avoid conflicts, but this is not a good idea when a continuation of problems and unmet needs may do damage to a relationship, assuming that the other does not turn abusive if confronted. Asking yourself "who, what, where, when, how" enables you to examine many more aspects of a situation to determine what the problem is, how it affects you and the relationship, and how you feel about it. You need to determine what you want (your goal). Ask yourself what is likely to happen if you don't receive what you want or what could happen to the relationship if you do. Once you have determined that you need to confront the other person, you need to try to think positively and encourage yourself to go through with it.

A way to prepare is through what is termed an **imagined interaction,** which is a form of intrapersonal communication in which you think about what you might say and another might say in response to you in a particular conversation.[19] Imagined interactions serve as a planning function. People who imagine interactions with others do not actually think about the interaction as they expect it to occur. Rather, they think about the interaction in an "if-then" kind of way: If he says "x," I will tell him "y"; if she says "a," I will say "b." In this sense, imagined interactions are much like cartoon strips. They are both visual and verbal, they happen sequentially, and the imaginer can rewrite the script if desired.

Imaginers also have powers similar to comic strip creatures: They can control a conversation to their satisfaction, they can read the minds of characters, and they can travel through time or back up action if they want to replay it.[20]

There is a downside to imagined interactions. When people are asked about thoughts they have concerning conflict situations, only 1 percent report thinking about the other person's view in the conflict situation.[21] People do try to make sense of conflict situations, however, by answering two questions: Who or what is responsible for the conflict? and How serious is the conflict? Unfortunately, simply focusing our thoughts on a conflict often makes it worse. People who dwell on a particular conflict tend to place the blame on the other person involved and overestimate the seriousness of it.[22] We find it useful not to simply ponder the conflict but to think about what the other person might say about it, what you would like to say, and how to do so in a "competent way." It is important not to mimic the findings of one study where results indicated that people imagine interactions with significant levels of verbal aggression and physical violence.[23] Imagining yourself acting competently in the conflict situation is most likely to result in competent behavior. After preparing for the confrontation, now is the time to arrange for it.

Tell the Person "We Need to Talk"

At the second step you tell the person, "We need to talk." Most people understand that the statement "we need to talk" is an invitation to confrontation, creating the initiation stage of the conflict process. Telling the person "we need to talk" may sound strange to you. To us, this step is like making an appointment or a reservation. We are simply saying that you both need to agree on a time to sit down and talk about what is bothering you.

You do this by asking the other person if you can meet and talk about something. Personally, we think you need to provide a little bit about the subject so that the other person has some idea about the topic of discussion, otherwise she or he may worry about something that has nothing to do with the meeting. You need to pick a time and place that is appropriate, but usually not over 24 hours from the time when you ask the other person to meet and talk. Working spouses, for example, usually don't want to engage in a serious discussion when they first arrive home from a hard day's work. Supervisors generally like to have some warning that a problem is afoot and usually have less busy times when they can meet with employees about problem areas. The point is this: Try to anticipate the other person's schedule so that the time to talk doesn't become one more crisis in a day full of them.

Pick a place that is relatively private and free of distractions. It's usually not a good idea to try to talk with the person with children, roommates, or others around or with the television set on. They are potentially distracting. An example of a way to ask for a meeting is: "I want us to talk about what happened last night. I know that now is not a good time, so can we discuss it tomorrow after your modern world class? We could go for a ride and talk." Once you have made the arrangement to meet, consider the next stage, the actual confrontation itself.

Interpersonal Confrontation: Talk to the Other about Your Problem

Stage three is the actual interpersonal confrontation, where you talk to the other about your problem, needs, or issues. This is the stage where assertiveness plays an important role because you call attention to a problem or issue and give voice to your wants, interests, or needs. When you want to assert yourself, follow these suggestions.

- Stand tall, or if sitting, lean slightly forward, but don't crowd the other person
- Keep at least a couple of feet between you both
- Look at the person, but don't stare (suggestion: focus on her or his forehead)
- Look serious, but don't frown, glare, or appear menacing
- Speak firmly, calmly, slowly, and don't allow yourself to become verbally aggressive
- Use open gestures and avoid any threatening gestures such as arm waving, pointing, standing up, or making a fist
- State your own point of view in terms of your needs, wants, interests, and concerns but find something on which you both agree.

While we are generally in favor of assertive responses to conflict situations, we need to point out that confronting others is not always advisable. You need to choose to assert yourself when the situation calls for it, however. Sometimes others cannot handle your assertiveness, and they may be someone who has a lot of influence over you or your future, such as your boss, teacher, parent, or romantic partner. Insecure people may become aggressive or passive-aggressive. One of the authors, Lee, likes to tell his students that the romantic, dating period is a good time to determine whether a future mate can handle one's assertiveness. When a problem occurs in your relationship, you can test your partner's ability to deal with conflict situations by confronting him or her. If that person turns abusive, walks out on you, becomes rigid and uncooperative, and you find yourself having to avoid or accommodate on all important concerns, you need to realize that such a person is likely to continue to mismanage conflict situations. On the other hand, if the person is not turned off by your assertiveness, takes you into consideration, and cooperates with you, then you may have discovered someone who is an effective conflict manager. The moral to the story is to try to surround yourself with people who are open with you and who can handle your assertiveness.

Consider Your Partner's Point of View

At stage four, you need to consider your partner's point of view. Researchers claim that empathy is an essential aspect of communication competence. "Empathic processes, or the tendency to consider another's beliefs and feelings, allow people to better judge appropriateness . . ."[24] Put yourself in the other's position and ask yourself how you would feel if requested to make the same change. Would you resent it? Would you think that such a request is reasonable? If you do not think it is, chances are the other doesn't either.

Assertiveness sounds self-oriented, but according to our view it is both self- and other-oriented. Self-orientation is standing up for your rights, interests, and concerns as discussed in Chapter 1. Other orientation means that you are attentive to, adaptive toward, and interested in others participating in a conversation. We shift to an other orientation when we start asking questions such as this: "What do you think?" "What do you want?" "How do you feel?" Other orientation is also seen in expressions of empathy and concern about the other's thoughts, wants, and feelings. It is manifested in behaviors such as listening well, providing relevant feedback to the other, and supporting and accepting what the other is saying as a true representation of who the other person is.

According to researchers, some individuals suffer from **informational reception apprehension,** which "triggers deficiencies in an individual's ability to receive, process and interpret, and/or adjust to information."[25] This concept is particularly relevant because people often fear what others may say in a conflict situation. They may blame us, bring up undesirable information, or remind us of past incidents. However, it is important that you open yourself to the other's point of view. Hopefully, you can see that the need to "hear the person out" outweighs the unpleasantness of what the other may say.

There are four skills for responding.

- You can rephrase.
- You can ask the other person what he or she means.
- You can provide a possible reason for a statement and see how the other responds.
- You can use an unfinished question and let the other person fill in the rest.

In responding, you need to try to keep your temper under control: Act; don't react. You do not have to accept what the other person says if it is incorrect.

When we listen to another's feelings, sensitivity is important. Perhaps one of the most disconfirming actions we can take is to tell others that they have no right to feel the way they do. Rather, focus on why others feel the way they do and what role those feelings play in the conflict instead of arguing about the legitimacy of the feeling. If a listener responds to a statement like "I get angry when I think you are taking advantage of me" by disparaging the feeling ("You can't really be angry over this"), the speaker will be less likely to continue the conflict episode to a mutually satisfactory ending. More likely, the person raising the issue will shut down and say something like, "Never mind. It doesn't matter," leaving both people feeling that the issue is unresolved.

Another disconfirming action is the response many people make when listening to others: "I know exactly how you feel." This is one message that does not belong in conflict language. You make such a statement to someone close to you when you're sharing an excited exchange or discovering mutual interests. But in conflict, such a statement belittles others because it negates the uniqueness of the listener's experience, and, in essence, represents a play for power. Rothwell refers to this as a "shift" response, as opposed to a "support" response.[26] The emphasis is on "I" (my wants, needs, desires, importance), not on "you" (your wants, needs, desires, importance). If you tell me how angry you are with me because I was on the phone when you expected an important call and I respond saying, "I know just how you feel. Last week I didn't get an important call, either," whose feelings become the focus of attention? Mine do. How is it different if I respond, "I didn't realize that you were expecting a call" or "You're really angry, aren't you"? This response makes your feelings the focus of my attention and, in doing so, acknowledges my responsibility in the conflict and my willingness to make amends. After determining how the other feels about the issue or problem, you can do the next step, resolve it.

Manage the Problem: Come to a Mutual Understanding and Reach an Agreement

An important step in managing conflict is coming to a mutual understanding and reaching an agreement. We sometimes find it helpful to put the agreement in writing for future reference ("You say I agreed to what?"). We need to request specific actions. The reason we request the action is shown in the expression of needs. Through the expression of specific wants and having reached an agreement, conflicting parties can give the outcome a try and attempt the last step, that is, review and reevaluation. Many interpersonal conflicts are resolved with rather simple agreements ("OK, I agree to do the dishes on days you work."). For more complicated ones, we make a number of suggestions for written agreements in Chapter 11, when we look at formal agreements that result from mediation.

Follow Up on the Solution: Set a Time Limit for Reevaluation

The entire confrontation process does not stop with an understanding, agreement, or resolution; it ends only after successful performance over time, which is determined (and more likely guaranteed) by a review at a later date, because a true resolution or agreement is one that works or is actually carried out. We suggest that you set a date with the other to return to the issue at hand and evaluate the progress made—reward yourself if successful or revise your agreement if not. After a few weeks, discuss to what extent the necessary changes have actually occurred.

In our discussion of the above six steps to confrontation, we purposely strove for brevity to give you more of an overview of the confrontation process. In the next chapter, we'll provide more detailed information on creating competent messages in conflict situations.

MANAGE IT

In this chapter, we describe the process of conflict and different ways conflict unfolds as people begin to experience issues with someone close to them. The key to effective conflict management is an understanding of both what gives rise to conflict (what we have termed the prelude to conflict and triggering event) and what occurs at the subsequent stages—the initiation phase, differentiation phase, and the resolution phase.

The prelude to conflict sets the stage by identifying the people, place, and time of the conflict. At the next stage, a triggering event functions as a stimulus, often leading to the initiation of conflict, followed by the initiation phase, which is the response to a triggering event. The subsequent differentiation phase is the ongoing interaction pattern in which most of the conflict communication occurs. Finally, in the resolution phase conflict participants come to a mutually satisfactory agreement or outcome.

Often people will get caught up in destructive cycles that do not allow their conflict to progress to some satisfactory outcome. The conflict avoidance cycle and the chilling effect are characteristic of a relationship between people whose first impulse is to avoid initiating conflict or to quickly withdraw when conflicts arise. They serve as examples of how unsuccessful conflicts become mired down in one of the first four stages, namely at stage two. In this case, the conflict has a prelude stage (e.g., one or more of the participants has a past history of poorly managing conflicts), followed by a stage two triggering event (e.g., one partner forgets an important date), but instead of progressing to stage three initiation, the offended individual does not initiate the conflict because she or he prefers not to engage in conflict. The chilling effect occurs in situations where one fears the outcome.

The competitive conflict escalation cycle has a *prelude* stage (e.g., one or more of the participants has a past history of poorly managing conflicts) followed by stage two *triggering event* (e.g., one partner forgets an important date) and moves through stage three *initiation*, but gets locked into stage four *differentiation*, instead of progressing to the final stage *resolution*.

The way we view our relationship with the other person, our past successes and failures in enacting conflict with the other, how we identify an issue, how we assign blame, and how we voice our complaint all affect our pattern of interaction in conflict situations. Potentially productive conflict behavior exists somewhere in the maze of options. In each stage of productive conflict we can choose to spin off into the avoidance, chilling effect, and competitive cycles. As with the destructive cycles, productive conflict behavior stems from attitudes and beliefs about conflict.

When we see conflict as a normal part of relationships and when we listen to others and assert ourselves, we are less likely to become mired down in a destructive conflict cycle. We have devised the following six confrontation steps to effectively manage interpersonal conflicts.

1. Preparation: Identify your problem/needs/issues.
2. Tell the person "We need to talk."
3. Interpersonal confrontation: Talk to the other person about your problem.
4. Consider your partner's point of view: Listen, empathize, and respond with understanding.
5. Resolve the problem: Make a mutually satisfying agreement.
6. Follow up on the solution: Set a time limit for reevaluation.

Although six confrontation steps may seem like a long list to remember, each and every step is an essential phase of the confrontation process. People often forget the last one, but we need to ensure that the process is complete and working as we intended.

We would like to say that confrontation always produces mutually satisfying results, but this is not true. Although confrontation works more often than not and sometimes with surprising results, there are times when the other person is uncooperative, the issue is too complex, and we don't have enough time or energy to do it right. As teachers, we authors encounter many pessimistic students who are reluctant to try the six steps; however, many report excellent results and a change of heart after applying them while confronting someone about a significant issue.

Think About It

1. In what ways do you take a nonprocess view of communication, relationships, or conflict? How can you change your thinking?
2. How have your conflicts typically played themselves out? Do you sense that there are patterns in your conflicts?
3. Think about several scripts that you perform regularly. What are the advantages and disadvantages of doing so?
4. Think of a time when you felt that you handled a conflict well. What did you do that seemed competent to you? How do those behaviors contrast with a time when you felt you handled a conflict poorly?

Apply It

1. Write out a description of a recent conflict that you experienced or observed. What would have happened if there were more or less individuals involved as parties to the conflict? How would the addition or subtraction of interested third parties or bystanders affect the conflict outcome? What effect would changing the time or place have had on the conflict?
2. Take a sheet of paper and draw three columns on it. Describe three recent conflict-triggering events that happened to you that involved people you know well. For example, a person at work is always borrowing your materials without permission. Compare the way you responded to each of these triggers. Did you respond the same way in each case? If so, why? If not, why?
3. Compare two conflicts in which avoiding worked in different ways—one conflict you avoided eventually resolved itself, and another you avoided that ended up getting worse because you put off confronting it.
4. Compare two conflicts—one that escalated and another that did not. What was the difference between the two? What were the outcomes?

Work With It

1. Using the process approach, identify each of the phases of the conflict cycle in the following narrative (prelude, triggering event, initiation, differentiation, and resolution).

   There are four secretaries where I work. Two of us have the same title because we are designated as the company "president's secretaries" and part of our job is to manage the workflow for the entire team of four. My coworker and I have to come to many agreements about phone schedules, work schedules, meetings dates, and lunch schedules. We both try to come up with ideas of our own to put to use for the team, and at times we have had arguments. We can sometimes come to an agreement and use one or the other's ideas.

   Recently, he and I met to talk about our new lunch schedule because we went from six secretaries down to four after layoffs. We both came up with our ideas on how to work lunch schedules and phone coverage. He liked his idea and I liked mine, but this time we really didn't want to use the other person's ideas. After a few rounds of rethinking what to do, we finally made a new schedule together and bits and pieces ended up looking like both models. We needed to work together in order to see that there were things that the other was missing and unfairness in certain areas of phone coverage. We had to do the schedule five times to get it right. It sounds a lot easier but it's not. Everyone gets a day off phones but still has to cover phones during lunch time, even if it's her or his day off because we don't have enough people. Two people go to lunch at 12 pm and two go at 1 pm and when you aren't at lunch you cover phones. We had to swap times through the week to make sure at least two days a week two people are going to lunch at 12 and that everyone has a chance to go to lunch with a different person at least one day a week. Wow, what a project it turned out to be but we finally got a working schedule in place, after we did it together.

(Continued)

2. Using the process approach, read the following case study and determine what stages are illustrated.

I was having dinner with my parents. When the topic of politics arose, I made a negative comment about the current U.S. president, in response to which my father called me an idiot. I felt my dad wasn't even listening to my point of view but rather looking for ways to criticize me. I told him that he wasn't listening. This in turn angered him and he told me that I'm someone impossible to carry on a conversation with. I told him that he was regressing to the way he treated me when I was a child. He then said, "When is your attitude going to change? Are you going to ever grow up?" I told him I was trying but felt that he was too demanding in his expectations of my maturity. As usual, my mother was eating without saying anything.

a. What type of nonproductive conflict cycle is illustrated by this case study?
b. What do you think happens later in this situation?
c. By applying the ideas learned in this chapter, analyze the conflict to see what has gone wrong and what other choices could have led to better outcomes.

NOTES

1. Kenneth W. Thomas, "Conflict and Conflict Management," in M. D. Dunnett (Ed.), *The Handbook of Industrial and Organizational Psychology* (Chicago, IL: Rand McNally, 1976), p. 893.
2. In Greek mythology, Procrustes was an innkeeper with only one bed. If his guest was too short for the bed, he stretched the guest to fit; if the guest was too long, he cut off the guest's legs to fit.
3. Vernon E. Cronen, W. Barnett Pearce, and Lonna M. Snavely, "A Theory of Rule-Structure and Types of Episodes and a Study of Perceived Enmeshment in Undesired Repetitive Pattern ('URPs')," in Dan Nimmo (Ed.), *Communication Yearbook*, Vol. 3 (New Brunswick, NJ: Transaction Books, 1979), pp. 225–240.
4. Gregory Bateson, *Naven*, 2nd Ed. (Stanford, CA: Stanford University Press, 1958).
5. Rudolph J. Rummel, *Understanding Conflict and War: The Conflict Helix*, Vol. 2 (Beverly Hills, CA: Sage Publications, 1976); "A Catastrophe Theory Model of the Conflict Helix, with Tests," *Behavioral Science* 32 (1987), 238.
6. Michael E. Roloff and Danette E. Ifert, "Conflict Management through Avoidance: Withholding Complaints, Suppressing Arguments, and Declaring Topics Taboo," in Sandra Petronio (Ed.), *Balancing the Secrets of Private Disclosures* (Mahwah, NJ: Lawrence Erlbaum Associates, Publishers, 2000), pp. 151–163; Denise Haunani Solomon, Leanne K. Knobloch, and Mary Anne Fitzpatrick, "Relational Power, Marital Schema, and Decisions to Withhold Complaints: An Investigation of the Chilling Effect on Confrontation in Marriage," *Communication Studies* 55 (2004), 146–171.
7. Michael E. Roloff and Danette Ifert Johnson, "Reintroducing Taboo Topics: Antecedents and Consequences of Putting Topics Back on the Table," *Communication Studies* 52 (2001), 37–50.
8. Ibid., pp. 57–58.
9. Ann Buysse, Armand DeClercq, Lesley Verhhofstadt, Else Heene, Herbert Roeyers, and Paulette Van Oost, "Dealing with Relational Conflict: A Picture in Milliseconds," *Journal of Social and Personal Relationships* 17 (2000), 574–597.
10. Michael E. Roloff and Denise H. Cloven, "The Chilling Effect in Interpersonal Relationships: The Reluctance to Speak One's Mind," in Dudley D. Cahn (Ed.), *Inmates in Conflict: A Communication Perspective* (Hillside, NJ: Lawrence Erlbaum Associates, 1990), pp. 49–76.
11. Lorel Scott and Robert Martin, "Value Similarity, Relationship Length, and Conflict Interaction in Dating Relationships: An Initial Investigation," paper presented at the annual meeting of the Speech Communication Association, Chicago, IL, November 1986.
12. Ibid.
13. Theodore A. Avtgis, "Adult-Child Control Expectancies: Effects on Taking Conflict Personally toward Parents," *Communication Research Reports* 19 (2002), 226–236.

14. Several authors have noted that once a conflict is initiated, the greatest pressures are toward escalation rather than toward containment and management. See, for example, Morton Deutsch, "Conflicts: Productive or Destructive?" *Journal of Social Issues* 25 (1969), 7–41; Louis Kriegsberg, *The Sociology of Social Conflicts* (Englewood Cliffs, NJ: Prentice Hall, 1973); Dean G. Pruitt and Jeffrey Z. Rubin, *Social Conflict: Escalation, Stalemate, and Settlement* (New York: Random House, 1986); Robert D. Nye, *Conflict among Humans* (New York: Spring Publishing, 1973).
15. Dominic A. Infante and Charles J. Wigley, "Verbal Aggressiveness: An Interpersonal Model and Measure," *Communication Monographs* 53 (1986), 61–69.
16. See for example, Dudley D. Cahn (Ed.), *Family Violence: Communication Processes* (Albany, NY: SUNY, 2009); and Dudley D. Cahn and Sally Lloyd (Eds.), *Family Violence from a Communication Perspective* (Thousand Oaks, CA: SAGE, 1996).
17. Pruitt and Rubin, *Social Conflict*, pp. 7–8.
18. Rory Remer and Paul de Mesquita, "Teaching and Learning the Skills of Interpersonal Confrontation," in Dudley D. Cahn (Ed.), *Intimates in Conflict: A Communication Perspective* (Hillsdale, NJ: Lawrence Erlbaum Associates, 1990), p. 229.
19. James M. Honeycutt, Kenneth S. Zagacki, and Renee Edwards, "Imagined Interaction and Interpersonal Communication," *Communication Reports* 3 (1990), 1–8.
20. Renee Edwards, James M. Honeycutt, and Kenneth S. Zagacki, "Imagined Interaction as an Element of Social Cognition," *Western Journal of Speech Communication* 52 (1988), 23–45.
21. Denise H. Cloven, "Relational Effects of Interpersonal Conflict: The Role of Cognition, Satisfaction, and Anticipated Communication," Master's thesis, Northwestern University, Evanston, IL, 1990.
22. Denise H. Cloven and Michael E. Roloff, "Sense-Making Activities and Interpersonal Conflict: Communication Cures for the Mulling Blues," *Western Journal of Speech Communication* 55 (1991), 134–158.
23. Terre H. Allen and Kristen M. Berkos, "Ruminating about Symbolic Conflict through Imagined Interactions," *Imagination, Cognition, and Personality* 25 (2005–2006), 307–320.
24. Amy S. Ebesu Hubbard, "Conflict between Relationally Uncertain Romantic Partners: The Influence of Relational Responsiveness and Empathy," *Communication Monographs* 68 (2001), 402.
25. Paul Schrodt and Lawrence R. Wheeless, "Aggressive Communication and Informational Reception Apprehension: The Influence of Listening Anxiety and Intellectual Inflexibility on Trait Argumentativeness and Verbal Aggressiveness," *Communication Quarterly* 49 (2001), 57.
26. J. Dan Rothwell, *In Mixed Company*, 6th Ed. (Boston, MA: Wadsworth, 2007).

CHAPTER 3

Communication Options in Conflict

OBJECTIVES

At the end of this chapter, you should be able to:

- Describe the three basic orientations toward others in conflict situations.
- Compare and contrast the four communication options for dealing with conflicts.
- Explain the three factors you should consider when choosing among the four conflict communication options.
- Describe the primary communication considerations that should influence your choice of a conflict communication option.
- List and explain the phases of collaboration.
- Discuss the advantages of collaboration.

KEY TERMS

accommodating
aggressive communication
assertive communication
avoiding
backstabbing
basic communication rights
collaborating
communication apprehension
communication considerations

competing
compromising
conflict communication options
forcing
gunny-sacking
nonassertive communication
nonverbally aggressive behavior
outcomes
other-centered orientation

passive-aggressive communication
personal stress
relationship-centered orientation
relationship stress
sabotage
self-centered orientation
strategies
verbally aggressive communication

Now that you have an overall view of what conflict is and how it unfolds in fairly predictable phases, we turn our attention to your behavior in the conflict situation. In this chapter, we provide a bird's eye view of the various choices available to people in conflicts before we elaborate in Chapters 4 and 5 on the choices we see as most desirable.

When faced with a conflict, people generally respond in one of three ways: They can respond in other-centered, self-centered, or relationship-centered ways. Depending on their initiation orientation with respect to the conflict, they may choose one of four **conflict communication options**, or ways of behaving toward the other: nonassertive, passive-aggressive, aggressive, or assertive. Each option leads in turn to a particular combination of **outcomes** (results of the conflict): lose–lose, lose–win, win–lose, or win–win. And each outcome contains within it **strategies** (verbal and nonverbal behaviors) people can enact to get the outcome they desire. The relationship of orientations, options, outcomes, and strategies is depicted in Table 3.1.

It's important to note that we are not saying that people always do or should respond in the same way. We want to emphasize that (1) we can choose how to respond in a conflict situation, and (2) the choices we end up making have consequences. It is not desirable to be locked into a particular style of communication, as this narrative illustrates:

> My husband, Peter, is a doctor who works in a hospital emergency room. He is used to making the decisions and giving orders. When he becomes impatient, he turns red and yells at the nurses and orderlies. So much of what goes on there is life and death where seconds really matter. The problem is that he can't leave his "dominant personality" at work when he comes home. He'll snap at me and the kids and even yells at us when he loses his patience. I tell him that we are not an emergency medical unit, just a family. He didn't always act like this, but years at the hospital have turned him into a tyrant.

We hope this reinforces the idea of individual responsibility for one's actions. When involved in a conflict situation, refraining from actions you would not like to receive and developing a sense of fair play are useful guidelines. The following sections explore some of the implications and factors that are relevant when considering conflict orientations and options, based on the assumption that with some instruction and practice many people are able to modify their behavior to better adapt to their circumstances. It is our desire that you learn to recognize when each of the orientations would be the appropriate option, although we admit that our bias is toward a relationship-centered assertive approach.

We also want to emphasize that this is not intended as an exercise in labeling people as personality types such as nonassertive or aggressive. Nor is this a psychological approach that digs for deep emotional problems that account for personality disorders. Our goal is to identify certain conflict communication behaviors that are viewed as good or bad habits or behaviors learned from good or poor models and apply them in problematic situations. Quite often we engage in destructive behaviors without realizing the harm they do to others. The important point about this approach to conflict is that if we have learned how to behave poorly, then we can unlearn it. The change is sometimes difficult, but it is possible.

Given this overview, then, we turn our attention to the first of the three orientations that a person can take in a conflict: the other-centered orientation that results in nonassertive behavior.

THE OTHER-CENTERED ORIENTATION: NONASSERTIVE COMMUNICATION BEHAVIOR AS AN OPTION

The first orientation one might take toward conflict is to be more oriented toward what others want than what you want. It's important to distinguish this from what some might consider humility or embrace of others.[1] The **other-centered orientation** represents a disregard for self that can result in unproductive outcomes. When one takes the other-centered orientation, nonassertive communication is the result, which is enacted through avoiding or accommodating strategies.

TABLE 3.1 Concerns, Communication Options, and Outcomes

General Concerns	Other-Centered	Passive-Aggressive	Self-Centered		Relationship-Centered	
	Nonassertive		Aggressive		Assertive	
			Verbally	Nonverbally		
Outcome	I lose–You win	I win–You lose	I win–You lose	I win–You lose	We both win and lose	We both win
Behavior Approach	Accommodating	Backstabbing and sabotaging	Competing	Forcing	Compromising	Collaborating
Message Behaviors	Giving in	Strategic stupidity	Prescription	Physical intimidation	Cost cutting	Description
	Deny conflict exists					
	Giving power to the other	Selective amnesia	Avoiding responsibility	Pushing/shoving	Prioritizing	Qualification
	Underresponsiveness					
	Smoothing	Lying	Presumptive attribution	Hitting	Objective criteria	Disclosure
	Changing topic					
	Process focus	Lack of cooperation	Hostile questioning	Use of weapons	Compensation	Soliciting disclosure
	Ambivalence	Nonverbal displays (tears, manipulating objects, etc.)	Rejecting			Negative inquiry
		Overscheduling	Faulting			
	Pessimism					Empathy/support
	Joking	Attack, withdrawn and apologize	Hostile joking			Emphasizing commonalities
						Accepting responsibility
						Initiating problem solving

Consider these two accounts of nonassertiveness in conflict:

> I was raised to be submissive. I obeyed my parents and other elders/authority figures; I never questioned what I was told. I believe this is because of my parents' culture and because of their ages (my mom is 41 years older than me and my dad was 53 years older than me). I am breaking free of the submissiveness (if you knew me about 6 or 7 years ago compared to now you would know I have changed), but I have A LOT more of breaking free to do. I have a hard time being vulnerable to people and admitting when I am angry. I have a tendency to accommodate people and avoid the situation and forgetting about it. I don't stay angry (and keep it in) for very long, it usually passes after a little bit.

> Previously, I saw conflict as a situation that needed to be addressed immediately. As I became more comfortable in how I handle conflict, I grew more discerning. I started trusting my intuition, and I felt comfortable in not always addressing conflict. I learned that there are occasions when people just really have a "bad day" and instead of always addressing conflict and being too concerned about what is going on, I learned that opting to just "let it go" works for me.

While for some people, nonassertiveness is a learned behavior, for others it can be a behavior they choose. We define **nonassertive communication** as the ability to avoid a conflict altogether or accommodate to the desires of the other person through the use of verbal or nonverbal acts that conceal one's opinions and feelings. When people decide to use nonassertive communication, they choose not to speak up for their interests, concerns, or rights. People may choose not to speak up for their interests in a number of different ways:

- They may do it in only one situation for a particular reason. Perhaps they let someone choose a movie to see that does not interest them because it was their friend's birthday.
- People may also choose to avoid conflict in certain types of situations or relationships. In this case, they may think that they should never argue with their father, boss, or aging grandparent.
- Finally, some may choose to avoid conflict altogether regardless of the situation. This happens when individuals do not think that others would or should take their needs into consideration.

People who are habitually nonassertive may regularly exhibit some distinguishing characteristics. They may allow others to interrupt them, subordinate them, or "walk all over them like a doormat." Sometimes they have poor eye contact, poor posture, and a defeated air about them. We may recognize the nonassertive communicator by her or his indecisiveness. People complain that when they confront someone who responds in a nonassertive way, the person often apologizes too quickly, refuses to take the conflict seriously, becomes evasive, stonewalls (avoids or ignores them), or walks out. A nonassertive communicator may sound sarcastic, but when confronted the person denies any wrongdoing. Nonassertive statements sound like these:

> "I don't dare say anything."
> "I want to avoid creating unpleasantness for myself."
> "What good would it do to speak up?"
> "I went along because I didn't want to offend anybody."
> "I don't want to make waves."
> "It's okay for you to take advantage of me. I don't mind."
> "I don't want to say anything that will make you uncomfortable, upset, or angry."
> "Whatever you decide is okay with me."

The concept of nonassertiveness is similar to **communication apprehension** or the level of anxiety a person feels in response to interpersonal, group, or public communication situations. Both terms describe people's failure to engage in conflict with others. For example, people who describe themselves as high in communication apprehension in interpersonal relationships prefer accommodation as a conflict style. However, in a group of people, they tend to prefer conflict avoidance, but if a conflict is unavoidable, they prefer to compete in an effort to end the conflict quickly. In any case, people high in communication apprehension find it difficult to use the assertive style when in conflict.

Nonassertive communication comes in two forms: conflict avoidance, where one stays away from the other person, doesn't speak to him or her, or won't discuss a problematic topic; and accommodation, where one simply gives in or goes along without giving a contrary opinion or agrees without voicing any complaint.

Avoiding as an Option

Avoiding means not addressing a conflict at all. When we avoid a conflict, we are choosing an outcome that is lose–lose. It is a lose–lose situation because the person who might have voiced the complaint loses a chance to improve his or her surroundings by reducing the source of conflict. The person giving rise to the complaint loses because he or she continues to be unaware that he or she has caused a problem for others.

Generally, people who avoid confrontation do so because they have a bad history of dealing with conflict in general. They may also think that the problem may simply go away on its own. We can add that they are not sufficiently concerned about solving a problem to risk confrontation or do not care enough about their relationship to use confrontation to improve or clarify the situation. Behaviors indicative of this strategy include choosing to withdraw, leaving the scene, avoiding discussing issues, or remaining silent.[2]

Hiding in the Sand. *Bobbi Foot's conflict artwork depicts her desire to avoid conflict and pretend it doesn't exist by keeping her head in the sand. Nevertheless, she does keep an eye out for problems coming her way.*

Accommodating as an Option

Accommodating means smoothing over conflicts, obliging others, and not making waves. People may say what they want or feel but are quick to give in to the other. Those who simply give in try to maintain the illusion of harmony. As a result, they suppress the conflict issue in this situation because they do not want to risk ill feelings. By accommodating, one gives up personal gains for the benefit of one's partner. Perhaps one is so concerned about the relationship and the other person that he or she suppresses personal needs, interests, and goals and thus does not make waves. While the partner of the one who is accommodating may derive considerable personal growth and satisfaction, the one who accommodates is not deriving similar benefits.

When they avoid dealing with the problems that plague them, both the people who choose nonassertive communication behavior and their partners lose. If they accommodate by giving in, their partners may win the fight, but the accommodators lose it. A person who gives in time after time may eventually believe that he or she has "had enough" and leave the relationship, so each ends up losing in the long run.

THE SELF-CENTERED ORIENTATION: PASSIVE-AGGRESSIVE AND AGGRESSIVE COMMUNICATION AS OPTIONS

A second orientation we can take to conflict is one that is centered on our own needs rather than on the needs of the other. People who hold a **self-centered orientation** often dominate, control, and force their decisions on others. They may not necessarily be uncaring about the other, but they favor their own self-interests or task accomplishment more than that of others. A person taking this orientation toward conflict runs the risk of appearing to others as argumentative, aggressive, controlling, and selfish in the conflict situation.

Within this orientation, two communication options are available: passive-aggressive communication and aggressive communication. Both of these options are oriented toward an "I win–You lose" outcome. In the passive-aggressive option, a person tries to win through subversion. In the aggressive option, a person overtly tries to get ahead at the other person's expense. We would like to stress that, while these are options available to you in a conflict situation, we do not find them advisable.

Passive-Aggressive Communication as an Option

> When I didn't like the way my team at work felt about something, I would go directly to the boss and win her over to my position. That way, it would look like the boss didn't like the group's idea. Admittedly, I did get nasty sometimes when I would tell her what was going on behind her back. She was always interested and would probe me whenever I was in her office. I know that members of my team suspected what I was up to. None of us much liked each other.

We define **passive-aggressive communication** as the ability to impose one's will on others through the use of verbal or nonverbal acts that appear to avoid an open conflict or accommodate to the desires of others but in actuality are carried out with the intention (or perceived intention) of inflicting physical or psychological pain, injury, or suffering. When people engage in passive-aggressive communication, they do not openly and directly stand up for their interests, concerns, or rights, but attempt to get what they want by underhanded means. For example, one may engage in **backstabbing** by going behind a coworker's back to undermine his or her project at work while telling the coworker how pleased one is with it. Alternatively, one might **sabotage** another's effort by failing to pass an important information or even destroying the other's property or work products.

At first glance, passive-aggressive communication behavior appears to be a type of aggressive behavior. However, the passive-aggressive communicator (seemingly like the conflict avoider or accommodator) does not openly and directly stand up for her or his interests, concerns, or rights. Instead, one might argue that passive-aggressive communication behavior is a type of nonassertive behavior. The problem with that claim is that this individual is really trying to win while making it appear that he or she is being cooperative. The passive-aggressive communication behavior is a type of its own with some characteristics from both the nonassertive and the aggressive types.

What communication behaviors do passive-aggressive communicators use?

- They may spy on others to get information to use against them.
- They may withhold something the other person wants, such as approval, affection, or sex, in order to get what they want.
- They may operate behind the scenes in an attempt to undermine others or to motivate outsiders to act against their adversaries.
- They may spread lies behind their adversary's back and engage in backstabbing.
- They may disclose some personal information to people they shouldn't after it was told to them in confidence.
- They might encourage attacks from outsiders.
- They may simply refuse to defend the adversary when others are attacking her or him.
- They may give away to others something of value to their adversary to make them think that they are perceived as friends when they are not.
- They may deny to one's face that a problem exists while at the same time fail to cooperate.

Scholars have compiled the following list of passive-aggressive behaviors, to which we have added a few of our own:

- forgetting promises, agreements, and appointments
- making unkind statements, and then quickly apologizing
- playing a stereo too loudly, slamming doors, banging objects
- not doing chores
- taking more time than usual to get ready
- getting confused, sarcastic, helpless, or tearful without saying why
- getting sick when one has promised to do something
- scheduling too much at once
- evading meetings so that others are inconvenienced

On occasion, we all get sick, make noises, fail to do a chore, or overschedule activities, but the passive-aggressive communication behavior is done with malicious intent. Initially, passive-aggressive communication behavior is of the win–lose variety. It may result in one getting what he or she wants while "doing in" the other. Eventually, however, the situation may turn into the lose–lose type, because when the victimized individual discovers the truth, he or she may end the relationship and have nothing more to do with the abuser.

There are times when we might try to convince ourselves that passive-aggressive behavior is a good option. For example, if your neighbors are having a noisy party and it is late, you might choose to call the police rather than simply ask them to turn down the music. Or if you discover that your acquaintance has cheated on an exam, you might simply report the incident anonymously rather than confronting the person with your knowledge. Such choices seem reasonable, but ultimately we abdicate responsibility in the situation. Choosing passive-aggressive behavior should be a last resort when all other options have been exhausted.

Aggressive Communication Behavior as an Option

> My father was a person who hit first and asked questions later when he was angry. I learned early in my life how to appease him so that I wouldn't get punished as frequently. But it took me a long time to realize that my husband wouldn't hit me because he was angry. I guess I just kept waiting for him to act like my father.

From a communication perspective, we define **aggressive communication** as the ability to force one's will (i.e., wants, needs, or desires) on another person through verbal or nonverbal acts done in a way that violates socially acceptable standards, carried out with the intention, or the perceived intention, of inflicting physical or psychological pain, injury, or suffering. The strategies that comprise this option are **competing** and **forcing**. While people may engage in "friendly competition," they may also partake in many other competitive events that intend physical harm or unwanted domination of others. When people decide to force others to give them what they demand, they advance their interests, concerns, or rights in a way that interferes with the interests or infringes on the rights of others. Their communication behavior reminds us of bullies when we were in grade school.

Aggressive communication behaviors range from mild forms of verbal intimidation to more severe beatings to extremely violent rapes and homicides. Aggression ranges from carefully planned attacks to sudden emotional outbursts that injure others. People use aggressive communication to get what they want at the expense of others in many different ways. They may choose aggressive behavior in only one situation for a particular reason, in certain types of situations or relationships, or regardless of the situation.

What communication behavior does an aggressive communicator give off? Aggressive communication may take two forms: physical and verbal aggression. Aggressive communicators tend to interrupt, subordinate, and stereotype others. They engage in intense, glaring eye contact, put forward an invading posture as they bear down on others, and emit an arrogant air about them. They try to dominate others by being loud, abrasive, blaming, intimidating, and sarcastic. We would call the following statements aggressive:

> "I have never lost an argument."
> "His stereo was so loud, I had to go over and pull the plug out of the wall. Then, he got the message."
> "I try to make others look bad, so that I look good. I try to get my way at all costs."
> "I am the boss. I know what's best."
> "I don't care what you think."

If they don't start a fight by getting physical, they react with violence the instant the other party "provokes them." Aggressive communicators often get nasty in an argument by "hitting below the belt" (using intimate knowledge against the other), bringing up unrelated issues, making promises they don't intend to keep, using other people (attack through friends or family), and demanding more.

People who resort to aggressive communication often win conflicts at the expense of their partners, because they care less about relational goals than their own.[3] Over time the losing partner may eventually "get fed up" and leave a relationship with one who is aggressive, so both end up losing in the long run.

Verbal Aggression

The realization that communication plays a role in violence has resulted in a new field of communication study focusing on "interpersonal violence" that studies both verbal and nonverbal aggression. In communication research, **verbally aggressive communication** is defined as a person's predisposition to attack the self-concept of another person in order to cause psychological pain for the other.[4] Verbal aggression takes the form of character attacks, insults, ridicule, profanity, and threats. Verbal aggression can also include stereotypes and prejudice.

A large body of research in a variety of settings demonstrates the importance of avoiding verbal aggression. Students are less likely to attend college classes taught by verbally aggressive professors.[5] A study of health workers found that incidents of verbal aggression caused as much, or more, stress on the job as compared to incidents of physical aggression.[6] Parental verbal aggression is linked to adolescent dissociative experiences.[7] College students describing patterns of aggression in their homes demonstrate the link between verbal and physical aggression. As the frequency of the verbal aggression between their parents increases, so does the incidence of physical aggression. Parents who attempt to solve conflicts through "rational" means (i.e., talking it over) are much less likely to engage in physical aggression during conflict episodes.[8] Verbal aggression is also a part of a pattern of escalation that frequently leads to episodes of physical violence in dysfunctional marriage couples.[9] Men who are exposed to family-of-origin violence are more likely to be verbally aggressive, domineering, and negative with their dating partners, showing potential for physical aggression.[10]

Verbal aggression often plays a role in conflicts that get out of hand. In actuality, physical (nonverbal) and verbal abuse often occur together, sequentially or simultaneously. While not all verbal aggression leads to violence, nearly all violent episodes begin with verbal aggression. Next we discuss **nonverbally aggressive behavior**.

Nonverbal Aggression (Physical Violence)

Nonverbal aggression, or physical violence, is often linked to initial verbal aggression, and it starts early in life. A study of sixth-grade schoolchildren found that physical aggression is seen as a natural response to certain kinds of verbal aggression, particularly those associated with attacks on physical characteristics, ethnicity, or race.[11] Infante and colleagues' work established that abusive husbands are more verbally aggressive than nonabusive spouses. They are also less argumentative, in that they are less able to verbally defend their position and refute the positions that others take.[12] Further research has linked verbal aggression in marriages to domestic violence.[13]

Research shows that men are more likely to resort to physical violence toward their female partners, although reports of female violence against dating partners suggest that roughly a third of women physically attack their male partners.[14] According to Marshall, males are more likely to hit or kick a wall, door, or furniture; drive dangerously; act like a bully; hold and pin; shake or roughly handle; grab; and twist an arm, whereas more females are at the receiving end.[15] Research also shows that male partners and fathers are more likely to physically harm their women and children than vice versa.[16]

One of the biggest difficulties in examining physical violence is the effect that social expectations have on violent behavior. In many cases, people see violent behavior as necessary and appropriate; indeed, sometimes it is the only acceptable solution to them.[17] In addition, the presence of bystanders to the conflict may escalate it into violence or reduce its likelihood.[18] Feld and Robinson found that the presence of bystanders decreased the use of violence by men toward women, but increased the use of violence of women toward men.[19]

Given the link between verbal aggression and physical aggression and the deleterious effects of physical aggression upon people and relationships,[20] we would argue that neither behavior is an appropriate first move in a conflict situation. Under extreme pressure, it is understandable that people may become verbally aggressive. When attacked, people may resort to physical aggression in self-defense. However, we maintain that initiating the use of either of these behaviors in a conflict situation is, at best, unwise and, at worst, destructive to the relationship.

THE RELATIONSHIP-CENTERED ORIENTATION: ASSERTIVE COMMUNICATION BEHAVIOR AS AN OPTION

The final orientation one might take in a conflict situation is relationship centered. Within this orientation, we recognize that both our needs and the needs of the other are important. Taking a **relationship-centered orientation** results in assertive communication behavior, which can in turn be enacted through collaborating or compromising strategies.

Using the preceding discussion of verbal aggressiveness makes identifying assertiveness easier. Assertiveness is a concept that became popular in the 1970s through various self-actualization programs that trained people how to say "no" to others in interpersonal confrontations.

> I am assertive with my daughter. When the issues are important (dating, car rides, new boundaries), I am an active and empathic listener. I allow her to focus her thoughts and views so I can understand and address them. Our arguments aren't loud or upsetting. I am calm and never raise my voice. I always try to use reason to try to find a solution. Resolutions to conflicts come about through compromise and collaboration.

A way of confronting others in conflict situations, **assertive communication** is defined as the ability to speak up for one's interests, concerns, or rights in a way that does not interfere with the interests or infringes on the rights of others. Of course this also means that one must allow the others to communicate their own feelings, beliefs, and desires. Assertiveness is seen as a middle ground between nonassertiveness, which is failing to stand up for your personal rights or doing so in a dysfunctional way, and aggressiveness, which is standing up for your personal rights without regard for others.

Although we may see unusual situations where nonassertiveness, aggressiveness, and passive-aggressiveness may serve a purpose, generally communication scholars advocate assertive communication behavior as a preferred means for managing a great many conflict situations because it combines a regard for the other with a regard for one's own personal goals. Because it tries to satisfy everyone, leaving no hard feelings, assertiveness is a concept linked to communication competence.

Asserting yourself appropriately means taking seriously your **basic communication rights**, which derive from those rights, concerns, or interests common to all communicators. You have the right to:

1. be listened to and taken seriously,
2. say no, refuse requests, and turn down invitations without feeling guilty or being accused of selfishness,
3. be treated as an adult with respect and consideration,
4. expect that others will not talk to you in a condescending way,
5. not feel what others want you to feel, to not see the world as they would have you perceive it, and to not adopt their values as your own,
6. your own feelings and opinions as long as you express them in a way that doesn't violate the rights of others,
7. have and express your interests, needs, and concerns as long as you do so in a responsible manner,
8. change your opinions, feelings, needs, and behaviors,
9. meet other people and talk to them,
10. privacy—to keep confidential or personal matters to yourself,
11. have others leave you alone if you wish,
12. ask others to listen to your ideas,
13. ask for help or information from experts and professionals, especially when you are paying for it,
14. not assert yourself, confront someone, or resolve a conflict, and
15. ask others to change their behavior when it continues to violate your rights.

There may be other rights that you could identify. Do some of these items surprise you? Are you violating the rights of others? With these rights comes responsibility. For example, in the next section, we present some **communication considerations**, or factors that influence the choice of one's approach, that may cause you to choose nonassertive communication behavior when it is appropriate. Moreover, to expect fair treatment from others, you must also respect the communication rights of others and treat them "as you yourself would like to be treated." As we enter into relationships, it becomes our task to help all involved to recognize and protect those rights. This is why we tend to favor collaboration over compromise, which may not protect all of the rights for both parties.

Assertiveness is the appropriate expression of one's point of view. Such messages reflect the premise that all persons should communicate in a manner that does not violate one's self-worth; the needs and goals of both persons have equal value. The outcomes of assertive behavior may include the accomplishment of goals, reinforcement of the self-concept, and relational development or maintenance.

Four defining features set assertive people off from other types. They are:

1. open in that they do not withhold information, opinions, and feelings,
2. contentious in that they take positions and define issues clearly,
3. not anxious in that they are not afraid to initiate relationships or conversations, and
4. not intimidated in that they choose to confront others rather than avoid them or simply give in to avoid "making waves."

Behaviorally, assertiveness is contrasted with aggressiveness, in which one's own needs are preeminent, and passivity, in which one's needs are underemphasized. Writers in the area of assertiveness claim that it promotes more caring and honest relationships with others, and they associate the concept with flexibility of response, arguing that assertiveness includes the ability to determine when not communicating one's rights is the best course.

What communication behaviors does an assertive person give off? Of course, assertive communication does not include the behaviors described above as nonassertive, aggressive, or passive-aggressive. Instead, assertive communicators tend to state their feelings, wants, and needs directly and in a responsible manner. Assertive communication includes good eye contact, straight posture, and an air of competence. People are assertive when they are able to disclose their feelings (both positive and negative), offer their opinions, and provide information as needed. Assertive communications consist of spontaneous expressions of warmth, humor, caring, and cooperation. Assertive people are also effective listeners, which requires that they determine how deeply the other feels about an issue and restate the other's feelings in their own words. We would consider the following statements as assertive:

> "I try to satisfy the other person and myself."
> "I like to consult others before I act."
> "I try to get everything immediately out in the open."
> "I'll tell you what I think, and I want you to tell me your ideas."
> "I am concerned about everyone. I don't want anyone left out."

The degree to which a person's behavior is labeled aggressive or assertive often depends on the observer. It also depends on who is performing the behavior. Generally speaking, a man and a woman can behave the same way in conflict and yet others may perceive each differently. For example, given the same behavior he is seen as assertive, but she is called aggressive. Despite sex differences in the way people are perceived, we can differentiate, at least on a general level, between aggressiveness and assertiveness in conflict situations. Both seek satisfaction of one's own interests, but assertiveness takes the other into consideration while aggressiveness does not or it even violates the other.

Compromising as an Option

Within the assertiveness communication option, one may be compromising or collaborating. Both have their place in conflict situations. A middle-of-the-road approach is compromise, which means making sure that no one totally wins or loses. People who are **compromising** in a conflict situation are interested in finding a workable rather than an optimal solution.

There are occasions where compromise can contribute positively to the outcomes in a conflict situation, especially in situations in which all parties cannot have what they want. However, compromise can also contribute negatively to the outcomes if all parties exchange offers and make concessions, and walk away from the conflict feeling unsatisfied with the outcome. As a strategy favoring trade-offs involving "give and take," it is designed as a realistic attempt to seek an acceptable (but not necessarily preferred) solution of gains and losses for everyone involved. This strategy is not ideal because regardless of the initial objective, in the end neither party may win using it, as they both lose at least some of what they had hoped to achieve. We elaborate on this approach in Chapter 5.

Collaborating as an Option

Collaborating means using integrative behaviors and developing mutually satisfying agreements to solve the problem once and for all. Collaboration, then, has two essential ingredients. First, it consists of integrative behaviors such as cooperation, collective action, and mutual assistance. When people collaborate, they work together toward the same ends in compatible roles. We call this teamwork. To an observer, the collaborators appear to work side by side and hand in hand. This approach is in direct contrast to opposing or competing individuals who counteract, antagonize, and work against one another.

Second, collaboration means that the partners have in mind the same goal, which is to strive for a mutually satisfying solution to the conflict. Mutually satisfying solutions are win–win outcomes. Collaboration emphasizes one's own self-interests but also respects the other's interests, needs, and goals. While collaboration may involve confronting differences, it requires a focusing on the problem and includes sharing information about everyone's needs, goals, and interests.

Avoiding Early Compromise

All too often, conflicting parties are too quick to compromise, when greater effort would produce a solution that completely satisfies both of them. For example, conflicting parties might settle for the following:

Examples of Compromise	Examples of Collaboration
Alternate driving the car	Go together to events.
Split driving 50:50	Take a bus/train.
Split housecleaning chores.	Hire a housecleaning service.
Alternate watching TV programs	Watch one and tape the other.
Alternate holidays with family	Combine families for the holidays.
Divide the money between them.	Increase the amount so that both get what they want.

When people chose not to engage in nonassertive or aggressive communication and instead speak up about their concerns, interests, and needs, they and their partners may both win. Assertive communication behavior gives others a chance, which is a good idea when a relationship is important to you. She or he says what the problem is so that the other may choose to do something about it. The other person may not respond in a manner that the assertive person would prefer, but at least the other is given a chance to do so.

Moreover, by asserting themselves, people may avoid **gunny-sacking,** or storing up hurts and anger until they explode. The strategy is harmful because one eventually explodes, perhaps turning violent. By not gunny-sacking, assertiveness may prevent a relationship from turning sour. All too often, people say, "If only he (or she) had said something. I never knew there was a problem." We shouldn't wait until it is too late or lose our self-control as it isn't fair to our partners or us. By getting troubles off our chests, we can monitor one another, adapt as needed, and avoid little problems turning into bigger ones. The relationship between assertive partners has the most opportunity for mutual satisfaction and growth.

COLLABORATION: THE PREFERRED APPROACH

Most writers favor collaboration for managing conflicts. It requires that a person believe that the concerns of the other person are as important as one's own and adopt the goal of finding mutually satisfying solutions to problems and resolutions of issues, which takes time and effort. Gross and colleagues demonstrated that people in temporary task-oriented dyads preferred a problem-solving approach and were critical of a controlling approach to the problem.[21] Research by Manning and Robertson suggests that "skilled negotiators tend to use low avoidance and high collaboration modes of conflict handling . . . [they] also show a preparedness to use accommodation and compromise, whilst avoiding competition."[22]

When you don't have the time or effort or find collaboration to be a problem, you can consider using an alternative strategy. However, as a general rule, we would like to see you adopt the collaboration strategy more often because it contributes less toward long-term personal and relationship stress and most toward personal and relationship growth and satisfaction. Therefore, we would like to spend the rest of this chapter on a more detailed description of collaboration and its related tactics, in addition to providing some good reasons for using collaboration.

Low Personal and Relationship Stress

In general, stress "comes from demands and pressures of the recent past and anticipated demands and pressures of the near future."[23] Stress can be personal or relational in nature, or a combination of both.

Personal stress occurs within a person and refers to wear and tear on one emotionally and physically. While a little stress is positive and pleasurable as when one experiences an uplift associated with falling in love, seeing a great performance, or watching an exciting athletic event, other stressors such as strong feelings of anxiety, frustration, and anger that are associated with life crises such as death of a family member, a divorce, a marriage, a new job, or a change in one's location may contribute to ulcers, heart disease, hypertension, migraines, and even suicide. Loneliness is also stress producing.

Psychologists have long argued that stress improves performance, but only up to a point, at which efficiency drops off sharply.

Relationship stress occurs outside the individual and refers to wear and tear on a relationship. Whereas personal stress goes on within the individual, relationship stress goes on between two or more persons. In long-term relationships, it is the "new social roles of the sexes" that is frequently mentioned as a relationship stress producer. Because of the omnipresence of interpersonal conflict, a little relationship stress is normal and unavoidable, but in the extreme, relationship stress results in relationship dissatisfaction and deterioration, which eventually may result in social disengagement such as breaking up, divorcing, or losing a job. Frequent reliance on collaboration to manage conflicts is the most advantageous alternative because it alone reduces one's emotional and physical stress as well as the stress on the relationship.

High Personal and Relationship Growth and Satisfaction

By failing to include one's self-interests, both avoidance and accommodation create conditions characterized by low feelings of self-worth and relationship satisfaction, and no opportunities for personal or relationship growth. By considering one's self-interests (but at the expense of others), competition creates conditions one may describe as high in personal growth, feelings of self-worth, and relationship satisfaction for the dominant party but low in personal and relationship growth for the other party to the conflict.

Thus, it may happen that people who frequently use accommodation and those who tend to choose to compete are attracted to each other initially but find that the stress and strain on the relationship as they grow apart often leads to relationship dissatisfaction for the one who gives in and eventual disengagement. By gaining some and losing some of one's interests, needs, and goals, compromise as a strategy contributes to moderate feelings of self-worth and relationship satisfaction, and moderate personal and relationship growth.

By allowing for self-interests, encouraging effective listening, and promoting an integrative approach to problem solving, collaboration, if enacted often enough, is the only strategy that contributes to high feelings of self-worth and relationship satisfaction for both partners and maximum personal and relationship growth. When successfully utilized as a mode for resolving interpersonal conflict aimed at developing an integrated consensus through argumentation and perspective taking, collaboration not only ends conflict but also modifies the perspectives of the individuals involved to a consensus framework that respects individual differences.

Collaboration is necessary for genuine and mutual understanding. With training, people can adopt a strategy of collaboration and find ways to develop mutually satisfying solutions to conflicts.

Enacting Collaboration

Given our emphasis on the desirability of collaboration, this section demonstrates how one might accomplish a collaborative process. Later, we use an extended example to illustrate it.

Clarification of Perspectives

When conflicting parties decide to confront one another in an effort to solve a problem, they need to clarify their points of view to one another. Collaboration calls for understanding the other as well as one's own position and respecting one another. To do this, we need to understand that good, well-intentioned people may hold opposing views, which do not diminish their humanity in any way. This narrative reports one person's frustration with a friend who cannot accept others' points of view.

> I don't know why, but often my friend and I get into huge arguments when we're driving somewhere. The other day he was talking about how repressed the United States is compared to Europe, and how we shouldn't have so many laws restricting our "natural inclinations." I replied that laws are often there to protect others from what we'd like to do, and he got really loud and said no reasonable person could see it any other way than his. This is what he usually says when he's tired of trying to make his point and doesn't want to listen to what I have to say, so I dropped it.

Rigid Goal but Flexible Means

When people collaborate, they are rigid in terms of the goal of developing mutually satisfying solutions, but they are flexible with respect to the means for achieving them. They are committed to a win–win outcome but are able to devise alternative ways to achieve it. Thus, they accept only high personal gains for themselves and their partners and tend to pursue many alternative paths in an effort to achieve a mutually satisfying outcome.

Developing Mutual Understanding

Resolving differences in opinion or points of view, in a manner that is mutually advantageous to everyone involved, usually first requires that partners increase their range of perspectives, solutions, or alternatives. Understanding the perspective of another person does not necessarily mean agreeing. It means only that you make an effort to see the problem as the other defines it, without deciding on the validity of the other person's perspective.

It also helps for you to try to see the difference between what you want for yourself and what might benefit both of you. One way of doing so is to think about what you want as end points on a continuum with many intermediate views. For example, if you and I argue over a dollar we both see on the sidewalk, we could change it into 100 cents and then see that one might settle for 90, 65, or 50 cents. A continuum often opens the door to many alternatives not previously seen.

Another technique for generating mutual understanding involves reordering the partners' views on the matter at hand, or helping the other person to see that the problem can be defined differently than his or her first impression of it. Such a shift can create an entirely new perspective. For example, when two sales representatives are arguing over who first contacted a client, one might say that the other could spend the sales commission on dinner for the both of them. That might make the other see the situation in a whole new light. Realizing that there are other possible solutions to the problem, each person must take a new look at the matter.

Implementation of a Mutual Understanding

While the discovery of a mutual understanding is often a challenging task, all the time and effort spent on its pursuit is wasted if appropriate measures are not taken to put the solution into effect. To implement means to undertake the solution as agreed on. Quite often, this requires a trial period. Sometimes minor adjustments are needed to make matters work out as intended.

In sum, Daniels and Walker describe the key aspects of collaboration as follows:[24]

1. It is less competitive.
2. It features mutual learning and fact finding.
3. It allows for exploration of differences in underlying values.
4. It resembles principled negotiation, focusing on interests rather than positions.
5. It allocates the responsibility for implementation across many parties.
6. Its conclusions are generated by participants through an interactive, iterative, and reflexive process.
7. It is often an ongoing process.
8. It has the potential to build individual and community capacity in such arenas as conflict management, leadership, decision making, and communication.

To illustrate the collaborative strategy in a real conflict situation, the following extended example is offered.

Case Study

Oganna and Adrian were married soon after graduation four years ago and each has worked ever since. This year they received a $20,000 inheritance (left to both of them). Now Oganna wants to take a year off from work and use the inheritance to pay for a year of her schooling. However, Adrian is against her taking a year off from work and favors banking the inheritance instead.

After giving the matter considerable thought and preparing for a possible conflict situation, Oganna decides to discuss her idea with Adrian, so she suggests that they talk about it after supper. She begins the confrontation by telling Adrian that she is unhappy with her present job and realizes that he would like her to continue working, but she would like to quit her job. She then listens to Adrian, who says that he realizes that she doesn't like her job, he is concerned about their future finances, and would prefer they both continue to work while they invest the inheritance, so that it would grow into a sizable nest egg.

Oganna states that she wants to take a year off from work to attend a local university to acquire a master's degree in business administration, which she says may advance her career in the long run. Adrian, who likes his job, is adamantly opposed to her taking a leave of absence because after four years of their paying off debts for an automobile and furniture for their apartment, he says that he would like to put the money in a bank to earn interest.

Both Oganna and Adrian indicate that they must resolve these differences of opinion because the issues are creating a strain on their marriage. They also say that a completely satisfactory understanding must not break up their marriage, but at the same time, must not result in either one having to give up ambitions, needs, and goals. In other words, they are rigid in their goals of achieving a mutually satisfying solution but flexible in how they might go about achieving it. At this point in the confrontation, they also shift from sticking to their positions or wants (I want to quit and go to school; I want you to make money) to a discussion of their interests or needs. While Oganna says she wants to have a job that is more satisfying, Adrian points out his need for future financial security. So, they agree that a solution must enable Oganna to advance in her career, and yet it must provide greater financial security for Adrian.

While Adrian and Oganna appear rigid with respect to goals, they report that they are willing to entertain a wide variety of means for attaining them. Here they begin to brainstorm a variety of options. Oganna could earn her degree on a full-time basis, on a part-time status, or not return to college at all and do something else instead. Adrian, meanwhile, could bank all $20,000 or $10,000 or $5,000 or none at all. At this point, however, a premature understanding that consisted solely of Oganna agreeing to return to school on a part-time basis and Adrian banking $10,000 would result in a compromise with both persons receiving less than they desire. They agreed that they would rather find a solution that is more satisfying to them both.

In addition to increasing the range of perspectives, the partners would benefit by trying to discover new perspectives, solutions, or alternatives that are related to the matter at hand, such as time, money, interests, security, and status or other factors that were not considered at first. Perhaps, in the case of Oganna and Adrian, they may introduce a time dimension in at least two ways. Oganna could attempt to complete the degree in one year or spread it out over two years or more. Adrian could invest the entire inheritance for an indefinite period or invest all of it now and some of it later. Moreover, because Oganna expressed a desire to do something different, she could consider not doing some aspect of her work that is especially bothersome to her. Perhaps a vacation or a change in her job situation such as a different task, new coworkers, or a different department (or even a new job) would satisfy her need for a change.

An idea occurs to Oganna that might help Adrian view the situation in a different light. She decides to go so far as to suggest that she could not remain in a marriage where a husband was not more interested in her happiness, needs, and interests. In fact, she states that obtaining a master's degree may make her more valuable to her employer and better guarantee her tenure and advancement in the long run. However, she adds that Adrian needs to realize that neither Oganna's desire for time off nor Adrian's desire for financial security is achieved in the event of a marital breakdown, especially if it means divorce. The threat of severe financial loss at this time which neither party wants may motivate the couple to see the value of the newly discovered alternatives to the problem, to realize that there may be a way to reach mutual understanding, and to make an even greater effort to achieve it.

It is hoped that Oganna and Adrian use interpersonal communication skills that are collaborative. Both are analytic, conciliatory, and problem solving in focus; attempt to clarify the issues and facilitate mutual resolution of the problem; describe behavior; disclose feelings; ask for disclosure from the other person; ask for criticism from the other person; qualify the nature of the problem; support the disclosures or observations the other person has made; and accept responsibility for each one's part in the conflict. Using the acceptable elements of the possible alternative opinions, points of view, and solutions, the partners work together to find a choice that meets the needs of everyone involved.

In the case of Oganna and Adrian, an example of an understanding that is mutually advantageous is as follows. As soon as possible, they could take a three-week camping trip that they both want. Oganna could return to her job after the vacation and enroll part time at the university for one year at which time she could request a leave of absence to attend to her studies full time, and then she could earn any remaining credits on a part-time basis. In the meantime, Adrian could bank most of the inheritance to draw interest for one year at which time Oganna could spend half of the inheritance on her education and the remainder could stay in the bank indefinitely. This solution has the potential of completely satisfying both Oganna and Adrian because while on a vacation with Adrian, Oganna is "getting away for a while" and on return she commences work on her degree and looks forward to a semester of full-time graduate student status next year, while Adrian banks most of the money for one year and half after that.

Although other agreements are possible, this is an example of how the collaborative strategy may actually enhance a relationship. During the confrontation and development of a mutually satisfying outcome, Oganna and Adrian have a greater understanding of each other's needs, desires, and beliefs. Each may believe that his or her position has a valuable contribution to make in the long run to their relationship, and that each needs to take the other's ideas into account in any decision the couple reaches. They may take pride in the fact that they asserted themselves and employed the collaboration strategy. As a follow-up, the partners need to reinforce these attitudes during the next few months to guarantee the successful implementation of the mutual understanding.

COMMUNICATION CONSIDERATIONS: CHOOSING THE APPROPRIATE COMMUNICATION OPTION

The idea we would like to foster is that flexibility, openness to alternatives, and adaptability are important interpersonal communication skills. However, we also favor a tendency toward the collaborative conflict strategy, which is proactive in nature and incorporates cooperative, integrative, and assertive behavior.

Although many advocates of nonviolence claim that physical aggression is never an appropriate response, it would seem that it is justified in a few specific cases (involving self-defense). However, we are unable to imagine a situation in which a verbally aggressive or a passive-aggressive response is appropriate. Effective communicators are assertive when it is appropriate and nonassertive when the situation justifies it. When is it appropriate for us to engage in assertive or nonassertive communication behavior? For effective communication one has to consider three aspects: the occasion, the other person, and your needs.

The Occasion (Including Time and Location)

In many respects, an occasion is like a situation. Recall from Chapter 1 that we said a "situation" exists when people play out particular roles in a given context that consists of a familiar setting at a particular time. You can think of a situation as being like a type of book—novel, nonfiction, collection of short stories, mystery, and so on. Just as there are many mysteries, novels, and nonfiction books, an occasion would be the equivalent of a particular book—this mystery, this romance, this thriller—where the time and place create unique expectations that guide our behavior. Like situations, occasions tend to recur—one mystery may seem similar to another. But just as different books call for different readings, so do different occasions call for different behavior.

The Other Person

Although the people involved and affected by your behavior are part of any situation, we want to call special attention to these elements because they must be taken into account in a conflict. We treat our parents, grandparents, significant others, siblings, children, employers, employees, and friends differently simply because of who they are and what they mean to us. We may find it more appropriate to be more assertive in one type of interpersonal relationship than another. Moreover, if we choose to be assertive, we need to consider the needs of the other person.

Your Needs

You are an important element in every conflict situation. You should consider your own needs and how you have prioritized them. Not all our needs constitute a life or death situation. We must satisfy at least some of our needs if we want to live a life worth living, but some needs are better put off at least temporarily or reduced to a less prominent position. Generally, we are more assertive on matters that make an important difference in our lives, which requires collaboration. In some instances, we can let go off less important concerns, such that we might end up in a compromise.

Consider the collaborative conflict style and assertive communication behavior:

- when a conflict is over something that is important to you
- if you will "hate yourself" later for not letting your feelings, ideas, or opinions be known
- when a long-term relationship between you and the other person is important
- when the other person can handle your assertiveness without responding with aggression or passive-aggression
- when the other person is cooperative
- when a win–win solution to a problem is possible

Consider the avoiding or accommodating styles and nonassertive communication behavior:

- when you think you are wrong or have a poor idea
- when the emotional hurt offsets any benefits that might result
- when something has occurred that is more important to the others than it is to you
- when a long-term relationship between you and the other person is important

Consider the competing style and aggressive communication behavior:

- when you have exhausted the other options, and you are in a physically threatening situation in which you must defend yourself to avoid being seriously injured or killed

Even in such a situation, use the minimum force necessary to overcome the threat. Let the police and the courts take the matter further.
- when a physically threatening situation exists for others and you choose to intervene on their behalf

Consider the competing style and passive-aggressive communication behavior:

- when you are in a physically threatening situation and you may have to go behind the other person's back and secretly report him or her in order to avoid direct confrontation where the other might seriously harm you

MANAGE IT

This chapter identifies the choices we can make in conflict situations. Just as there are many different types of conflicts and kinds of conflict issues, so there are different ways that we can respond to conflicts. Many people do not realize that they have options and can freely choose among them, with differing results.

A person may choose to respond to a conflict nonassertively by avoiding the conflict altogether or by accommodating the other person's goals. When the conflict is not important to us, avoiding and accommodating can be appropriate responses. However, when we take this other-centered orientation, we run the risk of ignoring important issues until they grow so large that it is difficult to address them effectively.

On the other hand, a person may take a self-centered orientation and respond to the conflict behavior of another competitively by responding with overt aggression or in a passive-aggressive manner. We maintain that physical aggression is seldom warranted except in situations of self-defense. Passive-aggressive behavior is warranted when there is implied danger in confronting the other, but it is not a good response over the long term.

Sometimes we choose a relationship-centered orientation and split the difference and compromise with the other person. In important conflicts, though, our best option is to choose collaboration by assertively speaking up for our interests, concerns, or rights in a way that does not interfere with the interests or basic communication rights of others.

Effective communicators are frequently assertive, sometimes nonassertive, and rarely aggressive. How does one determine when to choose one option over another? Three factors everyone should consider when choosing among the four conflict communication options are the occasion/time/location, the other person, and one's own needs. The communication considerations described in this chapter can help us decide when it is appropriate to use one type of conflict communication behavior or another.

Our first response in a conflict situation is not necessarily the best one. We need to slow down, think about the situation, and then respond to the other, using the skills discussed in this chapter. The only way to develop conflict skills is to use them in conflict situations.

In addition to learning about the communication options that exist in conflict situations, we need to identify the primary ways that people deal with conflicts. We present these in the next chapter.

Think About It

1. In dealing with conflicts, do you find that you tend toward one orientation over another? Are you satisfied with the outcome of conflicts when you act from this orientation? Do you favor the orientation all the time or are there exceptions?
2. In what kinds of situations has nonassertive communication behavior been called for? Were there disadvantages for you? Under what conditions, if any, might this behavior produce an advantage?
3. Does it strike you as strange to refer to swearing or name calling as a form of aggressive behavior? What do you think of the old saying "sticks and stones will break my bones but words will never hurt me"? Under what conditions, if any, might you gain advantages by using this communication behavior?
4. Sometimes abusive parents say they merely teach strict discipline. What do you think is the difference between punishing and disciplining a child? When do people overstep their parental authority to punish their children?
5. In what kinds of situations are you most likely to be assertive? Were there disadvantages for you? Under what conditions will being assertive produce an advantage?

Apply It

1. Take a piece of paper and write a description of a conflict you recently experienced or observed. Below your description, draw four columns and label them nonassertive, aggressive, passive-aggressive, and assertive. After reading the section on each type of communication behavior, describe how you could respond to your described conflict with that particular behavior. How effective would it be? Why?
2. Write out a description of a conflict you recently experienced or observed. If you had attempted the collaborative style, what actions would you have taken at each step of the conflict?
3. Take a piece of paper and write a description of a conflict you recently experienced or observed. Below your description, draw three columns and label them the occasion, the other person, and my needs. How does each aspect of the conflict impact the way you should react to the conflict you've described?

Work With It

1. Identify the correct communication option associated with the statement: aggressive, passive-aggressive, nonassertive, or assertive. After doing this exercise, check your answers against those at the end of the footnotes. If you have trouble with the answers, reread the relevant part of Chapter 3.
    a. I not only have a high regard for the other but also have a high regard for myself and my own personal goals.
    b. I allow other persons to interrupt me as much as they want. I believe that I am sensitive and subordinate to them. I am extremely indecisive and need time to think before settling a conflict. I often accommodate to the other person's view.

(Continued)

c. I find that I use this behavior a lot at work and with the people with whom I work. I find myself forgetting promises, appointments, and agreements; making unkind statements about others when they are not around; scheduling too many tasks to do at once; gossiping about the people I am in conflict with. I continuously deny that something is wrong but then fail to cooperate.
d. I don't let a lot bother me up to a certain point. Because of this, I do think I am letting other people get what they want and accommodating them. I know that I avoid serious conflicts in this manner. But when I am pushed past my limit my automatic system takes over and I shake like a leaf. It scares me into a sweat.
e. I always seem to try to impose my will onto others. I know that I need to chill out at times but sometimes my anger takes over when I am in a heated argument. I bring up topics that the other person wasn't expecting. I use this style in situations where I need to win. I am highly competitive.
f. I resort to swearing and other forms of verbal intimidation.
g. Conflict can just be unproductive. I just save my breath rather than trying to explain my point of view.
h. I make sure that my opinion is known and do the best I can to make sure my interests are known. But I also do not like anyone else to feel left out in a conflict situation. I am clear and concise in telling others what I believe the problem to be and the possible ways to remedy it. Another behavior I have in a conflict situation is to be listened to and taken seriously. I believe everyone should be taken seriously, especially in a conflict situation.
i. I try to be careful not to hurt anyone else's feelings with anything I say. I like to express myself in a responsible manner so as to not offend others.

2. Answer the questions following the description of the conflict. A and B married this past year, and A wants to spend the holidays with his or her side of the family. B wants them to go to his or her parents for the holidays. Neither wants to visit his or her relatives alone.

   a. What effective confrontation steps could A and B take before, during, and after discussing the issue? How could they clarify their perspectives using I-statements?
   b. What are their initial positions and what interests or needs lie behind them?
   c. What phases of collaboration should they employ?
   d. What additional techniques could they use?
   e. What might their final agreement look like if it attempts to satisfy both of their needs or interests?

NOTES

1. See, for example, Miroslav Volf, *Exclusion and Embrace* (Nashville, TN: Abingdon Press, 1996).
2. An interesting counterpoint to this idea is found in Julia Richardson, "Avoidance as an Active Mode of Conflict Resolution," *Team Performance Management* 1 (1995), 19–23, who argues that the lack of confrontation between management and teams can actually be an active strategy on the part of a less powerful team to accomplish their goals more covertly.
3. Randall C. Rogan and Betty H. La France, "An Examination of the Relationship between Verbal Aggressiveness, Conflict Management Strategies, and Conflict Interaction Goals," *Communication Quarterly* 51 (2003), 458–469.
4. Dominic A. Infante and Charles J. Wigley, "Verbal Aggressiveness: An Interpersonal Model and Measure," *Communication Monographs* 53 (1986), 61–69.

5. Kelly A. Rocca, "College Student Attendance: Impact of Instructor Immediacy and Verbal Aggression," *Communication Education* 53 (2004), 185–195.
6. Belinda R. Walsh and Emma Clarke, "Post-Trauma Symptoms in Health Workers Following Physical and Verbal Aggression," *Work & Stress* 17 (2003), 170–181.
7. Carolee Rada Verdeur, "Parental Verbal Aggression: Attachment and Dissociation in Adolescents," *Dissertation Abstracts International: Section B: The Sciences & Engineering* 63(3-B) (September 2002), pp. 1571.
8. Angea B. Swanson and Dudley D. Cahn, "A communication Perspective on Physical Child Abuse," in Dudley D. Cahn (Ed.), *Family Violence: Communication Processes* (Albany, NY: SUNY, 2009), pp. 1–26.
9. Sonia Miner Salari and Bret M. Baldwin, "Verbal, Physical, and Injurious Aggression among Intimate Couples over Time," *Journal of Family Issues* 23 (2002), 523–550; Dudley D. Cahn, "An Evolving Communication Perspective on Family Violence," in Dudley D. Cahn (Ed.), *Family Violence: Communication Processes* (Albany, NY: SUNY, 2009), pp. 135–153.
10. Kathy Skuja and W. Kim Halford, "Repeating the Errors of Our Parents? Parental Violence in Men's Family of Origin and Conflict Management in Dating Couples," *Journal of Interpersonal Violence* 19 (2004), 623–638. See also Kerstin E. Edin, Ann Lalos, Ulf Högberg, and Lars Dahlgren, "Violent Men: Ordinary and Deviant," *Journal of Interpersonal Violence* 23 (2008), 225–244.
11. Brenda Geiger and Michael Fisher, "Will Words Ever Harm Me? Escalation from Verbal to Physical Abuse in Sixth-Grade Classrooms," *Journal of Interpersonal Violence* 21 (2006), 337–357.
12. Dominic A. Infante, Teresa A. Chandler, and Jill E. Rudd, "Test of an Argumentative Skill Deficiency Model of Interspousal Violence," *Communication Monographs* 56 (1989), 163–177.
13. Clyde M. Feldman and Carl A. Ridley, "The Role of Conflict-Based Communication Responses and Outcomes in Male Domestic Violence toward Female Partners," *Journal of Social and Personal Relationships* 17 (2000), 552–573; see also George Ronan, Laura E. Dreer, Katherine Dollard, and Donna W. Ronan, "Violent Couples: Coping and Communication Skills," *Journal of Family Violence* 19 (2004), 131–137.
14. Emma Hettrich and K. Daniel O'Leary, "Females' Reasons for Their Physical Aggression in Dating Relationships," *Journal of Interpersonal Violence* 22 (2007), 1131–1143.
15. Linda L. Marshall, "Physical and Psychological Abuse," in William R. Cupach and Brian H. Spitzberg (Eds.), *The Dark Side of Interpersonal Communication* (Hillsdale, NJ: Erlbaum, 1994), pp. 281–311.
16. Ibid.
17. Loreen N. Olson, " 'As Ugly and Painful as It Was, It Was Effective': Individuals' Unique Assessment of Communication Competence during Aggressive Conflict Episodes," *Communication Studies* 53 (2002), 171–188; Loreen N. Olson and Tamara D. Golish, "Topics of Conflict and Patterns of Aggression in Romantic Relationships," *Southern Communication Journal* 67 (2002), 180–200.
18. Marie S. Tisak and John Tisak, "Expectations and Judgments Regarding Bystanders' and Victims' Responses to Peer Aggression among Early Adolescents," *Journal of Adolescence* 19 (1996), 383–392.
19. Scott L. Feld and Dawn T. Robinson, "Secondary Bystander Effects on Intimate Violence: When Norms of Restraint Reduce Deterrence," *Journal of Social and Personal Relationships* 15 (1998), 277–285.
20. See, for example, Sandra A. Graham-Berman, Susan E. Cutler, Brian W. Litzenberger, and Wendy E. Schwartz, "Perceived Conflict and Violence in Childhood Sibling Relationships and Later Emotional Adjustment," *Journal of Family Psychology* 8 (1994), 85–97, who argue that both witnessing parental violence and experiencing violence with siblings result in the use of physically aggressive behaviors later in life. See also Hendrie Weisinger, *Anger at Work* (New York: William Morrow & Company, 1995), pp. 161–164; and Suzanne M. Retzinger, *Violent Emotions: Shame and Rage in Marital Quarrels* (Newbury Park, CA: Sage Publications, 1991).
21. Michael A. Gross, Laura Guerrero, and Jess K. Alberts, "Perceptions of Conflict Strategies and Communication Competence in Task-Oriented Dyads," *Journal of Applied Communication Research* 32 (2004), 249–270.
22. Tony Manning and Bob Robertson, "Influencing, Negotiating Skills and Conflict Handling: Some Additional Research and Reflections," *Industrial and Commercial Training* 36 (2004), 108.
23. American Psychological Association, "The Different Kinds of Stress," retrieved October 26, 2005, from http://apahelpcenter.org/articles/article.php?id=21
24. Steven E. Daniels and Greg B. Walker, *Working through Environmental Conflict: The Collaborative Learning Approach* (Westport, CT: Praeger, 2001), p. 124.

CHAPTER 4

Responding to Conflict: The S-TLC System

OBJECTIVES

At the end of this chapter, you should be able to:

- Explain the S-TLC system for dealing with conflict situations.
- Explain how to "stop" and not respond habitually when in a conflict situation.
- Explain different ways to "think" about a conflict.
- Offer constructive advice to someone who doesn't "listen" well.
- Explain why the transactional model of communication is preferable to the linear model for managing conflict situations.
- Correctly create a four-part I-statement.

KEY TERMS

analyze
consequences statement
defensiveness
feelings statement
goal statement
identity goals

instrumental goals
"I" statements
listening
personalized communication
problematic behavior statement
process goals

relational goals
S-TLC
stopping
thinking
"you" statements

In Chapters 2 and 3, we defined conflict and discussed the many different types that have implications for how one should handle a conflict. Of particular importance are real, substantive conflicts that concern intangible issues. To manage them effectively, you need specific communication skills. You need to identify different types of conflicts and know how to fit the communication skills to the appropriate situation. The purpose of this chapter is to provide a general understanding of communication in general and describe our S-TLC system for managing conflicts over intangible issues.

COMMUNICATION IN CONFLICT SITUATIONS

You will recall that in Chapter 1 we talked about the way people communicate that they are in conflict with one another. We described both a "linear model of communication," which emphasizes accuracy in meaning, and a "transactional model of communication," which emphasizes managing and coordinating. We explained that from a linear point of view, our focus is on the end result, whereas in the transactional model we are more likely to see ourselves as mutually sharing responsibility for the conflict situation and working together to better deal with it.

The important thing to remember about communication is that it's not a one-way street: Just because you act competently doesn't mean you will resolve your conflict well. It takes two people to make the conflict and two people to manage or resolve it. Although you can learn these skills, it's important to remember that you can't make a conflict work all by yourself. You can control your own behavior, but there is still another person in the conflict situation responding to you.

THE S-TLC SYSTEM

The **S-TLC** system is an acronym for Stop, Think, Listen, and Communicate. We use the hyphen in *S-TLC* to help you recall the system because we all need a little TLC in our lives. Note, however, that our TLC stands for something different from Tender, Loving Care. By following these four steps, you can often resolve interpersonal conflicts through basic communication skills.

Step 1: Stop. When you realize that a conflict exists, begin by saying: "Stop!" Don't become so upset that you start to lose control of yourself. Instead, try to calm down and cool off. Try to control your mental faculties.

Step 2: Think. Think before you act! At an elementary level, try not to take the conflict personally. At a more advanced level, think about your goals, wants, and needs and those of your partner.

Step 3: Listen. Listen before you say anything! The tendency of most people is to justify themselves the moment they hear criticism rather than really listening to what the other person is saying. We believe that the ability to truly hear what the other person is saying is as important as what we say in a conflict.

Step 4: Communicate. Decide how to communicate and do it! You could react with violence or not. What are the outcomes if you react violently? What would happen if you don't? You could respond by communicating in a destructive way such as by using aggressive speech. You could respond by avoiding the conflict altogether or by simply giving in. You could sit down and discuss the problem with the other person. This chapter provides a particular method for approaching conflict, from our general S-TLC model through a confrontation ritual that provides opportunities for effectively managing the conflict. Let us begin with "stopping."

Stopping: Taking Time Out

Stopping is like taking a time out. For many people this is not too difficult. For others acquiring skills for slowing down the conflict is imperative. Some suggestions are these:

1. Exit temporarily to calm yourself. It is helpful to let the other person know that you are not abandoning the situation and will return.
2. Get a glass of water or some other beverage and take sips of the beverage before you respond to the other person.
3. Count backward from 100.
4. Change the problematic topic for a while to allow time for the air to clear.

It would help at this point for us to ask you to list as many ways as possible for stopping and taking time out in a conflict situation. Try to compare your list with as many people as you can. You will find there are a variety of ways to *Stop*. The important thing about this step is that it forces us out of a reactive stance into a proactive one. We now turn your attention to thinking about the conflict.

> In reading about the S-TLC process, I easily identified the first step as my primary weakness in the process. When presented with conflict I find that I am trying to resolve it before it has been completely presented to me. I realize now that by missing the first step—stopping and taking time out—I am not as effective in the TLC process as I could be if I had done. I actually skip right to the second step and start thinking about how to resolve it and in the process may miss important pieces of the message being communicated to me. This can be particularly destructive to good communication because I know people I am dealing with are quite aware that the wheels are turning.

Thinking about the Conflict: Analyzing Conflict Situations

Thinking is more than simply ruminating about the conflict; effective conflict managers effectively **analyze** the situation. You are more likely to have satisfactory outcomes when you think about a conflict ahead of time instead of going into it without thinking.[1] An important step in thinking about the conflict situation is to look at it as a whole, as depicted in Figure 4.1. It is helpful to keep these questions in mind as you examine a conflict. We call this mapping the conflict.

Thinking about Doing Nothing or about Changing the Other Person, Situation, or Self

The first step in thinking about a conflict is to understand that we have at least four options to contemplate: Although not advisable, we can do nothing and try to live with the situation. Sometimes that is our best choice, but usually it leaves a situation unchanged, continually eating away at us and making us more miserable. Many times, the other three options are considered better: We can try to change the other person, we can try to change the situation, or we can try to change ourselves. If you were the person described in the below example, how might you have handled the conflict she describes?

CHAPTER 4 Responding to Conflict: The S-TLC System

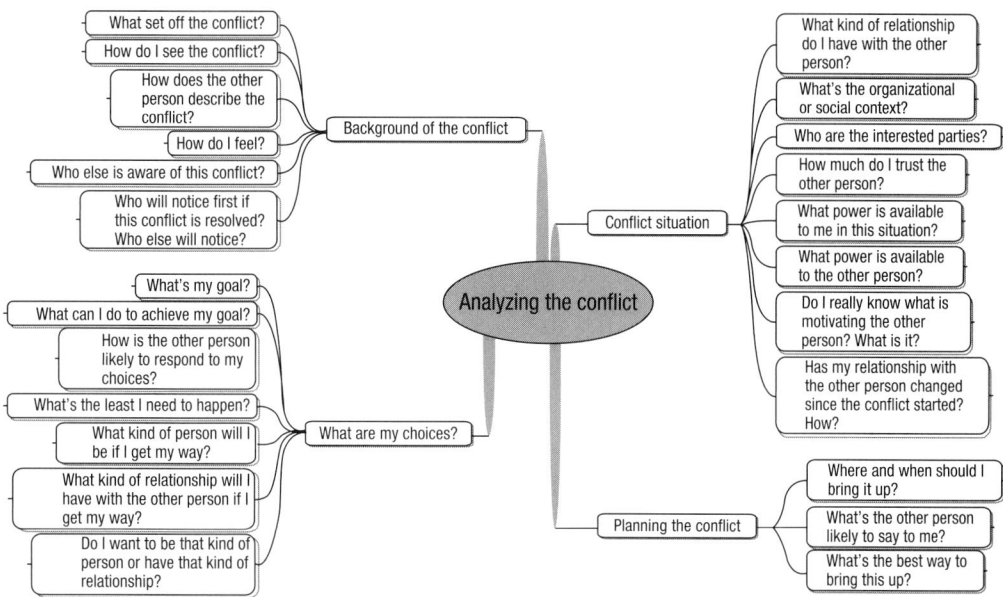

FIGURE 4.1 Mapping the Conflict

Both of our cars are old, and we definitely need to replace one of them. We really ought to replace both, but we can't afford to right now. We've been looking at different vehicles. My husband wants a truck because he goes camping a lot, but that means I'd be left with a barely functional car much of the time. I have to drive to work, which isn't far, but I have to ferry our teenagers around quite a bit to get to their various activities. And my car isn't that roomy, which means it's hard for me to negotiate with other moms to trade off chauffeuring the kids around. I think we need a minivan or a station wagon. It seems to me that one of those would benefit the whole family more, but all he can talk about is the fact that his truck is old and doesn't have air conditioning. Except for driving to his various campsites, he doesn't drive—he walks to work and doesn't spend much time driving the kids anywhere. I could trade in my car by myself, but I sure don't want to live with that kind of decision—I'll hear about it for years.

What are the various options open to this couple? They could decide to do nothing until a car breaks down and forces the situation. However, that option would be a crisis.

How can one person change another? Can or should we persuade the other to change his or her wants or needs? Perhaps the wife can convince her husband that buying the truck would neglect the needs of the family for a car that all can benefit from and enjoy. She could argue that spending family money should benefit the family as a whole.

How can people change the situation? This is a drastic step because it involves changing the situation, context, or relationship. It may mean finding new roommates, partners, or friends. It may mean changing rooms or moving to a different location that better meets everyone's wants and needs. A change in situation includes the possibility of breaking up with someone or changing jobs. The wife might decide that she could find a better paying job, so that the couple can afford to replay both vehicles. Because changing a situation is a major undertaking, we advocate trying to change the other person or one's self first, but sometimes those options don't work out.

How can people try to change themselves? Can or should they change their wants or needs? The wife could decide that the husband really needs and deserves his truck. She may decide she can live with her car for a couple more years. She could agree to the purchase of his new truck.

In established relationships, patterns of conflict become part of the way in which people relate to one another. Because of these established interaction patterns, people may think they do not need to analyze conflicts with the other person: They think they understand how the other person expresses desires and know automatically how to respond. While people often develop reliable tacit knowledge about the other, they generally fail as mind readers. It is important to bring that knowledge into our conscious thinking to make sure we really understand what is going on.

Thinking about Your Goals

A key factor to think about prior to confronting another person is your goal. What are the possible goals when a conflict presents itself? If you wish to reflect on your and others' goals in a conflict, you need to understand the three types of goals that are relevant. Wilson and Putnam argued that people pursue instrumental, relational, and identity goals in negotiation, some of which are generated ahead of time and some of which arise during the course of interaction. These goals are sometimes ill defined and may emerge during interaction or change as interaction progresses. Understanding the dynamic nature of goals can increase your options in conflict situations.

Instrumental goals are those that require the opponent to "remove a specific obstacle blocking completion of a task."[2] If you want a professor to change a grade, for instance, your instrumental goal is the actual changing of the grade as a result of your interaction with the professor. **Relational goals** involve attempts to gain power and to establish trust as the relationship between those in the conflict is established. Relational goals would include establishing your right to question the grade you received while not infringing on the professor's power. **Identity goals** concern how those in the conflict situation view each other. While people are generally motivated to maintain and support each other's self-image, they sometimes desire to attack the image of the other in a conflict situation. In questioning a grade, for example, you would want to make sure that you do not personally attack the professor; comments such as "your grades are unfair" or "you never give consideration to what I say" are attacks on identity. A more supportive comment is this: "I believe I met the requirements because I . . ."

A fourth type of goal people might pursue in conflict situations is **process goals,** which refer to alternative ways to manage communication and conflict. One party may prefer openness, consensus, and fairness, while the other prefers to keep feelings and wants private, maintain control, and win every argument. Parties need to first agree on their process goals before engaging in a conflict over an issue. The conflicting parties might raise and discuss such questions as, "Is their relationship important to them both?" "Is there one style of communication and conflict that would enhance their relationship more than others?" "What will happen to the relationship if only one person get's his or her way now or most times?" "Are both parties skilled in constructive conflict management techniques?" Sometimes competing process goals are making conflicts over issues difficult to manage or resolve.

Thinking about the conflict means that you bring your skills of analysis to the situation. In the next section, we discuss some means for improving your listening.

Listening in Conflict Situations

Most popular advice on conflict emphasizes speaking skills: Say it this way, at this time; assert yourself. But communication is the *interaction* of two or more people, and conflict occurs because the people have different and incompatible unmet needs and goals (or differ on the means for achieving the same goal). No one likes to hear "I can't believe you feel that way," or "You're wrong," when he or she is trying to explain feelings.

> Although I do believe I am a good listener, I find that while in conflict I am not such a good listener. I tend to see my views as being correct and then to be judgmental about what others are saying. I must also admit that thinking through a conflict can be a weakness for me. Sometimes I tend to be more reactive than willing to think through things, especially when it comes to conflicts with family.

Listening is a desire to pay attention to the other person. It is characterized by openness to the other person's views, willingness to suspend judgment during the discussion, and patience to hear the other out. Listening involves both an empathic response to the other person and a commitment to hear to all the other person has to say.[3] Listening does not come naturally, but it can be learned and the skills can be retained.[4] Rogers noted the following:

> Our first reaction to most of the statements, which we hear from other people, is an immediate evaluation or judgment, rather than an understanding of it. . . . Rarely do we permit ourselves to understand precisely what the meaning of his statement is to him. I believe this is because understanding is risky. If I let myself really understand another person, that understanding might change me. And we all fear change.[5]

We typically feel defensive when others have something critical to say about us. We do not want to know that we are not doing well or not doing all we should do. We want to think everything is fine. **Defensiveness** is "a somewhat hostile, emotional state which causes people to either partially or totally reject incoming messages and other stimuli which they perceive as being incorrect or contradictory to their point of view. . . . [It] affects both our perception and our subsequent behavior."[6]

Defensiveness arises from the interaction of people in a situation and occurs when people have a perceived flaw that they do not want to admit and they are sensitive to that flaw. When sensitive people believe that another has attacked their flaw, they respond to defend themselves.[7] Listening is a way of reducing both our own and others' defensiveness; people who feel listened to are less likely to feel attacked. We will have much more to say about defensiveness in later chapters.

Effective listening consists of several skills, some of which may seem obvious to you, and some that may seem new. As Ward et al. note:

> To be a good listener you have to be able to show you're listening. In dialog this includes the active display of attention, interest, understanding and/or willingness to let the other

person continue. This is accomplished in part with back-channels, also sometimes known as "response tokens", "reactive tokens", "minimal responses", and "continuers", that is, short utterances produced while the interlocutor has the turn. In English, these are typically short utterances such as uh-huh.[8]

In addition, you can engage in these behaviors to help make you a better listener in conflict situations.

First, shift your attention from whatever you are doing toward the other person. Others feel frustrated when you do not give them your full attention. One student, for example, reported that whenever she has a meeting with her boss, he continues to read and answer his e-mail as she is talking to him in the office about issues that need resolution. She rarely walks out feeling as though he knows what is happening in the office and what she is doing about it.

Second, look at the other person. It's harder to let your mind wander when you are making eye contact. While you are looking at the other person, also look for cues from the other person's face and eyes that add meaning to what is said.

Third, try to understand the other person's feelings rather than focusing on arguing with the other person. Remember that listening to and understanding others does not mean you have to agree with what they say. You are only trying to hear the person out before agreeing or disagreeing.

To concentrate only on one's own goals is to misunderstand the multifaceted nature of conflict. More importantly, though, listening is a way to affirm the value and worth of others. One author wrote that the feeling of being truly heard is so close to the feeling of being loved that most people cannot tell the difference.[9] Next, we turn to the topic of communicating.

Communicating in Conflict Situations: I-Statements

We hope you notice that communicating is the last set of skills for dealing with conflict. The simple fact is that most of us are ready to talk before we've stopped, assessed the situation, and listened to the other person. We want to emphasize how important the first three parts of this model are before turning to the primary verbal skill you will need for responding to conflicts: "I" statements.

Using I-Statements

Key to a productive conflict is the ability for the grieving individual to effectively communicate his or her desires for change without offending the person so much that he or she stops listening. Clearly, the way we state problems in a conflict situation affects the other person's response. An interesting research finding indicates that as a conflict progresses, people tend to repeat what they have said previously or use a more restricted vocabulary in describing their problems. In addition, they use fewer words that overtly connect sentence parts with each other, making their communication more abbreviated and harder for the other to understand. The researcher concluded that

> as participants move from simple disagreement to conflict, their levels of anxiety increase and apparently their perspective-taking skills decrease. . . . [T]he speaker begins to use talk

that is habitual and comfortable to the speaker, with less thought to the impact the words have on the other(s). Instead of "How can I say this so s/he understands (How can I persuade him/her)?" the response is to repeat what was just said with even less elaboration.[10]

Effective conflict behavior is assertive: It reflects both our rights as a communicator (to express our feelings) as well as our responsibilities (to communicate those feelings in a way that reflects ownership of them). Central to the notion of assertiveness is responsibility—for your actions, for your feelings, for your words, and for the consequences of all of them. This suggests that when we take responsibility for how we feel and act, we start to realize that in every conflict situation all parties to the conflict have contributed to it in some way.[11] As we have tried to emphasize before, understanding your own role in a conflict situation is vitally important to the resolution of it. One student wrote of the difficulty in adopting these skills:

> I wish they sold "assertive pills." I have a very difficult time expressing my thoughts and feelings. I have heard of the "I statement" theory before, but I have not given myself the opportunity to implement the conflict strategies that we are learning. In the past I have not been very good at expressing myself and have often found myself thinking, "I should have said this" or "why didn't I approach it from this direction instead." What was enlightening is while I want to focus on expressing my feelings, I also want to use the other person's point of view as a sounding board: what are you hearing me say? Maybe then I can have the opportunity to rephrase my thoughts and clear up my I statement. I need to actively seek out "safe" opportunities for conflict. A friend once told me that arguing with her husband was the best practice she had in becoming assertive. It was safe to "fight" with her husband because they love each other and would eventually forgive each other, but she learned to stand her ground and get her point across through safe practice. I'm not going to pick fights at random, but I am going to be more cognizant of expressing my "I statement" more often to work from tactic to conflict style

Probably the most important skill in conflict is the ability to use assertive **I-statements** that personalize the conflict by owning up to our feelings rather than to make them the responsibility of the other person. Saying "I feel" and "I think" is far less threatening to the other person than saying "You said . . ." and "You're wrong . . ." The ability to personalize communication comes from a basic assumption:

> If I experience myself as free, I am more likely to personalize my messages. If I am not free, I do not own my feelings. The two skills involved are (a) explicitly signifying that I am the one possessing the feelings, wants, and beliefs when that is what I mean and (b) refraining from holding others responsible for what is going on. Depersonalized communication is characterized by words like "they," "one," "it," and "people"; such words duck responsibility for what is going on and assign it to someone else.[12]

Unfortunately, we sometimes want to put the blame on the other person ("you make me") or to have the weight of a group's opinion ("most people think") rather than simply to express our feelings as our own. Instead of owning what they say and how they feel, people often tend to express themselves in impersonal or generalized language or blame someone else for their feelings and behaviors. As the examples in Table 4.1 show, when you own up to your statements and feelings, you take responsibility for them.

TABLE 4.1 Statements Demonstrating Responsibility

Escaping Responsibility	Taking Responsibility
He made me do it	I did it
She upset me . . . she made me angry . . . she got me all riled up	I was angry
The professor is too hard and insensitive	I think that the professor is . . .
That was a great movie!	I liked the movie a lot
Everyone knows that isn't true	I don't believe it
Adults don't behave like that	I don't approve of your behavior
Nobody likes her	I don't like her
Anyone with any sense at all would not	I don't understand why you would not
This is the way it has always been	I don't want to change it

A common type of responsibility avoidance is the use of **"you-statements**—language that emphasizes what we think is wrong with the other instead of identifying our feelings. While it is tempting to use these, we need to strive for the truth and accuracy, and take responsibility. You can see the difference between the statements in Table 4.2.

As we have noted, assertive behavior is characterized by **personalized communication**—language using "I" statements (i.e., I think, I feel) versus "you" or depersonalized statements (i.e., you always, most people think). You may find that learning assertive behavior and I-statements challenges you. Two misassumptions about others lead us to prefer depersonalized communication over communication that owns our feelings. First, we tend to confuse our perceptions of the other person with their qualities. Suppose, for example, your roommate frequently leaves a wet towel on the bathroom floor and hair in the sink after bathing. Which are you more likely to say to the other person (be honest!): "You're such a slob," or "It bothers me when you leave your towel on the floor and hair in the sink." The first statement puts all the blame on your roommate. With the second statement, you run the risk that your roommate may not care if it bothers you. And so the first statement seems less risky, but that is an illusion. Say to your roommate, "You're such a slob," and you create defensiveness. Even when joking, negative language creates an unsafe feeling for the other, resulting in defensiveness. Defensiveness, in turn, causes people to tune out your ideas.

TABLE 4.2 "You" Statements versus "I" Statements

You	I
You are too hard and insensitive	I think that you are . . . .
Your hair, hat, shoes is (are) terrible	I don't like your hair, hat, etc.
You have a warped sense of humor	I don't think you're being funny
You're too sarcastic	I don't like sarcasm

The second misassumption that seduces us into depersonalized communication is the thinking that others do not change much, and so we can predict their behavior. We can make some educated guesses about the way others react, and the better we know them, the better those guesses become. But making sweeping statements about the other person's behavior to make him or her "pay attention" belittles the other and indicates a lack of trust. We can say only that people respond to situational demands; we can estimate how they might perceive those demands and respond to them.

We need to overcome these misassumptions. Accepting responsibility linguistically is less likely to result in defensiveness from the other person. We need to express our feelings about the situation as specifically as possible and link them to behavior in some way. Only then is the other person likely to understand what is meant. Even if you first state the observation that your roommate left towels on the bathroom floor before declaring, "You're a slob," the other person is likely to become defensive and tune you out.

Components of I-Statements

To make effective I-statements, we have devised the following form to guide you:

I feel . . . when I . . . because I (think, believe) . . . I'd like (want, wish) . . .

The four parts of three types of descriptive statements are given below (see Table 4.3 for examples):

1. **Feelings statement:** A description of your feelings (e.g., feeling angry, neglected, offended, surprised, depressed, or unhappy). It is important to link our feelings to particular situations; vague feelings often create frustration in the listener.
2. **Problematic behavior statement:** A description of the offensive, upsetting, incorrect, selfish, problem-producing behavior (e.g., the other saying something insulting, nasty, or sarcastic, leaving clothes all over the room, or forgetting an important date).
3. **Consequences statement:** A description of the consequences the problematic behavior has for you or others (e.g., wastes your time, you have to expend the effort, you could

TABLE 4.3 Examples of "I Statements"

Feelings Statement	Problem Behaviors	Consequences	Goals
I feel annoyed	When I have to put gas in my car after you use it	Because I end up having to take the time to get gas	I'd like you to get gas after you use my car
I feel depressed	When I hear about all the fun others are having	Because the doctor says I have to remain inactive	I'd prefer to talk about other topics
I feel frustrated	When I study but still get a poor grade on a test	Because this could hurt my grade in this course	I would like to go over the chapters with you

lose friends, or your parents may get angry). The statement contains the word *because*. Ask yourself why you want the other person to change his or her behavior. What adverse impact does that behavior have on you? This may seem like stating the obvious but others do not always think about how their behavior impacts on you, so they need to be reminded.

4. **Goal statement:** A description of what you want specifically (e.g., one may want the other to appear on time in the future or call if delayed). It states what you want, would like, prefer, hope for, expect, or ask (avoid using words like *demand*, *require*, and *or else*). A major challenge is identifying what you really want and stating your position in a clear way that specifically describes what it takes to satisfy you.

Notice that every part includes "I," and ideally, none contains "you." While in theory, the best I-statements do not contain "you," you may find it difficult to avoid saying "you" when describing the problem. Test your recognition of specific need/feeling statements in Item 3 of the Apply It exercise on p. 81.

We need to point out that you can make longer I-statements than the above examples. You may choose to talk for a while about how you feel and then discuss what it was that made you feel this way and why. Because confrontation is a challenge for many, it may take a while before you eventually say what you want. This form is presented only to ensure that you address all four components when presenting your side of the conflict.

Finally, I-statements won't work unless they are accompanied by a calm, nonthreatening tone of voice and facial expression. If one is to avoid being perceived as judgmental, one must sound nonjudgmental in both what is said and how one says it. Otherwise, even the best worded I-statements won't work because they are accompanied by upset and anger, which contradict the words.

Advantages of Using I-Statements

By asserting yourself in this way, you provide much needed information, demonstrate honesty, and reduce defensiveness in others.

- You provide necessary information because the other person doesn't need to "read your mind" to determine what you are thinking, feeling, and wanting.
- You reveal your honesty by telling others what is on your mind, what you prefer, or what is upsetting you.
- You reduce defensiveness in others because you are not assigning blame or blurting out accusations.

Challenges Associated with I-Statements

I get too mad to be nice. Instead of using I-language, it is tempting to hit the other person where it hurts. This option seems particularly tempting when the other person has already hurt us. The nature of relationships, regardless of their setting, provides information that can embarrass or hurt the other person. Aggressive communication laden with blame, anger, and accusations may seem warranted in a particular conflict situation, but such communication behavior only makes matters worse because you cannot take back what you said. If you value your interpersonal relationship, you owe it to yourself and the other person to resolve the problem in a constructive and positive way. Owning your feelings, using the words *I think*, *I feel*, and *I want*, minimizes the possibility of regret over what is said. I-statements make one more assertive without producing ill feelings and provoking retaliatory behavior.

Moreover, remember that the S-TLC system reminds us to stop, think, listen, and then talk. You may need to stop and wait a few minutes, hours, or days until after you have "cooled down." Then, you may find it possible to express yourself using I-statements rather than abusive language.

It doesn't sound right or normal for me to talk that way. Many people have bad habits; they avoid, simply give in, or respond to conflict in aggressive ways. The problem is that over time, one's habits feel "normal," and any new behaviors seem "artificial" at first and require effort to learn as new habits. However, what one learns, one can unlearn. As you see the effect of using I-statements on others, you may prefer to use them more often. You need to give them a try and see how they improve your interpersonal relationships. As one student wrote:

> In the reading I also learned about being "assertive" and the importance of using "I" language. This is something I have been practicing for a while, and it was refreshing to find reinforcement of this practice in the book. But one of the problems I have encountered in using "I" statements is with the people who don't know about conflict management and misconstrue the "I" language for selfishness. I had several people tell me "why does it always have to be about you, all I hear is I, I, I." But after explaining that the "I's" simply mean I am taking responsibility for my actions, feelings, and consequences, they back off their attacks against me for using "I" language.

Remember that as a last resort, you can walk away from a conflict. If you find yourself overwhelmed by the situation, unable to remain in control of your emotions, and unwilling to listen to the other, tell the other person you need to leave and talk later about the situation. Walking away is not wrong if the alternative is losing control of yourself and ruining any chance to bring the conflict to resolution. Also, consider the possibility of bringing in a third party to help.

MANAGE IT

It's important to recognize that communication is not simply saying what's on one's mind. Communication (and, by extension, conflict) isn't something we do *to* the other person, but something we do *with* one another (like teamwork or like a dance).

In addition, this chapter introduces you to one of the most important tools in conflict management—the S-TLC system. The S-TLC system teaches us to stop, think, listen, and then communicate with the other person. By following these four steps, we can often resolve interpersonal conflicts through basic communication skills.

"Stop" means not reacting blindly and responding habitually to the other person. When we take time out, we can then consider our options and try to exercise them rationally. After we have stopped, we need to think, or analyze the situation to try to know what is really happening within it and the range of possibilities it presents. Rather than taking the conflict personally, we need to think about the consequences of doing nothing or about changing the other person, the situation, or ourselves. We need to consider the conflicting parties' instrumental, identity, relational, and process goals.

After stopping and thinking, it is important to listen to the other person. Listening to the other does not mean we have to agree with the other. It simply means that we consider the other's opinion important, and that we try to hear and understand it before we make a point or saying what's on our mind. Although our tendency is to become defensive when we hear a critical remark, listening without immediately defending oneself can make the difference between a productive and a destructive conflict.

To help students create assertive messages for expressing their feelings, wants, and needs during the fourth step of the confrontation process, we encourage them to use personalized communication—language using I-statements (i.e., I think, I feel) versus "you" or depersonalized statements (i.e., "you always," "most people think"). These I-statements consist of four parts: I feel (feeling statement), when I (problematic behavior statement), because I (consequences statement), and I'd like (goals statement).

Think About It

1. Think of a time when you felt that you handled a conflict well. What did you do that seemed competent to you? How do those behaviors contrast with a time when you felt you handled a conflict poorly?
2. How hard is it for you to stop a conflict? If you find it easy to not respond automatically, what advice can you give others who have trouble with this step? Whether you find this step difficult or not, what ways do you prefer if you try to take a "time out"?
3. What are you thinking about when others talk? Do you concentrate on what they are saying or do you think about your own ideas instead? After listing to someone, can you write down most of what that person told you? If not, why?

Apply It

1. Take a sheet of paper and make three columns. In each column, describe a conflict in which you thought the other person should change, you were able to change the conditions of the conflict, and you thought you should change yourself.
   Which of the changes was easiest to implement? Why?
2. Take a sheet of paper and make three columns on it. Label the columns instrumental goal, relationship goal, and identity goal. In each column, describe a conflict you experienced or observed with that goal. What made it a conflict? How did you resolve the conflict?

3. Look at the following statements. Which are correctly stated needs or feeling statements? Circle the correct statements. Check your answers against those provided at the end of the chapter.

   a. I feel disappointed that you are backing out of this show after you agreed to help me with it.
   b. You really irritate me when you don't show up for a date with me.
   c. I need assurance I am loved in a language I understand.
   d. I need for you to tell me where a class is going so that I can get excited about it.
   e. I feel like a single parent around here.
   f. You don't seem to contribute anything to our group project.
   g. I feel frustrated when it seems that I have sole responsibility for planning our dates.
   h. I feel like I am going crazy.
   i. I feel insecure when we don't have at least the equivalent of a month's salary in the bank.
   j. I am not the only person who's having trouble in your class.

4. Look at the following statements. Which statements are goal statements specifying a clear want? Circle the ones that do. Check your answers against those provided at the end of the chapter.

   a. Let's get together for lunch.
   b. I want us to spend more time together with the kids.
   c. I want you to attend this class with me.
   d. I wish we could play different kinds of music around here instead of yours all the time.
   e. I want to stop feeling overwhelmed.
   f. I don't want your pity!
   g. I wish you'd get off my case!
   h. I would like us to have one night a week, Wednesday, just for ourselves.
   i. I want you to exercise more.
   j. I want you to put your dirty clothes in the laundry and not on the floor.

5. Fill in the blanks with words that complete the sentence using the formula: I feel . . . when . . . because . . . I want . . .

   - I feel _____ when I have to wait and wait because I hate waiting around and wasting time. I want to leave at the time we agreed on.
   - I feel frustrated when _____ because I don't know what is expected of me. I would like some help on how to improve my grades.
   - I feel angry at myself when we stay out too late and drink too much _____ because _____. I want to get more sleep and cut down on my drinking.
   - I feel frustrated when I am the only one who cleans up this place because it's not fair to me. I want _____.

   Create your own I-statements:

   - I feel afraid when _____ because _____. I want _____ I feel _____ when _____ because _____. I want _____.

Work With It

1. Read the following case study and answer the questions that follow it.

   When engaged in conflict with my brother, Carl, we usually begin with a period of silence where we both contemplate our reasons for feeling as we do. We usually think the problem over thoroughly before we say anything. Then comes the verbal argument (I prefer to call it a discussion). We try to be compromising and focus on the problem. We are supportive, encouraging, direct, and honest. We express positive feelings for each other to let each other know that we care and want things to work out. We are careful about letting the other express himself while trying to understand his point of view. If you asked either of us, we could summarize the other's concerns quite accurately. I would say we believe in equal power. Finally after we get everything off our chests and get the matter resolved, we poke fun at each other and feel like a weight has been lifted off our shoulders.

   a. Did the parties use the S-TLC system for dealing with this conflict situation? How did they do so?
   b. What do you think the parties probably did to "stop"?
   c. What do you think the parties probably did during the "thinking" step?
   d. What techniques do you think the parties probably used during the "listening" step?
   e. Did the parties take a transactional view of communication? Why or why not?

2. Read the following case study and answer the questions that follow it.

   My friend and I both struggle with our emotional problems. Lately, we have both worked on areas in our lives. She is trying to assert herself more, and I am to the point where I cannot take any more advice on how to run my life. I need to start thinking about what I want to be, not what everyone else tells me I should be. Unfortunately, these two areas have run into each other. She feels she needs to tell me how she feels about everything, including how I act. For example, she told me the other day that I should just say, "I can't go with you today," instead of giving a long explanation. She told me when I give a long explanation it seems that I am trying to make up an excuse and that I just don't want to go with her. I told her I really couldn't handle that kind of criticism right now, and she said "no problem." Two days later, we got into it again when she got mad at me for something that wasn't my fault. She still believes she should assert herself and tell me exactly what is on her mind, and I still cannot handle it right now. It's a stalemate.

   a. What are the issues in this conflict? Are they intangible? Why or why not?
   b. Regarding the S-TLC system, do you think the parties tried to "stop"? According to the text reading, what could/should they have done? If you are good at doing this step, what advice will you give to others?
   c. What do you think the parties probably did during the "thinking" step? According to the text reading, what could/should they have done? If you are good at doing this step, what advice will you give to others?
   d. What techniques did the parties use during the "listening" step? According to the text reading, what could/should they have done? If you are good at doing this step, what advice will you give to others?
   e. Did the parties take a transactional view of communication? Why or why not?
   f. Did the parties try using I-statements? According to the text reading, what could/should they have done? If you are good at doing this step, what advice will you give to others?
   g. In what ways could the narrator change her friend, the situation, or herself?

NOTES

1. Rory Remer and Paul de Mesquita, "Teaching and Learning the Skills of Interpersonal Confrontation," in Dudley D. Cahn (Ed.), *Intimates in Conflict: A Communication Perspective* (Hillsdale, NJ: Lawrence Erlbaum Associates, 1990).
2. Steven R. Wilson and Linda L. Putnam, "Interaction Goals in Negotiation," in James A. Anderson (Ed.), *Communication Yearbook*, Vol. 13 (Newbury Park, CA: Sage, 1990), p. 381.
3. William H. Baker, "Defensiveness in Communication: Its Causes, Effects and Cures," *Journal of Business Communication* 17 (1980), 33–43.
4. Erik Rautalinko and Hans-Olaf Lisper, "Effects of Training Reflective Listening in a Corporate Setting," *Journal of Business and Psychology* 18 (2004), 281–299.
5. Carl R. Rogers, *On Becoming a Person* (Cambridge, MA: The Riverside Press, 1961), p. 18.
6. Baker, "Defensiveness in Communication," pp. 33, 35.
7. Glen H. Stamp, Anita L. Vengelisti, and John A. Daly, "The Creation of Defensiveness in Social Interaction," *Communication Quarterly* 40 (1992), 177–190.
8. Nigel G. Ward, Rafael Escalante, Yaffa Al Bayyari, and Thamar Solorio, "Learning to Show You're Listening," *Computer Assisted Language Learning* 20 (2007), p. 385.
9. David Augsburger, *Caring Enough to Hear and Be Heard* (Ventura, CA: Regal Books, 1982).
10. Mae Arnold Bell, "A Research Note: The Relationship of Conflict and Linguistic Diversity in Small Groups," *Central States Speech Journal* 34 (1983), 128–133.
11. Walter Isard and Christine Smith, *Conflict Analysis and Practical Conflict Management* (Cambridge, MA: Ballinger Publishing, 1982).
12. Herbert J. Hess and Charles O. Tucker, *Talking about Relationships,* 2nd Ed. (Prospect Heights, IL: Waveland Press, 1980), pp. 13–14.

CHAPTER 5

Managing Win–Lose Conflicts through Negotiation

OBJECTIVES

At the end of this chapter, you should be able to:

- Explain the difference between a tangible and an intangible conflict issue.
- Explain the assumption behind negotiation in which people try to minimize their losses and maximize their gains.
- Distinguish between competitive and cooperative negotiation and explain when each approach is most appropriate.
- Describe six ways to generate more options.
- List several additional ways that one can convert a potentially competitive negotiation into a cooperative one.
- Define BATNA and fractionation.

KEY TERMS

aspiration point
bargaining range
BATNA
behavioral issues
brainstorming
commonalities
compensation
competition
competitive negotiation
concession
conflict issues

consulting
control the process
cooperative negotiation
cost cutting
equifinality
fractionation
intangible issues
interests
language of cooperation
minimax principle
negotiation

objective criteria
personality issues
positions
prioritizing
relationship issues
resistance point
scarce resources
separating people from the problem
status quo point
tangible issues
thinking positively

In the preceding chapters we discussed how conflict managers can often clear up a misunderstanding by communicating their wants and listening to the other party. When confronted, the other often says, "Oh, I didn't realize you felt that way. Why didn't you say something sooner? Now that I know what you want, okay." The method we use, S-TLC, is very helpful where the participants tend to be more cooperative and willing to change. We hope that this is the case with most of your conflict situations. However, some conflicts simply do not lend themselves to this system. Where people feel a strong sense of their rights and feel they simply must prevail in the conflict, or where tangible issues are involved, we need more advanced conflict management techniques.

As we previously discussed, **conflict issues** are the focal point of the conflict, the "trigger" that people point to when they are asked what the conflict was about. In this chapter we consider two broad classes of conflict issues: those that concern intangible issues and those that concern tangible issues. We also distinguish between competitive and cooperative negotiation in the hope that you use them when most appropriate. We conclude with specific suggestions on how to engage in cooperative bargaining, where we combine interpersonal communication skills with negotiation techniques. After reading this chapter you can engage in effective negotiation for resolving conflicts over tangible issues.

INTANGIBLE ISSUES

When resources are not scarce, people do not have to gain at the other person's expense. Conflicts over **intangible issues** do not involve hard, physical, or observable assets. They center on love, attention, cooperative and beneficial behaviors, respect, power, self-esteem, and caring. Conflicts over issues that are intangible, and, thus, not truly scarce resources (even though conflicting parties may think otherwise), include situations like these:

- One partner has not been paying enough attention to the other partner (ignoring her or him).
- One person offends another by using sexist, racist, stereotyped, or otherwise offensive language.
- One person's behaviors, habits, or actions annoy or upset another person.
- One partner needs time alone or time out with friends.

Note that the common feature of these examples is that they all involve nonmaterial issues. Usually, we do not lose in situations where we are asked to spend more time with a partner. So in situations like this, being aware of the effects of one's behavior on others is not a win–lose situation. Asking one's relational partner to allow time for other friends or to leave one alone should not threaten the partner or take away from the relationship. Although these resources are often initially perceived as being scarce, this is a misperception, because conflicting parties can share them. When one is involved in situations like these, careful diagnosis of the conflict is needed. Except in cases involving major personality issues, conflicts involving resources that are not scarce are often resolved through interpersonal communication because assertiveness and cooperation can result in mutually satisfactory outcomes.

More detailed analysis of intangible conflicts shows that they usually involve personality, relationship, or behavioral issues. **Personality issue** conflicts focus on a whole constellation of behaviors such as being dominating, introverted, selfish, or achievement oriented. For example, "Alanna always does this." A lazy person presents problems for a highly productive, motivated individual. A shy person may make social life difficult for an outgoing, extroverted person. Behaviors are involved, but there is more going on. In cases involving distrust, power imbalance, or defensiveness, we offer advice in Chapter 6, where we discuss how to change these aspects of one's personality. Conflicts over intractable issues involve disagreements over value-based beliefs, such as the ethics of stem-cell research; foreign policies of the U.S. president; and so on. Such disagreements need not affect a relationship, but sometimes people are so committed to their positions that they are unwilling to "live and let live." We discuss intractable issues in detail in Chapter 15.

In cases where the conflicting parties differ on a way of life or values, they need to make deep-seated changes, seek therapy, or make major life changes, which are possible, but difficult and unlikely. Often personality conflicts do not result in mutually satisfying outcomes. How many times have we heard people saying, "I believe she or he will change after we marry"? While some do, many don't. Hopefully, your involvement with problematic personalities that refuse to seek help or change is only temporary and you can soon move on to others who can provide a more satisfying relationship.

Conflicts over **relationship issues** involve rules, norms, and boundaries that partners have tacitly or overtly agreed on.[1] Sometimes one friend decides to change the nature of the relationship to a romantic one, but the other person is caught completely off guard and finds the other's advances offensive or inappropriate because he or she wants them to remain "just friends." At other times one is upset with a romantic partner's lack of commitment. In Chapter 10, we examine violation of relationship rules and the relationship repair process when they are violated. Still other intangible conflicts involve **behavioral issues**, which concern specific and individual behaviors such as the way we handle money, time, space, and so on. The issue concerns *how* we have done something more than what we have done. Later, in Chapter 9, we discuss a special case of behavioral issues, often viewed as embarrassing moments, where one may lose face in a social situation.

We should not confuse behavioral issues with personality and relationship issues, which also consist of behaviors. Behavioral issues are generally specific to a situation and do not constitute a whole constellation of behaviors that make up a personality or an issue that define a relationship. When Mike is late to meet Sara, she might object because she was worried about him. If Mike is always late, undependable, and lazy, she finds herself dealing more with a personality issue. If Alex wants to push Kelly into a more serious relationship before she is ready, they end up dealing with a relationship issue. However, if Melody says you should be more considerate of her feelings, this may involve only one behavior that involves an intangible issue.

TANGIBLE ISSUES

Another kind of conflict issue revolves around tangible issues. Conflicts over **tangible issues** are often viewed as win–lose conflicts because they involve one's personal property, money, land, grades, promotions, water/food/air supply, natural resources (oil, timber, precious metals), awards/rewards, jobs, and so on. When tangible resources are scarce, conflicts involving them take more than interpersonal communication to resolve; they require more advanced conflict management techniques. Some examples of conflicts involving scarce resources include the following:

- Another person asks to move in with you and your roommate in an apartment or room designed for only two occupants.
- You and another must share only one car.
- There is not enough money for both of you to buy what you each want.
- Both parents want full custody of the children.
- An ex-spouse believes that she or he cannot maintain the current standard of living and at the same time pay alimony to the ex-partner.

Tangible, resource, or interest-based issues generally are conflicts that are countable and divisible, such as how we behave in regard to handling money, time, and space. Tangible issues are most susceptible to win–lose thinking and present a challenge for those who would create win–win outcomes. In many cases, a win–win outcome requires crafting a solution that is creative or ingenious. Of course this may take time and effort, as well as the many techniques we describe in this chapter, to open up more possibilities for consideration. In the case of a married couple discussing how to spend their vacation, let us say that she likes the fact that they "always go to the East Coast to visit her parents," but this time her husband wants to go to Hawaii. They do not have enough money to do both. A solution that would seem like "winning" to both of them might consist of a vacation package in the Caribbean that would allow them a stop on the East Coast. This narrative describes a behavioral conflict based on tangible issues.

> My parents wanted me to come back and attend school near them next year. My mom said she missed me and wanted me to go to school nearby so that I could commute from my parents' house. They're having a hard time letting me go. They tell me they can't afford this college. I work 30 hours a week and would pay for school on my own if I could take out more loans, but they are against that idea. There is so much tension in my family over this. I grew up in this state—my parents are the ones who moved. There's nothing for me there, and I don't want to leave here.

Tangible, resource-based issue conflicts are almost always important conflicts: They occur between interdependent people arguing over issues and possible solutions that could potentially affect their relationship. Table 5.1 lists the two types of conflict issues and gives examples of the way we might address them in a conflict situation.

Is a conflict involving a person being late to an event a tangible or intangible issue? Conflicts over time management can be difficult to classify. If there is enough time available but your friend or romantic interest chooses to spend little with you, you might call this to the other's attention, and perhaps that person may try to spend more time with you. In this case, time is an intangible issue. However, if he or she has three jobs and school, the other person may be too busy to do anything else without cutting back on the time he or she needs to spend elsewhere. Here time is a tangible issue.

We introduced you to the subject of conflict issues because conflicts involving tangible resources, which are hard, physical, or observable, require more than interpersonal communication to resolve; they require more advanced problem-solving techniques for generating more mutually satisfying outcomes. In this chapter, you learn how to resolve conflicts even

TABLE 5.1 Issues in Conflicts

Tangible Issues	Intangible Issues		
Concern material resources that are divisible in some way, such as money, time, etc. "I think we need new windows this year, even if we have to borrow the money to pay for them."	Involve immaterial resources that we value, such as esteem, power, love, etc.		
	Personality Issues "I wish you weren't so selfish"	**Relationship/ Normative Issues** "Because we are friends, you can depend on me for help when you need it."	**Behavioral Issues** "Why did you buy a new stereo we cannot afford?"

when they are over scarce tangible resources or at least those that initially appear as scarce. One way to do so is through negotiation or bargaining.

Negotiation is defined as "a particular type of conflict management—one characterized by an exchange of proposals and counter proposals as a means of reaching a satisfactory settlement."[2] Two people contemplating marriage might negotiate a prenuptial agreement, which usually involves tangible resources that the parties bring to the marriage. By agreeing to negotiate, people are agreeing (1) to engage in a conflict by confronting others rather than avoiding it and (2) to try to find an outcome that is mutually acceptable to all those involved in the conflict by exploring various options in the conflict. The terms *bargaining* and *negotiation* are often used in place of each other. This chapter is not intended as a full-blown discussion of all aspects of negotiation, but it rather focuses on tools used by negotiators for generating possible solutions.

In this chapter, we focus on resolving tangible conflict issues involving **scarce resources**; that is, people perceive there are not enough resources to go around. The resolution of these issues requires both interpersonal communication and basic negotiation techniques. There are some who believe that negotiation skills are fixed—that some people have the ability to keep at it and some don't. Research tells us, though, that people who believe they can acquire negotiation skills through practice more often wind up with more integrative outcomes that are personally beneficial.[3] It helps, then, to take the attitude that these skills can be acquired and perfected.

NEGOTIATION BASICS

One assumption behind negotiation is that people try to minimize their losses and maximize their gains—the **minimax principle.** This strategy is applied when both parties start bargaining with an **aspiration point** (their preferred option, which would maximize their gains) in mind. Both parties also have a **resistance point** (an identifiable amount that they are willing to concede to the other person with minimum loss). Between both parties exists a **bargaining range** (also known as a "zone of possible agreement" or ZOPA in some research) of resistance points and aspiration levels. If an agreement is not reached, parties return to their **status quo point,** or the position they occupied before entering the negotiation situation.

The status quo point may also be referred to as your **BATNA**, the acronym Fisher and Ury have given to the idea of one's "Best Alternative to a Negotiated Agreement." Your BATNA is determined on a number of levels. For example, if you can't come to agreement today with the other person, what's next best? If you can't come to an agreement with this person in the foreseeable future, what are your other alternatives? Considering your BATNA forces you to deal with reality. Maybe the BATNA is undesirable or worst—a disaster. Recognizing this may convince you to return to the bargaining session with a more cooperative attitude (see Figure 5.1).

We have a caution about BATNAs, though. They are most useful for determining what you might expect if you weren't going to reach agreement with the person in front of you. However, if the agreement you can reach with the other person is already better than your BATNA, the value of your BATNA in helping you get to agreement decreases. That is, if the offer the other person is making to you is better than your alternative to negotiation, then your BATNA isn't something you can use to get an even better deal. Your alternative is already worse. When this happens, your personal attributes, or what you can bring to the situation if a negotiation is reached, become more influential in the negotiation process.[4]

One implication of this idea is that one should expect to make some concessions. *This is not the same idea as a compromise, where you settle for less than what you truly want to achieve an agreement. Rather, you may need to set a higher goal than you think possible, knowing that you may need to settle for less in order to obtain what you truly want.* Research indicates that when people set their goals higher, they obtain better results than if they begin with goals closer to their resistance point.[5] Not only do people who set higher goals obtain better results, but those with specific goals do as well. Huber and Neale note:

> . . . if the aspirations of negotiators are too high, too easy, or nonspecific, the likelihood of an integrative win-win solution decreases dramatically. It seems that when goals are easy, negotiators acquiesce and compromise too soon; when goals are difficult, negotiators tenaciously seek high personal profit and subsequently fail to settle at a mutually beneficial level.[6]

You must understand the basic principle of identifying your aspiration if you are to engage in successful negotiation. Research demonstrates that engaging in successful negotiation benefits you not only in the present situation but also in the future: People who have failed to negotiate

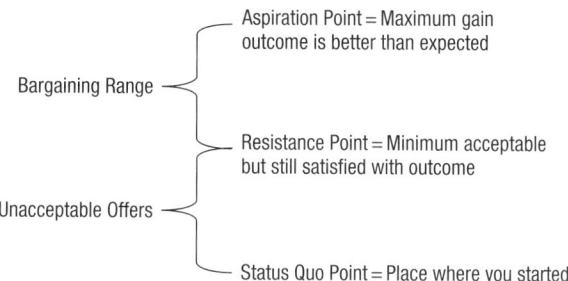

FIGURE 5.1 The Relationship of Different Bargaining Points in Negotiation

a good outcome in past situations are likely to repeat their poor performance in the future, regardless of whether they are dealing with the same person again.[7] Success begets success, so it is important to plan carefully and think about specific, attainable goals.

Competitive Negotiation

Competition often involves tangible issues.

> Competition . . . involves striving for scarce objects (a prize or resource usually "awarded" by a third party) according to established rules which strictly limit what the competitors can do to each other in the course of striving; the chief objective is the scarce object, not the injury or destruction of an opponent per se.[8]

The two different approaches to negotiation are competitive versus cooperative. A **competitive negotiation** pattern is an exchange in which one starts high, concedes slowly, exaggerates the value of one's concessions, conceals information, argues forcefully, and outwaits the other.[9] The competitive negotiator learns as much as possible about the other person's position without giving away her or his own position. Such negotiators believe that they must not show weakness in their positions or offer concessions too soon.[10]

Competitive negotiation often proceeds from a "fixed-pie" outlook; that is, there is an assumption that the outcome will necessarily be win–lose, leaving more for one person and less for the other. Going into a negotiation with this outlook frequently results in outcomes that are not integrative or beneficial for all involved.[11] Frequently, those who negotiate from this position wind up underestimating the size of the pie while at the same time believing that they have the larger slice in the end.[12]

If you decide to adopt this style of bargaining, you should base your decision on the demands of the situation. In cases that do not involve a significant interpersonal relationship, such as car or home buying, one might employ competitive negotiation to achieve the most value for the money. This is why negotiation is often taught in organizational communication courses. Because we sometimes are in situations that necessitate competitive bargaining, we should not simply reject it as a possibility but choose it purposefully and sparingly as needed.

Cooperative Negotiation

Early in this book, we drew attention to the value we place on our significant interpersonal relationships—family members, romantic partners, close friends, neighbors, and colleagues at work. For these people, we need to shift our attention from competitive bargaining situations to cooperative ones. **Cooperative negotiation** is an integrative form that combines formal bargaining techniques with many skills taught in basic interpersonal communication courses such as effective listening, assertiveness, supportive communication, and collaboration. Cooperative negotiation works best when the parties trust each other and the situation is one where mutually satisfactory outcomes are possible, even though the parties may not know that at the outset. One implication is that negotiators should assume that win–win solutions are always possible and work to achieve them because they often do in fact discover mutually satisfying outcomes eventually.

Given the various ways in which bargaining is studied, what findings can help us understand how bargainers reach mutual agreement through integrative behaviors in negotiation situations? Pruitt argues that integrative solutions occur when people are rigid in the goals they are pursuing but flexible in the means they adopt for those goals. In cooperative negotiation, the parties' goals are mutual gain, but they are open to a number of ways to achieve a win–win solution, known as **equifinality.** The formal definition of equifinality is that one cannot necessarily predict how something will turn out based on the way it started. In addition, Pruitt claims that information exchange leads to integrative agreements only when bargainers believe that the other is truly concerned with both their own needs and the other person's needs.[13]

According to Pruitt and Kimmel, when people think in terms of long-term rather than short-term results, they are likely to cooperate more. This is especially true if those involved understand that they depend on one another, that exploiting one another is not likely to achieve a good outcome, and that cooperating with the other probably generates more cooperation.[14] Further, people who view a past negotiation with high subjective value (as opposed to the actual outcome, which may not be as high) are more likely to be willing to engage in cooperative negotiations with the same person again.[15]

Finally, Fisher and Ury, who headed the Harvard Negotiation Project, identified several ways to generate a variety of possibilities before deciding what to do.[16] These include a variety of ways to generate more options, and other means to control the situation.

Generating More Options

Brainstorming. Rachel and her husband, Rick, haven't gone to a vacation spot in years. The only place she could think of was a trip to Hawaii, but she knew they couldn't afford to do that. She is bothered by the fact that they aren't having more fun and opportunities to travel. What should she do?

You are probably aware that the first solution that occurs to you is not necessarily the best one. But how do you move beyond your first solution? **Brainstorming** is a process that requires you to list all possible solutions, irrespective of their initial feasibility. Not all the options are workable, but when you have examined all the possible solutions you can think of, it is easier to focus on one. Here is what happens to Rachel when she tried brainstorming with her husband.

> I wanted to go somewhere on a vacation but realized that financing it was a problem. I brought up the subject with my husband and said I thought we should just list a lot of places to go to for fun. I told him not to laugh or criticize any of the suggestions and he promised to do the same. We each came up with a number of possibilities when something affordable and fun suddenly occurred that either of us would have never thought of on our own.

Brainstorming works best when everyone feels free to say whatever comes to one's mind, even if it sounds ridiculous at the time, because even a bad idea may cause someone to think of a good one.

Focus on Interests rather than Positions. Jamie wants to go out, but Ray says he doesn't want to. What should they do? Jamie could get so angry with Ray that she stomps out the door, slamming it behind her, and goes out alone to grab a bite to eat, but is that the best way to resolve this conflict? When conflicting parties focus only on their positions, they often blind themselves to other ways to resolve their conflicts. One way to increase their options is to shift their perspective from their positions to their interests. What is the difference between interests and positions? Think of **positions** as the final part of an I-statement (the goal part of the statement—what you want). Think of **interests** as needs that are satisfied by different positions. When a conflict is first identified and people begin to make their opinions about the matter known, it is easier to identify the various positions people have taken than it is to identify the interests each party has in resolving the conflict.

It would appear that Jamie and Ray are at a standoff with her wanting to go out and him not wanting to. That is how it all looks if we only consider their positions or wants. However, what happens if we move to a higher level and examine their needs or interests? We may find that Jamie wants to go out to eat *because she is hungry*. Her position is to go out, but the reason is she wants to go someplace to eat. Meanwhile, Ray wants to stay home *because he wants to cook and try out a new recipe*. His position is to not go out, but the reason he wants to stay home is to try out a new recipe. Their reasons reveal their needs and interests. When their needs or interests become known, Jamie agrees to stay home so that they can eat a meal prepared by Ray (which, it is hoped, can be prepared quickly). She can satisfy her hunger, and he gets to try out his new recipe. Both win.

Here are more examples of focusing on interests rather than positions:

> My boyfriend and I are always trying to help each other out. Sometimes, when I need to use his car, he carpools with his friends on the way to work so that I can use his car. I also drop him off at his friend's house so that I can accomplish some tasks instead of the car sitting in a driveway. If I know that he is really busy with something, but still needs to get other tasks done, I take time out from my day to assist him. I do this also because I know he is not the best at multi-tasking.

> When one of my high school friends was planning to visit a mutual friend and me, we looked around for an empty bed he could sleep in, but it seemed as though everyone was staying in town for the weekend. We were about to schedule his visit for another weekend, but it turned out to be OK for him to stay with his cousin's friend. They talked to each other on the phone, the arrangements were made, and a weekend was not wasted.

> Yesterday my friend Kerry wanted to go to town and she needed someone to go with her, but I had to do laundry at my apartment complex. We decided that first I would go with her to town and then she would drop by my apartment so I could get my laundry, and I would do it in her dorm. We both got to do what we wanted to do; we just figured out a different option.

People may change their positions if you show them how to meet their interests or needs. Thus, a good way to resolve win–lose conflicts is to shift from positions (where we really want the same object) to interests (where different positions/wants may satisfy our needs).

Cost Cutting. Maria is planning a vacation with her husband and children, but the price of airline tickets is too much for all four of them to go right away (her kids are 17 and 18). Should she simply give up on the idea because it costs too much, or should she and her family just go, knowing that they cannot pay their bills? Situations like these are not an either–or situation or win–lose. There are probably other ways to view the situation, and cost cutting can help. In **cost cutting,** one party to a conflict reduces the price of an item so that the other is more easily able to accept and live with the solution. In the following negotiation example you can see how one person reduces the price or cost to the other.

Maria would like to not give up on the family vacation but doesn't want to exceed their budget either. She and her husband decided to leave on Friday night and have their kids fly out on Sunday morning. This solution reduces the overall cost of the vacation. Maria and her husband also like the idea as they can have some alone time together. They still get a family vacation, but at a cheaper cost!

In other examples of cost cutting,

> The family of my boyfriend, Scott, was planning a two-week vacation to St. Martin and wanted us both to go with them. I was busy with school and he was overloaded with work. We both really needed to take a vacation, but for financial reasons, Scott couldn't afford to take two weeks' vacation from work. After some discussion, we came up with the idea that I would leave a week early with his family and he would join us the second week. This worked great because I not only got the time to get away, which I really needed, and get to know his family more, but we also had a wonderful time together the second week. He really enjoyed the much-needed vacation, and he didn't have to take the full two weeks from work.

> I was hesitant about renting a particular apartment because I wanted to have a home office but no telephone jack exists in the second bedroom. The landlord settled the deal by installing a more convenient telephone jack, solving my need for the office setup.

Compensation. Andrew's girlfriend, Vannamarie, found a job after graduation and moved to a city 2 hours away. He will continue going to college full time for another year before he graduates and finds a full time job, hopefully in the same city where she is now working and living. The problem is that she isn't getting enough time off to make the trip to his place, and he spends too much money trying to see Vannamarie. Should they see each other less? Should they consider breaking off the relationship because they are finding the distance between them too challenging?

There are always options, but we are often blind to them. One option these two young lovers might want to consider is compensation. **Compensation** occurs when Party A provides something of value (often monetary) to Party B to make up for losses caused by A's behavior or that result from A's demands. Vannamarie goes on to say that:

> I would like to continue seeing Andrew, and I know he feels the same way about me. Since I am working and have a larger source of income than Andrew has, I offered to reimburse him for his trips. He can see me without it creating a financial problem back at his college. Of course Andrew liked the idea, too, and is continuing to come see me.

Prioritizing. Megan, Julie, and Bettina are sisters, but Bettina, the oldest, is engaged, getting married this weekend, and moving out of the home she grew up in. She told the family that she would no longer need her room and many toys, games, and stuffed animals now that she was moving on with her life. Megan and Julie, who share a room, immediately got into a fight over who would get what. Should the strongest get everything she wants? Should their mother sell all Bettina's possessions at their next yard sale and use her old bedroom for a guest bedroom? Different items vary in value for conflicting parties. Some are more important to one person than to the other and vice versa. It is more difficult to bargain over items that are extremely important to one person, while other items may be more easily traded. A good system for working through the distribution of items that vary in value is called prioritizing (or logrolling). **Prioritizing** is a process in which each side grants to the other those issues or objects that the other gives top priority. "You can have items one and two if I can have numbers three and four." Both parties more easily bargain over some issues or objects, but not on those to which they give top priority. Conflicting parties desire several items (not just one) but only insist on the top priority because of its importance and not the others because they are less important. In the following example, Megan and Julie use prioritizing.

> Each of us made her own list of Bettina's items, ranking them from most wanted to least wanted. We agreed to let each other have the top items on their lists. After that exchange, both went to the next time, and so forth until we found we were both interested in the same items. At least we agreed on top 3 items for each of us.

Now the sisters would have to turn to other bargaining techniques to resolve the remaining issues.

The following are other examples of prioritizing.

> I just wanted to watch a movie (top priority) while crocheting the other day and my housemate really wanted to play cards (top priority) and also liked to listen to music. You cannot listen to music (not his top priority) and watch a movie at the same time. Also, you cannot crochet (not my top priority) and play cards at the same time. Of course we argued about it first with neither of us giving in. We finally realized we were wasting time and getting nowhere so I agreed to play cards with him if we first watched the movie.

> I wanted to help with finishing an installation job on a van, but my fellow worker Trish wanted to go to lunch before I did that same day. We discussed the matter and decided that Trish could help me first with the van and then she could go to lunch early while I would cover for her. Each of us had our main concern dealt with. We gave into the other on something that was low priority for ourselves but high for the other.

Base Decisions on Objective Criteria. Getting back to our case study involving Megan and Julie, after swapping items highest on their list, they now find that there are some of Bettina's possessions they both want.

Some of these may be decided along objective lines. One way is to try to base the decision on **objective criteria,** or guidelines we apply across a variety of situations to ensure fairness. Actually, we do this often in everyday situations when decisions are made on the basis of trade-offs, sharing, and turn taking. For example:

- It's my turn this time to go first, and you can go first next time.
- Majority rules.
- Let's toss a coin or draw straws to see who gets it.
- He needs it more than she does.

> Megan and Julie could decide to alternate who gets what on the remaining items on the list or flip a coin over some items. Take Bettina's room for example. Maybe Julie is older than Megan and they may agree that the oldest sibling should have first choice. Then Megan

can have Julie's room now and probably will get Bettina's room later. Or maybe Julie is further along in her education and needs more facilities at home to support her studying at home. Or they could simply draw straws, and the winner gets the room. These are common objective criteria we all use on occasion to settle everyday conflicts over scarce resources.

Additional Techniques for Converting Competitive Negotiation into Cooperation

Separating People from the Problem. One of the most important actions we can take in a conflict is to keep our perceptions of the other person separated from our perceptions of the problem or issue. It is easy in a conflict to confuse how we feel about the issue with how we feel about the person involved with it. Because this can work in either positive or negative ways, our like or dislike of a person can cloud our decision-making processes.

An example of focusing on the problem rather than those involved is found in this narrative.

> As a driver of a school bus, I get to know some of the parents and kids, some well. I occasionally have conflicts with students, and sometimes these spill over to conflicts with their parents. That is usually when the principal, Mrs. Cummings, who is my boss, gets involved. Recently, parents complained that they felt I had falsely accused their son, Ariel, of misbehaving on the bus. They saw the "referral for misbehaving" as an attack on their child by me. When the meeting occurred in the principal's office, they immediately began by attacking me and questioning my judgment as though I had something personal against their son. Mrs. Cummings really did a good job of separating their son and me (as people) from the problem, which was really Ariel's behavior, which led to conflicts with other children on the bus.

Offering Concessions. A person makes a **concession** when he or she grants something highly valued to the other person without asking anything in return, or when he or she drops a demand on the other. Researchers in social psychology suggest that, in general, bargainers who make concessions are more likely to elicit cooperative behavior from the other than are those who make demands or who make no concessions at all.[17]

Seeking Commonalities. Your point of view makes a difference. We know, for example, that it is difficult to cooperate and collaborate with others if you start out focusing on what you disagree on with them. That disagreement may produce distrust and competition. If instead you focus on areas of agreement, you are more likely to trust and cooperate, as this narrative demonstrates.

> I once had a professor who divided my discussion class into two groups, which he assigned to different classrooms. He then gave each group different instructions, initially. He told one group that they would begin by listing their **commonalities,** which could range from physical (all men, all strong, all tall, etc.) to nonphysical items (all communication majors, all enrolled at the same college, all living in town). He told the other group to begin by listing their differences. These also could range from physical (mixed group of men and women, differences in eye color, sizes, height, etc.) to nonphysical items (where they were born and went to school, parent's occupations). As it turned out, the group that started listing their similarities worked together in a more cooperative manner than did the group that began their discussion by focusing on their differences.

Talking Cooperation. Unlike some of the conflict messages we wrote of earlier that take responsibility for feelings and wants, the **language of cooperation** is "we-based": "We both want this," or "We both think this." This is important to everyone concerned. Cooperative language is also tentative: "What would you say if . . . ." or "Do you think that's a good idea?" Cooperative language leaves space for people who think differently, so that they aren't backed into corners.

Consulting before Acting. This skill is of paramount importance. Don't assume that you know what the other wants. Don't assume that you know what is best for the other person. Instead, check your statements to make sure they are right, or even more conservatively, ask what the other person wants before tendering an offer. **Consulting** means to seek input before taking action.

Communicating Frequently. As conflicts escalate, people have a tendency to shut down communication. They become entrenched in their positions and conclude that since they are at an impasse, they should say nothing more. Although communication is not a magic cure-all for conflict, frequent and non-hostile communication keeps those in the conflict from making too many unchallenged assumptions about the other. Recall our definition of transactional communication, which suggests working with others rather than trying to always dominate, avoid, or give in to others.

Controlling the Process, Not the Outcome. If an election is fair and honest, everyone has a good chance of getting elected. Controlling the election process can guarantee a fair outcome, but we still don't know who is going to be elected. We can have a similar approach to negotiating. By agreeing on procedures, steps, and goals, which are ways to **control the process,** the parties can create the conditions for a fair and honest problem-solving discussion, but we can't predict the outcome with certainty. One has to have *faith* that creating a cooperative negotiation process should produce a mutually satisfying outcome.

Thinking Positively. People often resemble the characters in the children's book *Winnie the Pooh.* Some people are Rabbits, compulsive about everything, wanting to control all events. Others are like Piglet, worried that the sky might fall in. Some are happy-go-lucky Poohs. They are content to take life as it comes, which is a way to **think positively.**

In contrast, there are the Eeyores. They're pretty easy to recognize. They make comments like, "I wasn't invited to the party, but I wouldn't have had fun anyway." Eeyores are not positive people, and their pessimism can really make it difficult for others to believe that they are making progress. Eeyores are the ones who shoot down all the solutions during a brainstorming session (dooming it to failure), who don't believe the parties can create any objective criteria to judge solutions to a problem, and who don't think any mutual interests exist when people are in conflict.

Moods indeed do have an effect on our bargaining and negotiation outcomes; people who have felt unsuccessful in the past tend to approach a present task pessimistically and subsequently do worse than those taking a positive approach.[18] A positive mood is significantly related to higher levels of cooperation and less competition in negotiation situations. On the other hand, negative moods tend to trigger higher levels of competition and lead to lower outcomes in negotiation situations.[19] Anger, in particular, may seem like a good negotiating tactic when used in movies or television shows, but studies indicate that it can backfire in negotiating situations, resulting in worse outcomes than if anger were not communicated.[20] You are rarely likely to benefit from communicating anger unless you clearly have more power than the other person in the negotiation.[21] Other emotions such as guilt and disappointment can affect bargaining outcomes as well; if you project guilt while bargaining, you will probably wind up with worse outcomes than if you project disappointment over the process.[22] So, beware of self-fulfilling prophecies! Don't become an Eeyore!

Engaging in Fractionation. In addition to calculating a BATNA, people in the conflict may also engage in fractionation in order to work through the problem.[23] **Fractionation** is a matter of breaking down the problem into its smallest pieces and then dealing with each piece one at a time. This account shows how fractionation helped solve the problem of repairing a house.

> We bought a lovely little house in a great location. Unfortunately, despite its great layout and look, it needed a lot of work. I would have rather done all the remodeling at once—preferably before we moved in! That simply wasn't possible. So, we finished out the garage so my son could use it as a bedroom and we fixed the fence to keep the dogs in. We repaired the roof before winter rains came and painted the house because it made sense to do it at the same time. Inside issues have taken much longer. Inside we made replacing the windows the first priority. After that we moved to refinishing the wood floors and replacing the old linoleum with tile. It will take about five years to get it all done, but it's a lot easier to handle one task at a time.

It is usually easier to get cooperation from others on small tasks than on much larger ones. Fractionation enables the conflicting parties to cooperate on something small and more manageable before moving on to other issues.

In this chapter, we have focused on ways of addressing conflicts over tangible resources that appear to be win–lose. Successful resolution of these conflicts depends on our ability to assess the situation and decide how important it is to achieve our initial goal in the situation. Situations occur when we decide to back off the conflict, giving more importance to the relationship. At other times, we need to argue more forcefully. In most cases, though, finding a solution is a matter of learning how to "color outside the lines."

MANAGE IT

The type of conflict issue makes a difference because we should manage some conflicts differently from others. Some conflicts are over tangible issues and others focus on intangible issues. What is the difference between a tangible and an intangible conflict issue? Intangible resources are emotional, mental, and psychological assets, and are not limited by nature. Consequently, issues related to intangible resources are often resolved through interpersonal communication. In contrast, tangible resources are physical and observable. Because tangible resources are often scarce, conflicts involving such issues take more than basic interpersonal communication skills to resolve; they require more advanced conflict management skills, in particular, negotiation techniques.

When confronted with a conflict over an intangible resource, skilled conflict managers follow the minimax principle to minimize their losses and maximize their gains. They start bargaining with an aspiration level but also have a resistance point in mind. While negotiating, a skilled conflict manager considers her or his Best Alternative to a Negotiated Agreement as a standard by which to measure the value of offers from others. One implication of this idea is that one should expect to make some concessions, so it pays to set a goal higher than one thinks possible to attain. Negotiators who make concessions are more likely to elicit cooperative behavior from the other party than are those who make no concessions at all.

Skilled conflict managers also strive for a win–win outcome. Such outcomes are more likely to occur when the parties trust each other and the situation is one in which mutually satisfactory outcomes are possible, even though the parties may not know that at the outset.

Whether we approach a conflict from a minimax principle or a win–win orientation, it is important for the conflicting parties to expand the solutions to the problem by brainstorming, focusing on the interests of the people involved rather than on their articulated positions, cutting costs for the other party, compensating, logrolling, and trying to agree ahead of time on objective criteria.

How do effective conflict managers employ additional means to convert a potentially competitive conflict into a cooperative one? They do this by separating people from the problem, making concessions, seeking commonalities, talking cooperation, consulting before acting, communicating frequently, controlling the process, thinking positively, and engaging in fractionation.

Think About It

1. When does the urge to compete affect your relationships? How do you make sure that both you and the other person understand that the competition is "friendly" rather than something more serious?
2. In which common situations would you most likely resort to competitive negotiation? In which for cooperative negotiation?
3. Can you list some situations in which a different objective criterion is applicable? For example, list one that involves "majority rules" and others that involve other generally accepted standards.
4. Can you think of examples where people either focused on the other person or tried to deal with the problem or issue instead? Discuss the outcomes.

Apply It

1. For the following situation, identify the bargaining range, aspiration point, resistance point, and status quo point.

    I recently was working on a client's insurance renewal and was talking with the company underwriter about the account. I was asking if we would be able to move the customers' worker's compensation coverage into a preferred pricing tier, since a large claim was no

longer within the "rating window" of 5 years. The underwriter was hesitant to do that because the account had a relatively high number of low dollar (under $1,000) claims. So I proposed to the underwriter that we put a "deductible" on all worker's compensation claims at $500, meaning that the customer would pay all claims under $500 out of pocket instead of submitting them to the company. I knew doing this would be helpful to the underwriter/company, because they wouldn't be doing paperwork or processing on low dollar claims . . . . something that is costly to them. I also knew going into the preferred pricing class would save the customer quite a bit, since they have a high payroll. The result was the underwriter was happy to make the change in pricing tier, provided the deductible was in place. The deductible was acceptable to the customer, because it saved them over 25 percent on the worker's compensation rates, which far exceeded historical costs for these under $500 claims. So all in all it was a win for the company and the customer and built up a lot of good will for me with the customer.
2. Write out examples of times you have used cost cutting, compensation, and logrolling in scarce resource conflicts. What clearly distinguishes each example as one type or the other?

Work With It

1. Read the following case study and answer the questions that follow it.

    Last week I met with a colleague, the Division Chief for Right of Way (I am Division Chief of Planning), to discuss our mutual need to staff a receptionist position on the eighth floor of a new office building we will occupy beginning next month. She will have about eighty employees working on this floor, while my staff will total around forty. For security and customer service reasons we need to place a receptionist at a cubicle opposite the elevator where visitors can be greeted, screened, and directed as they enter the floor. We do not currently have this problem in our existing building as the organization has a guard hired to check visitors in and out of the only public entrance to the building. Since the Right of Way Division has twice the number of employees and many more visitors than we do in Planning, I attempted to convince her to agree to staff the position out of her budget. I have had some previous history negotiating with this division chief and have found her difficult to work with. This meeting was no exception. I tried to convince her that equity demanded she pay for the position or at least two-thirds of the costs. She refused, arguing that I should bear the entire cost because her budget had been reduced this fiscal year.

    After posturing for some time, it was clear that she was not going to budge in her negotiating position. I had more important issues on my plate that day and also I did not want to take this issue to our mutual boss, the district director, to resolve. In light of this, I proposed that we split the costs 50:50, which she agreed to almost immediately. The problem I have is that this really is not a fair decision for my division and is another example of where I should have been more aggressive in sticking to my position, instead of looking for resolution through a compromise.

    a. To what extent did the parties apply the four principles of negotiation (people, interests, etc.)? If not, how could they?
    b. Did the parties use any of the four ways to generate more options (logrolling, bridging, etc.)? If not, how could they?
    c. Did the parties incorporate any of the recommendations for converting competitive negotiation to cooperation (talking cooperation, fractionation, etc.)? If not, how could they?

(Continued)

2. Recall a recent conflict you observed or experienced that concerned a tangible issue or problem that is a scarce resource (not enough time together or money, a single object or place you can't share, etc.). The conflict should be one that you resolved or have managed for the time being. Write a short description of the conflict and then analyze it by answering the following questions.
    a. How did you apply the four principles of negotiation (people, interests, etc.)?
    b. How did you use one or more of the four ways to generate more options (logrolling, bridging, etc.)?
    c. How did you incorporate the recommendations for converting competitive negotiation to cooperation (talking cooperation, fractionation, etc.)?

NOTES

1. Dudley Cahn, "Friendship, Conflict and Dissolution," in Harry Reis and Susan K. Sprecher (Eds.), *Encyclopedia of Human Relationships* (Thousand Oaks, CA: Sage, 2009).
2. Linda L. Putnam, "Bargaining as Organizational Communication," in Robert D. McPhee and Phillip K. Tompkins (Eds.), *Organizational Communication: Traditional Themes and New Directions* (Newbury Park, CA: Sage, 1985), p. 129.
3. Laura J. Kray and Michael P. Haselhuhn, "Implicit Negotiation Beliefs and Performance: Experimental and Longitudinal Evidence," *Journal of Personality and Social Psychology* 93 (2007), 49–64.
4. Peter H. Kim and Alison R. Fragale, "Choosing the Path to Bargaining Power: An Empirical Comparison of BATNAs and Contributions in Negotiation," *Journal of Applied Psychology* 90 (2005), 373–381.
5. William A. Cohen, "The Importance of Expectations on Negotiation Results," *European Business Review* 15 (2003), 87–93.
6. Vandra L. Huber and Margaret A. Neale, "Effects of Self-and Competitor Goals on Performance in an Interdependent Bargaining Task," *Journal of Applied Psychology* 72 (1987), 197–203.
7. Kathleen M. O'Connor, Josh A. Arnold, and Ethan R. Burris, "Negotiators' Bargaining Histories and Their Effects on Future Negotiation Performance," *Journal of Applied Psychology* 90 (2005), 350–362.
8. Raymond W. Mack and Richard C. Snyder, "The Analysis of Social Conflict: Toward an Overview and Synthesis," in Fred E. Jandt (Ed.), *Conflict Resolution through Communication* (New York: Harper and Row, 1973), p. 34.
9. David A. Lax and James K. Sebenius, *The Manager as Negotiator* (New York: Free Press, 1986), p. 32.
10. James A. Wall, *Negotiation: Theory and Practice* (Glenview, IL: Scott Foresman, 1985).
11. Carsten K. W. de Dreu, Sander L. Koole, and Wolfgang Steinel, "Unfixing the Fixed Pie: A Motivated Information-Processing Approach to Integrative Negotiation," *Journal of Personality and Social Psychology* 79 (2000), 975–987.
12. Richard P. Larrick and George Wu, "Claiming a Large Slice of a Small Pie: Asymmetric Disconfirmation in Negotiation," *Journal of Personality and Social Psychology* 93 (2007), 212–233.
13. Dean G. Pruitt, *Negotiation Behavior* (New York: Academic Press, 1981).
14. Dean G. Pruitt and Melvin J. Kimmel, "Twenty Years of Experimental Gaming: Critique, Synthesis and Suggestions for the Future," *Annual Review of Psychology* 28 (1977), 363–392.
15. Jared R. Curhan, Hillary Anger Elfebein, and Heng Xu, "What Do People Value When They Negotiate? Mapping the Domain of Subjective Value in Negotiation," *Journal of Personality and Social Psychology* 91 (2006), 493–512.
16. Roger Fisher and William Ury, *Getting to Yes: Negotiating Agreement without Giving In* (Boston, MA: Houghton Mifflin, 1981), p. 11.
17. Edwin Bixenstine and Kellogg V. Wilson, "Effects of Level of Cooperative Choice by the Other Player in a Prisoner's Dilemma Game," *Journal of Abnormal and Social Psychology* 67 (1963), 139–147; see also Marc Pilisuk and Paul Skolnick, "Inducing Trust: A Test of the Osgood Proposal," *Journal of Experimental Social Psychology* 11 (1968), 53–63; Gerald Marwell, David Schmitt, and Bjorn Boyesen, "Pacifist Strategy and Cooperation under Interpersonal Risk," *Journal of Personality and Social Psychology* 28 (1973), 12–20.

18. O'Connor, Arnold, and Burris, "Negotiators' Bargaining Histories and Their Effects on Future Negotiation Performance."
19. Joseph P. Forgas, "On Feeling Good and Getting Your Way: Mood Effects on Negotiator Cognition and Bargaining Strategies," *Journal of Personality and Social Psychology* 74 (1998), 565–577.
20. Eric van Dijk, Gerben A. van Kleef, Wolfgang Steinel, and Ilja van Beest, "A Social Functional Approach to Emotions in Bargaining: When Communicating Anger Pays and When It Backfires," *Journal of Personality and Social Psychology* 94 (2008), 600–614.
21. Gerben A. Van Kleef, Carsten K. W. De Dreu, and Antony S. R. Manstead, "The Interpersonal Effects of Emotions in Negotiations: A Motivated Information Processing Approach," *Journal of Personality and Social Psychology* 87 (2004), 510–528.
22. Gerben A. Van Kleef, Carsten K. W. De Dreu, and Antony S. R. Manstead, "Supplication and Appeasement in Conflict and Negotiation: The Interpersonal Effects of Disappointment, Worry, Guilt, and Regret," *Journal of Personality and Social Psychology* 91 (2006), 124–142; Van Kleef, De Dreu, and Manstead, "The Interpersonal Effects of Anger and Happiness in Negotiations," pp. 57–76.
23. Frank Tutzauer and Michael Roloff, "Communication Processes Leading to Integrative Agreements: Three Paths to Joint Benefits," *Communication Research* 15 (1988), 360–380.

CHAPTER 6

Managing the Conflict Climate

OBJECTIVES

At the end of this chapter, you should be able to:

- Describe the role that climate generally plays in conflict situations.
- Describe the role played by an imbalance of power in a conflict situation and explain how to equalize power.
- Describe specifically the role played by competition in a conflict situation and explain how to encourage cooperation.
- Describe specifically the role played by distrust in a conflict situation and explain how to create trust.
- Describe the role played by defensive behaviors in a conflict situation and explain how to engage and encourage supportive behaviors.
- Explain how the concept of defensive behavior differs from that of power imbalance.

KEY TERMS

climate
competition
conflict climate
cooperation
defensive behaviors
distrust
harmful conflict climate
healthy trust
mixed motive situation
neutral speech
nurturing conflict climate
power
power abuse
powerful speech
powerless speech
Prisoner's Dilemma (PD)
supportive behaviors
threats
thromise
trust
unhealthy trust
win–lose outcomes
win–win outcomes

Why do some conflicts escalate, get out of hand, and perhaps turn violent? Why do we feel out of control in some conflict situations? Why is it that sometimes we can deal with an issue calmly and at another time the same issue sets off an emotional reaction in us? These are important questions if we want to understand how conflicts escalate and sometimes turn violent. One factor that contributes to the escalation of conflict is the climate in which it occurs.

What is meant by **climate** in a communication situation? As you move from one location to another, you are aware of changes in the emotional tone of voices, the looks on people's faces, their body movements, dress code, room décor, which can reveal expectations for behavior. If you enter a location where a party is held, you are likely to encounter noise, a crowd of young people, loud music, a lot of social interaction, and a dress code that fits the occasion. You might smell cigarette smoke and alcohol. Many partygoers view a party as a positive experience and conducive to socializing or else they would leave. Conversely, at another location such as a hospital's patient ward, you probably encounter a quiet, highly restricted place of interaction with and access by the public. There is no drinking of alcohol, smoking, or use of cell phones, and you'll see many people in a variety of medical uniforms. Perhaps you smell a sterile environment that you associate with hospitals. If you were not visiting a close member of the family who is a patient, you would probably want to leave the hospital as soon as possible, probably immediately at the close of visiting hours. Depending on the event or place, there is a climate or an atmosphere that makes you feel comfortable or uncomfortable in a psychological as well as physical sense.

In Chapter 2, we described conflict from a process point of view. We know that physical processes, such as plant growth, depend on their physical environments to nurture them. Similarly, social processes like conflict management depend on a nurturing social climate. Although the concept of social climate is difficult to describe in concrete terms, we are still aware of it and its effects on our interactions. Of the many factors or properties that are part of the climate, we limit our scope of a **conflict climate,** or the psychological atmosphere impacting a conflict, to these opposing concepts: imbalance of power versus equity, competition versus cooperation, distrust versus trust, and defensive versus supportive behavior.

Conflict management fails to produce constructive and positive results when it suffers from a **harmful conflict climate,** consisting of the threats of power abuse, competition, distrust, and defensiveness, which foster avoidance and accommodation (possibly resulting in avoidance and chilling effect cycles) or competition (meeting force with force, which may foster a competition cycle that eventually becomes violent). Conversely, conflict management is successful in other situations because it benefits from a **nurturing conflict climate,** consisting of a balance of power, cooperation, trust, and supportive behavior that encourage openness, assertiveness, collaboration, and mutually satisfying outcomes.

The purpose of this chapter is to describe the role played by the climate in conflict situations and to explain how to engage in specific behaviors that contribute to a nurturing conflict climate and how to avoid creating a harmful one. We begin by explaining the role of power in conflict climates.

THE THREAT OF POWER ABUSE

> Recently my parents and I argued about my job. My parents don't want me to work while in school because they think it could interfere with my studies. But in reality they don't give me enough money to do what I want to do. While talking to my parents they feel that only their opinions are legitimate. They do not even consider what I have to say and very rarely even give me a chance to speak.

In general, **power** is the ability to influence or control events. People have power over us to the extent that we depend on them, can affect our goal achievement, and have resources we need to accomplish our goals. In our daily routine, we encounter people who are more or less powerful than we are, and these are often cases of legitimate power differences, such as the boss–employee, commander–troops, parents–children, and teacher–student. In the case above, the young man is still living at home, letting his parents pay his bills, and resents the fact that he is a dependent, powerless teen.

Legitimate power recognizes that a situation often exists in which someone must take control to accomplish a task or to protect the welfare or interests of the group. In such cases, we should hold that person responsible for performing certain leadership tasks and grant him or her authority over us and work with that person to successfully accomplish the tasks. Because we all vary in our capabilities and resources, power often shifts from one situation to another, creating opportunities for different people to have power over others at different times.

Power contributes to a harmful conflict climate when it is perceived as threatening. When this occurs, we call it **power abuse.**

> As a Captain, I once taught counseling to a group of high-ranking Army officers. When I finished a list of dos and don'ts for officers counseling enlisted personnel who had personal problems that might affect the performance of their duties, which included hanging one's military jacket and hat (both covered with rank insignia) on a coat stand before meeting with the individual, Colonel Johnson suddenly stood up, turned to face the class, and said, "I am a Colonel

Often, people use physical space to emphasize power differences. In this case, standing over someone at a desk might be interpreted as power abuse by the person who is sitting.

in the United States Army and when someone comes into my office to see me, he or she is going to know I am a Colonel." There was a moment of silence. I then asked the class, "How many of you would go to Colonel Johnson, if you had a personal problem?" Everyone laughed, and someone even said "No way." Not receiving the support for his position that he expected, the Colonel suddenly grew embarrassed, said he got the point, and sat down. He told me later that he hadn't really thought about the problems he created by "pulling rank" on people.

Obviously we tread on hallowed ground here. The idea of sharing power may seem radical or even shocking to some people like the colonel above. After years of graduate study and passing extremely demanding exams, they have attained Ph.D., M.D., D.D.S., or J.D., so the last thought they may have in mind is to sacrifice the status and power that comes with such extraordinary achievement. We could say the same for those who worked their way up from the lowest to the highest levels of any organization and worked hard to attain a position of influence. Because they made great sacrifices, overcame difficult barriers, and demonstrated high abilities to earn their rank or position in an organization, they believe that they have paid their dues.

Now we come along and ask them to share their hard-earned respect, power, and status with others. We recognize that we are asking a lot for privileged people to set aside their perceptions of themselves as outranking the rest of us, to treat us with mutual respect, and to work with us as their equals. We can hear their response: *Forget it!*

However, those who abuse their power create worry, anger, and resentment in the less powerful. In such cases power has a stifling effect. *Powerful people may be seen as intimidating or threatening.* Powerless people respond by avoiding, accommodating, or not asserting themselves. When power is abused, we do not expect to resolve conflicts in a mutually satisfactory way.

Some power differences are institutionalized, formal, and official. The police, judges, teachers, parents, officials, administrators, and bosses are given some powers over the rest of us in limited contexts, such as the courtroom, classroom, public office, or workplace. However, in other relationships we are more equal, but one person may assume power over another. In these cases power is not a finite quantity but something produced by human transactions. For example, a friend or romantic partner may try to take control of a relationship and dominate the other. Recall from Chapter 1 that communication is transactional and not linear. If we extend this idea to dominant–submissive interpersonal relationships, we realize dominant people do not have authority over another unless the other person grants this power to him or her. We are, of course, talking about situations in which people are communicating verbally and not using the threat of physical violence or weapons to create their dominance over the other.

As in the situation where power is institutionalized, dominant people abuse their power when they rely on threats to intimidate others and stifle input. Flagg noted that there are distinct differences in patterns of language used between people who are perceived as power abusers and those perceived as power-sharers.[1] **Threats** are statements that link the other person's noncompliance with negative outcomes. In addition, the dominant individual may use a **thromise**—a message that sounds like a promise (i.e., if you do x you will receive y) but operates like a threat because there is a penalty associated with noncompliance that may hurt the recipient. The recipient doesn't simply fail to receive a benefit.[2] You have probably experienced a thromise in your educational experiences. An instructor may have told you that you could do some extra work to raise your grade, but may also have indicated that failing to do so would result in being graded more harshly at the end of the semester as it would indicate a lack of interest in the class.

Like subordinates in more formal situations, submissive friends and partners respond to the more powerful or dominate people by avoiding dealing with issues, accommodating to the dominant others, and failing to assert themselves. Conflicts do not get resolved in a mutually satisfactory way.

Besides avoiding the use of threats and thromises, how does one dominate others less? One way is to rely more on neutral speech, which we define as neither powerful nor powerless speech. **Powerful speech** refers to verbal and nonverbal messages used to dominate and control others. Powerful speech can occur in different degrees. At one level it includes interrupting others, speaking loudly, controlling the topic of conversation, and sounding like one knows he or she is right (implying that the other is wrong). At another level it also includes talking down to people, put-downs, efforts to belittle others, interrupting the other, talking through the other, and talking louder than the other. At the extreme it includes very aggressive behaviors.[3] These could include verbal threats, swearing, name calling while shouting, standing up to the other, or standing over that person accompanied with menacing facial expressions.

Erickson and his colleagues identified some differences between powerful and powerless speech. Powerful speakers used more intensifiers (e.g., very), fewer hedges (e.g., I guess), especially formal grammar, fewer hesitation forms (e.g., uh, you know), more controlled gestures, fewer questioning forms (e.g., rising in intonation at the end of a declarative sentence), and fewer polite forms when addressing others.[4] Some examples of how people gain and maintain their power in interpersonal relationships are also found in gender studies. Van Dijk summarized this area of research as follows: "Women generally do more work than men do in conversation, by giving more topical support, by showing more interest, or by withdrawing in situations of conflict . . . men tend to interrupt men more often."[5]

Powerless speech is talking up to others; making requests or asking questions (showing that one is in need or is uninformed); speaking softly; and sounding tentative, uncertain, or unsure of oneself. Powerless speech includes hedges (It could be that . . .), disclaimers (I've only thought a little about this), and tag questions (I don't know, what do you think?). More speech devices are included in Chapter 9 on the topic of "face management." When people are nonassertive, as we discussed in Chapter 3, they also engage in powerless speech.

When one employs **neutral speech,** she or he does not talk down or talk up to the others but talks to them as equals and relies on objective language. People in authority may go by their first names and ask others to treat them as a colleague or an equal rather than as a superior. A person using neutral speech both seeks out and values input from others. He or she doesn't make decisions and simply announce them but engages others in the decision-making process. There is a true sense of equality when listening to neutral speech.

The idea of neutral speech that is neither powerful nor powerless is similar to the distinction we made in Chapter 3 between assertive behavior on the one hand and either aggressive or nonassertive behavior on the other. Like the nonassertive individuals, powerless and submissive people fail to effectively stand up for themselves, while aggressive people do it in a way that violates the rights of others. Only assertive people treat others as they want the others to treat them by striving for outcomes that benefit all conflicting parties and not just one of them at the other's expense. Assertive behavior serves as a goal for the powerful or dominant people (who should take the other into consideration) and for the powerless or submissive speakers (who should stand up more for themselves).

Sharing Power

To improve the conflict climate, change in the power dimension needs to come from the powerful people, such as bosses, parents and other older family members, and teachers. They must value the input of others and seek to focus on resolving problems. We have all heard of the expression, "two heads are better than one." However, in conflict situations where one person outranks the other, there is a high likelihood that only "one head" prevails, and the powerful or dominant party fails to seek the input from others for better ideas. Why surround yourself with advisors who are simply "yes men" or "yes women"? You could just as easily disband the group and make the decisions by yourself. In addition to making the best decision because of input from others, people are more satisfied in situations where they have some say or influence. However, they are less likely to speak up if they fear the consequences or believe that the powerful person may not listen to their ideas.

Those who do not wish to abuse their power should initiate and employ solution-oriented behavior rather than abusive power-perpetuating behavior.[6] People in powerful positions or dominant roles should consider the idea that "we are all in this boat together," in that we share a sense of purpose and the primary goals of the college class, athletic team, family, military unit, or work organization. Because there is a job to do, a task to accomplish, we should focus on the task and not on the preservation of status or power. The powerful and powerless all benefit by success of the class, team, unit, or organization, so stop worrying about sharing power and actively seek ways to share it.

There are ways conflicting parties can avoid abusing their power. One way is to give up some of the more obvious power resources and symbols of authority. By removing his hat and jacket, loaded with rank insignia, Colonel Johnson in our previous case study gives up power resources and status symbols that intimidate subordinates. By abandoning a podium or large desk to sit with the students, a teacher does the same. Bosses who leave the secure confines of their offices to walk among their employees to see firsthand how they are doing and what they need are also giving up power resources.

Another way to avoid abusing power is to make power resources accessible to everyone in the group. With regard to some responsibilities in a relationship, there are times when person A is the more powerful person, and in other times person B is the more powerful. When leaders or authorities turn over responsibility and control to subordinates even temporarily, they raise the subordinates' status and equalize the playing field. The aforementioned colonel may appoint a subordinate to take command in his absence. When people in authority delegate tasks to subordinates, they need to delegate some of their power for them to do the job. The teacher may let students give reports or conduct discussions in class rather than lecture, thus giving them more responsibility for the learning that takes place in the classroom. Examples of power sharing are given below.

The boss decides everyone's part-time work schedule. However, he notices low morale, frequent arguments over working hours, minor theft, and employees calling in sick. So, he announces a flexible work schedule allowing employees to turn in a schedule of preferred work hours. He also holds a meeting to discuss the problem of working during exam weeks and holidays. The employees see the problem of work coverage and that the boss better understands their school and home pressures. New workers are then added to the schedule just to cover difficult periods. Workers' morale greatly improves, there are no arguments over working hours, and they seldom call in sick.

The students in a marketing class were assigned to work in groups, with one person designated as a group leader. In Lynn's group, she made it known that she had worked in a marketing company over the summer and "knew more than the others did." She started ordering group members around and made all the decisions by herself. As members lost interest in the project and started not showing up to group meetings, she began to do all the work by herself. Finally, it became apparent that the project was taking too much time, and she could not do a good job without help. With some effort, she was able to get everyone together to explain the problem. For the first time she listened to everyone's complaints about her role as leader. Lynn agreed to let the group have more say and help define her role along with everyone else's. She pointed out that everyone's grade depended on the quality of the group project. Everyone's knowledge, ideas, and thoughts then made the group stronger as a whole. By combining the power in the group, no one person was overwhelmed by the project and the final result showed the efforts of everyone.

Yet another way to share power is for the one with the least interest in a relationship to increase his or her level of interest. Perhaps the other person has a terrific personality or brings certain advantages to the relationship. Better yet, the one with the least interest might better appreciate the commitment and attention received from the other, and he or she should see that as a fair exchange for his or her own assets. After all, teachers need students to teach, leaders need followers, and bosses or supervisors need workers to do their jobs. In any case, the more powerful person may change his or her perception of the other and increase her or his own level of interest or investment in the other person, which may distribute power more equally.

Finally, the powerful or dominating person can give power to the relationship that exists between the friends, romantic partners, or workplace members by acknowledging their relationship, making commitments to it, and taking it into consideration as they behave. For example, when two people marry, they change their perspectives on themselves and each other, because they now have their marriage to consider. This also happens if romantic couples have children. They may change their perspectives on themselves because they are part of a family, which must be taken into consideration now. From this day forward, they engage in actions *because they are married or because they have a family*. Whatever the relationship, it can become a third entity that can exercise power over the partners. As married persons, fraternity brothers or sorority sisters, roommates, friends, romantic partners, or workers, we avoid some behaviors and engage in some others for the sake of relationships with others. This change in perspective of who we are and of our relationship to one another results in our delegating some of our power to the relationship itself.

As powerful people create conditions for equalizing power in a conflict situation, previously powerless, submissive, or nonassertive persons need to be responsible and respond by asserting themselves more. Does this surprise you? The suggestion that you challenge someone you perceive as the authority or dominant person may strike you as unnatural, disrespectful, or even mutinous. However, when the powerful offer to work with you in a more equitable manner, it is our position that you should take advantage of this opportunity. All too often, subordinates fail to adequately step into a position of authority and do not exercise responsible leadership. For example, when the students are asked to discuss the subject, they sometimes fail to adequately prepare themselves for their participation and fail to seize the opportunity to act responsible for their learning and exercise some authority and control in the classroom.

While we have discussed many ways in which the powerful may, at least temporarily, set aside their power resources and symbols, stop using threats and thromises, and rely more on neutral speech, we now ask what the powerless can do to equalize the conflict situation. Like all perceptions, we need to consider alternate views of situations. Maybe you have more power than you think, or the stronger person may relinquish more power to you if you ask for it, but you are choosing to remain powerless.

As a subordinate, you can test the water to see how your teacher, boss, or dominant partner responds if you try the following:

- be assertive, stand up for yourself, offer your opinion
- ask for reconsideration or appeal but use a different rationale
- offer suggestions, solutions, and your rationale behind them
- ask for more responsibility and show that you deserve it
- Let your feelings, wants, needs, and interests be known but let it be known that you are willing to be a team player
- ask for another chance but next time try harder to produce

Notice the shift in perspective required here: It isn't a question of who is superior but rather what is the best way to resolve the conflict. This brings up the factor of competition, which is another property of a conflict climate.

THE THREAT OF COMPETITION

My friends and I went out for a beer after a football game. At a local bar, one of the customers became belligerent. Nothing new. He wanted me to give in just so he could say, "You don't amount to crap." To really put my face in it, he started hitting on Kate, one of my friends. Well, I couldn't allow him to get away with that. I now wanted to stand up for my friend, Kate, and make this guy pay for his offensive behavior. I got into his face and tried to stare him down. He just responded with colorful words and imagery to tell me how he felt, which just got me more riled up. Neither of us was going to back down and I wanted to force him into submission as much as he did me. At this point we started pushing, and he took a swing at me. I have learned self-defense over the years and reacted instinctively to his punch, which landed him on the floor. Would you believe he later called the police and claimed I assaulted him? Kate had left the bar, and his friends, who were still there, said I caused the fight, so the police took me to their station and told me to call a lawyer, which meant I had go to court.

Another dimension that affects how we relate and interact with others ranges from competition to cooperation. In Chapter 3, we identified competition as a conflict strategy, which is characterized by dominating, controlling, and forcing one's decision on others, and the compromising and collaboration conflict styles, which aim for more mutually satisfying outcomes. In Chapter 5, we described competitive and cooperative negotiation techniques for resolving conflicts over tangible (scarce) resources. Also, we stressed on competitive communication behavior, such as competitive arguments, and how such behavior can contribute to a competitive escalation cycle. In this chapter we describe the role of competition and cooperation as dimensions of the conflict climate.

In **competition,** the parties are positioned against each other, emphasis is placed on winning, and outcomes are framed as win–lose. Americans often watch or participate in competitive events. Perhaps this is because we view competition as a challenge and a way to grow stronger or more skilled. Sometimes competition is healthy and fun. Competition contributes to a harmful conflict climate when it is perceived as threatening. This occurs when the parties perceive the resolution of the conflict in terms of **win–lose outcomes,** where the gain or loss is significant to those involved. We get that sense of competition, rivalry, and winner takes all from the above case study. The young man and customer in the bar engage in a series of put-downs, negative attitudes, getting even, and escalatory behaviors that play a role in the competitive escalation cycle (see Chapter 2). Neither of the men wanted to back down but rather force the other into submission. They think that, if they don't walk away as winners, then they are walking away as losers. The problem occurs when they take their losses in competition as reflections of their personal competence. *Then the situation is seen as threatening.* Competitive attitudes and desires have their impact on the atmosphere surrounding a conflict.

Cooperation is a situation in which we place greater emphasis on the quality of an interpersonal relationship than on the outcome. Cooperation means working together rather than against one another. A cooperative climate is characterized by the open and honest communication of relevant information between those involved. When communication processes lead to perceived cooperation rather than competition, participants have an increased sensitivity to similarities and common interests rather than a focus on differences or threats, and conflict becomes a matter of mutuality, a problem to be solved rather than a win–lose situation. Cooperation generally increases levels of trust, openness, and collaboration, which lead to win–win outcomes. In **win–win outcomes,** the parties are mutually satisfied with the resolution of the conflict.

How does one create a cooperative climate within conflicts situations? An effective conflict manager keeps the parties' focus on the issue involved, emphasizes the need to reach some agreement about it, and stresses mutuality. In Chapter 2, we listed the specific escalation behaviors that should be avoided if one wants to create a more cooperative atmosphere. In Chapter 3, we identified the compromising and collaboration conflict styles, which aim for more mutually satisfying outcomes. In Chapter 5, we described cooperative techniques for converting competitive negotiations into more cooperative ones to resolve conflicts over tangible (scarce) resources.

When we think that the other party is competing with us in ways that result in his or her winning at our expense, the conflict climate is more harmful than nurturing. We instead need to emphasize cooperation. This brings up the factor of interpersonal trust, which is another property of a conflict climate.

THE THREAT OF DISTRUST

> My best friend, Marilyn, and I knew each other for about a year. I was interested in another guy who also was friend with my best friend. Meanwhile, my ex-boyfriend was trying to come back into the picture. I didn't think Marilyn would tell my new love interest about my ex, but I was wrong because she did. You would think she would have had my interests at heart, and she would have been concerned about how the situation would affect me, her friend, in the end. After that situation I felt plenty of distrust toward her.

Just as an imbalance of power and competition produce a harmful conflict climate, so does a violation of trust. **Trust** is the belief that another is benevolent or honest toward the trusting individual, and that the other person's caring transcends any direct benefits the other receives as a result of caring.[7] In other words, we trust others when we think they have our best interests at heart and do not wish to hurt us. Trust reflects "people's abstract positive expectations that they can count on partners to care for them and be responsive to their needs, now and in the future."

Distrust means we lack confidence in another person, we do not rely on that person, and/or we are suspicious or wary of her or him. In the above case study, the young woman trusted her friend, Marilyn, who didn't behave as a friend she can confide in. In cases like this, breaches of trust are seemingly unforgiveable, a topic we treat in Chapter 10 on "emotional residues."

In addition, **unhealthy trust** means gullible. It is typically inflexible, rigid, and consistent in actions toward others, without regard for the situation. Those who trust pathologically have a tendency to confuse risk-taking and trusting situations, overestimating the probability of getting what they want or underestimating the negative consequences of not getting what they want. Pathologically trusting persons may also overestimate the benevolence of the trusted person or overestimate their power to affect the trusted person's behavior. An example of unhealthy trust is illustrated by the following conflict between two roommates.

> I own a great deal of expensive photography equipment, which I keep at my apartment because I often do my studio work there. My roommate has this weird idea that the world is safe—he leaves doors and windows unlocked all the time. He comes from the Midwest, where "people are decent" and he never locked a door in his life. I believe that he is just too trusting.
>
> This conflict used to arise when I would come home in the afternoon and find the apartment door wide open. Sometimes, if he went next door he would leave the door standing open, but most of the time he would go to work and leave everything unlocked and the windows wide open. If I confronted him, he would fall back on the fact that if God wanted us to have our material possessions then He would make sure that they were not stolen (since everything is God's and He lets us keep them or take them away).
>
> Then an incident happened. Without telling my roommate, I loaned my television to a friend. When my roommate came home early to an unlocked apartment, he found the set missing. Well, he panicked and called the police and had them looking our apartment over until I came home and straightened everything out. This taught him just how he would react in a real robbery situation and that he should exercise more caution in securing the apartment. After that incident, he did decide to lock the doors.

Both distrust and unhealthy trust are threatening to an interpersonal relationship when they contribute to a harmful conflict climate. To a great extent, **healthy trust** is earned. If our actions warrant it, we gain the trust of others over time. Although trust depends on the previous actions of those involved, it still requires a leap of faith. Most people go ahead and act as though a sense of security about the other is justified, because evidence for trustworthiness is seldom conclusive. Our initial trust is often rewarded. Research seems to indicate that, to begin with, trusting individuals are more likely to assume positive implications of behaviors than are distrusting individuals. Although they do not deny the negative elements in their relationships, they limit the implications negative events have for the relationship; distrusting individuals overemphasize the importance of negative events. Trusting individuals tend to see negative events in a larger time frame, stabilizing perceptions and making conflict less threatening.[8] In another study, couples who trusted one another were more optimistic, and they tended to report that their partner's motives were positive, even to the extent of saying that the other person's motives were more positive than their own. People who had high trust in their partners usually did not change their opinions of the other person's behavior. The authors speculated that the confidence and clarity of the core attitudes held by trusting individuals lead them to react affectively to the partner's behavior in a relatively automatic, positive way and that little consideration of its meaning typically takes place. The potential cost of this process is that individuals may take acts of caring for granted if the implications of events are not elaborated.[9]

How does one engender trust? People gain the trust of others when they:

- begin by trusting others,
- perform cooperative actions,
- avoid suspicious activity, and
- reciprocate in trusting ways.

We can see how trust or distrust develops in an exercise called the **Prisoner's Dilemma (PD).** PD is a classroom exercise played like a game based on a familiar situation: Supposedly, two people are caught burglarizing a building and are brought separately to the police station. These are their options: If both of them remain silent, they both go free, but an incentive to speak the truth exists—if only one confesses, the one confessing receives a reward and goes free and the other goes to jail. However, if both take the bait and confess, they both go to jail. In order to both benefit the most, then, they must trust each other to act in each other's best interest and not just one's own and remain silent. This is called a **mixed motive situation,** because those involved have incentives to both cooperate and compete, but they can choose to stick with just one.

The notion that you can choose to maximize your gains and expect others to choose to lose is unrealistic and unsupported by research.[10] If we think that you are trying to maximize your gains at our expense, we distrust you and choose to compete. When played in class, some students become angry when they find that they can't trust the opposition. They often accuse the others of ruining the game. Emotionally intense and lively discussion usually follows the PD exercise.

One interesting issue connected with trust is the illusion of self-interest. Often, if a person sacrifices his or her own goals for the group, the group gains but the person making the sacrifice loses. In some cases, though, the person making the sacrifice sees making a moral choice (i.e., sacrificing on behalf of the group) as serving their own interest. The altruistic choice is reframed as self-serving because it is in line with the person's moral outlook.[11]

Criticisms of the PD paradigm are widespread. Perhaps the most serious one concerns the artificial and limited conditions under which communication can take place in PD simulations. However, the simulation has increased our understanding of trust and suspicion in conflict situations. In a similar game situation called "the sequential dictator," researchers found that participants usually reciprocated altruistic moves made by the other.[12]

A harmful climate includes distrust, whereas a nurturing climate manifests trust that is earned. We cannot say enough about the importance of trust in conflict situations. The next section examines the role of defensive and supportive behavior in the conflict climate.

THE THREAT OF DEFENSIVE BEHAVIOR

> It was time for the annual review where I work, and my supervisor asked me to come into his office to administer my review. When I entered, to my surprise not only was my boss present but so was a friend of his who is a supervising manager from another department. My boss zipped through a lot of points very quickly. When he was finished, without asking for any input from me, he asked me to sign it. I told him that I did not have enough time to digest all that he said and I was not sure I agreed with some of it. I wanted to take time and go over it point by point and defend the inaccuracies. I was also uncomfortable discussing some of the points in front of the other supervisor. It was at that moment that he said, "I am your supervisor and this is your review." It was like he was ordering me to sign it.[13]

In the above case study, the young woman saw the situation as threatening because her boss engaged in a series of behaviors that created defensiveness in her—judgment of her behavior, an air of superiority, and an impatience with her feelings about the situation. Such behaviors help create a harmful conflict climate. When interacting in your own relationships, you should make an effort to establish a nurturing conflict climate by being supportive and avoiding behaviors that generate defensiveness in others, as well as avoiding being defensive yourself.

In a seminal article, Gibb identified communication behaviors that are defensive or supportive (see Table 6.1). These behaviors play a role in their respective conflict climates because they either encourage people to become closed and hostile toward one another or encourage them toward greater openness and cooperation.

TABLE 6.1 Defensive versus Supportive Climates

Defensiveness Arises From		Supportiveness Arises From
Evaluation	versus	Description
Control	versus	Problem Orientation
Strategy	versus	Spontaneity
Neutrality	versus	Empathy
Superiority	versus	Equality
Certainty	versus	Provisionalism

According to Gibb, **defensive behaviors** consist of evaluation, control, strategy, neutrality, superiority, and certainty, while **supportive behaviors** involve nonjudgmental description, problem orientation, spontaneity, empathy, equality, and provisionalism.[14] It helps to consider these behaviors as opposites in pairs.

- An *evaluation* consists of praise and blame, while a *nonjudgmental description* is worded in a way that does not threaten the other's self-esteem.
- *Control* refers to attempts to dominate another's behavior, whereas a *problem orientation* is a focus on the issue rather than preserve one' power over another.
- While *strategy* suggests motives and agendas, *spontaneity* is straightforward, unplanned, and captures the spirit of the moment.
- *Neutrality* refers to a lack of concern for the welfare of others (i.e., "that is not my problem"), while *empathy* involves taking an interest in others.
- *Superiority* means "pulling rank" on others, versus *equality,* which expresses a desire to cooperate and invites participation.
- *Certainty* appears dogmatic because it refers to statements that consist of "all" or "every," such as "you always do that to me" or "everybody does it," while *provisionalism* suggests tentativeness, a desire to withhold one's judgment until all the facts are in.

What is the relationship of defensive behavior to the concept of power discussed earlier in this chapter? You may notice that a few of these behaviors are sometimes associated with people in positions of power, such as evaluation (critical), control (domination), neutrality (uninterested in subordinate's problems), and superiority ("pulling rank"). We do not want to confuse the subject of defensiveness by associating it with power. Defensive behaviors are associated with anyone, even those in positions of authority, so these behaviors may appear irrespective of power. They are more consistently associated with the feelings of inadequacy, insecurity, fear, or uncertainty that make one turn defensive in a threatening situation. To the extent that powerful people manifest defensive behaviors, they probably also experience feelings of insecurity about their roles as supervisors, leaders, or parents. In romantic couples, defensive behavior is triggered by

> . . . communication that lacks, or is perceived to lack, a supportive tone or content. Specifically, defensive communication occurred when one or more romantic partners failed to communicate warmth, failed to communicatively share, or failed to award attention to the other.[15]

In the following narrative, we added Gibb's key terms in parentheses to connect this example with his description of a defensive climate. How would you feel if you were the husband or wife in this marriage? What impact does this husband have on the management of conflicts between him and his wife? Do you see where the husband may be failing to communicate warmth and acceptance to his wife?

> As a husband, I intentionally exercise a lot of influence over my wife (control). I do this by having only one car and keeping track of our household finances (strategy). I give my wife a certain amount of money for the week, and I tell her that after she has gone grocery shopping,

she can have what is left over to spend on herself. That way she is rewarded for finding the best deals and getting the most for our money (evaluation). She complains to me that I am too tight, but I don't listen because managing the grocery money is not my problem (neutrality). I want her to think of me as the boss (superiority) and that I know what is best for us (certainty).

As you read this narrative, how do you think the husband and wife feel? As it turns out, he is insecure and is afraid of losing control of their marriage. Do you feel sympathy for the wife? One would not expect that his forceful hand would result in any mutually satisfying outcomes.

Now consider this next narrative. We again added Gibb's key terms in parentheses to connect this example with his description of a supportive climate. How would you feel if you were the husband or wife in this marriage? What impact does this husband have on the management of conflicts between him and his wife?

I don't criticize my wife (nonjudgmental description). We tackle problems together regardless of what the problem is. I don't think that either of us is better at solving problems than the other, but together we can come up with the best way to spend and save money (equality). I believe that what is important is that we come up with the best solution to a problem (problem orientation) rather than think I have to make all the decisions for us. I value her input. I don't first attempt to solve the problem and then try to convince her of the solution (provisionalism) but rather wait until we can discuss it together, because I value her input (spontaneity). I care about her feelings, wants, and needs, so I want to take her into account (empathy).

One would expect that by working together in a supportive rather than a defensive manner, the couple would develop more mutually satisfying outcomes when in conflicts.

Although the above listing of defensive and supportive behaviors that make up harmful and nurturing conflict climates may appear in an "either-or" format, typically climates exist somewhere in between such extremes. This means that every conflict climate has some degree of defensiveness and supportiveness. However, the nurturing conflict climate has more supportive than defensive behaviors, while the harmful conflict climate has vice versa.

Mutually satisfying outcomes are more likely to occur when communicators participate in the decisions, agreements, solutions to problems, and resolution of conflicts that affect them. When we confront another, we need to express our needs and feelings, which is sometimes difficult to do, because we may feel vulnerable. To the extent that we feel safe enough to assert our interests, needs, and goals, listen to the expression of others and cooperate in the process of achieving an understanding, the more likely we feel free to cooperate and collaborate.

MANAGE IT

Our purpose of this chapter is to describe the role played by climate in conflict situations. Abuse of power, competition, distrust, and defensive behavior create a hostile, dangerous, and harmful conflict environment that produces unsatisfactory outcomes for one or both parties. Unabusive power or equity, cooperation, trust, and supportive behavior create a warm, friendly, and nurturing conflict environment that is more likely to produce mutually satisfactory outcomes.

Abusive power contributes to a harmful conflict climate because it is perceived as threatening. The more powerful person in the conflict situation has greater latitude in using power in abusive and unabusive ways. Those who abuse power may find that the other person responds in passive or passive-aggressive ways in order to avoid threats and abuse. Although it is difficult to embrace the idea of giving up power, sometimes doing so is one's best option in resolving conflict. At the very least, deemphasizing power differences leads to a nurturing conflict climate. Those with less power in the situation should also seek opportunities to be more assertive, use power-neutral language, and take responsibility for the outcomes in the conflict situation.

Competition becomes part of a harmful conflict climate when the parties view the conflict situation only in terms of win–lose outcomes. This perception results in the conflicting parties seeing themselves as individuals who must win at all costs. By shifting to a conflict in terms of win–win outcomes, the conflicting parties can view themselves as partners, where maintaining and preserving the relationship is as important, if not more, than winning an argument or forcing one's decision on another.

Both distrust and unhealthy trust are threatening to an interpersonal relationship when they contribute to a harmful conflict climate. Some people distrust others too much and some are too trusting. Earned trust contributes to a nurturing conflict climate. People maintain the trust of others when they continue to act in cooperative ways, avoid suspicious activity, and reciprocate in trusting ways to the actions of the other.

Critical to our success in conflict situations is the use of communicative behavior that is supportive and nonthreatening. Conflicting parties should try to establish a nurturing conflict climate by being supportive and not being defensive. The most significant steps toward creating a supportive climate are found in communication that describes behavior rather than judges it, that is oriented toward solving problems rather than assigning blame, that focuses on description and problem solution rather than a "you-orientation," that manifests an attitude of empathy rather than an attitude that is neutral and unconcerned, and that conveys a sense of equality with the other rather than a position of superiority. Finally, a supportive climate is created spontaneously rather than through behavior perceived as strategic and through talk that suggests that the conversation is still in process rather than certain and final.

The concept of defensive behavior differs from that of power imbalance. While a few defensive behaviors are sometimes associated with people in positions of power, such as evaluation (criticizing), control (being dominating), neutrality (lacking interest in subordinate's problems), and superiority ("pulling rank"), defensive behaviors may appear irrespective of power. They are more consistently associated with feelings of inadequacy, insecurity, fear, or uncertainty that make one turn defensive in a threatening situation. When powerful people manifest defensive behaviors, it is an indication of feelings of insecurity about their role as supervisor, leader, or parent.

Communicators who create nurturing climates are more likely to create mutually satisfying outcomes because they participate in the decisions, agreements, solutions, and resolution of conflicts that affect them. If we feel safe enough to assert our interests, needs, and goals; listen to others; and collaborate in interpersonal conflicts, we are more likely to achieve mutually satisfying outcomes.

Think About It

1. How does it feel when you are in an unbalanced power relationship? What is it like to have more power? Less power?
2. What situations tend to create defensive behavior in you? Why do you think this is so? What might you do to decrease your defensiveness?
3. Under what conditions are you likely to use powerful speech? Powerless speech? Neutral speech? Why would your choice be most effective in those conditions?
4. When have you ever lost your trust in someone? How did you react to the loss of trust? How was the trust restored?

Apply It

1. Think of a particular relationship where there is an imbalance of power. List the power resources and power symbols associated with that relationship and the powerful speech cues of the person in authority. Are there any power resources or power symbols that the stronger person has overlooked or not utilized? How might the person's use of power affect the situation if a conflict should arise? How might the situation change, if he or she shares power with you?
2. Arrange to play the Prisoner Dilemma game with other members of your class, some as individual contestants, others as pairs, and some with three members on each team. At the conclusion of the game, describe the role both trust/distrust and competitive/cooperative behavior play in interpersonal behavior, conflict, and outcomes. Discuss feelings about the opposition.
3. Take a piece of paper and draw two columns on it. Compare two past or present conflict situations, one in which the other engaged in supportive behavior and another in which the other resorted to defensive behavior. What role does the supportive or defensive behavior play in each conflict situation? How do you feel about the other person in these relationships?

Work With It

1. Read the case study and answer the questions that follow it.

    I had just bought a new computer and was in the process of getting it all set up. Space is a precious commodity in university housing. My roommate has had a laptop computer for over a year that obviously requires less space to operate than does a full-sized computer like mine. He also has a printer that is about half the space of mine. Prior to my computer being shipped, we realized we would need another desk in the room. We were able to find one that barely fits in our room, and we moved it in. The new desk was half again as big as the one already in the room, and he started using it first.

    Once I got my computer partially set up, I realized that it was going to be a tight fit to squeeze all the equipment into the available space, and I asked my roommate if we could switch desks. He quickly and firmly replied, "No." I asked why not, since my computer took up so much more space, and it was already cramped in the corner where my desk is, without

(Continued)

even having all the equipment set up. He replied that he simply liked the bigger desk so that he could spread out more. I half jokingly said I would pay him to switch, and he said, "This isn't a barter system, and you can't bid on this desk." I reminded him that he has used the smaller desk for a year and a half without any problems whatsoever. My roommate then reminded me that he was in this room a year before I moved in. He also felt he was a better judge of arranging the place than I was. "You always have such stupid ideas," he said.

   a. What are the issues in this conflict? Are they tangible or intangible?
   b. Define power and describe the role played by an imbalance of power in this situation. How might the parties equalize power?
   c. Define competition and describe the role it played (could have played) in this situation. How might the parties convert the situation from a competitive one to a cooperative one?
   d. Define trust and describe the role played by distrust in this situation. How might the parties regain one another's trust?
   e. Define defensive behavior and describe the role played by defensive behaviors in this situation. How might the parties engage in more supportive behavior?

2. Think of two different conflict situations with individuals you know well and see often.
   - In the first situation, the other person is subordinate to you (you have some authority over her or him at home, work, or school).
   - In the second situation, the other person is superordinate to you (has authority over you at home, work, or school)

Your purpose is to describe the communication and conflict patterns that exist in the two types of interpersonal relationships where you are superior or subordinate. Although you are to write about both relationships, divide each relationship into two parts. In the first part, describe how the powerful person (you in one case; the other in the next case) might try to retain all the power and use it against the other. Also, try to describe the likely outcome of the conflict as a result of holding most of the power. In the second part, describe how the parties might redistribute the power in a way that would benefit the relationship, group, or organization. Again, try to describe the likely outcome of the conflict as a result of trying to create a balance of power.

When you discuss your two relationships, describe the verbal and nonverbal communication patterns. Do you find that you use the same communication behaviors for both persons, or do you find that you tend to use some with one person but not the other? Also, thinking of each person one at a time, go through the list of examples of powerful, powerless, and neutral speech and determine which ones you tend to use with each person and which they use with you.

As you analyze the imbalance of power and its effects on your relationships, also consider the role of trust, competition, and defensiveness. Do you trust each person equally well? Do they trust you equally well? Is there a sense of competition in the air? Are you more defensive or supportive with one another?

NOTES

1. Murray Flagg, "An Exploratory Study of the Use of Language in the Abuse of Power," unpublished doctoral dissertation, Trinity University, 2005.
2. John Waite Bowers, "Guest Editor's Introduction: Beyond Threats and Promises," *Speech Monographs* 41 (1974), ix–xi.
3. Loreen N. Olson, "Compliance Gaining Strategies of Individuals Experiencing 'Common Couple Violence,'" *Qualitative Research Reports in Communication* 3 (2002), 7–14.
4. Stephen K. Erickson and Marilyn S. McKnight, *The Practitioner's Guide to Mediation: A*

Client-Centered Approach (New York: John Wiley, 2001).
5. Teun A. van Dijk, "Structures of Discourse and Structures of Power," in James A. Anderson (Ed.), *Communication Yearbook*, Vol. 12 (Newbury Park, CA: Sage, 1989), p. 33.
6. Larry Powell and Mark Hickson, III, "Power Imbalance and Anticipation of Conflict Resolution: Positive and Negative Attributes of Perceptual Recall," *Communication Research Reports* 17 (2000), 181–190.
7. Robert E. Larzelere and Ted L. Huston, "The Dyadic Trust Scale: Toward Understanding Interpersonal Trust in Close Relationships," *Journal of Marriage and the Family* 42 (1980), 595–604; John G. Holmes and John K. Rempel, "Trust in Close Relationships," in Clyde Hendrick (Ed.), *Close Relationships* (Newbury Park, CA: Sage, 1989), pp. 187–220.
8. John Holmes, "The Exchange Process in Close Relationships: Microbehavior and Macromotives," in Melvin J. Lerner and Sally C. Lerner (Eds.), *The Justice Motive in Social Behavior* (New York: Plenum, 1981), pp. 261–284; John K. Rempel, "Trust and Attributions in Close Relationships," unpublished doctoral dissertation, University of Waterloo, Ontario, 1987.
9. Holmes and Rempel, "Trust in Close Relationships," p. 205.
10. Gary Bornstein and Zohar Gilula, "Between-Group Communication and Conflict Resolution in Assurance and Chicken Games," *Journal of Conflict Resolution* 47 (2003), 326–339.
11. Jonathan Baron, "Confusion of Group Interest and Self-Interest in Parochial Cooperation on Behalf of a Group," *Journal of Conflict Resolution* 45 (2001), 283–295.
12. Andreas Diekmann, "The Power of Reciprocity: Fairness, Reciprocity, and Stakes in Variants of the Dictator Game," *Journal of Conflict Resolution* 48 (2004), 487–505.
13. In using this particular story, we'd like to point out that the supervisor violated basic human resource practices. An evaluation should never be given in the presence of another unless that person is also evaluating the subordinate. Further, you have the right to have time to reflect on your evaluation and respond to it before signing.
14. Jack Gibb, "Defensive Communication," *Journal of Communication* 11 (1961), 141–168.
15. Jennifer A. H. Becker, Barbara Ellevold, and Glen H. Stamp, "The Creation of Defensiveness in Social Interaction II: A Model of Defensive Communication among Romantic Couples," *Communication Monographs* 75 (2008), 97.

CHAPTER 7

Managing Stress

OBJECTIVES

At the end of this chapter, you should be able to:

- Identify four types of stress.
- Distinguish between hyperstress and distress.
- Identify the sources of hyperstress in your life.
- List some of the likely sources of distress in people's lives.
- Explain how hyperstress and distress affect your communication behavior in a conflict situation.
- List the three solutions for developing a more playful attitude.
- List some specific techniques for dealing constructively with hyperstress and distress.
- Explain the ABC model, differentiate between positive and negative beliefs, and apply the model to a conflict situation.

KEY TERMS

ABC approach
activating event (A)
beliefs (B)
conflict proneness
consequences (C)
distress
eustress
hyperstress
hypostress
overblown conflict
playful spirit
stress
stressor

There's a bumper sticker that reads, "If you're not living on the edge, you're taking up too much space." There are people who like stress. They like to live fast, drive fast, and eat fast. They may even like conflicts! But these people are generally the exception.

If you are like many of us, you don't enjoy stress. How do you feel when you read this help wanted ad for teachers?

> Wanted: Men and women with the patience of Job, wisdom of Solomon, and ability to prepare the next generation for productive citizenship under highly adverse and sometimes dangerous conditions. Applicants must be willing to fill gaps left by unfit, absent or working parents, satisfy demands of state politicians and local bureaucrats, impart healthy cultural and moral values—oh, yes—teach the three Rs. Hours: 50–60 a week. Pay: fair (getting better). Rewards: mostly intangible.[1]

These expectations seem overwhelming, job specifics ambiguous, working hours endless, responsibility challenging—all for "intangible rewards." In this case the stress we experience by reading this ad may be due to role demands exceeding our abilities and conflicting with our other lifestyle demands.

Before we relate conflict to stress, it is important to realize that **stress** is experienced subjectively as a biochemical reaction within the body because of the way in which we interpret and respond to external pressures, which may be positive or negative.[2] Stress does not cause this reaction; it *is* the reaction. Moreover, we want to emphasize that people are responsible for their reactions to stress, although not all people respond the same way to the same stressor.[3]

Some interpersonal conflict textbooks highlight the idea that conflict is stressful. Of course, when we are focused on a problematic situation affecting an interpersonal relationship, dreading a confrontation with someone important to us, and looking at conflict negatively, we are likely to experience stress. Researchers have found that, in particular, competing, avoiding, and accommodating are associated with high work-related stress.[4] So choosing to communicate or say nothing and choosing particular ways to manage conflict can play a role in adding stress to our lives.

However, we also believe the opposite is true: The stress we are feeling in our lives often erupts into conflict with others. Stress can be seen as an escalator in a conflict situation, one that makes a person more easily fly off the handle or even turn violent. One of the authors has witnessed these eruptions all too often.

> I learned early on in teaching that when a student would see me during my office hours and enter my office all upset, sometimes crying or extremely angry over a particular grade on a quiz, test, or paper, I found that if I asked the student questions about what else was going on outside of class, I would find that the student had other more serious problems, such as withheld grades, a problem with graduating that semester, problems with parents, a relationship or marital breakup, loss of employment, eviction from an apartment, or death in the family. It was a combination of two or more significant events that were upsetting the student. For that student, outside pressures were becoming unbearable, and now I added to the problem by failing the student on an assignment. Since we faculty at this institution also advise undergraduate students as well as teach, I would shift to my advisor role, and let the student elaborate on his or her other problems. I would offer suggestions about ways to deal with these outside pressures. After spending some time on these other problems, I would switch hats resuming my role as teacher, and we would then talk about the grade and how the student could do better on future assignments. All this seemed to have a comforting effect on the student, who often apologized for how he or she behaved initially.

We believe that when others explode, jump all over us, or overreact in a conflict situation, we often find that they have other personal problems (or sources of stress) that make it difficult for them to behave with greater restraint. These past problems have produced stress and one more problem now is too much for these individuals. More technically, we can say that outside stressors may amplify or magnify our emotional response to negative social exchanges (which often take place during an interpersonal conflict). In other words,

... (D)isagreements with social network members may become especially upsetting in the context of high life stress, making the effects of such disagreements substantially worse at high levels of life stress than at moderate or low levels of life stress.[5]

In this chapter, we consider the situation in which stress contributes to the escalation of conflict. We'll define the common types of stress, describe many common sources of stress, explain stress's impact on conflicts you have with others, and suggest ways to constructively deal with stress as a way to help you manage conflict in your relationships with others. To the extent that you accept our philosophy and welcome the techniques and suggestions offered in this book, you should find that stress management can go hand in hand with conflict management. Together they can help you deal with difficult situations and make your life more enjoyable.

TYPES OF STRESS

Eustress and Hypostress

Selye has identified four kinds of stress.[6] A good kind of stress, **eustress** is a short-term stress that encourages us to take more seriously and expend more energy on important activities. For example, hitters stepping up to the plate in a baseball game may experience eustress, if they are psyched up to perform. Students getting ready to write a paper about a subject they have mastered may also experience eustress. Speech teachers train speakers to avoid the more serious problem of stage fright but try not to eliminate all stress so that the speakers are motivated to give their best speaking performance. When eustress occurs, we experience some stress but still have control over the situation. We know that we are able to make choices and have the necessary resources to meet the demand.

A second kind of stress is **hypostress,** or underload. This happens when we're bored or unchallenged by our situations. If you are employed in a job that is repetitive and requires little adaptation on your part, you may experience hypostress and find yourself more and more unwilling to go to work. When an absence from pressure gets too long, we hunger to get back into action. "I can stay home sick for only so long without going crazy!" The authors have found that vacations can lead to hypostress. The first week of relaxation is fine, but if the vacation is "too long" we begin to feel anxious and irritable, because we know there are tasks to be completed, and we want to finish them, so they no longer linger in the background. Although we may seem irritable or antsy, our problem is easily resolved when we return home and get back to work.

Hyperstress

Hyperstress and distress are major factors in conflict. **Hyperstress** occurs when too many tasks and responsibilities pile up on us and we are unable to adapt to the changes or cope with all that is happening at once.[7] This is the kind of stress frequently experienced by students and teachers. If we had asked you for a general definition of stress, you probably would have said something like "it arises when we are asked to do more than we think we are capable of doing at the time." You are technically describing hyperstress.

What are the sources of hyperstress in your life? The authors can point to their respective children, spouses, the workplace, coauthors, and publishing deadlines. This does not mean we are dissatisfied with any of these people or factors, but they can, from time to time, add stress to our lives, just as we do for them on occasion. The problem becomes hyperstress when we fear that many of the sources are overwhelming us at a given moment, which often results in our momentarily flying off the handle. Perhaps this happens to you as well.

Both negative and positive events may lead to hyperstress. Few people would doubt that an Internal Revenue Service audit is stressful, and almost all people find enduring a root canal a high-stress situation. On the other hand, getting married, we presume, is a happy occasion, and yet it causes a great deal of hyperstress as the bride and groom make arrangements, meet their new in-laws, and commit themselves to one another. Giving a dinner party is also pleasurable, but the demands of preparation may cause the host or hostess a great deal of stress.

One distinguishing feature of hyperstress is that the source is identifiable and clears up quickly when eliminated. If in the same week that you have three midterms, your parents call you to tell you they are divorcing, your car won't start, and you receive notice of several bounced checks, you are definitely a candidate for hyperstress.

When hyperstress occurs, our reaction to it unfolds in three stages.[8] First, we experience alarm, where our hearts beat faster, blood gets redirected to skeletal muscles, and so on. Essentially, your body is preparing to fight or run away. Second, we experience resistance. Our temperature, blood pressure, and breathing are still high, and our body releases hormones that affect us both physically and emotionally.[9] Finally, if stress is not relieved, we experience exhaustion. We become more susceptible to illness or even collapse because we have few physical and emotional reserves left.

Hyperstress can lead to **overblown conflict,** which occurs when people greatly exaggerate their reaction in a conflict situation, generally using a relatively unimportant issue as a focal point. The conflict is overblown by one or more of the parties who invests far more emotion and energy than usual. This narrative illustrates an overblown conflict.

> In a meeting at work, the person who generally runs the meeting asked the group if we wanted to continue our habit of having an inspiration thought that people took turns preparing. Everyone was silent and looked at the table. It really bothered me, though, because everyone says how wonderful they are but no one had an opinion. I knew I shouldn't have said anything as I was in the middle of too many stressful situations to be calm, but this just took me over the edge. I started haranguing the group, asking why if we're supposed to be so cohesive and wonderful with each other that we can't even venture an opinion over something like an inspirational message. Finally, I blew up and said, "Forget it. I'm out of here" and walked out of the room. I had a lot of apologizing to do after that happened.

Clearly, the topic of the inspirational message wasn't what caused this person's stress nor was it the cause of the overblown conflict. It simply served as a focus for excess stress-generated energy. Overblown conflicts are often resolved when the person who has done the ranting and raving apologizes, usually making some excuse for the untoward behavior (e.g., "I was stressed out") that the target of the conflict accepts as a reasonable excuse. However, it is preferable to avoid overblown conflicts in the first place. This is done through more effective stress management. We'll return to the notion of overblown conflicts in Chapter 12, when we discuss psychodynamic theory.

How to Manage Hyperstress

Managing stress also heads off the escalation of conflicts that occur because of it. Walker and Brokaw suggest a number of different things that a person can do to manage stress.[10]

There are some habits that help us to keep stress from occurring as regularly. These entail eating sensibly, getting enough sleep and rest, living a balanced life. engaging in relaxing activities, spending time with good friends, saying "no" to requests you really can't take on, and accepting what you can't change. In addition, avoiding self-medication through the use of nicotine, alcohol, or drugs helps us keep stress at a minimum. However, it's not always possible to live so sensibly, and stress hits us anyway.

One of the most effective stress relievers is regular exercise. It doesn't necessarily have to be strenuous; even a stroll around the block can lower your blood pressure, regulate your breathing, and create a sense of relaxation. Yard work or other physical labor can also be effective. Making a piece of art or even coloring in a children's activity book can relieve stress. You can discuss a stressful event with a trusted friend. This doesn't mean you vent anger but that you seek advice from a more objective person, who can help you move toward resolution of the stressful situation. You can give in during a quarrel about something that isn't particularly important, heading off the stress before it starts.

Other means of managing stress involve your environment. Tackling your more difficult tasks first, and then finding a way to reward yourself with a pleasurable activity following it can be helpful. For example, you can tell yourself you'll watch a movie you've wanted to see when you finish a difficult task. If you anticipate a stressful event, you can rehearse it ahead of time to avoid overreacting while in it. You can also clean your living area, and organize or reorganize your work space, as this person does:

> One of my most effective ways of dealing with stress is to clean the house or my studio. I actually find it very satisfying and relaxing because I can think about the problem that's bothering me and the symbolic aspect of having my place cleaner when I'm done really helps me focus. When I'm really stressed, I move the furniture around in my studio. If nothing else, it helps me look at things in a new way.

Women, in particular, benefit from the company of other women when they are stressed. While men generally respond to stress with "flight or fight" responses, the more healthy response for women is to "tend and befriend." When women experience stress, a hormone called oxytocin is released in response. That hormone offsets the flight or fight response and moves women toward gathering together with other women. This in turn causes a calming effect. Men don't experience this because the testosterone surge they experience when stressed negates the oxytocin. Estrogen, however, enhances oxytocin. The author of this research concludes: "that the more friends women had, the less likely they were to develop physical impairments as they aged, and the more likely they were to be leading a joyful life."[11]

Finally, we suggest that you turn your attention to others as a means of reducing stress. Helping others, throwing a party, volunteering in a charity, and other means of reaching out can actually reduce your stress. Post and Neimark's remarkable research on the power of giving concludes:

> Generous behavior is closely associated with reduced risk of illness and mortality and lower rates of depression. Even more remarkable, giving is linked to traits that undergird a successful life, such as social competence, empathy, and positive emotion. By learning to give, you become more effective at life itself.[12]

The authors identify several ways of giving to others that can result in lower stress and lower rates for illness for the giver: expressing gratitude, helping others grow, speaking up for one's beliefs, listening to others, and engaging in creative activities.

Distress

In addition to eustress, hypostress, and hyperstress, people may experience **distress,** which arises when they don't feel that they have control over the situation and when the source of stress is unclear. While many students and teachers are familiar with hyperstress in their lives, distress is experienced more by some than others or occurs at different times in people's lives. One of the authors remembers when he dated in college and encountered distress.

> For a period of several months during my last year in college, whenever I went out on a date, my stomach became so upset that I felt like throwing up. I then had to "call it a night" and go home early. Needless to say that embarrassed me and disappointed and confused my date. I had no idea what was the matter at the time. Meanwhile, over the next several months, I was accepted to graduate school, graduated from college, and started graduate school. My stomach problem "magically" disappeared. Without realizing it, I was worried about graduation, acceptance to graduate school, and succeeding in graduate study. These must have been looming somewhere in the back of my mind and affecting me by upsetting my stomach. Once it became clear to me that I had cleared the major hurdles and was succeeding in graduate school, I stopped experiencing the upset stomachs when dating.

Distress is more encompassing than the other forms of stress. It relates more to our world view, personality (Type A, too controlling, workaholic, etc.), and self-fulfilling prophecy (or expectations). Because distress can make us appear difficult or act in ways that appear unpleasant to others, it can contribute to conflict proneness.

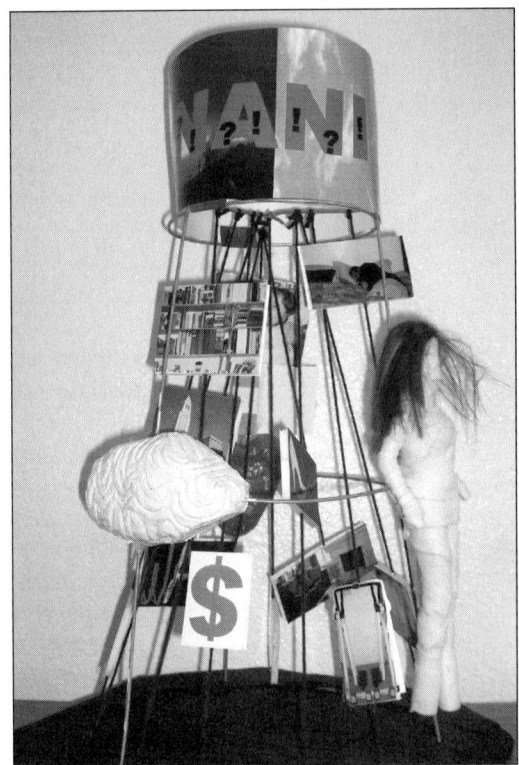

One source of stress is competing demands on our lives, as NiniLii Paxton has depicted in her conflict art.

Conflict Proneness

Conflict proneness due to distress occurs when people take themselves too seriously, don't enjoy what they are doing, or fail to see the humor in their everyday affairs. Distress makes people unhappy. Fearing that they are falling behind or not succeeding in achieving their goals, they have lost sight of the fact that they are not playing for fun. Instead, they are concentrating entirely on the end result. Athletes do this when they focus only on winning or outperforming others. Many of these people are not happy, having fun, or enjoying life.

You may have difficulty listing the likely sources of distress in your life. In fact, you may be among the lucky ones who are not experiencing distress. But there are those who may tell you that everything is OK but they aren't happy and find that they are having trouble getting along with other people. They may be experiencing distress. It may take the help of others to determine exactly what the problem is.

There are numerous reasons why modern living is stressful. Obviously, jobs can be a major source of distress and unhappiness. In his scholarly treatment of the subject, Brenner adds,

> ... (M)oney is important, but I believe that how we earn it is even more important ... there is a great letdown in our sense of joy from life, and in our self-respect, as a result of things we do that we are unconsciously apologetic for, or feel guilty about, in the course of our daily work. And to a person who is unhappy, life cannot be fun.[13]

Why are people not happy? There are many reasons. Consider this person's account:

> I have a good friend who was, for a time, homeless. He moved to this state without having a job lined up and found he couldn't get one. He ran through his resources and wound up living out of his car. It has really affected him. It's hard for him to spend money even on necessities, because he's terrified of being homeless again. The fact that he's making good money now and banking a good portion of it doesn't matter. As far as he's concerned, another rainy day is just around the corner.

People who take life too seriously often end up turning to alcohol, nicotine, and drugs; become addicted to something; or engage in compulsive spending, buying expensive items or taking vacations that they can ill afford.

We start our life as children with an obvious demand for joy. Even as adults, there is a child hidden in each of us, and this child would like to come out and play. However, later we learn to take everyday activities too seriously, such that they become obligations, which usually rob us of fun, joy, and merriment. Our preoccupation with achievement whether in winning or outperforming others makes us feel insecure. According to Brenner, "Unfortunately, the traditional repression of play, humor, and wit deeply changed our ability to enjoy life and to be content. It has turned us into severe, aggressive, function-oriented rather than people-oriented creatures."[14]

It is not enough that we take matters too seriously. Sometimes we turn play and fun activities into work. Professional sports may be an example where some "players" no longer enjoy the "game." It has ceased to be fun for them. The same might be said of some entertainers and actors who have lost the joy of "playing" before others. Those situations show the negative elements that exist, which also can be found in work and serious situations that are not viewed from a play or fun perspective.

Let's take an activity that should be fun like a vacation. Often people say they need a vacation to recover from their vacation! Why is that? Part of the reason is that they spend a great deal of time planning it, working overtime to pay for it, worrying that the experience might not live up to their expectations, and obsessing about how many tasks will be piled up on their desks when they return to work.

Why do we say that distress leads to conflict proneness? People who take themselves too seriously find it difficult to manage conflicts effectively. They fly off the handle too quickly, avoid too many issues, and perhaps become verbally or physically abusive of their loved ones. For these unfortunate persons, failing interpersonal relations may become a downward spiral that doesn't end until they have lost their friends and loved ones. Some may need psychotherapy but others may realize before it is too late that they must do something now and try to lead better lives. The question is how to do that? Our answer is to develop a "playful spirit."

How to Manage Distress: Developing a Playful Spirit

How do we change our attitudes and adopt a playful spirit? Play theorists encourage us to develop a **playful spirit** by changing our attitude toward life in a way that enables us to lighten up. The following techniques may be of help to you

- Don't blame yourself for everything that goes wrong or doesn't pan out.
- Look for situational factors that you may learn to accept rather than fight against.
- See irony in problematic situations.
- Visualize absurdities. Make a joke to yourself of something negative. An excellent example of this is the line of products promoted by Demotivators.Com. They sell "inspirational posters" that are a spoof of the high gloss photographs one often sees in offices.[15]
- Ask yourself: Am I happy right now? What can I do now to be happier?
- Learn to say "No," without feeling guilty.
- Take on a new role, which is more enjoyable than the present one.
- Do something you can succeed at, especially after failing something else.
- Hang a sign in your room or workplace: Success is happiness!

If you compare this list with the one in the preceding section for managing hyperstress, you can see that these are aimed more at changing the way you look at the world and making lifestyle changes, whereas the list for hyperstress tends to focus more on distractions, relaxation, physical exercise, and balancing work and play.

We can learn from those older people who avoid distress by grasping a playful attitude. Books have been written on the stress encountered by women over 50. The recent upsurge of "Red Hat Clubs," where women celebrate the fact that they're over 50 and deserve to be called "Queen Mother," is an example of how people may adopt this playful attitude. According to the official Web site of the Red Hat Club,

> The Red Hat Society began as a result of a few women deciding to greet middle age with verve, humor and élan. We believe silliness is the comedy relief of life, and since we are all in it together, we might as well join red-gloved hands and go for the gusto together. Underneath the frivolity, we share a bond of affection, forged by common life experiences and a genuine enthusiasm for wherever life takes us next.[16]

The use of humor in conflict situations is a double-edged sword. On one hand, used appropriately, it can alleviate some of the stress in the situation and help people express some of their negative emotions in a more positive way. Appropriate humor may also help maintain social order, channel hostility, or assist people in saving face. But if the humor is inappropriate, it can also make the conflict situation worse. The ability to use humor in a conflict situation, though, is an indicator of the level of trust in it—those who trust one another can laugh together.[17]

But, what if other people think that everything is just a big joke to you? If your parents are paying for your college education, your boss is taking a chance in hiring you, or your teachers think that you only do superior work if you take their assignments very seriously, then you fear that they may misinterpret your behavior. So, we are not saying that you have to act truly silly in the presence of others. Much of what we suggest may be accomplished covertly, that is mentally. We can see the world differently, talk to ourselves in a constructive matter, and make light of some matters as a mental state. Thus, we can feel less guilty and less anxiety. Meanwhile, we continue to be productive and do what is possible or what it takes to keep a job or earn good grades. Neale claims, "Those who have observed children at play have no doubts about their seriousness."[18] Rahner adds:

> The same things that give human play its unique character—the light-hearted relaxing of the mind, the charm of a certain smiling contempt for mundane things, the wisdom of ease and detachment—also make it possible for a person to kick the world away from oneself with the airy grace of a dancer, and yet, at the same time, press it to one's heart.[19]

According to Sutton-Smith, a playful spirit contributes to well-being and is associated with being an emotionally, socially, physically, and mentally healthier person.[20] Approaching our environment as a game to be played as well as taken seriously can convert an unhappy life into a happy one—or at least reduce one's conflict proneness.

CHANGING HOW WE LOOK AT LIFE'S CHALLENGES

Obviously, we need to take ourselves less seriously, see the humor in our everyday activities, and enjoy life more. We need to recognize that "in true success, the notions of 'noble character,' 'joyful living,' and the centrality of family and friends are key elements."[21] This means that we have to allow more time, plan some fun activities into our lives, learn to laugh more, and avoid making situations more complicated than they need to be. How do we do this? Essentially, there are three different ways to lighten up.

The First Solution

We can make a distinction between work and play. We can view work as what we do for the sake of something else, while play is what we do for its own sake. So, we can add to our week a few mindless entertainment and fun activities in an effort to balance work. You certainly could give this solution a try. However, it may not work because a few fun events in the evenings or on weekends may not be enough to balance 40, 60, or 80 hours of a demanding job during the week. It helps, but is it enough?

Moreover, the type of mindless entertainment and fun activities may lose impact if they are passive rather than active. Watching a movie may be somewhat relaxing, but more benefit may be gained from taking a walk or playing a game with someone.

Perhaps the greatest shortcoming of this approach is that it runs the risk of making you feel imprisoned by your job. If you can find some joy in your work, it is likely to reduce the stress associated with it. As Bakke points out:

> Many have heard the story of the visitor to a job site where workers were busy in a variety of construction activities. "What are you doing?" the visitor asked one of the workmen. "I'm laying bricks," he responded. A few minutes later, the visitor repeated the question to another workman. "I'm building a wall," he said. The visitor then put the question to a third workman. "I'm helping to build a great cathedral," he replied, leaving no doubt about his passion for his work.[22]

Bakke's point is simple but important: The attitude with which we approach our tasks has an important impact on the level of stress we will feel about them.

The Second Solution

The second way to lighten up is to take the view that "play is an attitude of mind that may pervade any human activity."[23] It isn't our actual experiences, but what we make of them, which gives meaning to our existence. It has been said that life can be easier than what we actually make it. It's as though we need to give ourselves permission to have fun. Mahan argues that

> ... (W)hat we'd most like to do is chuck the whole project of improving ourselves and with it our incessant and obsessive monitoring of our "progress" toward whoever it is we think we ought to be ... we long for a kind of self-forgetful yet fully engaged sense of immediacy, for a more graced and gracious way of being in this world, one that cuts deeper than the surface imagery sketched by our infernal preoccupation with some soon-to-be success or failure ... [24]

We can change the way we feel about our everyday activities at home, work, or school. We must find joy in the work we do. This is a far more encompassing than the first solution. It is a matter of seeing our work as a game, as a type of play. Miller puts it another way: Not that we should start playing and stop working, but rather, we should work as if at play, because that is what we are doing anyway—playing at work.[25]

We need to take ourselves less seriously, treat matters more gamefully, and designate all our activities as games that we play. We need to make the decision that if we must do our everyday activities, we might as well enjoy doing them. We need to catch ourselves every time we take ourselves too seriously. When we do that, we come alive—we lighten up.

The Third Solution

The third solution can be termed *integration*—one understands that joy and pain are often found in the same place, and that both are to be valued. Goldingay remarks:

> So many things we achieve are achieved only through struggle and conflict, not in easy ways. ... I have so longed to find somewhere in life some corner where joy is unmingled with pain. But I have never found it. Wherever I find joy, my own or other people's, it always seems to be mingled with pain .... The bad news is that there may be no corner of reality where joy is not related to pain. The good news is that there is no corner of reality where pain cannot be transformed into overflowing joy.[26]

In addition to the above useful suggestions for dealing with hyperstress and distress, we can learn a way of thinking that can help reduce or eliminate entirely either type. We have to begin by identifying the source of stress, or **stressor**.

SOURCES OF HYPERSTRESS AND DISTRESS

Stress can arise from a number of sources in our lives. Sometimes, we experience stress because there is a disparity between the kinds of activities we are engaged in and how we see ourselves (e.g., a moral person doing an immoral act). Quite often persons suffering from *hyperstress* can easily list the sources, while persons experiencing *distress* have to work harder to find the source, sometimes needing help in the process. Stressors, can include:

- anticipated life events (e.g., graduation, aging)
- unexpected life events (e.g., the death of a loved one, the loss of a job, or too much happening at once)
- the need to make tough decisions (e.g., should I go to grad school or marry or get a divorce?)
- struggle among the various roles we play and how much time and attention we should give to each one (e.g., perhaps you play all these roles: a student, a child, a friend, a part-time worker, and a romantic partner)

CONSTRUCTIVE AND POSITIVE THOUGHTS/BELIEFS AS RESPONSES TO HYPERSTRESS AND DISTRESS

You'll probably agree that overblown conflicts are a negative coping strategy that you should avoid as much as possible. But how do you cope with stress in a positive way? Personal characteristics affect the way people respond to stress. Some people, for example, are simply "hardier" than others. They are involved in their jobs and families, they believe they can control their lives, and they see change as a challenge rather than as a threat. Can you become hardy? It is partly a matter of the way you think about stressors, and, as shown below, you can change your way of thinking.

Probably the most important tool available for managing hyperstressful and distressful events is our thought process. How we think about matters affects the way we perceive the events we experience. This in turn has a major impact on how we choose to respond to them, and whether we need to engage in conflicts with others. McKinnon and colleagues claim, "The way in which a stressor is interpreted, more than the stressor's properties, predicts the intensity, nature, and duration of physiological and psychological response."[27] We can't escape decisions. We nearly always experience the pressure of time and role demands.

We begin with the observation that the same event produces different reactions in people. Some interpret practically any event as good, others as indifferent, and still others as a disaster. We believe that the difference lies in our way of thinking about the event. Our approach to stress management is called the **ABC approach:**

A = the activating event or stressor
B = our relevant beliefs or thoughts
C = consequences or effects and reaction to the stressor

The stressor "A" is the **activating event,** which produces the stress (boss at work, too many assignments due tomorrow). Of course, it is nice if we can change "A" and eliminate the source of our stress from our lives. There are two ways to do that: change something in the environment (turn off the computer if it is stressing you today) or change environments (pick up and leave; go somewhere else). In the news recently, an airline pilot became so stressed over his next flight that he refused to get on the plane. Of course, he needed professional help, but at the same time, the passengers had to appreciate the fact that he decided to avoid a situation that was too stressful for him to handle that day. Unfortunately, each life event we encounter (courtship, weddings, childbirth, taxes, death, applying for jobs, promotions, etc.) all produce some degree of stress. So, we can't always eliminate the stressor entirely even if we want to. In such cases, we can change "B," or our **beliefs** (or thoughts) about the stressor, and interpret, perceive, or label the activating event in a more constructive or positive way. When you cannot cope with your circumstances, we suggest that you try changing yourself (or at least the way you think or look at something).

To what extent should one change his or her beliefs to reduce stress? We should not overlook the fact that changing "B" may be difficult if not impossible in some cases. For many persons who have a reasonable well-grounded set of beliefs, they know when to compromise, give in, or assert themselves. Other people simply tolerate stress in their lives because they were taught to expect it and live with it.

> I expected to put in a lot of hours in teaching, low pay, and occasional encounters with difficult teachers, faculty, and administrators. I know I am experiencing stress quite frequently, but I expected that. It comes with the territory. I choose not to let it get me down. I think instead about the advantages of having a job with a roof over my head, heat, electricity, dependable pay, and occasional days off as well as the entire summer. Maybe this comes from my time spent in the military overseas where I was sometimes subjected to unbearable living conditions. I have come to appreciate a job like teaching.
>
> I tell my students that if the classroom is too hot and uncomfortable, imagine themselves living or working under worse conditions like the workers outdoors who are right now digging a trench around the building as part of a new campus hot water line project. Our situation looks pretty inviting to those workers.

In other cases, individuals who do not have certain life experiences or upbringing that lends support to demanding situations may find it difficult to manage conflict. These people experience a great deal of stress when they try to impose their prescriptive moral values on others at work or in the home. However, there is evidence that changes in beliefs can reduce stress.[28] While these persons may find it difficult to change many of their beliefs and values, we can suggest some beliefs that many people can change.

Let's begin with a common activating event (A) where someone rejects you. Maybe she or he doesn't ask you to go shopping, or vote for you, or call you when you want her or him to. It is at this point that we want to impress on you that you have a choice as to what to think (B) when confronted by "A." Our thoughts or beliefs color the event we perceive. This explains why two people may view the same event quite differently because they do not share the same point of view. Here is an example:

1. I am awful; no one accepts me; I am always rejected by others; I am a worthless person; I deserve this because I am unpopular; I wish someone could do some magic and change me into a better person.
2. I don't like this; I wish it hadn't happened; it was unfortunate, undesirable; we would have had a lot of fun together; I am good company, but he/she doesn't know what he/she is missing; I'll go do something I know that I want to do.

If you choose to think option 1, the **consequences (C)** consist of your becoming upset and disorganized, panicking, suffering severe anxiety, and maybe even going into depression. The next person to say or do the wrong behavior may push you over the edge, and you explode. If you choose to think option 2, the consequences (C) consist of your feeling sorrowful initially, and perhaps a bit regretful, irritated, or frustrated. However, there is no need for you to overreact and put yourself down. You can figure out a way to make the best of the situation. The next person to say or do the wrong action is not adding fuel to a raging fire, so you can respond in a constructive or positive way if you find yourself in a conflict situation.

The key point here is that *if you choose option 1, you upset yourself.* This is a self-fulfilling prophecy in that if you expect the worst, you are likely to receive it. Here is a list of thoughts that contribute to stress and the escalation of conflict: irrational thinking, ineffectual thinking, self-damaging thinking habits, self-damning, wishful thinking, intolerance, pessimism, expecting the worst, perfectionist thinking, expecting some magic, being superstitious, being dogmatic, blaming, or damning others for everything. In addition, being too other directed (or accommodating) is a problem, as one thinks too much about what others think of her or him. If your self-acceptance depends on what others think, you lose control of who you are—which is a stressful event! On the other hand, being too self-directed (or competitive) is also a problem when people think they must win every argument, always come out on top, and have to show up the opposition. If your self-acceptance depends on being Number One, the fear of failure is a constant source of stress.

If you are not hired after applying for a job, you can either blame yourself or realize that hiring is very complex and many factors are taken into account, so it is quite possible that you are not to blame. If you blame yourself, you will lose confidence, start feeling distressed, and stop looking for work, but if you understand that you may well not be to blame, then you can continue the job search with confidence.

So, how can you control your thoughts so as to reduce your stress? The first step is to discover the ways in which your "self-talk" contributes to your stress. Consider how these different ways of thinking about the same event, shown in Table 7.1, can increase or reduce stress.

We're not suggesting that you ignore the reality of the situation when you engage in supportive self-talk. What we are suggesting, however, is that if you can avoid "doom and gloom" thinking about situations and focus on the power and choices you do have within them, you can reduce your stress level. Ellis claims that it is not the events themselves that cause stress but how we talk to ourselves about the events that causes our stress.[29] Consider how this person handled a stressful situation.

> There's a coworker who is really unpredictable. I never know if he's going to snarl at me or say hello. It really depressed me, and I'd slink around the hallways hoping I wouldn't run into him. But whose life was being ruined? Mine. So, I decided I'd cheer up and greet him. To heck with him if he wants to be nasty. At least I'll know I acted like a nice person.

TABLE 7.1 The Effect of Self-Talk on Stress

Situation	Self-Talk Increasing Stress	Self-Talk Decreasing Stress
Romantic	I'll never find someone like him/her again.	I enjoyed my time with him/her and I know there's someone else out there.
Failing a test	I'm so stupid. I won't pass.	I can take other actions to bring up my class grade. I can study differently next time.
Getting a speeding ticket	Everyone was speeding. Why me?	I was going over the speed limit. I intend to concentrate more on my driving.

Therefore, if your point of view or thoughts and beliefs are not producing positive results, then you should consider adopting a different way of looking at the world.

Helpful self-talk is rational. Three unhelpful kinds of statements are "shoulds," "awfuls," and "overgeneralizations." "Shoulds" have to do with the expectations we have for ourselves, for others close to us, and for the world in general. "Should" statements also contain words like *ought*, *must*, and *have to*. Some of the shoulds are unreasonable, and create expectations that are impossible to meet. Consider how this person responds to "shoulds."

> Three of us meet regularly to gripe and complain to each other as well as encourage each other. All three of us come from rotten families and we have committed to letting go of the negative messages of our childhood. All three of us have lots of "shoulds" in our lives—I should parent better, I should spend more time with my spouse, I should work harder, I should do this, I should do that. When one of us starts to talk this way, we tell that person to stop "shoulding" on himself or herself.

Recognizing when you are "shoulding on yourself" is one way to escape negative self-talk. Another kind of negative self-talk includes "awful" statements. When people talk about how horrible their circumstances are, or the fact that it is simply unbearable, it is pretty easy to start thinking that nothing can change. Continuing self-talk that makes change seem unlikely probably results in situations that do not change.

The final means of negative self-talk, "overgeneralizations," contains words like *always*, *never*, *everyone*, and *no one*. Overgeneralizations happen when people think one event is indicative of their entire life. You failed a test, so you're a complete failure. Someone didn't listen to you in this one instance, and that person never listens to you, and so on.

Negative self-talk is a poor means of controlling your thoughts in a situation. It leads to stress and the need for more self-talk. When you are in a situation where you cannot control other people's responses, you still have control over your own. Recognizing that is a way of reducing the stress that you feel about the situation.

People can be socialized or trained in ways to reduce the stress they experience.[30] Avoiding overgeneralizations and learning more positive self-talk are constructive actions you can take. Once you realize that the unproductive outcomes you have experienced in the past are often due to the way you chose to look at situations, you see a way to improve your situation. It is up to you to make a difference and choose to think about problematic situations in more constructive ways. We can also try to find the humor in stressful situations. Some research suggests that the "tendency to tell jokes and stories . . . predicted perceiving events and situations in one's life as more predictable and controllable."[31] This is especially important when stress levels are excessive.

> Rediscovering personal responsibility by accepting the consequences of our decisions and accepting inevitable imperfection will go a long way toward coping with stress. . . . If . . . we are capable of making decisions and taking responsibility for those decisions, we can reduce stress.[32]

MANAGE IT

We began our discussion of stress by identifying it as a contributor to conflict. Stressed people may more easily fly off the handle and perhaps even turn violent. We also identified four types of stress. Eustress is a short-term stress that encourages us to take more seriously and expend more energy on important activities. Hypostress, or underload, occurs when we're bored or unchallenged by our situations. Because the eustress and hypostress are only temporary and do not lead to significant conflicts, we focused on hyperstress and distress, which offer greater challenges to the conflict manager. Hyperstress occurs when too many tasks and responsibilities pile up on us and we are unable to adapt to the changes or cope with all that is happening at once. One distinguishing feature of hyperstress is that the source is usually clearly identifiable and clears up quickly if we eliminate it. Hyperstress makes it easy to experience an overblown conflict, which occurs when people greatly exaggerate a conflict, generally using a relatively unimportant issue as a focal point. The conflict is overblown by one or more of the parties who invests far more emotion and energy than usual. Some specific techniques for dealing with hyperstress are listed in the chapter.

Distress arises when we don't feel control over the situation and when the source of stress is unclear. Distress is more encompassing than the other forms of stress. It relates more to our world view, personality (Type A, too controlling, workaholic, etc.), and self-fulfilling prophecy (or expectations). Because distress can make us appear difficult or act in ways that appear unpleasant to others, it can contribute to conflict proneness.

Conflict proneness due to distress occurs when people take themselves too seriously, don't enjoy what they are doing, or fail to see the humor in their everyday affairs. Distress makes people unhappy and difficult to work or live with.

While some specific techniques are listed in the chapter for dealing with distress, a more encompassing way to manage distress is to develop a playful spirit. We suggest three ways to do that: Make a distinction between work and play, striving for balance between them; turn work into play so that you enjoy what you do; and learn how to appreciate the bad with the good because some suffering makes us better appreciate good fortune when it occurs.

There is another more general way to deal with hyperstress and distress which is known as the ABC model. The letter A stands for the activating event or stressor; B means our relevant beliefs or thoughts; and C refers to the consequences or effects and reaction to the stressor. In addition to identifying stressors and relating them to consequences, the model also shows us the important role played by our thoughts and beliefs.

We can avoid stress by minimizing the number of irrational thoughts we entertain. We can monitor our emotional reactions to problematic situations and ask what feelings different events are arousing in us. We can record our self-talk and make sure it is positive rather than negative. When you write down what you are saying to yourself such as something like, "I am a failure because I received an F on this algebra test," it is easier to see that it is irrational. By writing down your self-talk, you can also dispute your irrational beliefs by writing down rational statements instead. If your negative self-talk includes a statement like, "I'll never understand this subject," you can dispute that by listing what you already do understand and listing places where you can seek help on this section.

If you are doing your best to alleviate hyperstress as it occurs, and to avoid distress when you can, you are much less likely to engage in destructive conflicts. When we are stressed, it is more difficult to practice good communication skills. Empathy is difficult during periods of hyperstress or distress. It is hard to hear another person out and want to respond to them. Keeping stress at an optimal low level is a way of ensuring competence in communication situations.

Think About It

1. When have you recently (or ever) blown up over something that was not such a big deal really? Can you think of times you got really upset but now can't remember why? Think back on these occasions and try to determine if there were other problems going on in your life. Did they put you on edge so that you felt overwhelmed and exploded?
2. Have you tried any of the techniques listed for reducing hyperstress? Which worked best? Do you know someone who should try some of these techniques?
3. Have you ever experienced distress as defined and explained in this chapter? If not, do you know someone who has? Were you or this other person able (at some point) to identify reasons for this distress? Did you or the other person try any of the techniques listed for reducing distress? Which worked best for you? Do you know someone who should try some of these techniques?
4. Look at your work and school commitments. How might you apply each of the "three solutions" to improve how you feel about your job and school?

Apply It

1. Take a piece of paper and draw three columns on it. In the first column, identify the various sources of stress you have in your life. In the second, indicate whether the stress factor is positive (leading to eustress) or negative (leading to distress, hyperstress, or hypostress). In the third column, list ways you can reduce the stress.
2. Take a piece of paper and draw three columns on it. In the first, list two or three stressors you are facing right now. In the second, list the kind of negative self-talk you are engaging in about that stressor. In the third, write a different self-talk message that can help reduce your stress level.

Work With It

1. Read the following case study and answer the question that follows it.

    With my roommate Elena, I've been unhappy and stressed out over the fact that my roommate may or may not be coming back next year to room with me. We have been the best of friends since our first days in elementary school, and I can't imagine anyone else as my roommate. (Note that the roommate does not seem to realize that this uncertainty is making her edgy and irritable.) Everything she does right now is getting to me. I don't like it when she comes in late and wakes me, doesn't study when I do, and is too busy with her other friends to eat with me. We don't see each other anymore and here we are roommates!

    Anyway, yesterday she left the room and took my laptop computer without asking me. I really erupted. I went hunting for her and found her in the library lobby typing notes with a couple of her classmates. I went right up to her and grabbed my laptop. I really told her off and left with it. She and her friends just stared at me.

    a. What are the issues in this conflict? Are they tangible or intangible?
    b. Which type of stress is the roommate experiencing?
    c. What specific techniques might she use to counter her stress?
    d. How might one develop a more playful spirit?
    e. How might the ABC model be applied in her situation?

2. Apply the ABC model to the major stresses in your life by listing the following in a four-column table.
    a. List activating events or stressors (triggering events, people, places, situations) in your life. Indicate which are temporary or short-lived stressors and which are longer term. Identify each as annoying or anger producing and disappointing or depression producing.
    b. List consequences (physiological effects/body reactions, behavioral effects, psychological effects—negative coping and defense mechanisms).
    c. List your internal pressures (irrational beliefs, self-damnations, thoughts, assumptions, wishful thoughts, intolerances). These are to include "should statements," "awfulizing statements," "overgeneralizations," and self-talk (or irrational beliefs).
    d. List the positive coping mechanisms that you would like to use.

NOTES

1. Susan Tifft, Who's Teaching Our Children? *Time* 132 (1988, November 14), 58–64.
2. Bruce W. Speck, "Defining Stress as Ethical Conflict," *The Bulletin* 56 (1993), 34–37.
3. Carolyn M. Aldwin, *Stress, Coping, and Development*, 2nd Ed. (New York: Guildford Press, 2007).
4. Warren A. Reich, Bonnie J. Wagner-Westbrook, and Kenneth Kressel. "Actual and Ideal Conflict Styles and Job Distress in a Health Care Organization," *The Journal of Psychology* 141(1) (2007), 5–15.
5. Kristin J. August, Karen S. Rook, and Jason T. Newsom. "The Joint Effects of Life Stress and Negative Social Exchanges on Emotional Stress." *The Journals of Gerontology: Series B: Psychological Sciences and Social Sciences* 62(5) (2007), S304–S314.
6. Hans Selye, *Stress without Distress* (New York: J. B. Lippincott, 1974).
7. Velma Walker and Lynn Brokaw, *Becoming Aware*, 6th Ed. (Dubuque, IA: Kendall Hunt, 1995), p. 315.

8. Thomas Berstene, "The Inexorable Link between Conflict and Change," *The Journal for Quality and Participation* 27 (2004), 4–9.
9. These hormones are often tied to the perceived power a person has in the relationship; see Timothy J. Loving, Kathi L. Hefner, Janice K. Kiecolt-Glaser, Ronald Glaser, and William B. Malarkey, "Stress Hormone Changes and Marital Conflict: Spouses' Relative Power Makes a Difference," *Journal of Marriage and the Family* 66 (2004), 595–612.
10. Walker and Brokaw, op cit.
11. Gail Berkowitz, "UCLA Study on Friendship among Women," retrieved January 6, 2003 from http://www.womenandhorses.com/article001.html. Summary based on Shelley E. Taylor, Laura C. Klein, Brian P. Lewis, Tara L. Gruenewald, Regan A. R. Gurung, and John A. Updegraff, "Female Responses to Stress: Tend and Befriend, Not Fight or Flight," *Psychological Review* 107(3) (2000), 41–429.
12. Stephen Post and Jill Neimark, *Why Good Things Happen to Good People* (New York: Broadway Books, 2007), p. 2.
13. Paul Brenner, *If Life Is a Game, How Come I'm not having Fun?* (Albany, NY: SUNY Press, 2001), pp. 87, 89.
14. Ibid., p. 90.
15. www.demotivators.com
16. Red Hat Society at http://www.redhatsociety.com/infonew/howitstarted.html
17. Wanda J. Smith, K. Vernard Harrington, and Christopher P. Neck, "Resolving Conflict with Humor in a Diversity Context," *Journal of Managerial Psychology* 15 (2000), 606–625.
18. Robert E. Neale, *In Praise of Play: Toward a Psychology of Religion* (New York: Harper & Row, 1969), p. 173.
19. Hugo Rahner, *Man at Play* (New York: Herder & Herder, 1972), pp. 7–8.
20. Anthony D. Pellegrini (Ed.), *The Future of Play Theory: A Multidisciplinary Inquiry into the Contributions of Brian Sutton-Smith* (Albany, NY: SUNY, 1995).
21. Brian J. Mahan, *Forgetting Ourselves on Purpose: Vocation and the Ethics of Ambition* (San Francisco, CA: Jossey Bass, 2002), p. 42
22. Dennis W. Bakke, *Joy at Work* (Seattle, WA: PVG, 2005), pp. 240–241.
23. Brenner, *If Life Is a Game, How Come I'm not having Fun?* p. 73.
24. Mahan, *Forgetting Ourselves on Purpose*, pp. xx–xxi.
25. David L. Miller, *Gods and Games: Toward a Theology of Play* (New York: Harper Colophon Books, 1973).
26. John Goldingay, *Walk On: Life, Loss, Trust, and Other Realities* (Grand Rapids, MI: Baker, 2002), p. 100.
27. William McKinnon, Carol S. Wiesse, C. Patrick Reynolds, Charles A. Bowles, and Andrew Baum, "Chronic Stress, Leukocyte Subpopulations, and Humoral Response to Latent Viruses," *Health Psychology* 8 (1989), 391.
28. Shevaun D. Neupert, David M. Almeida, and Susan T. Charles, "Age Differences in Reactivity to Daily Stressors: The Role of Personal Control," *The Journals of Gerontology: Series B: Psychological Sciences and Social Sciences* 62B (4), P216–P226.
29. Albert Ellis, "Overview of the Clinical Theory of Rational-Emotive Therapy," in Russell Grieger and John Boyd (Eds.), *Rational-Emotive Therapy: A Skills-Based Approach* (New York: Van Nostrand Reinhold, 1980), pp. 1–31.
30. Anthony D. Lamontagne, Tessa Keegel, Amber M. Louie, Aleck Ostry, and Paul A. Landbergis, "A Systematic Review of the Job-Stress Intervention Evaluation Literature, 1990–2005," *International Journal of Occupational and Environmental Health* 13(3) (2007), 268–341; Hieu M. Ngo and Thao N. Le, "Stressful Life Events, Culture, and Violence," *Journal of Immigrant Health* 9 (2007), 75–84.
31. Nathan Miczo, "Humor Ability, Unwillingness to Communicate, Loneliness, and Perceived Stress: Testing a Security Theory," *Communication Studies* 55 (2004), p. 222.
32. Speck, "Defining Stress as Ethical Conflict," p. 35.

CHAPTER 8

Managing Anger

OBJECTIVES

At the end of this chapter, you should be able to:

- Determine whether you are anger-in, anger-out, or anger controlling.
- Explain how anger can negatively affect a conflict situation.
- Identify the "primary emotion" that is being interpreted as anger.
- List ways to effectively control your anger and express it in constructive ways.

KEY TERMS

anger
anger controllers
anger-ins

anger-outs
interpersonal violence

secondary emotion
ventilation approach

Few people feel nothing during a conflict. For most of us, a conflict situation is often associated with a number of emotional responses—excitement, sadness, resentment, and anger among others. Phillips et al. claim, "It can be argued that in terms of social outcomes anger is the most important of all negative emotions in relation to the effects of anger expression on social relationships."[1] Of the emotional responses, anger can escalate and do the most damage to yourself and your interpersonal relationships,[2] because it is commonly believed by researchers that anger is the usual precursor to aggression.[3] Further, it is in our most important relationships that we experience anger:

> The overwhelmingly majority of anger episodes happened between people who had close interpersonal ties. That our close intimate relationships should generate anger more than other contexts is hardly surprising. There is more opportunity, people are more likely to care about and feel hurt over the actions of loved ones, and they are likely to feel more confident and secure about expressing anger.[4]

Anger is a strong feeling of displeasure, a synonym for antagonism and rage. Anger is different from feeling hurt or irritated. We experience these other emotions when someone or something frustrates our desires, but anger carries with it the desire to get even or seek revenge. Anger is associated with aggression, often because people expect that by behaving aggressively they will reduce their anger.[5]

Anger may lead to revenge and interpersonal violence. **Interpersonal violence** involves harming another person physically, emotionally, or mentally. We introduced you to verbal and physical aggression in Chapter 3, but we want to emphasize the idea that, in many cases, verbal abuse may escalate into physical aggression, when one or both parties physically attack the other. Later, when asked what they were fighting about or what started the argument, the two may not even remember, which is a sure sign that the conflict itself is unimportant, but anger and sometimes the desire for revenge blew the conflict all out of proportion. Verbal and physical abuse often characterize problematic relationships in need of help, although the partners may not think so.

Many of us have experienced anger and the escalation of conflict to a point where we wanted to inflict pain on the other person, either physically or emotionally by verbal abuse. One of the authors, Lee, tells this story:

> Sometimes when teaching conflict management, I like to pair off students, ask them to hold hands, and then role-play an interpersonal conflict. Even though the students were told to continue holding hands throughout the conflict, some simply couldn't do it and let go of each other. Others, who continued to hold hands, leaned away from each other or squeezed the other's hand uncomfortably hard while arguing with each other. In the class discussion that followed, students reported that it seems incongruous to argue and hold hands at the same time. They often admitted that when they got angry during a disagreement, they wanted to hurt the other person or at least not to welcome any warm and friendly contact.

Many students take classes to make themselves more successful supervisors, managers, or leaders. When in charge you may feel the pressure to set a standard for others and sometimes you have to make an example. Keeping your cool as leader is important because you do not want others to consider you a hothead.

We have all seen anger of different types. First, anger can occur instantly with no malice or forethought like the eruption of a volcano in people who are not generally viewed as hostile or aggressive. A second type of anger festers away for days, months, or even years such as when one plans for revenge. Still a third type is attached to people's personality, always lying just beneath the surface it would seem, but quickly manifesting itself in the form of hostility whenever these individuals feel pressured, defensive, or attacked. It may well be that anger lies along a continuum, ranging from a form that may be quickly brought under one's control to a form that requires a great deal of psychotherapy. Generally, anger "can be seen as a means of trying to get something done by forcing a change in the target's behavior, especially when one feels that one has power or control over the target."[6]

Some people have learned to turn this burst of energy into more positive or constructive endeavors. Although we have a tendency to see anger in a negative light, feelings of anger may be positive for the person experiencing them if, over the long term, that anger

People often respond with anger when they feel as though they are being forced to do something.

serves to change a situation or relationship that is currently unsatisfactory into something more acceptable.[7] Further, research suggests that if a person knows he or she will have to engage in a confrontation, that person is "sometimes motivated to engage in activities likely to increase their anger, despite the fact that such activities are less pleasant than alternative ones. . . . Angry participants performed better than excited participants in a confrontational task."[8] We want to emphasize the fact that sometimes anger can be used constructively. It can motivate us to get off our seats and stand up for our interests, needs, and wants or what we think is right.

Research indicates that people may actually have traitlike anger, which "is conceptualized as an enduring disposition to experience anger more frequently, more intensely, and for a longer period of time."[9] People who have high-anger trait process events in a way different from those who do not have high-anger trait. Such people are especially attuned to anger-related words (e.g., "Why did you do that stupid thing?") and respond to them more quickly than they do to words reflecting other emotions (e.g., You did a great job).[10] On the other hand, people who have low-anger trait tend to spontaneously reframe the circumstances in ways that deflect or inhibit their anger.[11]

While some hostile individuals may need the help of therapists, we believe that reading about anger and the principles of anger management can help many people bring their anger impulses under their control. We need to try to control our anger and attempt to avoid provoking anger in others. While there is a lot the other person could and should do to de-escalate a volatile situation, in this chapter we do not teach you how to avoid getting angry, but rather how to manage it more effectively. We concentrate on actions you can take to control your anger and to respond to angry people to keep a situation from getting out of hand.

EXPERIENCING ANGER

How do you know anger when you feel it? Which of these do you experience when angry?

- headache, neck ache, shoulders ache
- tightness in the face or chest, unable to breath, rapid breathing
- butterflies in the stomach, rapid heart rate
- hands clenched, gritting teeth, rigidity, twitching
- stare angrily
- sweating, feeling hot, feeling cold/chills
- numbness
- crying

What does the feeling of anger do to you? Does it feel threatening? How do you respond physically to an interpersonal conflict situation? Perhaps your heart rate increases, you may perspire, your breathing rate may increase, and your muscles may tense. People feel anger in different ways as these narratives suggest.

> I had invited my work group over to my house, but I really had hoped a particular person would not come. But he did and within a half-hour of his arrival I had a headache that wouldn't stop. I realized that my neck was really tense and my leg muscles hurt. For me it's the back of my neck that gets extremely hot. I feel hungry and nauseous at the same time. I always tense up my body, make a fist, and take quick breaths.

What causes you to feel angry? A friend calls you "stupid" and displays an obscene gesture, so you feel angry; a romantic partner is late for an important event, so you feel angry; a friend or romantic partner makes a rude comment about a member of your family, so you feel angry. What do all these instances have in common?

Although experts may agree that anger has some underlying emotional factor, they differ in their identification of the cause of anger. Stevens suggests that anger is caused by a perceived loss of control such as getting someplace on time or receiving unfair treatment from others.[12] Not getting what we want is frustrating. According to Hocker and Wilmot, the primary emotion is the fear that occurs when our personal security is threatened or our self-esteem is attacked.[13] Some psychologists claim that anger and hostility are cover-ups for insecurity, loss, and sadness.[14] If we are angry at or with someone, we feel more righteous about our emotions, and it is easier for us to lay the responsibility at the other person's feet, than if we say, "I fear . . ." or "I am disappointed." Anger protects us; admitting our fears or disappointments may make us feel vulnerable.

Regardless of the cause of anger, we usually know who or what made us angry. It is the person who offended you, the romantic partner who is late, or the person who offended a member of your family. In any of these situations, we may react with aggression, hostility, and revenge. These reactions may permanently harm an interpersonal relationship, such as a romantic partnership. For those who disrupt frequently or carry their resentments over a long period of time, they may suffer cardiovascular problems and heart attacks.

There are some interesting differences that occur when researchers examine gender and age differences in anger and aggression. First, men and women experience anger that results in aggression in different ways:

> . . . the anger experience is different for women because of the power differential between women and men. For men, anger is empowering because they have more power, and being angry ensures the continuation of that power especially if it is accompanied by threats and/or violence. Women's anger, on the other hand, emerges out of feelings of frustration and powerlessness.[15]

When expressed anger turns to aggression, men and women also differ in their explanation they give for becoming aggressive. For most women, acts of aggression produce anxiety and unpleasant emotions, and "women believe that such [aggressive] acts reflect a loss of self-control."[16] On the other hand, men see aggression as a challenging behavior; it is a way of exerting control over others in order to gain important social rewards such as respect.[17] Campbell and Muncer conclude that gender differences in aggression are largely attributable to "women's greater ability to suppress or divert the expression of aggressive behavior,"[18] most likely because they do find the expression of aggression to be unacceptable on a number of levels.

Some researchers have found that as people grow older they are less likely to exhibit trait anger. Anger for older adults (~50s and up) is less frequent and less intense. In addition, older adults are less likely to engage in external anger displays, such as slamming doors or being verbally aggressive.[19]

Do you lose control of your anger? Or does it work as an impetus for change and make you more productive? While your ability to control your anger is likely to improve with age, it is possible to make improvements now if you understand the nature of anger and how to manage it.

MANAGING ANGER: THREE DIFFERENT WAYS OF EXPRESSING OR NOT EXPRESSING ONE'S ANGER

People tend to manage their anger by not expressing it or by expressing it in one of the following three different ways: anger-ins, anger-outs, or anger controllers. Keep in mind that these three avenues have to do with the expression of anger and may not bear a direct relationship to trait anger. A common feature of **anger-ins** is that they do **not** express their anger to the person who has upset them. They are people who:

- have a hard time even admitting that they are angry
- know they are angry with someone but do not want to tell the other person
- tell others about their anger but not the one who upsets them
- may be passive-aggressive.

Joelle says:

> I have a difficult time admitting to others that I am angry. I always try to put others first so sometimes I think that if I avoid letting my angry emotions show that I am protecting those

> around me from a conflict. When I'm angry my mood becomes melancholy, and I avoid those who anger me. Because I don't like to argue with people and do not like to rock the boat or make a scene, I sometimes let problems bottle up inside.

As you may recall from our discussion of gunny-sacking in Chapter 3, one of the problems with bottling the anger inside is that one may eventually erupt. The above narrator goes on to say:

> Then after holding in my anger for weeks or months, I would just erupt over some little thing and let the other person know what I thought of him or her and how that person made me feel. Usually that person would be shocked at my reaction. I know this is not the best way to deal with my own anger.

Another type of anger-ins is the passive-aggressive individual, who wants to get even without directly confronting the persons they are mad at.

> One of my suitemates, Michelle, got really angry at us all. She reacted by taking everything she owned in the common area such as videos, pots and pans, some arts and crafts things, furniture, and so on. Everyone has contributed something for us all to use. What she did was, she basically waited until she was alone in the suite, she looked around and collected everything she saw she owned (including some decorations that she donated to the common room). When we all got home, we noticed that Michelle was gone and so was her stuff. She had gone to the city for the day and didn't get home until one in the morning. She wasn't communicative. Instead of talking to us about her problems and concerns, she locked herself in her room until we left and then got her revenge.

Anger-ins' response to anger is generally avoidant, passive, or accommodating. They may sulk around, expect you to read their minds, and become even angrier. Eventually, they might become bitter or resentful toward you and turn passive aggressive, thereby burning dinner or forgetting to give you an important telephone message. Anger-ins generally aren't people who respond with overt hostility.

Contrary to popular conceptions of the way men and women act, males score consistently as "anger-ins."[20] Many believe that suppressing anger can cause stress, which in turn may lead to both mental and physical illnesses. In addition, it may be harmful to those experiencing chronic pain, as suppressing anger heightens perception of the pain and magnifies its impact.[21]

We would include as anger-ins people who vent their anger to others, like a friend, parent, colleague, or bartender, rather than the offensive person. This is called the **ventilation approach.** In some cases, ventilation may be beneficial, such as times where it is not a good idea to confront the offensive personal directly—a boss who gets angry, an abusive partner, a defensive, insecure person who cannot take criticism. In addition, venting sometimes elicits helpful advice from the other to help one get a better understanding of the problematic situation, devise constructive ways to handle it, and receive encouragement to confront the problem person. In this case, venting may be useful.

> If I feel I have to talk to someone I will talk to my friend Jessica. She is a very good listener and does not criticize, but gives me advice on how to approach the person I am angry with.

She also will sympathize with me, but she will also tell me if I am the one that did the wrongdoing. By talking to my friend I am able to get up the courage and have a plan of action for confronting the person and the problem.

However, there are many other times when venting is problematic. When you talk about how angry you are at the other person, you may only focus on the wrong done to you and minimize the part you may have played in the problem. The biggest problem in cases like these is that simply expressing anger, without directing it toward the person responsible or toward problem solving, actually increases it, particularly when we rehearse repeatedly through different tellings. Ventilating through aggressive behavior is not an instinctive catharsis for anger. It lowers our inhibitions about acting aggressively and makes us more prone to aggressive behavior. Talking out anger does not rid us of it: Talking rehearses the anger and makes us feel it even more deeply. In addition, tantrums and rages do not forestall neurosis: They increase it.

We would suggest, then, that these anger-in behaviors are ways of how not to respond to conflict. They are the direct opposite of anger-outs.

Anger-outs are people who are quick to express their anger, vocally or physically to the person who upsets them. Adam says:

When growing up, I would lash out at my father and criticize him. I was always afraid that one of us would start punching the other. I often felt bad after the argument and sad that I had hurt my father. But I was upset and angry and just let him have it. We usually ended up with a strong sense of resentment for one another. It is hard to change after fighting this way all these years.

Anger-outs express their energy outward often aggressively rather than hold it in. These are the door slammers and screamers. If they continue in their anger, they may humiliate the object of their anger or slander or ostracize that person. Sometimes, they are moved to bully the other or damage that person's reputation. Anger-outs tend to engage in:

1. automatic reactions, are quick to criticize, blame, and accuse
2. minor aggressive acts such as bickering
3. verbal aggression
4. physical aggression, force

Does one sex tend to have a greater number of "anger-outs"? Actually, "men and women are equally likely to keep quiet when they feel angry, or talk it out, or scream it out, or even get violent.... It does not depend on gender and it does not depend on personality."[22] As was discussed, previously, though, men and women experience and interpret anger and aggression in different ways, even though there are few differences in the way they express it.

One should not overlook the social context and the consequences of anger. You don't want your expressed rage to result in another person physically attacking you. Likewise, these anger-out behaviors are ways of how not to respond to conflict:

- When the other person says what is bothering him or her, come back with a "Well, you . . ." response and attack, accuse, or deny.
- Listen closely so that you can pick apart what the other person is saying.

- Argue over the way something is stated rather than what is being said.
- Call the other person names.
- Remind the other person of every stupid behavior he or she has ever done with respect to the issue at hand.
- Disregard the other person's feelings. Tell the person, "You shouldn't feel that way."
- Tell people that you know their situation better than they do (i.e., "I know exactly how you feel").
- Make threats.
- Fail to cooperate if it isn't your idea (i.e., "If I can't have my way, I won't do anything at all").
- Indicate that nothing can change and you're both doomed to failure anyway.
- Ask the impossible of the other person.

While many people are either anger-outs or anger-ins (that is why we have textbooks on conflict management), people can choose to become anger controllers, who are those who practice S-TLC. Tracy says:

> My boyfriend and I used to scream and say nasty things to each other, but we both realized that was pointless and just made us more upset. Now we communicate more with each other. When something is bothering either of us, even if the other doesn't want to hear it, we bring it up and try to talk it out. If one of us gets really angry, it shows and the other knows that the problem is important and deserves out undivided attention. We sometimes take time outs to just cool down.

In another instance:

> When a problem arises, let's say noise during quiet hours, we resident halls staff must enforce the rules. Rather than running out of the office yelling and screaming that the residents are being too loud and they need to quiet down, I will sit in the office, take a deep breath, think about how I am going to approach them, take another deep breath and remain calm, but stern and tell them that it is quiet hours and they need to lower their voices. Most of the time if I say it seriously with no smile and raise my eye brows (some nonverbal communication!) they will get the idea that I am not messing around.

Anger controllers are assertive individuals who do not let their feelings control how they respond in conflict situations. This is not to say that anger controllers do not express their anger. They still "get it off their chests," but they do it in more constructive ways than do the anger-outs. They put into practice what is recommended in the previous chapters. Anger controllers tend to:

1. think positively about conflict and try techniques to better manage it (Chapter 1)
2. use assertive communication behavior; employ the steps of the interpersonal confrontation ritual (Chapter 2)
3. collaborate and work together toward mutually satisfactory solutions (Chapter 3)
4. use the S-TLC system (Chapter 4)
5. negotiate (Chapter 5)
6. manage the conflict climate (Chapter 6) and stress levels (Chapter 7)
7. manage their anger by expressing it effectively and heeding the dos and don'ts listed later in this chapter.

However, before conflicting parties can learn these behaviors, they need to gain control over their feelings. Controlling anger is a matter of (1) practicing new habits so that we don't lash out during our flight-or-fight anger episodes and (2) learning to express the underlying emotion when we experience the slow-building kind. How we learn to control anger depends on the more general habits we have about it. Some of these habits occur before we express our anger, and others later.

Before Expressing Anger

How we think about a situation determines whether we experience anger or not. When someone is late, when someone has disappointed you, when someone has said something hurtful, how do you frame the event? Your interpretation of the event is probably the best indicator of how angry you feel and how you choose to express it. Do you assume that the other person has hurt you on purpose? Do you look beneath the person's behavior? Do you look for causes that are beyond the other person's control? We are not suggesting that you consistently make excuses for another person. But the kinds of inferences, assumptions, or conclusions you make about another in a conflict situation affect the way you respond to the other. When you believe the other has acted in a way that constrains your behavior, that such action was intended to harm you, and that such action is uncalled for, you respond with anger. Further, we tend to draw different conclusions about others than we do about ourselves—we make excuses for our failures but attribute the failures of others to personal shortcomings. So, how are you making assumptions about the other? Is it possible that the other is innocent of intent to harm you, as this person suggests?

> It may make me sound like Pollyanna to say this, but I do find that if I say to myself, "Thanks for not running into me," rather than accusing another driver of "not having the brains God gave an amoeba," my blood pressure generally doesn't rise and my anger is momentary rather than lasting. In addition, if I try to assume that a person cutting me off simply didn't see me rather than assuming he or she is an idiot, I also contain the amount of anger I feel while driving. It takes practice, and quite honestly, it's harder on a day when I'm tired or upset about something.

In general, when you find yourself in a situation where you are becoming angry, there are three sets of specific techniques that have proven useful for many people: take time out, relaxation exercises, self-talk, and seeking alternative ways to release your anger.

Take Time Out

Exit temporarily if you can. Some people report that counting backward from 20 (or 50) helps them cool off.

> A student of mine, named Tara, visited my office to discuss her grade on the last test. She was unhappy about it and clearly would not accept any responsibility for her grade. I tried to explain how the grade was derived and how she could improve on future tests, but she became angry. Suddenly she stood up and bolted out of the room. I thought the situation unfortunate, especially for the student who probably would continue to be angry to her own detriment. But after twenty minutes, the student suddenly appeared at my office door and

in a nice manner, said, "I shouldn't have acted like that. I was upset and started to lose it. I thought it best to leave and cool off. Now I want to find out what I have to do, so that I can do better on the next test."

Relaxation Exercises

Controlling your physical responses is also helpful. Shut your eyes, tighten muscles (clench your fist, tense your body), and fantasize your anger—imagine it, feel it all over your body, then suddenly release the tension, and picture something serene and relaxing. Monitor your body as you release the different muscles. Breathe slowly and regularly. Concentrate on relaxing your muscles—tense them up and then release them again. Being aware of how you are physically responding to the situation can help.

Self-Talk

Engage in helpful self-talk before, during, and after a conflict. Before a potential conflict (if you can see one coming), tell yourself, "I'm not going to let so-and-so get to me." During the encounter, tell yourself that the other doesn't know what she or he is saying, is really upset at something, and doesn't mean to hurt you physically or psychologically. After successfully surviving a potentially threatening situation, compliment yourself for getting through it so calmly. Tell yourself that you have really improved in the way you handle situations like that.

Anger-ins need to take time to think about why they are angry and what they would like to change in the situation. Rather than thinking about ways to get back at the other person, anger-ins must focus on problem solving.

Seek an Alternative Way to Release Your Anger

Anger-outs need to find some way to dissipate the energy that can escalate a conflict. Physical exertion, like running or other exercise, helps to focus the anger-out. Would you believe that something like housework, particularly cleaning toilets, is helpful? (And quite symbolic!) So is gardening and pulling weeds. Art and music are also ways anger-outs can learn to express anger in healthy ways. Once the energy of the anger has worn off, the anger-out needs to reflect on the situation and discover the source of the anger.

Overall, dealing with anger requires first that we build habits of positive rather than negative and destructive responses to anger-provoking situations. It is also necessary that we determine the underlying source of the anger and that we decide what, if anything, we need to do to alleviate that source of anger. The realization that anger is a cover-up for other emotions we are reluctant to admit suggests that another trick to controlling emotion is to determine what unmet need or desire is being frustrated that creates the fear or hurt.

Uncover the Emotion that Is Disguised as Anger

Anger is a **secondary emotion,** meaning that its origin is in other emotions such as fear, disappointment, hurt, and frustration. Communication scholars suggest that the primary emotion is the fear that occurs when our personal security is threatened or our self-esteem is attacked. Some psychologists claim that anger and hostility are cover-ups for insecurity, loss, and sadness.[23] As Rosenberg elaborates:

> At the core of all anger is a need that is not being fulfilled. Thus anger can be valuable if we use it as an alarm clock to wake us up—to realize that we have a need that isn't being met and that we are thinking in a way that makes it unlikely to be met. To fully express our anger requires full consciousness of our need. In addition, energy is required to get the need met. Anger, however, co-opts our energy by directing it toward punishing people rather than meeting our needs.[24]

The realization that anger is a cover-up for other emotions we are reluctant to admit suggests that another trick to controlling emotion is to determine what unmet need or desire is being frustrated that creates the fear or hurt. For example, a teacher may feel frustrated because not all members of her class may pass an exam. Her fear is that she is not teaching as well as she could or should. So if she gets a lot of questions during a review session prior to the exam, the teacher may suddenly turn angry and accuse her students of not studying enough. Her apparent anger is really a response to her fear that the students may fail and make her look bad as a teacher. Once the teacher realizes that, she is much less likely to act angry toward her students.

Expressing Anger Effectively: Dos and Don'ts of Anger Management

We know that anger can escalate a conflict and help cause it to get out of hand. If one chooses to do so, how is it best to express one's anger to the offender? Unfortunately, many of us have learned destructive ways to deal with anger from our families and peers.[25]

Of course, we wish to change the way many people manage their anger. We believe that the best verbal response to anger is contained in the skills we discussed in the chapters leading up to this one. However, there are additional specific actions than escalation or de-escalation, so we have compiled a list of dos and don'ts. Let's begin with the actions we must avoid doing: "The Don'ts."

There are many communication behaviors that increase anger both in the person expressing the anger and the person hearing it. Most of these should be obvious to you. Speaking more loudly or yelling increases anger, as does standing over another person or invading his or her personal space. Making threatening gestures or going so far as to poke or push or shove another person will certainly aggravate the situation. Swearing and cursing are unlikely to keep the situation under control. Engaging in threats or using a "thromise" (a promise of reward if the other cooperates and a threat of punishment if they do not) escalates conflict and heightens anger. Obviously, if you know of issues sensitive to the other, you will increase his or her anger by mentioning them, particularly if those issues are not really relevant to the conflict at hand. Mocking the other, working to increase a competitive atmosphere, or encouraging rivalry engenders anger. Not listening to the person at whom you are angry and allowing yourself to be egged on by bystanders is also dangerous. Finally, expressing anger under the influence of alcohol or drugs is a bad idea. In vino veritas aside, we are likely to regret what is said under such circumstances. When people introduce drugs or alcohol into the picture all bets are off. Those times are not good ones to get into an argument or disagreement. Alcohol has a way of bringing out the worst in some people. Someone you know is normally calm and can effectively manage stress and anger, but then he becomes a different person when drunk. You cannot expect a reasonable discussion if engaging in a conflict with someone who is drunk or on drugs. Leave them be until they sober up.

In addition to calming our emotional reaction in a conflict situation, we can choose how we respond to anger provocations. Anger is best expressed and most effective when several conditions are met.[26]

First, it is best to express anger not when one is overcome with a sense of rage but sometime later after cooling down. Recall in Chapter 4, we recommend that when you realize that a conflict exists, begin by saying, Stop! Don't become so upset that you start to lose control of yourself. Instead, try to calm down and cool off. To gain greater control over your mental faculties, take a time out. We suggest that you exit temporarily to calm yourself, go for a glass of water, count down from 100, or stop discussing the problematic topic for a while to allow time for the air to clear.

Second, you must direct your anger at the target of the anger. Suppose, for example, you are really angry with your boss because she or he changed your hours without consulting you, and the new schedule now conflicts with your classes. You probably do not believe that you can yell at your boss, so instead you go home and slam objects around the house and yell at your roommate. The trouble is that such actions are unlikely to reduce your anger. Instead, you are probably angrier when you are through going on a rampage, because you find additional shortcomings with your boss as you remember all the other inequities you have experienced in your job.

Third, when you express your anger, there has to be a feeling that you have restored your sense of justice and of control over the situation while not inflicting harm on the other person. Going into your boss's office and screaming might make you feel good, but he or she is unlikely to then give you what you like—changing your hours. And if your boss changed your hours simply because of forgetfulness rather than because of a malicious intent, screaming at the boss is too severe a reaction for the situation.

Fourth, and this not necessarily up to you, the expression of anger is likely to be effective if it gives you a sense of control over the situation and if that expression changes the behavior of the other person (your boss says, "I'm sorry, I forgot that you had class on Monday and Wednesday afternoons") or if it provides new insights (you realize you cannot work for this person and must find a new place of employment).

Finally, for the effective expression of your anger, the target must not retaliate in anger. This last condition is unfortunately the hardest to create. We have yet to meet more than a handful of people who can let others express anger at them without responding in kind. To help meet this last condition, we must express anger responsibly and with tact. Tavris noted, "The result of the ability to control anger is that people feel less angry, not more."[27] As Brian discovered at work:

> I am reminded of my boss at work, who had to make some tough decisions, sometimes not to everyone's liking. I can still see one of my colleagues, who stopped our boss on his way out his office. He stood right in front of him and started yelling at him. Interestingly, our boss did not respond in kind. He lowered his voice to almost a whisper, and looked like he was very concerned about the issue. My colleague stopped raving when he realized that we

were all staring at him and he was the only one making a scene, which embarrassed him. When he stopped yelling, the dean invited him to go back to his office, where they continued the "discussion" without all of us watching.

There is more that you can do to be sure that your expression of anger is appropriate. Be aware of your behavior. Try to see multiple nonjudgmental interpretations of what is being said now rather than thoughts having to do more with past moments.[28] In addition, try to anticipate the effect that your words and actions have on others. It does minimize the amount of conflict you need to experience. Try to keep the other focused on the here and now. Past history should stay out of the conversation as much as possible.

You should be open to what others have to say. Let them say what they are feeling and accept it as a legitimate feeling, if not a legitimate criticism. On the other hand, it is important to negotiate acceptable boundaries with others. Controlling your anger does not mean giving people permission to hurt you or use you.

A good lesson to remember is found in Aesop's fable of a man, his son, and the donkey. A man and his son are walking from the countryside into town alongside the donkey. In response to one person's criticism that they are not using the donkey efficiently, the man puts his son on the donkey. Another person criticizes, so he rides the donkey while the boy walks. Another person criticizes, so both ride the donkey. Another person criticizes, and they decide to carry the donkey, strung upside down on a stick over their shoulders. On the town bridge over a river, they accidentally drop the donkey into the river, and, being bound, the donkey drowns. Do not react to or act on everything a person says. *Don't drown the donkey!*

Responding to Another's Anger

One of the more difficult challenges we must face in a conflict is the anger and possible rage an anger-out person is feeling. Often, our fear about the way another may react affects our ability to solve a problem, as this narrative suggests.

> Over the years, my husband has become calmer, but he still can lose his temper over unimportant issues pretty easily. When he loses his temper, he scares me. He's a big guy, and seeing all that muscle tense up makes me want to hide. I kept trying to hide a credit card bill from him, because I was afraid to tell him what a mess I had made. I was afraid he might even hit me when he found out. He finally picked up the mail before I did, and I prepared myself for the worst.

When you are dealing with someone who is extremely angry, it is important to do what you can to stay calm and not feed his or her anger. Often, people are loudly angry because they fear no one listens to them unless they yell and scream. Listening and reflecting are important skills in responding to another person's anger.

Equally important is acknowledging the importance of the source of anger. If you say something to the effect of "I can't believe you are reacting this way" or "I think you are being childish," you fuel that person's anger rather than subdue it. When a person is on the verge of rage, it is not the time to express your anger about the situation. You need to focus on calming that person down before raising any issue of your own.

If your attempts to acknowledge the other person's source of anger and the legitimacy of her or his feelings fail, and the person continues to rage and fume, it is often a good idea to exit the situation. Saying something such as "I can see you're really angry, and I think I'd like to give you some time to cool off before we talk about it" acknowledges that you sympathize with the other and have a commitment to work out whatever problem is there, but postpones the conflict until both people are calm and ready to talk about it.

We not only need to know how to respond to anger-outs, but we also need to adapt to anger-ins.

As one fellow says:

> Being an anger-in type of person I chose to hold my anger inside and vent to my wife or my friends. While unknowingly applying the ventilation approach while "venting" this would in fact re-enforce my thoughts that were at the root of my feelings of anger and frustration and give cause for retaliation.

Anger-ins probably have the hardest time figuring out what the underlying issue is. Give anger-ins a safe space where they can express their thoughts. They need to figure out why they're really angry.

MANAGE IT

Anger is a strong feeling of displeasure, a synonym for antagonism and rage. Anger is different from feeling hurt or irritated. We experience these other emotions when someone or something frustrates our desires. While we recognize that sometimes anger can be used constructively by motivating us to get off our seats and stand up for our interests, needs, and wants or what we think is right, destructive anger carries with it the desire to get even or seek revenge.

Research indicates that people may actually have traitlike anger. In addition, there are gender and age differences in anger and aggression.

People tend to manage their anger in one of the following three different ways: anger-ins, anger-outs, or anger controllers. A common feature of anger-ins is that they do not express their anger to the person who has upset them. We would include as anger-ins, people who vent their anger to others, like a friend, parent, colleague, or bartender, rather than the offensive person. Another type of anger-ins are the passive-aggressive individuals, who want to get even without directly confronting the persons they are mad at.

Anger-outs are the direct opposite of anger-ins. They are people who are quick to express their anger, vocally or physically to the person who upsets them.

Anger controllers are those who practice S-TLC, the confrontation ritual (including assertiveness and I-statements), and cooperative negotiation techniques. The chapter also includes some useful dos and don'ts when responding to angry people.

While there may be people who are clearly one type of anger manager than others, many people are more likely a combination of all three. In a situation where you fear the reaction of another person or know you have no effect on that person, you may chose to be an anger-in. In another case, you find that the only way to motivate a person is show some emotion and reveal some anger. Lastly, you may know individuals who listen and cooperate, and who can control their anger by following the S-TLC model, and express it effectively through the use of I-statements. In all cases, the skillful manager is sensitive to the way she or he is feeling, thinking, and behaving in a conflict situation. Knowing which type one currently manifests and how to correctly and effectively manage one's anger in a conflict situation results in more mutually satisfying interpersonal relationships.

Experts differ in the cause of anger as some underlying emotional factor. Some say it is caused by a perceived loss of control. Others say that the primary emotion is the fear that occurs when our personal security is threatened. Still others say it is a cover-up for loss of self-esteem and sadness. In all these cases, anger protects us; admitting our fear or disappointment may make us feel vulnerable. We must find the underlying fear and deal with it.

Think About It

1. Are you a person who tends to blow up, do you express your anger calmly, or do you simply not express it at all? What are the outcomes of expressing anger in this way?
2. Under what conditions have you found yourself expressing your anger appropriately? How was the situation different from a time that you felt your anger was out of control? What do you think you could do to duplicate the situation under which you expressed your anger constructively?
3. Have there been times when you have realized that the anger you are experiencing is a mask for another emotion such as frustration or disappointment? What characterized that situation?
4. What are some ways you use to work off your anger before talking to another person?
5. How do you feel when another person is angry at you? What do you do to keep yourself calm in those situations?

Apply It

1. What makes you really angry? For one day, keep a journal of the way you are reacting to problems around you. You can do this by keeping track of your data in three columns. In the first, list the situation to which you reacted angrily. In the second column, rate how angry you were, with 1 = mildly irritated, 5 = extremely angry. In the third column, write down why you thought you were angry. How might you have reacted differently?
2. Go to a public space, such as a shopping mall. As unobtrusively as possible, observe when people are angry. What do they seem to be angry about? How long does their expression of anger last? How do they seem to resolve their anger? Are there differences in anger expression because of the gender, age, and/or ethnicity of the people you observe?

Work With It

Read each of the case studies and answer the following questions:

1. Which cases illustrate an anger-in, an anger-in who is venting anger, an anger-out, or anger controller?
2. In each case, was the anger managed effectively? If not, identify the "primary emotion" that is being interpreted as anger and explain how anger affected the communication behavior.
3. List suggestions for better managing the anger in those situations that were not handled well.

Cases

A. When in conflict, one of my housemates always avoids everyone when she is upset, so we never know if she is upset at someone, or simply in a bad mood. It is very hard to read her and we never know how to react, but yet she always expects us to understand how she is feeling. Those of us who live in the house are incessantly conflicted on what to do because we do not know how to respond to her avoidance.

B. My partner and I don't let our feelings get overwhelming. We express how we feel. We do not keep things bundled up inside and we definitely do not like to explode and let a conflict get out of hand. We take a time out, do relaxation exercises, or engage in self-talk. To take a time out, we can either exit temporarily or count to 100 backwards. My partner always stops and goes for a walk when he gets angry to blow some steam off. Relaxation exercises help to control our physical responses. I like to exercise or go to the gym when I feel overwhelmed or very angry. Sometimes I do yoga-like exercises and breathing techniques and it really seems to help. Then, after our time out and we have calmed down, we can talk and listen to each other without losing our cool.

C. My roommate is really messy. She constantly throws her things around the room, leaving her items in the middle of the room. Then, she had the nerve to tell me that I do not clean the apartment enough. Why should I have to clean up her things that she leaves around? In fact, I do not even know where she would want me to put her things away. Instead of me confronting her about my anger, I went behind her back and talked to my best friend about the situation. I was just complaining about my roommate, and one complaint would lead to another, and eventually I was making myself more mad than I was in the beginning of the situation.

This weekend, my boyfriend and I got into an argument. I wanted to resolve the conflict right away but my boyfriend got so angry that he walked to his car and sat in it for 10 minutes while I waited outside his house. I had handed the matter badly, by shouting when I didn't get my way, and being impatient and demanding an immediate resolution to the problem, and in this case that wasn't happening as speedily as I wanted it to. I yelled at him and interrupted him a lot, told him he was ruining my night, and stated everything I wanted him to do not asking him what he wanted to do to resolve this conflict.

NOTES

1. L. H. Phillips, J. D. Henry, J. A. Hosie, and A. B. Milne, "Age, Anger Regulation and Well Being," *Aging and Mental Health* 10 (2006), 250, 250–256.

2. Marie-France Lafontaine and Yvan Lussier, "Does Anger towards the Partner Mediate and Moderate the Link between Romantic Attachment

and Intimate Violence?" *Journal of Family Violence* 20(6) (2005), 349–361; see also Kenneth D. Locke, "Interpersonal Problems and Interpersonal Expectations in Everyday Life," *Journal of Social and Clinical Psychology* 24(7) (2005), 915–931.
3. Anne Campbell and Steven Muncer, "Intent to Harm or Injure? Gender and the Expression of Anger," *Aggressive Behavior* 34 (2008), 292, 282–293.
4. Virginia Eatough, Jonathan A. Smith, and Rachel Shaw, "Women, Anger and Aggression: An Interpretive Phenomenological Analysis," *Journal of Interpersonal Violence* 23 (2008), 1771, 1767–1799.
5. Hermina Van Coillie and Iven Van Mechelen, "Expected Consequences of Anger-Related Behaviours," *European Journal of Personality* 20 (2006), 138, 137–154.
6. Agneta H. Fischer and Ira J. Roseman, "Beat Them or Ban Them: The Characteristics and Social Functions of Anger and Contempt," *Journal of Personality and Social Psychology* 93 (2007), 104, 103–115.
7. Ibid.
8. Maya Tamir, Christopher Mitchell, and James J. Gross, "Hedonic and Instrumental Motives in Anger Regulation," *Psychological Science* 19 (2008), 328, 324–328.
9. Dominic J. Parrott, Amos Zeichner, and Mark Evces, "Effect of Trait Anger on Cognitive Processing of Emotional Stimuli," *The Journal of General Psychology* 132 (2005), 69, 67–80.
10. Ibid., p. 75.
11. Benjamin M. Wilkowski and Michael D. Robinson, "Guarding against Hostile Thoughts: Trait Anger and the Recruitment of Cognitive Control," *Emotion* 8 (2008), 582, 578–583.
12. Tom G. Stevens, *You Can Choose to be Happy* (Seal Beach, CA: Wheeler-Sutton, 1998).
13. William Wilmot and Joyce Hocker, *Interpersonal Conflict,* 6th Ed. (New York: McGraw Hill, 2001).
14. John Gottman, Robert Levenson, and Erica Woodin, "Facial Expressions during Marital Conflict," *Journal of Family Communication* 1 (2001), 37–57.
15. Eatough, Smith, and Shaw, "Women, Anger and Aggression," p. 1771.
16. Campbell and Muncer, "Intent to Harm or Injure? Gender and the Expression of Anger," p. 285
17. Eatough, Smith, and Shaw, "Women, Anger and Aggression," p. 1770.
18. Campbell and Muncer, "Intent to Harm or Injure? Gender and the Expression of Anger," p. 282.
19. Phillips, Henry, Hosie, and Milne, "Age, Anger Regulation and Well Being," p. 254.
20. Carol Tavris, *Anger: The Misunderstood Emotion* (New York: Touchstone, through Simon and Schuster, 1989), p. 203.
21. Phillip J. Quartana and John W. Burns, "Painful Consequences of Anger Suppression," *Emotion* 7 (2007), 400–414.
22. Tavris, *Anger.*
23. Gottman, Levenson, and Woodin, "Facial Expressions during Marital Conflict."
24. Marshall B. Rosenberg, *Nonviolent Communication: A Language of Life* (Encinitas, CA: Puddle Dancer Press, 2005), p. 144.
25. Denise D. Quigley, Lisa H. Jaycox, Daniel F. McCaffrey, and Grant N. Marshall, "Peer and Family Influences on Adolescent Anger Expression and Acceptance of Cross-Gender Aggression," *Violence and Victims* 21(5) (2006), 597–610.
26. Ibid., pp. 152–154.
27. Ibid., p. 189.
28. Karen Wachs and James V. Cordova, "Mindful Relating: Exploring Mindfulness and Emotion Repertoires in Intimate Relationships," *Journal of Marital and Family Therapy* 33(4) (2007), 464–481.

CHAPTER 9

Managing Face

OBJECTIVES

At the end of this chapter, you should be able to:

- Explain the role of face and face saving in conflict.
- Explain the difference between positive face and autonomous face.
- Identify at least three preventative strategies you can use to avoid threatening the other person's face in a conflict situation.
- List three general ways and three specific techniques you can use to support another's face during interaction in a conflict situation.
- Compare and contrast three conflict situations using the repair sequence: one where you offer an account, one where you make a concession, and another where you offer an apology.

KEY TERMS

account	disclaimers	positive face
acknowledgment	excuses	positive face management
apologies	face	preventive facework
autonomous face	facework	remedy
autonomous face management	impression (face) management	repair sequence
concessions	justifications	reproach
corrective facework	offending situations	supportive facework

In Chapter 5, we introduced you to conflicts based on behavioral issues and highlighted that a special case of behavioral issues, often viewed as embarrassing moments, occur when we lose face in a social situation. Take the following narrative as an example:

> My boyfriend, Rich, and I got in a little disagreement the other day. He was talking about his friend Mike, and I said something in a way I probably should not have. While he was telling me a story about his buddy, I said, "yea, Rob is really funny. He's a

great guy." Well Rich took that the wrong way. He said, "I should hang out more with Mike because he is funnier than I am and such a great guy." I realized that inadvertently I had put Rich down. He felt like I did not like him, or that I thought he was not funny.

A fundamental assumption that underlies our approach to interpersonal conflict is that people are motivated to create and maintain impressions of themselves. By *impression,* we mean what sociologist Goffman termed **face,** or people's image of themselves.[1] The concept of face is basic to who we think we are. One of the authors, Lee, likes to have his students do the "Twenty Statements Test." He asks his student to take out a sheet of paper and write down as many answers as they can to the question, "Who am I?" He tells them to shoot for 20 answers. When finished, Lee points out to the students that the answers are a way to look at the faces they present to others.

Another assumption we make is that people generally work to support one another's face when socializing and communicating. We call this behavior **face management**. Face is what one does; face management is the face that results during interaction with others, who may support, alter, or challenge one's process. According to Goffman, we all have images of ourselves, and we project that image (our face) in interactions with others.[2] As we interact, we also look for confirmation of the face we present.

In his classes, Lee points out to his students that their answers to the "Twenty Statements Test" represent specific and important aspects of themselves that need to be supported in interaction with their friends, family, and romantic partners. If one writes: I am a student, communication major, daughter, and so on, then they want others to see them as such, and they do not appreciate negative remarks about their student status, major, family, and so forth. They might include in their list qualitative items such as I am intelligent, hardworking, reliable, on time to class, and so on. Again they want others to see and recognize them for these attributes and will feel threatened if others call them stupid, lazy, undependable, and ignorant of the time of day. The "Twenty Statements Test" is a good way to identify the characteristics each of us present to others and want to be supported in interaction. This support serves the basis for peace and harmony in our friendships, family, and romances.

The projection of face is cooperative—as long as the image we project seems consistent and believable, others usually accept it and respond to it as presented. For example, we attempt to appear as competent teachers (or present our "face") and trust our students to support us in our roles (i.e., manage our "face" in the classroom, hallway, or faculty office). Similarly, the students act like prepared and motivated individuals and expect the faculty to respect their image of themselves. Of course, the situation is made more complicated by the many factors that affect our perceptions, understandings, and actions, but this example can give you an idea of how we present and manage face in everyday interaction.

In this chapter, we want to address an important skill in developing competent conflict management behavior and that is the ability to maintain one's own impression and that of others to avoid escalating the conflict and to restore a relationship if face is lost. We help you identify people's face, identify techniques to prevent the loss of face, describe general and specific ways to support the other's face in conflict situations, and describe steps you can take to correct a situation after it has occurred.

UNDERSTANDING THE DEMANDS OF FACE

The mutual cooperation involved in projecting face is a principle of interaction that is taken for granted. Being able to create and sustain an identity for oneself, as well as helping the other person to create and maintain an identity for himself or herself, is a fundamental component of communication competence, according to Cupach and Metts. In the past, intercultural communication researchers claimed that everyone has face concerns during conflict, but members of different cultures present, protect, lose, and save face in different ways because of different levels of face concerns. However, recent research suggests that these cultural differences are not as great as we think.[3]

Not only are people striving to present a particular face and hoping that it can be maintained in interaction with others, this motivation may create a conflict situation. A person may think he is smart, funny, and lovable, but when challenged she or he is likely to be offended. In fact, the remark may so anger him that he walks out of the room and has nothing more to do with the other person. Face is something that lurks behind the scene and may or may not make a difference in a conflict situation. However, when aroused, it may make all the difference in the world. The lengths to which people may go to maintain and repair face are wonderfully summarized in a recent book called *Mistakes were Made (but not by me)*, which examines years of research examining how we justify our actions when faced with the possibility that they are wrong. The authors note:

> If letting go of self-justification and admitting mistakes is so beneficial to the mind and relationships, why aren't more of us doing it? If we are so grateful to others when they do it, why don't we do it more often? First, we don't do it because, as we have seen, most of the time we aren't even aware that we need to . . . . Second, . . . even when people are aware of having made a mistake, they are often reluctant to admit it, even to themselves, because they take it as evidence that they are a blithering idiot.[4]

In addition to creating conflict situations, threats to face can also make them worse. Negative comments about the state of a romantic couple's relationship have been found to be more face threatening than those concerning either partner's personality, physical appearance, or specific behaviors.[5] However, something as simple as answering cell phone calls and the length of the phone conversation when on a date with a romantic partner can produce negative face threats and negative feelings.[6] In fact romantic partners confront potential face threats when initiating, intensifying, or ending romantic relationships.[7] Any interaction is potentially face threatening; but in conflicts, where people face incompatible goals or activities and share the feeling that the other is somehow interfering with their own pursuit of rewards and goals, face threats are present.

In Chapter 2, we introduced you to the idea of the competitive conflict escalation cycle. One source of these dysfunctional cycles is the introduction of face issues, which add an extra issue to the initial conflict problems. Because face is so important to people, they try to repair their damaged image before the initial conflict issue is settled. Threatening the other person's face is a good way to guarantee that the conflict does not enter the resolution phase. The introduction of face issues into a conflict can escalate the severity of the conflict, making it difficult for people to resolve the original issue.

One of the reasons that face issues may so complicate conflict situations is that when people feel as though they have lost face they often experience shame or guilt. While both emotions are reactions to untoward behavior, shame is more self-focused (e.g., I am such an idiot) and guilt is more behavior focused (e.g., What a dumb thing I did). Of the two, guilt is the more productive emotion. While guilt "causes us to stop and re-think—and it offers a way out, pressing us to confess, apologize, and make amends,"[8] shame does not lead to those outcomes. When we feel shame, we are more likely to withdraw and avoid others, denying our responsibility for the situation and shifting the blame to others. Guilt tends to lead to a felt need for restoration; shame leads to defensiveness. Thus, our interaction with others must try to especially avoid shaming others.

When people lose face they may also seek retaliation. Aggressive responses to face-losing situations are more likely when people believe that the other person in the situation has caused it. Such situations are as mild as someone criticizing you in public (e.g., a teacher criticizing a student in class) or teasing you. It is sometimes more serious, such as one friend picking a fight with another in public.

TWO TYPES OF FACE: POSITIVE AND AUTONOMOUS FACE

In a seminal work, Brown and Levinson concluded that people experience two kinds of face needs.[9] **Positive face** means that people want others important to them to like and respect them. A person's **positive face is managed** when it is supported by others who appear to value what the person values, express admiration for the person, or show acceptance of the person as a competent individual. **Autonomous face** is that part of us that longs for some independence, privacy, recognition for our contributions, or time alone.[10]

> Autonomous [or negative] face is the desire to maintain one's own autonomy. Individuals in any culture want to be shown proper deference and respect and not have their privacy and space invaded, their resources spent, and their actions restricted without just cause.[11]

While each of us enjoys the company of our loved ones, family, and friends, there are times when we want to engage in a creative activity (writing, painting), spend some time in reflection (walking or sitting and thinking), prepare for a big event (get our act together), contribute to some large project, or simply rest after a lot of socializing. We **manage autonomous face** when people recognize, encourage, support, and approve the activity. We also want to put some of ourselves into the products and services we provide for others, which is another way to look at our autonomous face. When others recognized the personal contribution we made as well as the time and effort we put into the activity, our autonomous face is again supported. Problems arise when others do not accept our autonomous face or reward us for our efforts.

> My roommate, Sarah, only gets paid if the woman she works for, Anna Marie, actually uses her designs. Keep in mind that Anna Marie constantly calls Sarah and takes up a lot of her time. The designs take many hours and even days to do, but there is no guarantee that Sarah will benefit from all her time and effort in the end. She has a lot of school work and not

enough time to stay on top of it all. Anna Marie should pay Sarah for her time and effort, not just if she occasionally uses one of her designs.

The desires for positive and autonomous face, under the best of circumstances, can create a dilemma. One may communicate support of another's positive face by expressing admiration for that person, spending time with that person, and so on, but by doing so, one can encroach on the person's autonomy.

> On a recent television show, an elderly but wealthy woman took an interest in a family struggling to make ends meet. At first the parents were delighted to be invited to the wealthy woman's home and enjoy her many luxuries. The problem occurred when the woman started spending a great deal of time with the children, took over the parents' roles, buying the children whatever they wanted, giving them a room of their own in her house, letting them do whatever they wanted such as painting on the walls of the children's room. She even crawled into bed with the parents one night when they were watching TV in her guest bedroom. The parents enjoyed her hospitality up to a point but that ended when they felt that their privacy and independence was threatened along with the challenge to their parenthood.

Supporting a person's positive and autonomous face requires a balance under the best of circumstances. Consider how these competing needs are threatened in a conflict situation.

> I would say that the biggest conflict in my life arises when my girlfriend gets emotional. Of all the girlfriends I have had, I have never dated one as emotional as my current girlfriend. The conflict usually comes when I have had a hard day and still have work to do in the evening. My girlfriend will come over and yell at me for ignoring her and not really loving her, because I have been gone all day. When I try to tell her I have been busy and still have much to do, the conflict gets worse. She starts to cry and becomes crazy. At this point, I cannot deal with the situation and want to hide under a rock. The conflict usually has to defuse itself by me leaving and not speaking to her until later that evening or the next day. If she follows me out the door, I have to stop and order her back inside and not answer her calls for a few days. When she becomes calm, the situation gets resolved, but sometimes it can last for a week or so.

While the man's positive face is supported by his partner's desire to spend time with him, his autonomous face is threatened by her need for too much of his limited time. According to O'Sullivan, it is unlikely that people would perceive a particular encounter as strictly positive or negative.[12] So, in the above example, the man's and his partner's conflicts would arise out of the need to support both positive and autonomous face.

Sometimes our individual needs smoother another's need for autonomy. Take this case with Aron for example.

> Last semester, my friend, Aron, started seriously dating Vicky. In the beginning of their relationship, he hung out with me and our mutual friends. But, as things progressed, he seemed to cling to his girlfriend, and completely ignore the rest of us. We know he enjoys our company and likes spending time with us, but as his relationship with Vicky progressed,

he simply disappeared. She demanded his total time and attention and completely shut out his other friends and interests. He needs to gain a balance between her demands and his own personal needs (i.e., independence from the girlfriend).

Sometimes face threats occur unexpectedly. A study of 911 calls, for example, claims that the required questions for information asked by the operators "can threaten callers' desire to be treated as trustworthy, intelligent, and of good character, as well as threaten their need to feel unimpeded in their requests for timely police service."[13] And while most of us would agree that being told we are cared for is good, a directly affectionate message, while supporting our positive face, might threaten our autonomous face.[14]

To help solve the dilemma posed by competing desires for positive and autonomous face, we offer a before, during, and after set of recommendations. Before committing loss of face, people may take steps to prevent it. During interaction, they can go a step farther by supporting the other's face in general or specific ways. Finally, if a threat to face is made, they can use corrective facework: using constructive responses to loss of face in a conflict situation.

FACEWORK

Facework is a process by which people establish and maintain their impressions of themselves to others, as well as supporting or denying the impressions that others are making. Domenici and Littlejohn claim, "Face is an accomplishment of interaction as communicators work together over time to negotiate face issues."[15] There are four factors in facework: the act (what is or should be said or done?), the conversation (what do I think is happening right now?), the episode (how does this fit into a larger pattern of interaction with the other?) and the lifescript (who am I?). All four factors are interconnected—as changes occur in one they will occur in others. That is, as you choose different conversational strategies, as you interpret different episodes, it will affect your lifescript, and vice versa. Facework is generally one of three kinds: preventive, supportive, or corrective.

Preventive Facework

By avoiding or minimizing threats to face, **preventive facework** forestalls becoming embroiled in face-saving issues during conflict situations.

- One way to use preventive facework is to try to see the situation from the other's perspective—how the issue affects the other and the other's self-image.
- Another way is to accept what the other person says at face value (no pun intended). Unless there is a good reason to the contrary, it is best to accept what the other person says as an accurate reflection of his or her feelings.
- A third way to avoid face-saving issues is to accept the other person's right to change his or her mind. No one can predict the future with any degree of accuracy. The fact is that goals change, people change, and life changes. To treat a change in goals as a sign of the

other person's insincerity or instability threatens the other person and sets up future conflicts concerning that very issue.
- Fourth, people can also avoid threats to face by avoiding face-threatening topics (which is almost impossible in a conflict situation) or by employing communication practices that minimize threats to face.

The last approach of avoiding threats to face consists of communication practices such as politeness and **disclaimers** (additions to the message that soften the forcefulness of the message) that help to minimize threats to face before they happen.[16]

This narrative illustrates how to maximize a face threat.

> Just recently, my mother was expressing her dissatisfaction to me about the host in the dining room at the retirement home where she lives. She had come a little late to lunch and found that "her" table had dishes all over it. Instead of moving to a different table or asking someone to take away the dishes, she turned to the host and said, "When are you going to start doing your job?" As she told me the story, she was amazed that the host had subsequently been rude to her. I tried explaining conflict message skills to her, but someone with as much practice at engaging in nasty behavior as my mother is not likely to change.

In the above conflict situation, for example, the person making the complaint could have used either of the following disclaimers to soften the effect of the complaint:

- *Hedging:* indicating uncertainty and receptivity to suggestions. "Is this my table? It doesn't seem to have gotten cleared yet."
- *Cognitive disclaimer:* asserting that the behavior is reasonable and under control, despite appearances. "I don't want to sound demanding, but I'd really like to sit down now and the dirty table is bothering me."

Other disclaimers available in a conflict situation include the following:

- *Credentialing:* indicating you have good reasons and appropriate qualifications for the statement you intend to make. "I am your friend and I care about you, so I want to say . . ."
- *Sin license:* indicating that this is an appropriate occasion to violate the rule and one should not take the violation as a character defect. "Well, this is a special occasion and . . ."
- *Appeal for suspended judgment:* asking the other to withhold judgment for a possibly offensive action until it is explained. "Hear me out before you get upset . . ."[17]

The above prevention techniques are illustrated in this person's situation:

> A conflict situation in which face-saving was an issue is when I had to address my fellow sorority members about a bad situation. We had a fundraising event on an upcoming Friday night, and with 30 women in the sorority, only five were planning to help out. The problem is, we could not do the fundraiser with only five people there to help out. It looked like we might have to cancel the event. I was very upset by this and decided I needed to say something about it at our next meeting. I was worried about my "face" because the girls are important and I would like them to like and respect me, and the problem was pretty touchy. Some preventative strategies I employed to avoid threatening their faces were: seeing the

situation from their point of view, avoiding face-threatening topics, being polite, and using disclaimers. In this specific conflict situation, I decided to assume that those who were unable to make the event had legitimate reasons they could not attend, and I did not question anyone's absence, to avoid threatening others' faces. I also understood that the fundraiser was not their priority. I used the cognitive disclaimer when I started off by saying "I don't want to sound like your mother, but we really need people to be there on Friday, and because not everyone could come together, we stand to lose out on raising any money." I used another disclaimer when I said "I don't want anyone to take personal offense by this, but. . . " By using the disclaimers I was able to minimize threats to face.

Supportive Facework

When in a conflict with someone, use **supportive facework** to help reinforce the way the other is presenting himself or herself. In a general way, people want others to like them, respect them, encourage them, consult them, include them, appreciate them, reward them, make references to them, ask them for their opinion or input, smile at them, greet them warmly, help when needed, and make them feel safe. Ask yourself if you do the following when in a conflict:

1. Do I try to make the other feel important?
2. Do I try to make the other look good to other people?
3. Do I try to make the other think that they are winning?
4. Do I try to make the other feel secure?
5. Do I try to make the other believe that I am honest and trustworthy?

We can support others in a general way by what we do and what we say. If we don't include, consult, ask, reward, or help others, they may feel put down by our actions. It is also possible to put down people verbally by insulting them or showing disrespect.

We can also support others in a more specific way. To do this, you need to determine what traits or characteristics the other perceives in himself or herself and point out the ones you have in common or are capable of supporting.

You like to fish? Well, so do I.
I like people with red hair.
You're a jogger, so let's jog together next time.
You have taken three classes from Professor Hamad. I hope to take a class from her soon.
We both want to lose weight.

One of our students illustrates this more specific type of support for the other in the following situation:

> I wasn't close with one of my housemates when we first moved in. One day it was just the two of us home, and she was watching TV in our common living room. I didn't know her well but wanted to put in the effort. So I came in and sat down, and we started talking about our mutual love of the particular show she was watching. By having that in common with her we both started to open up and get along much better.

When people say they don't like others with a particular color hair, and you have that hair color, they may put you down. Because they say they don't exercise regularly, you may see that as some kind of disapproval for your doing it. If their goal in a conflict is to inflict serious mental harm on you, they can resort to verbal abuse and put you down. If their goal is to solve a problem, then they want to avoid abuse and support your face.

In the earlier example of a sorority member trying to get her sisters to participate in a Friday fundraising event, she goes on to describe how she supported their faces in the ongoing interaction.

> First, I tried to make the others feel important, secure, honest, and trustworthy. Second, I specifically recognized their individual needs and interests by saying "We all want money for the dance festival that is coming up . . . " and "We are sisters. We feel the need to come together . . . " and "I know that everyone is really busy right now . . . "

Corrective Facework

When a threat to face has been made, you should use **corrective facework,** or statements meant to ameliorate the effect of face-threatening messages. When you are the one whose face has been threatened, one means of corrective action is simply to act as though no threat to face has been made, ignoring the action that caused a face threat. This is a good strategy for minor issues, but ignoring a major face threat may result in a larger conflict later on.

Other forms of corrective action have been generated by Thomas and Pondy, who viewed **impression management** (ensuring that the image one projects is the one that others perceive) as critical in moving a conflict to its resolution phase.[18] People's beliefs about the other's intent affect the conflict strategies they choose and how they interpret the other's strategies. Thomas and Pondy found that when people were asked to recall what conflict resolution mode they had used, the majority (74 percent) were most likely to recall using "cooperative" modes: collaboration, compromise, and accommodation. However, the majority (73 percent) also recalled that the other person in the conflict had been competitive rather than cooperative. Thus, people are not being perceived as cooperative even when they think they are being cooperative.

The authors identified a number of ways in which people can work to manage the impression they make in a conflict to help ensure that the image they project is the one the other person perceives. Some of their suggestions are these:

- The first activity is scanning, or checking out the perceptions being created. We can question the other to confirm that we are "on the same page."
- A second activity is explaining, used when we perceive that the other has not taken our message in the way we meant it.

Repair Rituals

What should we do if we realize that we have offended the other person? We have available to us a ritual known as a repair sequence, which has these four steps:

Offending situation: the other's behavior is seen as intentionally hurtful, whether or not that person did intend it
Reproach: request for an explanation of an offense from the one offended
Remedy: an account, concession, or apology supplied by an offender
Acknowledgment: evaluation of the account supplied by the one offended

The **repair sequence** is a specialized version of the conflict process where a triggering event is followed by initiation, differentiation, and perhaps resolution. The difference is mainly in the relationship of the issue to the episode. Whereas in conflict both people perceive that the other is interfering with their goals or engaging in incompatible activities, in a repair sequence there is a clear distinction between the offender and the offended party. The offender has created a problem (i.e., the offender has not acted in accordance with the image she or he has created for the other person) and must explain his or her actions. Let us consider each of the phases or steps in the repair sequence.

Offending Situation

Offending situations are those in which a person believes that the other has acted in an intentionally hurtful way. Usually, the offense is face threatening in nature. Nothing is more awkward than having to continue interacting with a person who has offended you and refuses to acknowledge it or appears unaware of it.

Reproach

People are unlikely to walk away from an offense without saying anything at all, although that can happen on occasion, especially when the consequences are minimal. In more significant cases, one can call attention to an offense by simply commenting on it or confronting the offender and asking him or her for an explanation (e.g., "What do you have to say about the broken window?"). In some cases, one can make an offender aware of an offense even by remaining silent. The other may perceive this as "the silent treatment," realize what caused it, and come forward with an explanation. Finally, the offended party may also use nonverbal cues (e.g., slamming doors, dirty looks) to let the offender know an offense has occurred, which assumes that the offender knows what he or she did to upset the other.

Remedy

Reproaches create a need for us to take an action that rectifies matters. However, it is possible that an offender may respond to a reproach by refusing to act, the most aggravating response. Refusals include denying that one was even involved in the offending event or that the event took place (which may mean lying). A person can also refuse to act by turning the reproach around and questioning the right of the offended person to make a reproach. In cases where one cannot deny the event or one's role in it, there are three broad types of actions an offender can take to restore a relationship: offer an account (through excuses or justifications), make a concession, or offer an apology; one can also act in a way that combines any of these. (See Table 9.1 for a listing of actions.)

An **account** is explanation for behavior when questioned. Accounts are also part of the conflict interaction (when a person is challenged on an issue and must respond) or its aftermath (when a person tries to explain what was done and said in a conflict situation).

TABLE 9.1 Image Restoration Strategies

Less Restorative	**Excuses**
↓	I didn't do it, someone else did.
	I was forced to do it; you made me do it
	I lost my head; I didn't know what I was doing.
	I didn't mean to do it
	Justifications
	I meant well
	It was a one-time thing; it's not characteristic of me. You know me better than that.
	It looks a lot worse than it really is.
	It actually was a good thing to do given the circumstances
	Concessions
	Let me give you something for your pain.
	I will make the offense right; I will change my ways
	Apology
More Restorative	I am so ashamed and so sorry this happened. Please forgive me.

Accounts serve an important function in that they explain how people interpret the situation at hand.

Accounts may take the form of excuses or justifications. **Excuses** admit that the offense occurred but deny responsibility for it. The offender can claim

- impairment (e.g., "I was drunk"),
- diminished responsibility (e.g., "I didn't know"),
- scapegoat status (e.g., "they made me do it"), or
- that she or he is a "victim of a sad tale," in which the offender recounts a series of misfortunes that have resulted in the way the offender is today. Sad tales are often the staple of courtroom drama, in which defense attorneys try to prove their client incapable of responsibility in a crime.

In contrast to offering an excuse, the offender may choose to offer a justification, which diminishes the meaning of the offense rather than diffusing responsibility for it. **Justifications** may acknowledge that an act was committed while claiming that

- it hurt no one (e.g., "it was just a practical joke"),
- the victim deserved it (e.g., "he hit me first"),
- other people who have committed similar offenses were not punished,

- he or she had good intentions when choosing to commit the offense, or
- the offense was needed because of loyalty to others (e.g., the reasons used by various political subordinates when explaining why they broke various laws).

Because not all excuses or justifications are acceptable or sufficient in themselves, the offender may need to make some sort of concession. **Concessions** admit the offender's guilt and offer restitution. For example, a husband brings his wife flowers, she does something with him that he enjoys doing (play golf, sail, or watch a football game), one gives a gift to the other, and a relative buys the other tickets to a basketball game. Concessions are often done in combination with excuses or apologies.

Apologies are admissions of blameworthiness and *regret* on the part of the offender. Apologies allow a person to admit to blame for an action, but they also attempt to obtain a pardon for the action by convincing the offended person that the incident is not representative of what the offender is really like.

Schlenker and Darby have identified several levels of apology, which are used progressively by actors as the offense committed becomes more serious and as the actor's responsibility for the offense increases. An apology can include a simple "pardon me" or something more complicated, including statements of remorse (e.g., "I'm sorry"), offering to help the injured party, self-castigation, or direct attempts to obtain forgiveness. In one study, respondents were asked to imagine that they had bumped into another person in a public place, either in a crowded shopping mall or in a hallway at school between classes. The degree of felt responsibility was manipulated by explaining that the actor was either knocked from behind, thus bumping into the victim, or had not been paying attention and bumped into the victim without noticing. Offenses of varying degrees were that the victim had been bumped on the arm (low), knocked to the ground but was unhurt (medium), or knocked to the ground and was moaning in pain (high). Respondents were asked whether they would use one of the levels of apology, respond in nonapology (e.g., saying or doing nothing, or responding nonverbally), or respond in justification ("I'm glad to see you're not hurt") or excuses ("I didn't see you"). According to Schlenker and Darby,

> If the apology is viewed as sincere by the audience, the actor appears to have repented, appears not to require further rehabilitative punishment, and should be forgiven. The social interaction can then return to its normal course and the actor has minimized the negative repercussions.[19]

Apologies are particularly important when one is faced with the reality of having offended a high-trait hostility person. When a person is faced with an offending situation, his or her blood pressure and pulse rises. Those who rate high on trait hostility or anger have much higher increases in blood pressure and pulse when subjected to verbal harassment. But, if after the experience they are given a sincere apology, their blood pressure and pulse returns to normal much faster than if they receive an insincere apology.[20]

Acknowledgment

After an account has been rendered, the offended party responds with an acknowledgment in one of several ways. The most mitigating way is to honor the account, accepting its content and signaling, verbally or nonverbally, that the "score is even." The offended party may also retreat from the reproach, dropping his or her right to make it (e.g., "I didn't know that you were forced into action"). The offended party may also simply drop or switch the topic, moving away from the reproach without resolving the issue. More aggravating is *rejection* of the account, either by taking issue with it (e.g., "I can't believe you expect me to believe you") or by simply restating the reproach as though no account was given.

In an effort to apply the repair ritual in his own life, a student writes:

> Some of my old high school buddies visited during Home Coming at the college. One night after one too many beers, I started getting a little rowdy with one of them, and friendly child play turned into drunken wrestle-mania right there in the bar. After taking the rest of the night to sober up and cool off, I felt I needed to say something to break the ice due to the fact that my buddy wasn't speaking to me. I decided that I should be the one to explain and apologize for my actions because I realized that I instigated the whole mess. So instead of ignoring the situation and pretending like nothing happened, I admitted to my friend (the person I offended) that my behavior was unacceptable but I also explained that it was unintentional. I had one too many drinks that night. After I explained myself to him, he was completely understanding and forgiving. I offered to treat him to breakfast, so we went out. If I hadn't tried to excuse my behavior, tried to apologize, and bought him breakfast, my friend and I would still not be talking to each other. However I realized that taking responsibility for my offending behavior the night before was my best bet to get out of the dog-house.

Let us authors hasten to add, that we do not condone using the excuse of alcohol or drugs for inappropriate, immature, or offensive behavior. Some excuses are more acceptable than others; however, the above scenario illustrates the repair ritual in a way that some students can identify with and understand.

RESPONDING TO OTHERS

In a recent study, Benoit and Drew examined the ways in which people respond to impression-management strategies. They had people rate how appropriate and effective various strategies are when someone has damaged one's impression. The scenario was one in which person A bumps into person B, spilling something on B's favorite coat. B accuses A of ruining B's clothes, and A replies with denial ("I didn't do it"), evasion of responsibility for the event ("it was an accident; it wasn't my fault"), reducing the offensiveness of the event ("it's not that bad"), corrective action ("I'll have the clothing cleaned"), or apology ("I'm so sorry"). The results indicated, not surprisingly, that apologies and offering some corrective action were seen as the most appropriate and effective ways to restore one's image in this kind of circumstance.[21]

Unfortunately, Elana didn't do all she should have done:

> I do not think I used the right remedy after offending my boyfriend. I just said I didn't mean to upset him and that I thought what I said was no big deal. I never said that I was sorry for upsetting him, and I never showed regret.

CONFLICT AND IMPRESSION MANAGEMENT IN CYBERSPACE

A newly developing area of communication study is online conflict that occurs in real-time chat rooms or asynchronous discussion forums. In their study of online conflict, Smith, McLaughlin, and Osborne found that few people replied to reproaches and seldom completed the traditional repair sequence.[22]

How can you explain this difference between online and face-to-face conflicts? We suggest that it is much easier to "walk away" from an offending situation online than it is face-to-face, especially where there is a relationship between the parties involved. In many of these online offending situations, there is no (previously established) relationship to repair. When face-to-face, if you call me on the carpet for something I said or did, I may feel obligated to respond and seek your acceptance of my excuse, apology, or concession, but in an online discussion group, I might find it easier and less awkward to simply exit the discussion.

Smith's research is corroborated by others examining the difference between face-to-face (FTF) conflict and conflict in computer-mediated communication (CMC). Zornoza and colleagues, for example, found that negative conflict behaviors were more frequent in CMC than FTF, and the number of positive conflict management behaviors actually decreased over time.[23] In addition, Dorado and colleagues found that there were higher levels of avoidance and lower levels of forcing in computer-mediated negotiation, while FTF negotiation displayed more forcing and compromise.[24] Finally, Hobman and colleagues' research indicated that CMC groups displayed more process and relationship conflict than FTF when first starting, but those differences disappeared after the first day.[25]

Another line of research in cyber communication involves the creation of impressions and their management by users of Social Network Sites (SNSs) such as *My Space* and *Facebook*. Teachers who use *Facebook*, for example, and allow students access may be perceived as more accessible and similar to students, which may result in higher student participation and more positive attitudes toward the class and the instructor.[26] Among students, the number of friends one has, the descriptions that one makes about oneself, and the comments made by others are related to the impressions people make on others in SNSs. Specifically, the number of friends one has on *Facebook* is related to perceptions of popularity but only up to a certain point. People having fewer than 100 friends or more than 300 friends are viewed as less popular than those in the middle, but for different reasons:

> Individuals with too many friends may appear to be focusing too much on *Facebook*, friending out of desperation rather than popularity, spending a great deal of time on their computers ostensibly trying to make connections in a computer-mediated environment where they feel more comfortable than in face-to-face social interaction.[27]

While the number of friends is related to positive impressions of the person being rated, the number of friends one has does not have any particular relationship to ratings of physical attractiveness.[28] However, the attractiveness of the friends who leave messages on person's wall in *Facebook* affects impressions of that person's attractiveness.[29] Further, the comments made by others about a person on his or her profile are more influential in creating impressions than statements one makes about oneself.[30] While it has been commonly expected that people seek out online relationships because of their inability to handle face-to-face ones, research does not bear that conclusion out. While people who are anxious about FTF communication do use *Facebook* to pass the time and assuage feelings of loneliness, they have fewer friends. The author concludes: "Such results seem to justify the rich-get-richer hypothesis, which states that the internet primarily benefits extraverted individuals. Our results are in contrast to findings that socially anxious individuals are more likely to form relationships online."[31] Still another study demonstrated the utility of *Facebook* for solidifying relationships that might otherwise be weak and for creating social ties linked to a sense of community.[32]

MANAGE IT

Some other cultures more openly discuss face and face-saving techniques than we do here in the United States. However, the concept is no less important for Americans. One of the primary reasons conflicts escalate or get out of hand is due to face threats.

The truth is that people everywhere are motivated to create and maintain favorable impressions of themselves; this impression or image people have of themselves is called *face*. There are two types of face that are important to every one of us: positive face and autonomous face. A person's positive face is supported when others value what the person values, express admiration for the person, or show acceptance of the person as a competent individual. Autonomous face is the desire people have for recognition for their contributions and freedom from constraints and impositions. When others recognize what one does and respect a person's independence, the person's autonomous face is supported.

The desires for positive and autonomous face, under the best of circumstances, can create a dilemma because it requires balance. This balancing act is referred to as impression management.

Impression management means ensuring that one's message is not mistakenly taken as face threatening. To do this, an effective conflict manager adds to the message (before the other receives it) disclaimers such as hedging, cognitive disclaimer, credentialing, sin license, or appeal for suspended judgment.

Once engaged in conversation with another, an effective conflict manager can employ general ways and specific techniques to support another's face in conflict situations. In a general way, people want others to like, respect, encourage, consult, include, appreciate, and reward them. They want others to ask them questions, greet them warmly, help them when needed, and make them feel safe. We can also support others in a more specific way. To do this, we need to determine what traits or characteristics the other perceives in himself or herself and point out the ones we have in common or are capable of supporting.

In a conflict situation in which we lose face, we can employ a repair sequence to regain it. A repair sequence has these phases or steps: the offending situation, a reproach (request from the offended person for an explanation of the other's offense), a remedy (an account from the offender such as an excuse or justification, a concession, or an apology), and an acknowledgment (evaluation of the account).

Some offenses are worse than others. When the violation creates more than an offending situation, a relational transgression occurs, which we examine in the next chapter. When relational transgressions occur, forgiveness and perhaps reconciliation are necessary to restore the relationship.

Think About It

1. How have you seen issues of autonomous and positive face create conflicts in your experience? What have you done to resolve issues of autonomous and positive face? Are the strategies you use for each different?
2. What are your general and specific face needs? In general, what actions could others take that would show support for your face needs? What specific actions could they take?
3. If you are a member of *Facebook*, *My Space*, or another Social Network Site (SNS), think about the way you use it. How do you present yourself? What impression do you hope people will get from reading your profile? Have there been times people have posted something on your profile that you wished they hadn't?

Apply It

1. Imagine that you have to say something potentially face threatening to a friend. Explain how you could use each of these disclaimers to soften the complaint:
   a. hedging
   b. cognitive disclaimer
   c. credentialing
   d. sin license
   e. appeal for suspended judgment
2. Visit a number of different SNS sites. How does the site itself describe its purpose? How do you see the profiles of people within the site exemplifying that purpose? What are the differences between the various sites?

Work With It

1. Read the following case study and answer the questions that follow it.

   A long-lasting conflict centered on the amount of time and affection Frank's wife, Judy, was spending on their cat, Lucky. This conflict took place a number of times, usually whenever Frank was feeling neglected. Whenever Judy entered the house, she lavished the cat with affection. In fact every time she passed the cat in the hallway, she would stop and caress her, talk to her, and go out of her way to make the cat feel loved. From his perspective, Frank felt that Judy always had time to give the cat the affection she needed (and more) while never having time to provide the affection he felt that he needed. He inferred from her actions that she was never too busy for the cat but rarely had enough time for him. He was jealous of the cat.

   From Judy's perspective, the cat was helpless and her lavishing attention was only because the cat was so "cute and defenseless." Judy didn't realize that Frank would really enjoy short, quick doses of affection throughout the day like she was giving the cat.

(Continued)

Because of a few instances where Judy interrupted Frank while he was working intensely on something and he responded a bit negatively, she also felt that he might put a damper on her affectionate overtures toward him by not being responsive, or by failing to "purr."

   a. What is the likely outcome of this conflict situation?
   b. How could the characters have supported one another's face using general techniques? How could the characters have supported one another's face using specific techniques, and what would then have been the likely outcome?
   c. Suppose you recommend corrective actions to the couple. Describe the steps in the repair sequence as they would apply to this conflict. Also, what role could accounts, concessions, and apologies play in this case study?

2. Read the following case study and answer the questions that follow it.

   A group of us live together in a sorority house. One of our sisters, Gina, is normally quiet and easygoing. However, one day she suddenly verbally attacked each one of us and accused us of plotting against her behind her back. I said to her, "What? Where is this coming from?" We were all shocked at her suddenly different behavior. She even threw a textbook at one of her sisters and stormed out of the room. That evening she rejoined the group but said nothing about the incident. At first, a couple of us raised the issue, but she just smiled and said, "I don't know what you are talking about."

   a. Is this an offending situation?
   b. Does a reproach occur?
   c. Was a remedy offered? If not, what might it be? As for acknowledgment, what remedies would likely receive rejection from the narrator? What remedies might receive acceptance?

NOTES

1. Erving Goffman, *The Presentation of Self in Everyday Life* (New York: Overlook Press, 1959); *Interaction Ritual: Essays on Face-to-Face Behavior* (New York: Pantheon Books, 1967).
2. Ibid.
3. John Oetzel, Stella Ting-Toomey, Tomoko Masumoto, Yukiko Yokochi, Xiaohui Pan, Jiro Takai, and Richard Wilcox, "Face and Facework in Conflict: A Cross-Cultural Comparison Of China, Germany, Japan, and the United States," *Communication Monographs* 68 (2001), 235–258; John Oetzel, Stella Ting-Toomey, Martha Idalia Chew-Sanchez, Richard Harris, Richard Wilcox, and Siegfried Stumpf, "Face and Facework in Conflicts with Parents and Siblings: A Cross-Cultural Comparison of Germans, Japanese, Mexicans, and U.S. Americans," *Journal of Family Communication* 3 (2003), 67–93.
4. Carol Tavris and Elliot Aronson, *Mistakes Were Made (But not by Me)* (Orlando: Harcourt, Inc., 2007), pp. 221–222.
5. Shuangyue Zhang and Laura Stafford, "Perceived Face Threat of Honest but Hurtful Evaluative Messages in Romantic Relationships," *Western Journal of Communication* 72(1) (2008), 19–39.
6. Amy Ebesu Hubbard, Hae Lin Han, Whitney Kim, and Leanne Nakamura, "Analysis of Mobile Phone Interruptions in Dating Relationships: A Face Threatening Act," paper presented at the International Communication Association, San Francisco, CA, 2007.
7. Adrianne Kunkel, Steven Wilson, James Olufowote, and Scott Robson, "Identity Implications of Influence Goals: Initiating, Intensifying, and Ending Romantic Relationships," *Western Journal of Communication* 67(4) (2003), 382–412.
8. June Price Tangney and Rhonda L. Dearing, *Shame and Guilt* (New York: The Guilford Press, 2002), p. 180.
9. Penelope Brown and Stephen Levinson, *Politeness: Some Universals in Language Usage* (Cambridge: Cambridge University Press, 1987).

10. Originally the research literature referred to this concept as "negative face." Because the term seemed misleading, we chose to refer to the concept in a more descriptive way as "autonomous face."
11. Steven R. Wilson, Carlos G. Aleman, and Geoff B. Leatham, "Identity Implications of Influence Goals: A Revised Analysis of Face-Threatening Acts and Application to Seeking Compliance with Same-Sex Friends," *Human Communication Research* 25 (1998), p. 65.
12. Patrick B. O'Sullivan, "What You Don't Know Won't Hurt Me: Impression Management Functions of Communication Channels in Relationships," *Human Communication Research* 26 (2000), 403–431.
13. Sarah J. Tracy, "When Questioning Turns to Face Threat: An Interactional Sensitivity in 911 Call Taking," *Western Journal of Communication* 66 (2002), p. 152.
14. Larry A. Erbert and Kory Floyd, "Affectionate Expressions as Face-Threatening Acts: Receiver Assessments," *Communication Studies* 55 (2004), 254–270.
15. Kathy Domenici and Stephen W. Littlejohn, *Facework: Bridging Theory and Practice* (Thousand Oaks, CA: Sage Publications, 2006), p. 22.
16. Renee Edwards and Richard Bello, "Interpretations of Messages: The Influence of Equivocation, Face Concerns, and Ego-Involvement," *Human Communication Research* 27 (2001), 598.
17. John Hewitt and Randall Stokes, "Disclaimers," *American Sociological Review* 40 (1975), 112.
18. Kenneth W. Thomas and Louis R. Pondy, "Toward an 'Intent' Model of Conflict Management among Principle Parties," *Human Relations* 30 (1997), 1089–1102.
19. Barry R. Schlenker and Bruce W. Darby, "The Use of Apologies in Social Predicaments," *Social Psychology Quarterly* 44 (1981), 272.
20. Jeremy C. Anderson, Wolfgang Linden, and Martine E. Habra, "Influence of Apologies and Trait Hostility on Recovery from Anger," *Journal of Behavioral Medicine* 29 (2006), 347–358.
21. William L. Benoit and Shirley Drew, "Appropriateness and Effectiveness of Image Repair Strategies," *Communication Reports* 10 (1997), 153–163.
22. Christine B. Smith, Margaret L. McLaughlin, and Kerry K. Osborne, "Conduct Control on Usenet," *Journal of Computer-Mediated Communication* 2 (1997), retrieved on April 7, 2005, from http://jcmc.indiana.edu/vol2/issue4/smith.html.
23. Ana Zornoza, Pilar Ripoll, and Jose M. Peiro, "Conflict Management in Groups that Work in Two Different Communication Contexts: Face-to-Face and Computer-Mediated Communication," *Small Group Research* 33 (2002), 481–508.
24. Miguel A. Dorado, Francisco J. Medina, Lourdes Munduate, Immaculada F. J. Cisneros, and Martin Euwema, "Computer Mediated Negotiation of an Escalated Conflict," *Small Group Research* 33 (2002), 509–524.
25. Elizabeth V. Hobman, Prashant Bordia, Bernd Irmer, and Artemis Chang, "The Expression of Conflict in Computer-Mediated and Face-to-Face Groups," *Small Group Research* 33 (2002), 439–465.
26. Joseph P. Mazer, Richard E. Murphy, and Cheri J. Simonds, "I'll See You On 'Facebook': The Effects of Computer-Mediated Teacher Self-Disclosure on Student Motivation, Affective Learning, and Classroom Climate," *Communication Education* 56 (2007), 1–17.
27. Stephanie Tom Tong, Brandon Van Der Heide, Lindsey Langwell, and Joseph B. Walther, "Too Much of a Good Thing? The Relationship between Number of Friends and Interpersonal Impressions on Facebook," *Journal of Computer-Mediated Communication* 13 (2008), 542, 531–549.
28. Ibid.
29. Joseph B. Walther, Brandon Van Der Heide, Sang-Yeon Kim, David Westerman, and Stephanie Tom Tong, "The Role of Friends' Appearance and Behavior on Evaluations of Individuals on Facebook: Are We Known by the Company We Keep?" *Human Communication Research* 34 (2008), 28–49.
30. Joseph B. Walther, Brandon Van Der Heide, Lauren M. Hamel, and Hillary C. Shulman, "Self-Generated Versus Other-Generated Statements and Impressions in Computer-Mediated Communication: A Test of Warranting Theory Using Facebook," *Communication Research* 36 (2009), 229–253.
31. Pavica Sheldon, "The Relationship between Unwillingness to Communicate and Students' Facebook Use," *Journal of Media Psychology* 20 (2008), 67.
32. Nichole B. Ellison, Charles Steinfield, and Cliff Lampe, "The Benefits of Facebook 'Friends:' Social Capital and College Students' Use of Online Social Network Sites," *Journal of Computer-Mediated Communication* 12(4), retrieved on March 7, 2009, from http://jcmc.indiana.edu/vol12/issue4/ellison.html.

CHAPTER 10

Managing Conflict through Forgiveness

OBJECTIVES

At the end of this chapter, you should be able to:

- Distinguish relational transgressions from other types of problematic situations.
- Explain which relational transgressions are hardest to forgive.
- Distinguish forgiveness from forgetting and reconciliation.
- Explain the advantages of forgiveness and reconciliation following relational transgressions.
- Describe the steps one must take to forgive.

KEY TERMS

core relational rules
deception
emotional residues
forgiveness
helping orientation

reconciliation
relational transgressions
revenge
self-fulfilling prophecies
transforming the meaning

truth bias
unforgiveness
victimization

In the previous chapter, we introduced the idea of an offending situation that exists when people have acted in ways that threaten the face of another person or that seem intentionally hurtful. Accounts, concessions, and apologies are ways of rectifying problematic situations. But when "offending situations" take on crisis proportions and become more intense than a simple face-management problem, we call them relational transgressions.

Some hurtful actions may not need forgiving, such as annoyances, slights, or disappointments. Smedes notes, "It is wise not to turn all hurts into crises of forgiving.... We put everyone we love on guard when we turn personal misdemeanors into major felonies."[1] However, when others do commit relational transgressions against us, how do we handle the situation? In this chapter, we discuss conflict situations that involve central relational issues, the nature of forgiveness, its effects, the means people use to forgive one another, and the ways in which we may reconcile our differences. You are expected to learn how to distinguish forgiveness from forgetting, distinguish forgiveness from reconciliation, explain the advantages of forgiveness and reconciliation following relational transgressions, and identify the steps you can take to forgive others and, if you choose to do so, to reconcile with them.

RELATIONAL TRANSGRESSIONS

Relational transgressions are extremely problematic situations in which core rules of a relationship are violated, leaving high emotional residues. We'll explain each of these elements—rules and residues—in turn.

Core relational rules define our expectations about the way we should behave toward others as well as the way they should behave toward us. We treat strangers one way, friends another way, and our romantic partners still another. We relate to our parents differently from our more distant relatives. Part of the socialization process has taught us the rules that govern each type of social relationship such as romantic pairings, friendship, and being roommates. Relational transgressions occur when those rules we take for granted as "sacred" are broken by someone important to us.

In Chapter 5, we introduced you to the idea of relationship rule as one type of intangible issue that often occurs in interpersonal conflicts, where the parties are interdependent. Among friends, for example, a core relational rule becomes an issue when a person who claims to be your friend fails to help in your time of need. "Imagine that a person runs out of gas outside of town and calls someone she considers a good friend to come and give her a ride. Suppose the other responds with 'Why call me? Why don't you call a taxi?' If one fails to help in time of need, the friendship is in trouble."[2]

Another relationship rule is that you should not lie to your best friends. Lying to an acquaintance about why you do not want to go to the beach is different from lying to your best friend, because best friends are supposed to trust each other. This is particularly true because as we develop friendships with others, we tend to develop a **truth bias** toward them: We assume that they tell us the truth. This truth bias makes us more vulnerable and less accurate in detecting deception when it occurs. In addition to the cognitive effects, research indicates that the more involved people are with another person, the more intense their negative emotions when they discover that the person has lied to them. In addition, the more important the information lied about, the more intense negative emotions are on discovering the deception and the more likely it is that the future of the relationship is in jeopardy. Lying to one's best friend is a relational transgression.

Rules govern our romantic relationships as well. In a committed romantic relationship a core relational rule is that you should not cheat on your partner. Metts asked respondents to rate relational transgressions in order of their difficulty in resolution and found that sexual infidelity was identified as the most difficult to deal with.[3] But sexual infidelity in romantic relationships is not the only relational transgression.

Another romantic relationship rule consists of intentional deception and lies. **Deception** is generally classified as deliberately altering information to change a person's perceptions about an issue. Certainly, "social lies" and lies used to avoid sticky situations (e.g., "I really can't go with you to the beach because I have to study") are part of our social fabric, whether or not we approve of them. They become a relational transgression, however, when the lie breaks core relational rules.

Another rule is that you should not physically or verbally abuse those you love. We introduced you to the topic of interpersonal violence in Chapter 8. One expects his or her partner to love and protect. This occurs because as we develop romantic relationships with others, we tend to take a **helping orientation** toward them: We assume that they love us and desire to help rather than hurt us, as we do them. Verbal and physical abuse run contrary to a helping orientation. Clearly, interpersonal violence in a romantic relationship constitutes a relational transgression, a violation of expected behavior. Violence, when it occurs, is an event progressing from an out-of-control conflict episode, and it creates an issue that the relational partners have to deal with if they are to continue their relationship.

We have chosen to focus on rules of friendships and romantic relationships, because Americans expect romantic partners to also be good friends. Romantic and married partners are expected to actually share two relationships, a romantic relationship and a friendship. Therefore, many conflicts in romantic rules occur because of the violation of core relationship rules of either love or friendship.

In addition to violating core relationship rules, relational transgressions produce highly **emotional residues** in a relationship; that is, people experience lingering emotional responses to the memory of the transgression. Transgressions result in negative emotional, cognitive, and behavioral responses. If a good friend or romantic partner has lied to you, you may experience shock, disbelief, hurt, anger, and/or betrayal. You may wonder whether you can trust what that person says in the future. It may even cause you to verify the truth of that person's communication for a while. People in long-term relationships face a need to forgive and perhaps reconcile the transgression in some way.

WHY STUDY FORGIVENESS AND RECONCILIATION?

The need to study forgiveness and reconciliation is based on the assumption that conflicts are cyclical and repetitive (see schismogenesis, URP, competitive escalation cycle, and chilling effect in Chapter 2), affected by what has come previously and affecting what comes after. Our ability to break out of dysfunctional conflict cycles and respond appropriately to conflicts in the present is in no small way dependent on our ability to forgive those close to us.

While once the province of religious discourse, forgiveness is an established part of the communication and psychology research literature. How then are we to understand this gift and bestow it appropriately?

DEFINING FORGIVENESS AND RECONCILIATION

Forgiveness and reconciliation are related but separate processes with the former generally preceding the latter. **Forgiveness** is a cognitive process that consists of letting go of feelings of revenge and desires to retaliate.

Overall, forgiveness occurs when a person lets go of his or her feelings of revenge and need for retaliation, and changes his or her thoughts about the transgression and the transgressor. It starts with anger over a transgression and moves toward **transforming the meaning** of the event, or changing the way we view the event in light of other events in our lives. Forgiveness is something that happens over time as "negative unforgiving emotions [are replaced] with positive other-oriented emotions . . . [and] negative emotions are repeatedly whittled away."[4] Forgiveness is "reframing of how one views the world . . . . [It is] in reality a case of acting in one's own enlightened self-interest."[5]

Writers in the field of forgiveness focus largely on the "victim's development of empathy toward the perpetrator as a necessary step in forgiveness";[6] lasting forgiveness results from the ability to see the perpetrator as a human being rather than as a stereotyped victimizer. It is a necessary step in growing as a person; the choice not to forgive is essentially an unhealthy one. However healthy a choice it may be, forgiveness cannot be rushed. "Premature forgiveness that takes place before self-affirmation and empowering are under way is deleterious. Frequently, it does not even seem to be forgiveness at all, but is instead a cover for passivity and anxiety."[7]

We can distinguish forgiveness from both unforgiveness and revenge. **Unforgiveness** is a cognitive process in which one doesn't let go of feeling of revenge and maintains a desire to retaliate. **Revenge** is a behavior based on the notion of "an eye for an eye." One wants to follow evil with more evil. Revenge characterizes the cycle of violence in which each aggressive act is followed by more aggressive behavior. The best way to stop the cycle is to switch to forgiveness and perhaps initiate reconciliation.

Reconciliation is a behavioral process in which we take actions to restore a relationship or create a new one following forgiveness. It is a process distinct from forgiveness. As Freedman et al. argue, "Forgiveness . . . is *one* person's response toward another in a hurtful situation; reconciliation is the process of *two* people, together, negotiating and working out differences."[8] The evidence indicates that forgiveness is an important mental process that should follow traumatic conflict. Reconciliation, on the other hand, involves a series of actions we may choose to avoid, particularly if the offender is likely to violate us again.

Forgiveness does not obligate us to reconciliation or creating a new relationship. It is not simply forgetting that something happened. It does not release the other person from the consequences of his or her behavior. It does not deny anger. It does not put us in a position of superiority. It is not a declaration of the end of all conflict or of ever risking again with the other person (or anybody else). It is not one way. When forgiveness takes any of these forms, it feels demeaning, as though the other is simply waiting for a time to even up the score.[9]

The widespread assumption by many people that forgiveness and reconciliation are virtually simultaneous is disturbing to us, because that assumption often moves people toward reconciliation before such action is actually warranted. One writer calls this reconciliation via *cheap forgiveness,* which is a "compulsive, unconditional, unilateral attempt at peacemaking for which you ask nothing in return . . . when you forgive cheaply, you seek to preserve the relationship at any cost, including your own integrity and safety."[10] Reconciliation via "cheap forgiveness" is often driven by fear of the offender's anger, fear of the offender leaving, or fear of harming the offender. It is based on an unhealthy need to preserve a relationship that may not survive the cost of avoiding the conflict. In our experience, this usually only prolongs the painful period leading up to the eventual break up of the relationship. The desire for reconciliation must be tempered by recognition of the possible dangers involved within it.

We do not forgive to become martyrs to the relationship. We forgive because it is better for us and better for the other person. We forgive because we want to act freely again, not react out of past pain.

ADVANTAGES OF FORGIVENESS

Forgiveness Benefits Our Mental Health

Most writers in the area of forgiveness have argued that holding onto grief and hurt is psychologically unhealthy. By placing blame on other people, we relinquish our control over our emotions and give that control to another.

Holding grudges constitutes an egocentric position wherein we view those who have hurt us only in terms of what we need, what we wish, or what we long for.[11] Those who not only do not forgive but additionally seek revenge do so " . . . based on the belief that . . . it is possible to measure the magnitude of an offense, to receive an equal amount of retribution somehow balances the account."[12]

Forgiveness is linked to both mental and physical benefits. For example, research examining social adjustment and the ability to forgive found a high correlation between the two: As a person's social adjustment score went up, so did the person's ability to forgive.[13] More recent research on the role of forgiveness in counseling and mental health has demonstrated that teaching people about forgiveness and training them in "forgiveness strategies" helped increase recovery from divorce (restoring positive feelings about oneself, etc.), decreased feelings of guilt, and decreased feelings of depression and anxiety.[14] Among other benefits, forgiveness intervention has been effective in reducing depression and anxiety,[15] raising self-esteem,[16] improving perceptions of self-efficacy,[17] and increasing self-esteem and feelings of hope while lowering depression and anxiety for incest survivors.[18]

Some people who forgive others cannot forgive themselves and vice versa. Researchers have found that the process of forgiving oneself is different than that of forgiving others, and being able and/or willing to do one does not mean a person is willing or able to do the other.[19] People who are unable to forgive themselves have higher levels of loneliness, although which causes what is not yet understood. It may be that people who are lonely overestimate the severity of their offenses and so do not forgive themselves. Or, it may be that people who do not forgive themselves for offenses cut themselves off from social contact. Whatever the direction of the relationship, learning forgiveness toward both others and self is an important skill.[20]

Forgiveness Benefits Our Physical Health

Not only is forgiveness related to our psychological health, it is related to our physical health as well.[21] College students who report an ability to forgive others perceive their health to be better than those who do not.[22] Additionally, people who have high levels of trait-like unforgiveness tend to experience higher levels of pain than those who have lower levels.[23] In general, those who are able to forgive sleep better than those who don't.[24] And senior citizens who manifested greater abilities to forgive others reported better physical health than those who reported less ability to forgive others.[25]

Trait-like forgiveness or unforgiveness has some widely demonstrated links to cardiovascular health. People with higher trait-like forgiveness experience lower blood pressure and better recovery from incidents that raise blood pressure than those with low trait-like forgiveness.[26]

Harms resulting from the inability to forgive often involve anger and stress. We experience physical damage when this flight-or-fight mechanism, which was designed for short-term emergency responses to situations, becomes a long-term ongoing response.[27] The desire for revenge may play a role in physical damage to our bodies making us more susceptible to physical illness.

WHY DON'T PEOPLE FORGIVE?

Given the number of mental and physical benefits to forgiveness, one would think that people would see the good in embracing it. We know this is not always the case. But why? There are several explanations for a lack of forgiveness in a relationship.

The most frequent reason people don't forgive is that the other has not admitted wrongdoing, apologized, or asked for forgiveness. One study examined the way people describe transgressions, how they have come to forgive or not forgive the other person, and whether or not they attempted reconciliation. When people report that they have not forgiven the person who offended them, the primary reason for not forgiving is that they have not received an apology or an explanation from the other. Since the other has admitted no wrongdoing, they are not willing to forgive. In addition, people report refusal to forgive when the other continues in offensive behavior.[28]

Research has also demonstrated a link between a person's perception of an apology and whether or not it is accepted. When a person is offended, being offered an apology that is too elaborate for the offense or too simple may result in a lack of forgiveness.[29] Further, since people often refuse to forgive when the other has not offered an apology or explanation, they also might believe that by withholding forgiveness, they can prevent the transgressor from hurting them again.[30]

There are others who don't forgive because they prefer the role of victim. In a related manner, a few do not want to give up their right to hold a grudge; it gives them a sense of power to hold their hurt over the other person. Sometimes, being hurt has created a loss of face for the person who was offended, and forgiving the transgressor would cause an even greater loss of face. And fear of vulnerability and giving off what might be perceived as "signs of weakness" are often a barrier to forgiveness.

People with higher levels of empathy find it easier to forgive others, although they may have difficulty forgiving themselves for offenses they have committed.[31] In addition, empathy has a stronger relationship for forgiveness in men than in women; while women are more empathic in general, it does not affect their levels of forgiveness. However, men with higher levels of empathy are more forgiving than those with lower levels.[32] Those who are able to see themselves as potential offenders are also more likely to forgive than those who cannot imagine themselves as offenders; again, this effect is more pronounced for men than women.[33]

Age is also a factor. One study found that college-aged students, who were hurt in previous dating relationships, found it more difficult to forgive than any other age group who had similar experiences.[34]

Perhaps most importantly, some people don't forgive because they don't know how and no one offers support for doing so; in fact, some people think a forgiving person is stupid or naive.[35] People may learn to forgive while in short-term therapeutic intervention but will revert back to a place of unforgiveness over time when there is no continued support for their forgiveness processes.[36]

WORKING THROUGH FORGIVENESS

Learning to Forgive

Recall that we differentiated reconciliation from forgiveness. Whereas forgiveness is a cognitive process that consists of letting go of feelings of revenge and desires to retaliate, reconciliation is a behavior process in which we take actions to restore a relationship or create a new one. Because they are different processes, forgiving the other cognitively does not necessarily lead to reconciliation behavior. Many people forgive, but at a distance. They let go of their need for revenge but do not choose to put themselves in a position where the other can hurt them again.

In his seminal work on forgiveness, Smedes lists the key stages that the process goes through, namely hurt, hate, healing, and coming together.[37] We now know that "coming together" need not be taken in a physical sense but rather in a psychological, mental, and emotional sense, where you might cognitively forgive another without behaviorally reconciling.

Can people be taught to forgive? The answer is yes. While "unforgiveness tends to fade naturally . . . specific training tends to speed and deepen the process."[38] The skills people need to learn in order to facilitate forgiveness are listed in Table 10.1. Further, the type of training in forgiveness that people receive affects their levels of forgiveness in the future.

Levels of Forgiveness

Figure 10.1 illustrates the various levels a person may go through in seeking to forgive another. Each successive level, we would argue, results in greater personal transformation for the person who forgives. At higher levels, a person will feel greater levels of empathy and greater awareness of his or her own limitations. At any of these levels, a person may simply forgive and not move into reconciliation, but reconciliation without forgiveness creates a dangerous emotional position for the one who has been hurt.

TABLE 10.1 Learning to Forgive

- Understand that forgiveness is a process.
- Start by acknowledging how the other hurt you.
- Allow yourself to experience anger.
- Don't adhere to the "victim" stage.
- Find people to support your forgiveness process.
- Recognize that the other person may not treat you any differently than in the past. Focus, then, on your responsibility in the situation and your responses to it.
- Try to see the other person as someone like yourself—human, having flaws, and making mistakes. This helps you escape from the villain or victim mentality.
- Try to see yourself as a person like the other—capable of hurting people, capable of doing something wrong (not necessarily that you are capable of the same offense). This helps you escape from a position of superiority with respect to the other.
- Think about what you have learned from the situation, and how you have grown as a result of it. Events usually have a positive and negative side to them, so you may often switch from a negative view to a positive view of the same event.

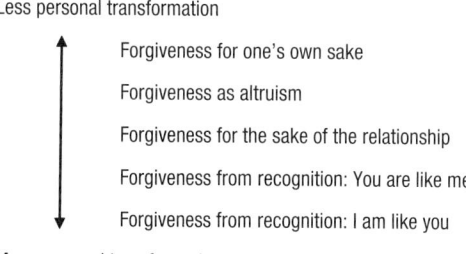

FIGURE 10.1 Levels of Forgiveness

At the first level, a person may forgive because it is a healthy to so; forgiving makes us feel better. This is the most common understanding of forgiveness in one study of college students and community laypersons.[39] Forgiveness at this level is accomplished because the victim realizes that not forgiving hurts the victim rather than the offender. In some cases, such forgiving does enable reconciliation.

At the second level of forgiveness, a person might forgive because of empathy for the other, understanding that the other needs forgiveness. Worthington observes that "this is a difficult sell . . . . Yet most people . . . come to see that anger, resentment, hostility, rate, and hatred destroy . . . . lasting satisfaction comes more often with creating."[40] While this type of forgiveness may not necessarily lead into processes of reconciliation, it does make reconciliation more probable.

The third level of forgiveness moves a person from forgiving for the sake of the other to forgiving for the sake of the relationship. Moskal describes this type of forgiveness as something that "lies at the place where three roads meet: the ethics of obligation, in the matter of forgiving what was done; the ethics of virtue, in the matter of the motive of love and the virtue of creativity; and the ethics of [authenticity], in implying a deep and abiding concern for the other who has disclosed."[41] This kind of forgiveness is generally precipitated by expressions of remorse and regret by the offender as well as promises of change in the future and is generally the inception of reconciliation processes in the relationship.

The fourth and fifth levels of forgiveness are unlikely to occur except in the instance of a relationship that is in the process of reconciliation and recreation. These two levels of forgiveness require high levels of empathy on the part of the forgiver and generally can occur only in close contact with the offender.

In the fourth level, the person begins to see the offender as "like me." Feelings of estrangement and separation, feelings that the offender is a separated other begin to diminish. Empathy increases. This results in a lessening of the victim–villain characterization of those in the relationship.

When forgiveness deepens, the victim is not only able to see the offender as "like me," but the victim is able to say, "I am like the offender." This is a very difficult cognitive move. It requires that the victim see himself or herself as a person capable of harming others. As the research discussed above showed, however, it is associated with higher levels of forgiveness. It does not require that the victim believe that he or she is capable of the same offense, but in this stage the victim is capable of seeing how he or she has inflicted pain on others and has received forgiveness for those offenses.

WORKING THROUGH RECONCILIATION

Levels of Reconciliation

As a person works through levels of forgiveness, he or she will also consider how to move through levels of reconciliation (see Figure 10.2). The first level involves no reconciliation at all, even if the other has been forgiven. This is not an uncommon outcome. Indeed, most of those reporting that they had forgiven others in Lulofs' study indicated that they had no desire to continue the relationship with the other person. They had forgiven for reasons of self-benefit or altruism but had not expressed a desire to restore the relationship, even though in some cases the offender had attempted to remedy the situation in some way.[42]

If a person does decide to reconcile (possible reconciliation), it is usually because the transgressor admits guilt for the relational transgression, perhaps accompanying the admission with an explanation. This creates the possibility that a relationship may be reopened and regrown between the two. Conditional reconciliation may occur when the transgressor communicates some level of regret for the offense and offers an apology. Processual reconciliation takes place as the offender attempts to remedy the harm done. Restoration is achieved as trust is rebuilt and the relationship is recreated.

If reconciliation is desired, the offended person may communicate her or his forgiveness to the transgressor. Sometimes, people do not state their forgiveness but simply behave in ways that communicate it. In doing so, the prior relationship is reestablished or converted into a different one. Trust rebuilds. And as trust rebuilds and the offender continues to act in trustworthy ways, the actions of each confirm that forgiveness and reconciliation have occurred; behavior constitutes the reality. The relationship between forgiveness and reconciliation is shown in Table 10.2. Where there is no forgiveness, reconciliation is, at best, a managed truce between people who try not to talk about the event. Where forgiveness is granted, reconciliation may not occur, but if it is, reconciliation can move through the levels discussed here.

Steps toward Reconciliation

In this section, we describe a series of steps for effectively managing a conflict situation in which an offender and the offended party attempt to work through the issues necessary for forgiveness and reconciliation, if desired by both parties.

Less relational transformation

No reconciliation, even if forgiveness has taken place

Possible reconciliation when offender admits culpability

Conditional reconciliation when offender communicates regret for the offense and offers an apology

Processual reconciliation offender attempts to remedy the harm done

Restoration when trust is rebuilt and the relationship is recreated

More relational transformation

FIGURE 10.2 Levels of Reconciliation

TABLE 10.2 Interrelationship of Forgiveness and Reconciliation

Forgiveness Not Granted		Forgiveness Granted	
No Reconciliation	**Pseudo-Reconciliation**	**No Reconciliation**	**Genuine Reconciliation**
• Event may be repressed, or alternatively, used to establish victim status • Bitterness • Lack of trust with similar others	• People interact but maintain distance • Event generally not discussed; if discussed, may be used as means of maintaining power • Blaming cycles • Often sets stage for further conflict	• Victim forgives for own sake • Event is reframed over time • Distance kept from offender, or interaction only under limited circumstances	• Victim forgives for own sake as well as for the sake of the relationship • Victim forgives because the offender is in need of forgiveness • Over time, victim sees other like self • Over time, victim sees self like other • Relationship is recreated

Step One: The Account and the Apology

The transgressor may explain her or his offensive behavior and offer an account and an apology. When people report to communication researchers that they have not forgiven the person who offended them, the primary reason for not forgiving is that they have not received an explanation and an apology from the other. Because the other has admitted no wrongdoing, they usually are not willing to forgive. In addition, people report refusal to forgive when the other continues the offensive behavior. Clearly, the process should begin with the transgressor understanding, recognizing, and admitting the offensive nature of his or her behavior; offer an account; follow the explanation with an apology; and ask for forgiveness. We say that this step is optional because not all offenders explain and apologize; where it is to one's advantage, the offended person may choose to forgive without the transgressor taking the first step.

As indicated above, except in cases of sexual infidelity and emotional attachment or intimacy (to someone else), research shows that people tend to let the transgressor off the hook by accepting accounts and apologies. In explaining behavior to the offended party, research indicates that the transgressors tend to rely most on justification or apology.

Step Two: Acceptance of Account and Apology or Its Absence

Here the offended person may chose to forgive the other if the transgressor has changed or is truly sorry for the transgression. The offended person makes a judgment call. Some people are willing to change, do in fact change, realize the errors of their ways, and are truly sorry for their transgressions, and others are clueless. The offended person needs to separate those who warrant forgiveness from those who do not. In deciding to forgive the other, the offended person must decide that it is a good idea to let go of any feelings of anger, resentment, and revenge.

An offended person may chose to forgive without any input from the offender. In the absence of an explanation and apology, the offended person may decide unilaterally that it is no longer in her or his best interests to continue feeling angry, resentful, and revengeful. Harboring such feelings is costly and drains one emotionally. Of course, when hurt by someone we trust and care for, it takes some time before we reach a point where we question the value of maintaining these feelings. If you are deciding to forgive without actually having discussed the transgression with the offender, it helps to keep these points in mind:

- With few exceptions, forgiveness is not equated with forgetting about the transgression.
- Forgiveness is generally conceived of as a process through which people move on with their lives after experiencing some hurt.
- Forgiveness involves reframing the event: One reframes the event so that it becomes less central in a person's life or in the life of a relationship.
- Forgiveness also includes reframing our perception of the other person: We see the person who hurt us in a different light. We may come to again value the other person—that is, we see that person as having worth regardless of the hurt he or she has caused us. We may see the other as equally precious. We may decide to trust again and take risks until it is seen by both people as authentic; however, forgiveness is not necessarily equated with the restoration of trust. We may love that person again.
- When we forgive, we recognize that we cannot change the past; we know that we can influence future events; we accept the fact that the past is past.

Step Three: Forgiveness May or May Not Be Communicated

At this point, the offended person decides whether or not to explicitly communicate his or her forgiveness to the offender. If it is not communicated explicitly, the offended person behaves in ways that imply forgiveness has taken place. In some cases, we may choose to restore or alter the relationship when the other person convinces us that he or she has truly changed or no longer poses a threat to us emotionally or physically. If we decide to restore the relationship eventually, then it is important to risk telling the other about our hurt. It is a risk because, as research shows, the other person may tell us that our feelings are not justified or that we have no right to feel hurt. Such an action makes it more difficult to forgive the other.

It is easier to forgive when the other person admits guilt or offers an account and an apology. Even so, depending on the offense, we may have a problem in trusting again. A frequently asked question is this: "Does this mean I have to trust the other person like I did before?" We think the answer is no unless the person earns your trust over time.

Injuries heal, and scars do remain. But the difference between forgiveness and simply moving on is that there are stories for where you have been. You neither ignore your scars nor focus on their ugliness. Injuries are not forgotten, but they do not always dictate the way you behave. We believe that forgiveness occurs when we no longer define our emotions, our desires, or our behaviors in terms of our injuries. Those scars become a part of us, not the whole of what we are.

Step Four: Transforming the Relationship, if Desired

If desired by the parties, reconciliation may result in a transformed relationship between the parties in the transgression—we may feel less enthusiasm than before, we may feel better than before, or we may create an entirely different type of a relationship. For example, a relational transgression is often a reason for separation between spouses. Let us assume that two spouses are unable to forgive one another and seek revenge in the courts, where they spend most of their financial assets; expend considerable time, effort, and emotion seeking revenge against each other; and reaffirm their negative opinions of the other spouse. She blames him for his infidelity and he blames her for laziness and squandering. The courtroom is filled with anger and resentment. They may think they have no reason to communicate or relate to one another ever again, and they may not have to if the divorce occurs early in their marriage as they have no children. However, suppose they were married several years and do have children. Issues related to alimony and child support may make it unlikely that the spouses can avoid each other in the years to come.

Let us say that in another case, a couple with children suffer a relational transgression followed by a temporary separation but then decide to "kiss and make up." In addition to forgiving each other, let us say that they also restore their relationship and continue as husband and wife. All assets remain in place, and the spouses continue as parents to their children. In this case forgiveness and reconciliation restored the relationship. Of course, the relationship may not be exactly the same, because the spouses may have agreed to some changes to the issues that led to the conflict in the first place, but we would say that in most respects life is continuing as before the blowup. If the couple is willing, though, the relationship can become stronger than it was before the transgression, but this takes considerable time and effort at reframing the transgression.

In still another case, let us consider a family where the spouses suffer a relational transgression and decide to forgive one another, but they want to convert their relationship (i.e., they no longer want to remain husband and wife). However, due to the need to maintain alimony and child support, they want to continue to work together in the future. They end up divorced but maintain open lines of communication and consult each other from time to time. Perhaps the ex-husband continues to maintain the residence where his ex-wife and children live. Maybe the ex-wife visits her ex-husband when he is ill or in the hospital. Maybe they decide to share the same home (not together), with each living there for six months, so that the children can remain in one school. While the nature of this relationship may vary in its degree of warmth, former spouses may redefine their relationships as friends who help each other, especially in times of need and as parents as they continue to take care of their children while separated physically.

Step Five: Actions Confirm Forgiveness and Reconciliation

The role played by actions is found in research examining **self-fulfilling prophecies,** in which people act toward us in the way that we expect. If you act toward the other as though he or she is not trustworthy, the other may begin to act in untrustworthy ways. If you act toward the other as though the relationship is strained, he or she may come to believe it is strained and act in ways that reflect this belief.

As discussed in the previous section, reconciliation does not mean you simply forget what happened, but you do move forward in your relationship, rebuilding trust and reestablishing intimacy. Acting in ways that signal forgiveness creates expectations of a renewed relationship or a different relationship and the possibility of change. Reconciliation means acting in ways that do not lock the present situation into constant reexamination of the offense.[43]

Social construction theory suggests that we make our social worlds by the way we talk about them, and we act within our social worlds based on the way we have made them through our talk. For example, a couple that is beginning to date might say, "We are just friends," and act accordingly. Later on, they may agree to move to a definition of "dating partners." This change in the definition of their relationship occurs with a change in their behavior toward one another. In a circular way, their affectionate behaviors increase because they change the definition of the relationship, and as the affectionate behaviors increase they give labels to their relationship that define it as more serious. Thus, in the communication–reality loop, the way we communicate about our behavior helps to constitute the reality of it. As we describe our behavior, we affect the way we behave; as we behave, we affect the way we describe our behavior.

The process of forgiveness and reconciliation works in the same way.

1. After forgiving one another, we tell each other that the act is forgiven, which allows us to act without reference to the offense.
2. In turn, we feel better about our relationship with one another and can talk about our relationship without reference to the offense.
3. In turn, our actions confirm what we said so that our behavior constitutes the reality of our forgiveness.

This approach highlights the role of communication in the aftermath of conflict and views forgiveness and reconciliation as social constructions: Those in a fractured or stressed relationship must create a meaning for the concept they term *forgiveness* and must create the actions necessary to make forgiveness seem real to them. Constructing reconciliation is the process of integrating what has become problematic into the realm of the unproblematic in relationships. Small conflicts may only cause people to temporarily pause and ask about the fit of the conflict into the total relationship. Transgressions interrupt their everyday reality, forcing them to reconcile vastly different pieces of the relationship. Accounts and apologies offer new definitions for the offense and its role within the relationship; reconciliation is the process of enacting that new definition so that it becomes permanent.

Thus, expressing forgiveness after conflict becomes a self-fulfilling prophecy when enacted correctly: We say forgiveness is possible; we act toward the other as though we have forgiven; the other, in turn, feels forgiven; and we are able to have a relationship that has moved beyond a relational transgression to where the transgression no longer defines the relationship. Here we have a communication process (involving verbal and nonverbal language, attributions, expectations, and confirmation) that is also a conflict resolution process. When any of these steps break down—if we say we forgive but do not act as though we have, or if we continue to refer to the offense as though it has not passed—forgiveness is almost impossible. Instead, we become victims of the relational transgression, and the transgression defines us and our relationship with the other. We can avoid the role of victim by forgiving and reconciling with the transgressor.

Although some therapists think that forgiveness is grasped quickly in some cases, most researchers in the field argue that the process of forgiveness takes time. The key in getting to the point of forgiveness is the ability to transform the meaning of the event that has occurred and to see it as an event among many in a relationship instead of the central event that defines the quality of the relationship. It is time-consuming and cannot occur if people are not willing to explore and reconcile the different feelings that arise as a result of transgressions.

MOVING BEYOND VICTIMIZATION

If reconciliation is not advisable, the offended person may forgive without engaging in communication with the transgressor. This is why we say that the reconciliation step is optional. One may chose to forgive without reconciling. In some cases, it is appropriate to forgive at a distance, so to speak, when the other person has not changed, has shown no willingness to change, continues to engage in offensive behavior, or poses harm to us mentally or physically. Under these conditions, contacting the other and becoming vulnerable again by expressing our anger and our hurt may cause more harm than good, so we forgive for our own sake—to let go of the offense, to move on with our lives, and to approach new relationships freely.

We tend to look for others outside of ourselves to blame. But it is the ability to move beyond **victimization** or the feeling of being a victim that leads to a state of forgiveness:

> We had a family friend who lived with us throughout my childhood years. He molested me numerous times over the course of my childhood. I never told my parents until long after he had died. I thought I had worked through most of my forgiveness issues when I found out that my parents had let him live with us knowing that he had served time in jail for child molesting. What were they thinking? How could they let him spend time alone with me? How couldn't they know? I had forgiven my molester, and I had stopped thinking of myself as a child abuse victim, but in some ways it was harder to forgive my parents.

You may never experience a traumatic event like physical or sexual assault, or have someone lie to you about an important issue.[44] In the course of your everyday conflicts, however, you may at times think you are victimized (used, manipulated, or abused) by another. Perhaps the feeling results from having secrets you told to the other in trust used as weapons against you later in a conflict. It may arise from having your personal possessions taken or destroyed.

Forgiveness is a process. It may take days, weeks, or years. Forgiveness allows us to act freely again. Without it, we are held by the event that victimized us; with it, we move forward.

> I am unable to forget the time I took a trust and openness class in which the topic was "Someone in my life whom I want to forgive." As a group exercise, we discussed the steps to forgiveness and then we each had to contribute a personal experience of unresolved and unforgiving conflict with someone. You would not believe what happened. Adult men and women alike told shocking stories of wrongs done to them, and they talked about their anger and rage. The facilitator told us that we have suffered long enough. He asked us to picture our antagonists as children. Picture what was being done to us as being done to them as little children. He said we know that people do to others that which was done to them often as children. He asked us to free them from their wrongs and see them as the wronged, needy people they are. Instead of distancing us from those who had wronged us, he brought us together as mutual victims who are suffering together. I have difficulty believing what then happened. There were changes and healing like I have never seen before. We were all overwhelmed by what was happening. Some cried, some held hands, some hugged the facilitator and then one another. I couldn't help but wonder what would happen if everyone in the world went through a group experience like this.

If you cannot disengage people from their past, you enslave yourself to an ugly emotional affair. You may have unresolved conflicts with others, especially with family members. These unforgiving experiences are now serving as a barrier between you and that person, preventing you from having the positive relationship both of you need. Someday you may realize that these people are only doing the best they know how. They brought "past baggage" with them. Now you are in a good position to drop the baggage you are carrying in favor of new tools. You no longer have to act based on your past. As you move forward in your new ways, you can also let go of your feelings that "justified" your old ways. You can stop seeking revenge and choose to forgive. A new outlook, it is hoped, alters or reestablishes a much needed relationship. If the other doesn't respond, drop it. Forgiveness is your benefit alone to enjoy.

SEEKING FORGIVENESS

An unfortunate side effect of the recent surge of research on forgiveness is its tendency to focus on the person doing the forgiving instead of the person seeking forgiveness. Part of the reason for this is that we tend to overestimate how badly we have been hurt by others and underestimate how badly we have behaved.

Ashby has suggested that seeking forgiveness mirrors some of the stages of forgiving. In the first stage, the person who has committed the offense against another experiences feelings of shame and guilt for the offense. Having experienced these feelings, in the second stage, the offender makes a decision to seek forgiveness. While we have a tendency to be judgmental about those who have hurt us, the decision to seek forgiveness in a genuine way is humbling to the offender and makes that person very vulnerable. In the third stage, the offender expresses remorse and repentance. This includes "apologizing, confession, taking on the pain of the other, making amends, and changed behavior." It is important that the offender acknowledge the extent of the impact that the offense had on the other. Sometimes it is impossible for the offender to make up to the injury he or she has caused to the other. All the offender can do is express a desire to restore whatever is possible to restore and sincerely demonstrate that such an offense will not happen in the future.

The final stage of seeking forgiveness is waiting, which in some cases may be the most difficult part. Just because a person has sought forgiveness in a sincere way, hoping to make amends, does not mean the other will accept the apology and render forgiveness. When this is the case, the best people can do is remind themselves that they have done the right thing and then let it go.

MANAGE IT

We believe that forgiveness is the most important part of conflict management. We can properly analyze a serious conflict involving relational transgressions, choose the right strategy, say all the right words, and come to an agreement without actually letting go of hurt associated with the conflict. If we cannot forgive the hurt and truly reconcile with the other person, and if we cannot transform the meaning of the event we have experienced, we tend to repeat our mistakes in ways that often become increasingly more destructive.

Why do we reengage in destructive conflict without forgiveness? The reason lies in the fact that relational transgressions involve core relational issues and leave emotional residues, such as abusing or cheating on romantic partners and lying to them or our friends.

Not every conflict necessitates our entry into forgiveness and reconciliation processes. But the conflicts that involve outcomes important to us in our intimate relationships almost certainly leave behind bad memories and bad feelings, including memories and feelings that we must come to terms with if we want to live differently in the future.

Forgiveness is a cognitive process that consists of letting go of feelings of revenge and desires to retaliate. We give up our right to change the future based on the past. While we may never forget a transgression, forgiveness begins with a decision to reduce our focus on event as a defining characteristic of our relationship with the other person, or indeed, our entire lives. The ability to move beyond victimization leads to a state of forgiveness.

Reconciliation is a behavior process in which we take actions to restore a relationship or create a new one. Once we forgive the other for the relational transgression, we do not have to reconcile unless we want to. We may wish to forgive at a distance and not communicate our forgiveness to the transgressor, or we may decide that we wish to reestablish a relationship or create a new one, so we choose to reconcile.

Critical to our understanding of both forgiveness and reconciliation is the understanding that they are not one-time events. Often, we return to an event cognitively and emotionally, but we deal with different parts of it. Like the ability to analyze conflicts and the ability to effectively communicate feelings and desires, the effective use of forgiveness and reconciliation strategies to cope with difficult conflicts characterizes the competent conflict manager. Through the processes of forgiveness and reconciliation, we can forge new relationships or repair former ones and move forward by letting go of the past. We must understand the kind of response necessitated by various transgressions and develop a repertoire of responses designed to remediate problematic situations. Of all the skills in conflict, we must learn how to put a conflict into perspective and move forward, otherwise our relationships become unstable; without forgiveness, our relationships eventually come to an end.

Think About It

1. Was there a time when a "truth bias" worked against you in a relationship? What kind of relationship was it? How were you deceived? In retrospect, does it seem as though you should have known the other was lying to you?
2. Is there an event in your life that you find difficult to forgive? What is it? What makes it so difficult to forgive the other person? If you are not experiencing a difficult event now, describe a past event that you found difficult to forgive.
3. Seven years ago a thief broke into your home, went through your personal belongings, and stole many of your possessions. He was caught, much of your property was returned to you (but some was damaged), and he was sentenced to seven years in a state prison. Are you now in a position to forgive him for what he did to you? Should we forgive all convicted felons after they serve their time in prison? Do you feel differently if the crime was committed against you? Would you feel differently if you were the one convicted?
4. Return to the incident you described above in 3. What would it take for you to forgive the other person? What are the consequences of forgiving the other person? Of not forgiving the other person?
5. Anne Lamott wrote that "not forgiving is like drinking rat poison and waiting for the rat to die."[45] Are there times when we should not forgive? How does this affect us?

Apply It

1. What constitutes a transgression in your relationships? Compare two relationships you are in, one with a close friend and one with an acquaintance, and list three transgressions.
2. Do an Internet search using the terms *forgiveness*, *reconciliation*, and *revenge*. What kinds of sites do you find? Which term produces more sites? Why do you think that is?
3. Write out a description of a conflict involving a relational transgression that moved through the reconciliation process. Describe what happened at each step of the process. How long did it take? Was it worth it to you? Why?
4. Watch a movie that features a relational transgression that occurs between two or more people. How does it follow the model of forgiveness and reconciliation that was presented in this chapter? Some suggestions for viewing (in alphabetical order): *Atonement, Changeling, Notes on a Scandal, The Painted Veil, There Will Be Blood.*

Work With It

Analyze the case study below in terms of the key ideas discussed in this chapter. You, personally, may not want to forgive anyone in this case study, but you are asked to take the necessary steps in forgiveness as an exercise to illustrate and apply the process. We selected a case study rather than have you describe an actual situation in your life so that you might analyze the conflict situation objectively and see ways to implement the suggestions in this chapter.

> Write an essay on the case study below in which you answer the following questions. What did Jeanne do that upset Mark? Does his behavior constitute a problematic situation or a relational transgression, and why? What probably makes it difficult for Mark to forgive Jeanne? What would he and she have to do for him to forgive her? Why would forgiveness and reconciliation help Mark? Apply the steps of forgiveness to this situation and describe what Mark must do at each step if he is to truly forgive her. Explain how he might forgive her but not forget the incident and change the nature of their sibling relationship.
>
> Everyone in my family is stupid about money. Some of us are more stupid than others. I've been trying to make things better and slowly but surely I'm working my way out of debt.
>
> My sister came to me two years ago and asked to borrow some money. She was desperate. She thought I could just take a loan against a credit card. I refused. I knew my wife would be furious if she knew I had lent the money as my sister already owes us thousands of dollars.
>
> She wouldn't let up. She actually came to my office to talk to me so my wife wouldn't know about it, and wouldn't leave. She finally convinced me to take out a loan through one of those pay-advance places that charges an enormous amount of interest. She promised me she would pay it back. Of course, she didn't. I had to take a loan from my retirement account to pay it back because the interest accumulated faster than I could

> pay it off. Naturally, my wife found out about it and she was furious, as I knew she would be.
> I feel like Charlie Brown when he listens to Lucy promise him that she'll hold the ball in place so he can kick it. She always pulls it away at the last moment and he winds up on the ground. I'm looking up at the sky wondering if I can ever trust her again, much less recover such a large amount of money. It really set my plans to retire debt back.

NOTES

1. Louis Smedes, *Forgive and Forget: Healing the Hurt We Don't Deserve* (San Francisco, CA: Harper & Row, 1984), p. 15.
2. Dudley D. Cahn, "Friendship, Conflict and Dissolution," in Harry T. Reis and Susan K. Sprecher (Eds.), *Encyclopedia of Human Relationships* (Thousand Oaks, CA: SAGE, 2009), http://www.sage-ereference.com/human relationships/Article_n226.html.
3. Sandra Metts, "Relational Transgressions," in William R. Cupach and Brian H. Spitzberg (Eds.), *The Dark Side of Interpersonal Communication* (Hillsdale, NJ: Lawrence Erlbaum, 1994), p. 4.
4. Everett L. Worthington, Jr., Suzanne E. Mazzeo, and Wendy L. Kliewer, "Addicting and Eating Disorders, Unforgiveness, and Forgiveness," *Journal of Psychology and Christianity* 21 (2002), 259, 257–261.
5. Donald Hope, "The Healing Paradox of Forgiveness," *Psychotherapy* 24 (1987), 242; see also Albert Ellis and Robert A. Harper, *A New Guide to Rational Living* (North Hollywood, CA: Wilshire Book Co., 1975), who claim that forgiving leaves us sane and realistic.
6. Ann Macaskill, John Maltby, and Liza Day, "Forgiveness of Self and Others and Emotional Empathy," *The Journal of Social Psychology* 142 (2002), 663, 663–665.
7. Donna S. Davenport, "The Functions of Anger and Forgiveness: Guidelines for Psychotherapy with Victims," *Psychotherapy* 28 (1991), 141, 140–144.
8. Human Development Study Group, "Five Points on the Construct of Forgiveness within Psychotherapy," *Psychotherapy* 28 (1991), 495, 493–496.
9. R. C. A. Hunter, "Forgiveness, Retaliation, and Paranoid Reactions," *Canadian Psychiatric Association Journal* 23 (1978), 167–173.
10. Janis Abrahms Spring with Michael Spring, *How Can I Forgive You?* (New York: Harper Collins, 2004), p. 15.
11. Heinz Kohut, "Narcissism and Narcissistic Rage," *The Psychoanalytic Study of the Child* 27 (1972), 379–392; Jared P. Pingleton, "The Role and Function of Forgiveness in the Psychotherapeutic Process," *Journal of Psychology and Theology* 17 (1989), 27–35.
12. Hope, "The Healing Paradox of Forgiveness," p. 240.
13. James G. Emerson, *The Dynamics of Forgiveness* (Philadelphia, PA: The Westminster Press, 1964), used the Rogers and Dymond q-sort test of emotional adjustment, adding items concerning feelings about one's ability to forgive (Carl R. Rogers and Rosalind F. Dymond, *Psychotherapy and Personality Change* [Chicago, IL: University of Chicago Press, 1954]).
14. Mary F. Trainer, "Forgiveness: Intrinsic, Role-Expected, Expedient, in the Context of Divorce" Doctoral dissertation, Boston University, 1984; Mellis I. Schmidt, "Forgiveness as the Focus Theme in Group Counseling" Doctoral dissertation, North Texas State University, 1986; John H. Hebl, "Forgiveness as a Counseling Goal with Elderly Females" Doctoral dissertation, University of Wisconsin, 1990.
15. John H. Hebl and Robert D. Enright, "Forgiveness as a Psychotherapeutic Goal with Elderly Females," *Psychotherapy* 30 (1993), 658–667.
16. R. H. Al-Mabuk, Robert D. Enright, and P. A. Cardis, "Forgiveness Education with Parentally Love-Deprived Late Adolescents," *Journal of Moral Education* 24 (1995), 427–444.
17. F. M. Luskin, K. Ginzburg, and Carl E. Thoresen, "The Efficacy of Forgiveness Intervention in College Age Adults: Randomized Controlled Study," *Humboldt Journal of Social Relations* 29 (2005), 163–184.
18. Suzanne Freedman and Robert D. Enright, "Forgiveness as an Intervention Goal with Incest Survivors," *Journal of Consulting and Clinical Psychology* 64 (1996), 983–992.
19. Scott R. Ross, Matthew J. Hertenstein, and Thomas A. Wrobel, "Maladaptive Correlates of the Failure to Forgive Self and Others: Further Evidence for a Two-Component Model of Forgiveness," *Journal of Personality Assessment* 88 (2007), 158–167.

20. Liza Day and John Maltby, "Forgiveness and Social Loneliness," *The Journal of Psychology* 139 (2005), 553–555.
21. Everett L. Worthington, Jr., Charlotte Van Oyen Witvliet, Pietro Pietrini, and Andrea J. Miller, "Forgiveness, Health, and Well-Being: A Review of Evidence for Emotional Versus Decisional Forgiveness, Dispositional Forgivingness, and Reduced Unforgiveness," *Journal of Behavioral Medicine* 30 (2007), 291–302.
22. Tobi Wilson, Aleks Milosevic, Michelle Carroll, Kenneth Hart, and Stephen Hibbard, "Physical Health Status in Relation to Self-forgiveness and Other-forgiveness in Healthy College Students," *Journal of Health Psychology* 13 (2008), 798–803.
23. James W. Carson, F. J. Keefe, V. Goli, A. M. Fras, T. R. Lynch, S. R. Thorp, and J. L. Buechler, "Forgiveness and Chronic Low Back Pain: A Preliminary Study Examining the Relationship of Forgiveness to Pain, Anger, and Psychological Distress," *The Journal of Pain* 6 (2005), 84–91.
24. R. Stoia-Caraballo, M. S. Rye, W. Pan, K. J. Brown Kirschman, C. Lutz-Zois, and A. M. Lyons, "Negative Affect and Anger Rumination as Mediators between Forgiveness and Sleep Quality," *Journal of Behavioral Medicine* 31 (2008), 478–488.
25. Judith A. Strasser, "The Relation of General Forgiveness and Forgiveness Type to Reported Health in the Elderly" Doctoral dissertation, Catholic University of America, 1984.
26. J. P. Friedberg, S. Suchday, and D. V. Shelov, "The Impact of Forgiveness on Cardiovascular Reactivity and Recovery," *International Journal of Psychophysiology* 65 (2007), 87–94; see also K. A. Lawler-Row, J. C. Karremans, C. Scott, M. Edlis-Matityahou, and L. Edwards, "Forgiveness, Physiological Reactivity and Health: The Role of Anger," *International Journal of Psychophysiology* 68 (2008), 51–58; Kathleen A. Lawler, Jarred W. Younger, Rachel L. Piferi, Eric Billington, Rebecca Jobe, Kim Edmondson, and Warren H. Jones, "A Change of Heart: Cardiovascular Correlates of Forgiveness in Response to Interpersonal Conflict," *Journal of Behavioral Medicine* 26 (2003), 373–393; Jeremy C. Anderson, Wolfgang Linden, and Martine E. Habra, "Influence of Apologies and Trait Hostility on Recovery from Anger," *Journal of Behavioral Medicine* 29 (2006), 347–358.
27. Kathleen A. Lawler, Jarred W. Younger, Rachel L. Piferi, Rebecca L. Jobe, Kimberley A. Edmondson, and Warren H. Jones, "The Unique Effects of Forgiveness on Health: An Exploration of Pathways," *Journal of Behavioral Medicine* 28 (2005), 157–167.
28. Roxane S. Lulofs, "Swimming Upstream: Creating Reasons for Unforgiveness in a Culture that Expects Otherwise," paper presented to the Speech Communication Association Convention, San Antonio, TX, November 1995.
29. Alexander G. Santelli, C. Ward Struthers, and Judy Eaton, "Fit to Forgive: Exploring the Interaction between Regulatory Focus, Repentance, and Forgiveness," *Journal of Personality and Social Psychology* 96 (2009), 381–394.
30. Julie Juola Exline and Ray F. Baumeister, "Expressing Forgiveness and Repentance: Benefits and Barriers," in Michael E. McCullough, Kenneth L. Pargament, and Carl E. Thorsen (Eds.), *Forgiveness: Theory, Research, and Practice* (New York: The Guilford Press, 2000), 133–155.
31. Macaskill, Maltby, and Day, "Forgiveness of Self and Others and Emotional Empathy", see also Varda Konstam, Miriam Chernoff, and Sara Deveney, "Toward Forgiveness: The Role of Shame, Guilt, Anger and Empathy," *Counseling and Values* 46 (2001), 26–39.
32. Loren Toussaint and Jon R. Webb, "Gender Differences in the Relationship between Empathy and Forgiveness," *The Journal of Social Psychology* 145 (2005), 673–685.
33. Julie Juola Exline, Roy F. Baumeister, Anne L. Zell, Amy J. Kraft, and Charlotte V. O. Witvliet, "Not So Innocent: Does Seeing One's Own Capability for Wrongdoing Predict Forgiveness?" *Journal of Personality and Social Psychology* 94 (2008), 495–515.
34. Michael J. Subkoviak, Robert D. Enright, Ching-Ru Wu, Elizabeth A. Gassin, Suzanne Freedman, Leanne M. Olson, and Issidoros Sarinopolous, "Measuring Interpersonal Forgiveness," paper presented at the American Educational Research Association Convention, San Francisco, April 1992.
35. Doris Donnelly, *Learning to Forgive* (Nashville, TN: Abingdon Press, 1979).
36. James N. Sells and Leslie King, "A Pilot Study in Marital Group Therapy: Process and Outcome," *Family Journal* 10 (2002), 156–166.
37. Smedes, *Forgive and Forget*, p. 15.
38. Alex H. S. Harris, Frederic Luskin, Sonya B. Norman, Sam Standard, Jennifer Bruning, Stephanie Evans, and Carl E. Thoresen, "Effects of a Group Forgiveness Intervention on Forgiveness, Perceived Stress, and Trait-Anger," *Journal of Clinical Psychology* 62 (2006), 729, 715–733.
39. J. W. Younger, R. L. Piferi, R. L. Jobe, and K. A. Lawler, "Dimensions of Forgiveness: The Views of Laypersons," *Journal of Social and Personal Relationships* 21 (2004), 837–856.

40. Everett L. Worthington, Jr., *Forgiving and Reconciling* (Downer's Grove, IL: InterVarsity Press, 2003), p. 25.
41. Jeanne Moskal, *Blake, Ethics, and Forgiveness* (Tuscaloosa, AL: University of Alabama Press, 1994), p. 9.
42. Lulofs, "Swimming Upstream."
43. For further reading on forgiveness after serious offenses, see Ruth Anna Abigail, "Forgiving the Unforgivable? Processes of Forgiveness and Reconciliation after Episodes of Family Violence," in Dudley D. Cahn (Ed.), *Family Violence: Communication Perspectives* (New York: SUNY Press, 2009).
44. For those who have experienced childhood trauma, two excellent resources are James E. Kepner, *Healing Tasks: Psychotherapy with Adult Survivors of Childhood Abuse* (San Francisco, CA: Jossey-Bass, 1995); and Gina O'Connell Higgins, *Resilient Adults: Overcoming a Cruel Past* (San Francisco, CA: Jossey-Bass, 1994).
45. Anne Lamott, *Traveling Mercies* (New York: Anchor Books, 1999), p. 134.

CHAPTER 11

Managing Others' Disputes through Mediation

OBJECTIVES

At the end of this chapter, you should be able to:

- Define mediation and contrast it with the other alternatives to dispute resolution (ADRs).
- Describe the difference between formal and informal mediation.
- Explain when a third party should intervene as a mediator.
- Describe the role of the mediator.
- List and describe the steps of mediation.

KEY TERMS

adjudication
ADRs
arbitration
behavioral commitments
caucus
common ground
conciliation
dispute
fractionation
framing
intake
mediation
mediator
ombudsperson
opening statement
reframing
rules

Till now, we have concentrated on those concepts, principles, and skills that are most useful when you are personally involved in a conflict with someone you know. You can apply what you have learned so far to better manage or resolve the conflicts you yourself are having with others.

This chapter is different in that it focuses on what you need to know to help others who are having a conflict. Perhaps they invite you as a third party to intervene on their behalf. The nature of the conflict is different because it is one that the conflicting parties cannot handle by themselves. They need the help of a third party—a role you can perform after you study the subject of mediation.

In this chapter, we apply the principles taught in formal mediation training to the management of conflicts in informal or everyday settings. Basic information is provided on mediation concepts, skills, steps, and techniques, so that you can help your friends, family, and coworkers resolve their interpersonal conflicts. However, if you want to practice mediation on a more formal basis, you need certification, which means mediation training by an approved university program or state agency. For our purposes, you need to learn how to explain the alternatives to dispute resolution (ADRs), define mediation and dispute, describe the role of the mediators, explain when it is useful to include mediators in conflict situations, explain the advantages and limitations of mediation, and effectively perform the steps you would take to mediate an informal dispute. We begin first with an overview of the dispute resolution process in which mediation is one alternative.

ALTERNATIVES TO DISPUTE RESOLUTION

Mediation is one alternative to what is called dispute resolution. In fact, you cannot fully appreciate the idea of mediation without first understanding the concept of a dispute. A **dispute** is defined as "a conflict that has reached a point where the parties are unable to resolve the issue by themselves due to a breakdown in communication, and normal relations are unlikely until the dispute is resolved."[1] Not all conflicts are alike. Conflicts become disputes when participants realize that they confront a communication barrier, preventing normal relations. The parties seek help from a third party because they cannot resolve the issues by themselves.

When a dispute occurs, the conflicting parties sometimes resort to violent means. Our prisons are full of people who took "justice" into their own hands by taking violent action against someone with whom they disagreed. For those who use their heads instead of their fists and guns, the following alternatives to dispute resolution (**ADRs**) exist:

- **Arbitration:** a neutral third party considers both sides of a dispute and makes a decision, which is more binding than that of a judge in the legal system if both parties have agreed in advance to abide by the decision (no appeal).
- **Adjudication:** a neutral judge and jury in the legal system hear attorneys who prosecute or defend people and decide a case, which either party may later appeal.
- **Ombudsperson:** one who cuts through the red tape on behalf of individuals who feel abused by the larger system (often governmental agencies) in which they work, study, or seek support.
- **Conciliation:** a neutral third party practices "shuttle diplomacy" by traveling back and forth between conflicting parties who are unable to meet together for any one of a variety of reasons.
- **Mediation:** a neutral third party facilitates communication between the conflicting parties so that they may work out their own mutually acceptable agreement.

We are focusing on mediation in this chapter because many studies have found that mediation produces superior results to adjudication.[2] It is less costly than other ADRs. If one disputant thinks he or she is better off pursuing a legal recourse through the courts, for example, it can greatly increase the costs to the other person. Mediation conducted well reduces the likelihood that either of the disputants will seek legal remedy. Most importantly, it also has unique advantages that appeal to communication scholars:

1. Mediators help to restore communication and normalize relations.
2. Mediation allows for full participation by the conflicting parties.

3. Mediation has a high success rate. It is estimated that "once the disputants have agreed to mediate, at least 80% of the time they are able to work out an agreement that is acceptable to both of them."[3]

FORMAL VERSUS INFORMAL MEDIATION

As it turns out, there are cultural differences in mediation[4] and several different approaches to mediation, each with its own set of techniques, but the approach advocated here does not require the mediators to take sides, engage in psychotherapy, or play the role of advocate. Rather, mediators are viewed here as unbiased facilitators of communication between the parties in a private setting. In many formal settings where it is normally more satisfying, cheaper, and faster than litigation, this form of mediation has become a popular alternative. In such formal settings, one party typically calls a local mediation center for a mediation, and a first meeting between the parties and mediators usually occurs within the next few days or weeks. In any case, community and school mediations are often free or offered on a sliding scale that is cheaper than lawyers' fees.

In formal mediations, satisfactory agreements are often worked out at a single mediation session lasting 1–3 hours, although complex cases such as divorce settlements involving child custody may require weekly sessions until all the details are worked out. Disputing parties are often more satisfied with mediated agreements than they are with the courtroom decisions of judges and juries and are more likely to comply with mediated agreements than they are to court orders because they have more control in the resolution of their dispute.

There are formal programs that train and certify mediators. Community and campus dispute resolution centers offer mediation for a wide range of conflicts including noisy neighbors, sexual and racial harassment, minor assault, breach of contract, landlord–tenant and buyer–seller disputes, small claims, bad checks, trespassing, and a variety of interpersonal issues such as gossip and rumors, misunderstandings, friendship issues, and post-breakup disputes. Although experience has shown that it is beneficial, mediation is still relatively unused in union labor disputes.[5] Mediation is a method of parental intervention in children's disputes.[6] Rapidly becoming a popular alternative to the courts,[7] divorce mediation is a branch of family mediation that deals with issues associated with child custody, visitation, child financial support, and the redistribution of marital property. Today, divorce mediation training is offered to workers from a wide variety of occupations, including family law attorneys[8] and family counselors and therapists.[9] However, communication among the mediator and disputants lies at the basis of all these mediation training programs. Before one can deal with child custody, emotional issues associated with divorce, the children's interests, or dispose of marital property, the mediator must create a communication climate that is conducive to a mutually satisfactory settlement. This can be particularly difficult with parents who use children as a bargaining chip in divorce proceedings.[10] Among experts in mediation, there is a concern with the growing number of lawyers involved in mediation processes. They note,

> . . . some lawyers are approaching mediation in the same way as litigation, by using adversarial techniques within the process. If the parties relinquish their autonomy in choosing the way mediation is conducted, then . . . .[m]ediation may in the long term not provide a

"true" alternative to litigation . . . introduction of procedural conventions, increasing adversarial conduct and rising mediation costs are, perhaps, an inevitable downside of evaluative mediator practice as, parties select leading lawyer-mediators.[11]

For those who have gone through formal training, it is clear that it offers a practical application of many skills taught in undergraduate interpersonal communication and conflict management courses. In the following sections, we apply the formal mediation process to the management of everyday conflicts. First, we focus specifically on the role of the mediator.

THE ROLE OF THE MEDIATOR

The **mediator** is defined as a neutral third party who has no decision-making power regarding the outcome of the mediation. Although it may seem as though the mediator plays only a minor role, the mere introduction of a third person converts a private affair into a matter of social concern. Compared to private conflicts that tend to occur in the privacy of one's own home or involve only the partners themselves, mediation brings conflict to a social, public, and cultural level. The Chinese refer to this phenomenon as "the principle of three."[12] From the Chinese perspective, a culture of two is not a public affair and encourages a win–lose situation when two individuals engage in conflict. However, in a culture of three, the third party is there to remind the disputants that their behaviors are being viewed by others, thus bringing the behavior under social control and increasing the likelihood of social justice. The mere presence of mediators enables them to encourage cooperation rather than competition, strive for reasonable decisions that meet social concerns, and create and enforce rules to guide the interaction.

In informal situations, people can help others without their being formally trained and certified. Thus, everyone can benefit from receiving training that is available to the general public and is similar to that required for certification. The focus on mediators' attitudes, skills, and knowledge can form a basis for orienting third parties to their role as mediator. Basically, mediators attempt to create a safe and constructive environment to encourage the disputants to communicate, cooperate, and work out their own mutually satisfying solution.

Who should take the role of the "third person" and function as the mediator? In the view that dominates mediation, mediators are expected to be neutral. This means that mediators are unbiased, and there is no reason for them to take one party's side against the other. In formal or informal cases, it is not a good idea to mediate if one knows one party better than the other. Mediators must also make every effort to demonstrate their neutrality by equalizing the speaking time, giving the same amount of time and attention to both parties, and not spending time alone with one of the parties without spending the same amount of time with the other during the mediation. Certainly, mediators are not to take sides in the dispute.

Another approach to the role of the mediator has been developed through the Center for Mediation and Law at Harvard Law School. In their view, the mediator should develop a "subjective neutrality," in which he or she honors the validity and truth of each person's story without deciding who is right or wrong.[13]

Second, because mediation offers the disputants an opportunity to openly talk to each other about their feelings, needs, goals, and reasons for behaving as they do, mediators must maintain confidentiality. They are not to make public the names of the conflicting parties, disclose the words spoken during the mediation, or retain notes after terminating mediation. In formal cases, trained mediators learn rules that cover a few legal exceptions, which they include in their opening remarks and make explicit on the mediation consent form, which is signed by both parties before mediation begins. In informal settings, mediators can simply state in their opening remarks that the mediation is considered confidential and ask the parties if they can agree to keep what is said "among us." It is this guarantee of confidentiality that makes self-disclosure possible in mediation.

Third, the mediators are competent in communication. In practice, you must manifest these effective communication behaviors:

- Be descriptive rather than judgmental. (e.g., you might say, "It seems like you are raising your voice," rather than "It sounds like you are angry.")
- Be specific. (e.g., "You have mentioned how bothered you are by your colleague's work habits. What specific habit bothers you the most?")
- Focus on behaviors that one can change.
- Give feedback when it is requested.
- Give timely feedback making it as close as possible to the behavior being discussed.
- Speak only for yourself. (e.g., "I understand you to say . . . " "I take it that you feel . . . " "I want you both to . . . " "I prefer to keep my opinions to myself.")
- Check what you see or hear with the other parties.[14]

Fourth, mediators are trained to facilitate communication by encouraging cooperation and discouraging competition between the parties.[15] Essentially, a mediator's objective is to create a safe and constructive environment for the parties to discuss emotional and substantive issues and reach agreement. The process of mediation is successful to the extent that it moves from a competitive to a cooperative orientation because competition creates a defensive communication climate and cooperation creates a supportive atmosphere. Competitive communication is self-promoting because it serves as a vehicle through which individuals attempt to distort the other's perceptions of the situation in order to gain an advantage. A cooperative orientation consists of behaviors characteristic of organized action (e.g., working together) and a thought process known as consensus (e.g., shared understanding, actual agreement). It also facilitates attempts to discover areas of common interest regarding issues.

Fifth, mediators have no decision-making power with respect to the outcome of the mediation. Initially, the parties often have expectations about the role of the mediators such as expecting them to solve their problems. Mediators must resist the temptation to solve the disputants' problem and need to inform the parties that they have no authoritative decision-making power.[16] However, because many disputants who entered mediation have found it difficult to communicate, relate, or work with each other in the past, mediators instruct the conflicting parties in constructive communication by announcing and enforcing communication rules. This topic is described in detail in the next section.

We just described the role of the mediator. To understand how mediators gain control over the mediation process to produce mutually satisfying outcomes, we need to examine in detail a particular approach to mediation known as the rules or structural approach and the mediator's responsibility as a communication rules enforcer.

Mediators as Communication Rules Enforcers

To appreciate the idea that mediators primarily control the communication process to give them greater influence over the outcome of the interaction, one must understand how mediators are trained to create and enforce communication rules. **Rules** are obligations (they tell us what we must say, what we should say) and prohibitions (they tell us what we had better not say in certain situations). Many of the rules we abide by were learned through our families and other important people in our lives; for example, many of us learned that "If you can't say something nice, don't say anything at all" (which may be a reason so many people dislike conflict). At other times, we know a rule has been broken because others call our attention to our behavior with direct comments or indirect behaviors such as glaring at us or moving away. For example, at a friend's wedding, it is customary to congratulate the groom and convey best wishes to the bride. Saying "congratulations" to the bride is considered in poor taste, and if you do so, others may give you a disapproving look. The rule is there, but it is not a strong one because so many people forget and get away with congratulating brides. On the other hand, laughing at a funeral is almost unheard of. It is prohibited, and anyone who breaks the rule gets escorted out of the room.

Thus, a pattern of behavior is rule-governed when there exists mutual expectations or a consensus regarding what is appropriate behavior in a given situation. Although rules are social conventions, which are violated or changed by individuals or groups, it is argued that when people know the rules, they tend to conform to them. Mediation is viewed as a structured social activity guided and defined by rules designed to convert competitive orientations and actions into cooperative ones.

In their opening statements, mediators lay down the communication rules for the mediation.

- They enforce those communication rules.
- They steer the disputants through the steps of mediation.
- They manage the tone of the discussion.
- They ask disputants to cease discussing some topics and focus on others.

It is no accident that even early practice in divorce mediation was based on a rules approach.[17] As communication rules enforcers, mediators establish and enforce the rules by which participants interact. Some common rules that are useful for directing the communication process toward positive outcomes are as follows:

- taking turns to talk without interruptions
- talking without expressing hostility to one another
- creating a positive climate with no put-downs
- focusing on the future (what the parties will do) rather than the past (what was done)
- striving for a win–win solution with no one feeling dissatisfied or agreeing to something unacceptable
- striving to solve the problem rather than attacking or blaming the other person

- being honest and sharing your thoughts and feelings without fear of criticism or publicity
- adhering to time constraints set by mediator
- agreeing to abide by additional rules as announced by the mediator during the session

Anxious to delve into an actual mediation? You first need to study the steps mediators take from the beginning to the end of the mediation.

THE MEDIATION PROCESS: STEP BY STEP

In an effort to pull together much of the advice and principles of mediation, we have devised a list of steps that are common to mediating both (1) formal disputes conducted by certified mediators in divorce, community, or organizational settings and (2) informal disputes conducted by noncertified (but trained) third parties in family, friendship, or workplace settings. Once the conflicting parties realize that a dispute exists, the following steps are taken:

- One or both disputants seek mediation, or mediators talk them into it (the intake process).
- The mediators bring the disputants together and make an opening statement.
- Following the mediators' opening statement, they ask each person to take a few minutes to describe the dispute from his or her point of view without interruption.
- The mediators find common ground on which to build agreement.
- The mediators write up the final agreement.
- The mediators end the mediation.

In the rest of this chapter, we explain and illustrate these steps in detail. Let us begin with the fact that the conflicting parties realize that a dispute exists. This is to say that they are at a point where they realize that they cannot manage the conflict without help. They initiate the mediation process by taking the first step, which means requesting that someone take the role of a third party and mediate their conflict.

Intake

In formal mediation, the preliminary phase in which the parties seek help from a third person who decides to intervene is called **intake.** While informal mediations are often less methodical and sometimes seem quite chaotic initially, the parties eventually end up with someone who agrees to help them resolve the dispute. They may engage in "intake" without calling it that.

The decision to include a third party to mediate the conflict is an important one and involves the realization that such a person is necessary and that the parties must pick an appropriate person for the role. Both disputants may seek help from a third person, who becomes the mediator. If only one seeks help, the third person may contact the other disputant to see if she or he is agreeable to mediating the dispute. If neither disputant seeks help, a third person who is aware of the dispute may contact the disputants to see if they are agreeable to mediating the dispute. Asking to intervene in the conflict of others, however, should be done carefully. Uninvited mediation may seem like meddling rather than help.

Who should take the role of the "third person" and function as the mediator? As discussed above, mediators are neutral and unbiased, have no decision-making power with respect to the outcome of the mediation, must maintain confidentiality, communicate with competence, and encourage cooperation and discourage competition between the parties. This rules out people who are more involved with or familiar with only one of the conflicting parties, those who think they know what is best for the parties and dominate the mediation by talking most and advising them, people who can't keep secrets, who are not competent communicators, or those who encourage competition between the parties.

Opening Statement

Obviously, if mediation is to take place, mediators must arrange for a first meeting with the disputants where they make an opening statement. After all, mediators are responsible for initiating, managing, and terminating the mediation sessions. Mediators must select a location free of interruptions and distractions. The conflicting parties should sit and face one another with the mediators at the end of the table.

At the first meeting, mediators make an **opening statement,** where they explain the purpose and process of mediation, including their role as facilitators of communication and lay out the communication rules that structure the mediation. Mediators also use the initial remarks as an opportunity to re-establish communication between the disputants and redirect it in a more positive direction. At this initial meeting, mediators make the following rules clear to the disputants:

- That their participation in mediation is voluntary and the mediator or conflicting parties may terminate it at any time.
- That the mediator is unbiased (impartial toward either disputant).
- That what is said in mediation is confidential.
- That the goal is a written agreement with which both parties are satisfied or at least comfortable.
- That the disputants are to trying to work out a mutual agreement between them with the help of the mediator, who is an unbiased facilitator of discussion and does not make decisions for the disputants (not a judge or jury).

The mediators also inform the participants that they are to adhere to a few communication ground rules to include the following:

- The parties are encouraged to talk to and look at one another rather than at the mediator.
- The parties are asked to take turns talking without interruptions.
- The parties are required to adhere to time constraints set by the mediator.
- The parties are asked to strive to solve the problem rather than attack or blame the other person. Mediators have to help the parties learn to talk without expressing hostility to one another and to create a positive climate with no put-downs (focus on the problem, not the other person).

- The parties are encouraged to focus on the future (what they can do) rather than the past (what was done).
- The parties are told that they can openly share thoughts and feelings without fear of criticism or publicity.
- The parties are required to strive for a win–win solution with no one feeling dissatisfied or agreeing to something either party finds unacceptable.
- The parties are asked to agree to abide by additional rules as announced by the mediator during the session.

All of this sounds like a lot for an opening statement, and it is. Sometimes not everything is included in the opening statement, but the mediators add to it as the mediation continues. As you gain experience mediating, you can keep the opening statement to essentials and then add the other rules and suggestions later as the need arises.

Note the essential items that the mediator chose to include in the following opening statement. Do you agree with his or her choice?

> I am glad that you both decided to try mediation and am pleased that you have asked me to help out here by serving as mediator. Let me start off by saying that your participation is entirely voluntary. I don't see any reason to say anything to others, so if you want to keep what we say just among us, that is fine with me. Is that what you want to do? OK, my role here is to help you work out your own agreement, one that you both feel comfortable with. In addition to not making your decisions for you, I must avoid siding with either of you or showing any favoritism. I may stop you to ask you questions, and I may make some notes, so that I can keep track of the issues and help you write up a mutually acceptable agreement. During the session, I may have to establish some ground rules. For example, let's agree right off not to engage in any name calling, and if the conflict escalates, I'll have to stop the session.
>
> I am going to ask each of you to tell us your side of the story, while I try to write down the key points, so we can discuss them. When one of you is talking, the other is not to interrupt. Are there any questions? If not, let's begin with Marisa. After hearing your side of the story, Georgia can tell us hers.

Describing the Dispute

Mediators usually begin with the person who initiated the complaint against the other. For example, a neighbor who is upset about the other neighbor playing basketball in the driveway early in the morning, which annoys him, is probably the person who initiates the complaint (against the noisy neighbor). This person describes the problem from his or her point of view, explaining what happened and how she or he feels about it. The other person listening must not interrupt the speaker, but must hear out the speaker in his or her entirety. As soon as the first party finishes the opening statement, mediators ask the other party to explain what happened from her or his point of view, again without interruption. After each opening statement, mediators summarize back to the disputant the issues raised and how the mediators believe that the disputant feels about them. Mediators ask for confirmation of their summary from that disputant, and sometimes ask disputants to summarize what they heard from the other party. From these opening remarks, mediators identify the issues that are to comprise the agenda for discussion. At this early stage of the mediation, mediators may tolerate some venting of feelings for a short period to help get them out of one's system, but later they discourage the strong expression of feelings, which can escalate the conflict.

Sometimes it is useful for mediators to **caucus,** in which the mediator steps aside with one disputant for a private discussion to request the disclosure of information that the disputant doesn't want to make in the presence of the other. This technique is especially useful when the parties are at an impasse. In the private meeting, the mediator may help one of the parties to better understand how to contribute more positively to the discussion. To maintain an unbiased position, it is important that the mediator meets with both parties, separately of course, for about the same amount of time. Mediators should ask permission from each party before introducing into the discussion something disclosed in the caucus.

The following case might be a good place to caucus. The description of the dispute revealed the following:

> These two disputants are romantic partners, living in the same house and relying on only one car to drive to campus and town. Robert decided that he needed a "break" from his involvement with Cherene, which she initially agreed to. He wanted to stay in the same house (and move to another bedroom) and share the car. They had shared a bank account, but he withdrew half of the money and opened a new account of his own. Cherene had originally signed for the apartment, so she felt obligated to pay the rent, but she didn't have enough money now in her account to pay the bills unless he would give her his share of the expenses, and lately he became reluctant to do so. As time went on, she continued to act as his primary romantic interest even though he was looking to distance himself from her. That is why she told everyone she knew that "everything was fine between them." Consequently, he became more and more aggravated with her actions and his reactions hurt her a great deal. When he said that he might bring home other female friends of his, she told him that he better not do that, or she would do some serious damage to the car (which was originally his). Robert had met her parents, and they were visiting this weekend. Because they liked him, she didn't want to tell them about Robert's recent behavior. There is a lot of miscommunication between the two since and the situation is progressively getting worse with many quarrels and screaming matches.

In this situation, the mediator might want to caucus with each person and ask him or her how one truly feels about the other person and the relationship. Do they love each other? Do they want out of the relationship entirely but don't know how to do it? Each person may not want to talk about these feelings in the presence of the other but may open up to the mediator. The mediator might help convince the other person to strive for more openness and honesty later when they resume the mediation.

Common Ground

Mediation sessions usually begin with a broad and confused discussion of issues seen from competitive orientations, but when mediators are successful, the discussion proceeds to more detailed and specific statements out of which cooperation and consensus (shared meanings) emerge. The techniques mediators use are fractionation, framing, reframing, and common ground.

Mediators begin with the easiest issues to resolve, leaving the most difficult for last. While thinking about the issues and discussing them, the mediators may rely on a useful technique for resolving conflict over an issue called **fractionation,** which we defined on page 97 as breaking down complex issues into smaller, more manageable ones. After separating issues into their smallest components, the mediators can ask the disputants to deal with each issue one at a time, which builds a feeling of success on small issues, until the larger issues are successfully resolved.

Another technique is known as **framing,** where mediators ask neutral or friendly questions that avoid blame or passing judgment and summarize issues. One more technique is **reframing,** where mediators restate negatively loaded, biased, or accusatory statements made by one of the parties in more neutral terminology or restate positions in a way that makes the disputants look at the issues differently. Finally, mediators highlight **common ground,** which consists of attitudes, values, behaviors, expectations, and goals the parties share and can serve as a basis for an agreement.

As soon as it seems appropriate, the mediators ask the parties what they want as an outcome of the dispute. Sometimes people do not know what they want and need time and encouragement to determine what they want. Once the wants are expressed, sometimes the opposing party discovers that the want is not what she or he expected to hear or as extreme as originally thought. This clarification of wants may lead to a quick settlement, but oftentimes it does not. In any case, the mediators succeed in getting the positions on the table as soon as possible.

Because the parties' interests and needs are broader than their specific positions or wants (see Chapter 5 for a discussion of interests versus positions), the mediators facilitate discussion of the interests that lie behind positions taken by the disputants. For example, the mediators discover that the complaining neighbor wants the other neighbor to stop playing basketball, but what he really needs is to sleep in mornings without noise and interruption. However, the opposing neighbor says he wants to play basketball in the morning, but what he really needs is practice at shooting baskets sometime most days. As it turns out, he doesn't really need to shoot baskets in the early morning.

In addition to discovering interests and needs, the mediators also reframe the disputants' statements and positions. The mediators do this by helping the parties restate their comments in less offensive language and reword their utterances as proposals. For example, the mediators might say, "You say that your neighbor's basketball is keeping you awake in the early morning, but are you asking that he play later in the day instead?"

As the discussion progresses, the mediators request proposals or solutions to the problem that would satisfy the interests and needs of both parties. The mediators also help the parties brainstorm alternative proposals. In many group communications, students of communication learned how to brainstorm solutions to problems. The idea is not to criticize or limit the proposals in any way, but simply to create as long a list as possible. Sometimes one suggestion, even if corny or ridiculous, triggers the parties to think of something better. Brainstorming plays an important role in expanding the range of options for reaching an agreement.

Throughout the discussion, mediators identify, highlight, and reinforce points of agreement, encourage positive contributions, and show attentiveness by responding verbally or nonverbally to comments by both parties. This positive feedback encourages the parties to continue the mediation and work toward agreement.

Try seeking common ground, perhaps as a member of a small group. Consider the list of issues you discovered from the above case study, involving a dispute between two romantic partners, Robert and Cherene. See if you can fractionate any of the issues into subissues. Then brainstorm solutions to the problem. Determine a list of points you think the two might agree on.

Final Agreement

Usually, the mediator keeps track of areas of agreement as the mediation progresses, so that eventually she or he has a rough draft of all points of consensus. Mediators learn early on in their training that wording of these commonalities is important. While it helps to list the different points of agreement, mediators need to employ the following format and say that "X agrees to this . . . Y agrees to that . . . " Mediators attempt to keep the agreement simple. They use clear, specific details (spelling out who, what, where, when, how). It helps to think of the agreement as a list of **behavioral commitments** because it enumerates the specific observable actions each party needs to take to fulfill the agreement. When there are co-mediators, one usually takes the responsibility of keeping track of this list of behaviors, while the other encourages the conflicting parties to communicate effectively. In developing the agreement, mediators should strive for balance or "something for everyone." The agreement also needs to address questions of feasibility and practicality because the parties should find the agreement workable. Finally, the culminating step occurs when the mediators ask both parties to sign the agreement.

Because it is important that mediators take a neutral role, they should not comment positively or negatively about areas of agreement. Mediators are not the ones agreeing to the behavioral commitments, so they should refrain from commenting one way or another. This is not a negotiation in which both are trying to win the most they can from one another. Sometimes, one party settles for less than expected in a mediation simply because he or she knows that the other is more likely to live up to the agreement. Of course, mediators can raise questions of feasibility. Is this idea doable? Can each of you actually do this?

In the following scenario, we offer an initial draft of the behavioral commitments as an example.

> Daria, who is a communication major and college senior living at home, often finds herself in the middle when her mother and her teenage sister engage in conflict. Both have come to rely on her to help them resolve their conflicts (or play the role of mediator). In this case, the sister wants more freedom and responsibility, which her mother is against before the mediation.

After facilitating the mediation, in which both parties explain their views, Daria, who has kept track of areas of consensus during the mediation, drafts an agreement as follows:

Agreement between Mother and Sister dated _____.

Mother agrees to not wait up for the sister to return when out with friends or on a date on Friday and Saturday nights.

Sister agrees to tell her mother whom she is with, the places they plan to go, and return home by 1 a.m.

Mother agrees that sometimes plans change and sister may go places not originally intended.

Sister agrees to not go to places that her mother is concerned about (namely, Mr. G's in town, Mathew's home when his parents aren't there, Linsey's home when her parents aren't there).

Mother agrees to stop criticizing her boyfriend to his face.

Sister agrees to come home by 10 p.m. on school nights.

Mother agrees to let her use her car in cases where she has to meet her friends.

Sister agrees to not drive and drink alcohol.

Signed by _____ and _____ (Sister)

Witnessed by _____ (Daria as mediator)

As you consider the above case, keep these points in mind. First, as mediator, Daria personally may not think this is a good agreement. She may think the mother is too strict or too lenient or the daughter too young or too old, but as mediator, she is not the one who is bound by this agreement. If this is what the mother and sister agree to, then Daria should keep her opinions to herself and encourage the two parties. Second, although the sister probably initiated the complaint, Daria tried to balance the agreement so that each party leaves the mediation with something she wants. Also, rather than say something vague or indefinite, such as "Mother doesn't want sister going out just any old time, staying out as late as she wants, or going to places that she doesn't approve of," Daria strove for specificity by clarifying the exact days, times, and places or people by name. Finally, Daria kept responsibilities clear by using the simple format, "X agrees to do . . . Y agrees to do . . . " Although mediators don't keep notes of the mediation after it is terminated, Daria may want to keep a copy of the agreement for future reference if the participants think that is a good idea or do not object.

Ending the Mediation

The mediators give each disputant a copy of the handwritten, signed agreement. Where appropriate, the mediators set up a date for reviewing and evaluating the agreement. They thank the parties for using mediation and wish them well. Unlike formal mediation, the mediators in an informal dispute usually do not need to file paperwork, have the agreement typewritten, or mail it to the disputants.

The agreement, whether written or not, culminates the process of mediation. The process as a whole works well in many everyday situations. Even young children can learn conflict mediation, making a difference in their lives and the lives of those around them.[18]

Following training in mediation in class, some students of one of the authors made comments such as these:

> I could relate to this subject because it reinforced my training as a Resident Assistant on campus. I have dealt with different issues in the building where I lived, where I have used mediation to solve conflicts among residents and staff members.

> I did not realize that I act as a mediator almost daily at work. I work with children. Children often find themselves in some sort of dispute or conflict with one another, it is my job to act as a mediator for them so that they can work out their own mutually satisfying outcomes.

> Teachers, day-care providers, and others who work with kids are mediators all day long. Mediating conflicts between children may seem simple or small, but they are important to the children involved.

I think mediation happens almost every day on a more informal level. This can happen between roommates, families, coworkers, and so on. If there is a problem, a third party might intervene to help the resolution run more smoothly.

I thought this subject helped me to see different ways of handling conflict situations and how important it is to sometimes have a third party involved. Many times I find myself in conflict with someone and we cannot come to a resolution but with the help of someone else we come to a resolution that is fair to both of us. I see that having a neutral third party can be very helpful when trying to deal with certain issues.

Like these students, we hope you may find mediation useful in your everyday life.

MANAGE IT

The study and practice of effective mediation is a natural fit for students of communication and conflict. For those who have gone through formal training, it is clear that it offers a practical application of many skills taught in undergraduate interpersonal communication and conflict management courses. However, we must shift our thinking from dealing with our own conflicts to helping others resolve theirs.

When should we intervene in other people's conflict? Help is needed when a dispute exists, meaning that the two parties are unable to resolve the conflict on their own. Unlike other alternatives to dispute resolution, such as conciliation, ombudsperson, arbitration, and adjudication/litigation, mediators are unbiased third parties who facilitate communication between the conflicting parties so that the conflicting parties can work out their own agreement.

A typical mediation usually proceeds through the following steps:

- One or both disputants seek mediation or a mediator may talk them into it.
- The mediator brings the disputants together and makes an opening statement.
- Following the mediator's opening statement, each person takes a few minutes to describe the dispute from his or her point of view without interruption.
- The mediator finds common ground on which to build agreement.
- The mediator writes up the final agreement.
- The mediator ends the mediation.

When drafting the agreement, mediators need to employ the following format: X agrees to this, and Y agrees to that. The mediators should attempt to keep the agreement simple. They use clear, specific details (spelling out who, what, where, when, how). It helps to think of the agreement as a list of behavioral commitments because it enumerates the specific observable actions each party needs to take to fulfill the agreement. In developing the agreement, the mediators should strive for balance or "something for everyone." The agreement also needs to address questions of feasibility and practicality—both parties should find the agreement workable. Finally, the culminating step occurs when the mediators ask both parties to sign the agreement.

This chapter concludes our presentation of the core concepts involved in effective conflict management. The afterword presents an overall view of the effective conflict manager.

Think About It

1. Did you receive mediation training in elementary, middle, or high school? Did you find the training useful? What disputes did you mediate? If you did not receive such training, would you like to? Does your college or university offer mediation training?
2. What experience, training, and abilities do you possess that would make you a good mediator? Where are you weak? What could you do to become a better mediator?
3. Have you studied rules in other communication courses? What are communication rules? How do mediators enforce communication rules?
4. How might you use techniques such as fractionation, framing, reframing, and common ground for solving problems that don't involve interpersonal conflicts?
5. Why should communication majors make good mediators? Why might lawyers and psychotherapists find it difficult to effectively play the role of mediator?

Apply It

1. Now it is your turn. Imagine yourself as a mediator and write an opening statement for the following case.

   Two roommates, Mr. X and Mr. Y, have differences of opinion on what they like to listen to on the stereo, what they like to eat, when they have visitors, when they wake up or quiet down at night, and when they use the room for study.

2. Read the following case study, and identify the issues that the conflicting parties should discuss.

   Two employees, Brian and Jon, have come to you because of clashing work habits. Both work in the same enclosed office and there are no other spaces available where either could be shifted. Brian likes to work with the door open, but Jon likes the door closed. Brian tends to shift tasks frequently, talking on his cell phone or speaking to people going by, while Jon prefers to do one task at a time. Jon tends to talk to himself as he is working. Jon also likes to put large post-it notes on the wall to visualize what he is working on, while Brian works primarily on his computer. Brian likes to spread a number of different items out to refer to as he is working and tends to leave them on the ground and all around his desk until he is finished. Both are claiming that each other's work habits are preventing each other from working to full capacity.

   For the above case, write out at least four statements that demonstrate fractionation, framing, reframing, and common ground.

3. Read over the following scenario and draft an agreement using the format, "X agrees to this and Y agrees to that." Strive for balance as much as possible.

   One roommate cares about the cleanliness of the apartment, but the other has shown no interest. However, in the course of mediation between roommates over their messy apartment, they agree to divvy up the household chores and times/days to do them.

   Imagining the typical chores and considering a reasonable schedule for the two roommates, draft an agreement that you intend to ask both roommates to sign. Use the appropriate format recommended in this chapter.

Work With It

1. Apply the chapter objectives to the following case study.

   My mother allows my 13-year-old sister, Leanne, to publish a blog [online journal]. She did not know what Leanne was writing about online until she started receiving long distance telephone calls from older men asking for her by name. Both my mother and sister complain to me about the other. My mother tells me that she would like to start reading her blog daily and would like to delete any content that she finds inappropriate. Leanne tells me that her blog is like a diary, and she doesn't want her mother to read it. Both are really upset with each other.

   - Define mediation and explain whether you think a third party should intervene as a mediator, and why.
   - Describe the role of mediator for whomever intervenes as a third party.
   - List and briefly describe the steps the third party should go through for this hypothetical mediation.

2. Take turns playing the role of mediator or co-mediator and conflicting parties, so that everyone has an opportunity to role-play a mediator. Then, discuss the mediation and ways to improve it.

You may wish to devise your own role play. If not, then select one of the following situations to mediate and assign roles of two conflicting parties and one or two mediators. If needed, others may serve as observers, but they cannot participate in the mediation. Mediators should start with their opening statements and follow the mediation steps.

   a. Family members: Your father and his sister (your aunt) have asked you to mediate their dispute. Your father thinks that your aunt took an expensive piece of furniture from their father's house after he passed away without discussing it with him. Your aunt took care of their father in his final days and had a key to his house. Your aunt was also in control of their father's finances and your father thinks she took all his money during his final days. Now your father is angry at his sister.
   b. Two romantic partners, Lacey and Henry, are living in a house with a third person, you. You treat them both equally. Recently Lacy decided that she wants to watch some TV programs, even though they were on the same time as sports. Meanwhile, Henry wants to watch the sports on the weekend and some weekday nights. The negative atmosphere is so bad in the house that you asked each of them to let you mediate the conflict, and they both agreed to let you do it.
   c. Two romantic partners are having a conflict over time management. He wants to spend time with his buddies and even invites one or two to join them when they go out together. She doesn't approve of all of his friends and finds two to be offensive and a bad influence on him. She wants to go out more often as just the two of them. She also wants more time with him without his buddies hanging around.
   d. Two roommates: Ms. X spends too much money. She likes to buy a lot of clothes. She never has enough for meals or gas, so she is always asking her roommate money, Ms. Y, to buy food or gas. She wants money to help pay for her books and sometimes doesn't have enough to help pay their room expenses. Ms. Y is fortunate to have enough money, but thinks it is unfair that her roommate isn't pulling her share and needs money from her so often. Ms. X often doesn't pay back the money she owes her roommate.

(Continued)

e. Two roommates: Bryon comes home late and rowdy from the local bars on Thursday, Friday, and Saturday nights. Roommate Lee has Friday classes and needs to go to work early every weekend.
f. Two sisters: A borrows B's clothes without her permission. B occasionally snoops through A's room and tries to find her diary and other personal items.
g. Married seniors: Husband recently retired and now spends all his time in the house. He doesn't do any household chores and gets in his wife's way.
h. Two neighbors: Pearson's dog barks, and when loose makes messes in his neighbor's yard. Recently the dog ripped open the garbage container when the neighbor placed it at the end of the drive for pickup.

NOTES

1. Nancy A. Burrell and Dudley D. Cahn, "Mediating Peer Conflicts in Educational Contexts: The Maintenance of School Relationships," in Dudley D. Cahn (Ed.), *Conflict in Personal Relationships* (Hillsdale, NJ: Erlbaum, 1994), p. 79.
2. See, for example, Robert E. Emery, David Sbarra, and Tara Grover, "Divorce Mediation: Research and Reflections," *Family Court Review* 43 (2005), 22–37; Frank E. A. Sander and Robert C. Bordone, "Early Intervention: How to Minimize the Cost of Conflict," *Negotiation* 21 (2005), 1–4; Lisa B. Bingham, "Employment Dispute Resolution: The Case for Mediation," *Conflict Resolution Quarterly* 22 (2004), 145–174.
3. Bruce C. McKinney, William Kimsey, and Rex Fuller, *Mediation: Dispute Resolution through Communication*, 2nd Ed. (Dubuque, IA: Kendall Hunt, 1990), p. 146.
4. Sook-Young Lee, "Mediation Techniques of an Informal Intermediary in Intercultural-Interpersonal Conflict," *Human Communication* 11 (Winter 2008), 461–482.
5. Camille Monahan, "Faster, Cheaper, and Unused: The Paradox of Grievance Mediation in Unionized Environments," *Conflict Resolution Quarterly* 25 (2008), 479–476.
6. Afshan Siddiqui and Hildy Ross, "Mediation as a Method of Parent Intervention in Children's Disputes," *Journal of Family Psychology* 18 (2004), 147–159.
7. James A. Wall, Jr., John B. Stark, and Rhetta L. Standifier, "Mediation: A Current Review and Theory Development," *Journal of Conflict Resolution* 45 (2001), 370–391.
8. Stephen K. Erickson and Marilyn S. McKnight, *The Practitioner's Guide to Mediation: A Client-Centered Approach* (New York: John Wiley, 2001).
9. Robert Coulson, *Family Mediation: Managing Conflict, Resolving Disputes* (San Francisco, CA: Jossey-Bass, 1996); Stephen A. Giunta and Ellen S. Amatea, "Mediation or Litigation with Abusing or Neglectful Families: Emerging Roles for Mental Health Counselors," *Journal of Mental Health Counseling* 22 (2000), 240–252.
10. Robert B. Silver and Deborah C. Silver, "Practice Note: Divorce Mediation with Challenging Parents," *Conflict Resolution Quarterly* 25 (2008), 511–520.
11. Penny Brooker, "An Investigation of Evaluative and Facilitative Approaches to Construction Mediation," *Structural Survey* 25 (2007), 233, 220–238.
12. Wenshan Jia, "Chinese Mediation and Its Cultural Foundation," in Guo-ming Chen and Ringo Ma (Eds.), *Chinese Conflict Management and Resolution* (Stamford, CT: Ablex, 2001), p. 290.
13. Gary J. Friedman, Jack Himmelstein, and Robert H. Mnooking, *Saving the Last Dance: Mediation through Understanding* (Cambridge, MA: Harvard Law School, 2001). Video.
14. Joyce L. Hocker and William W. Wilmot, *Interpersonal Conflict*, 4th Ed. (Dubuque, IA: Wm C. Brown, 1995), p. 238.
15. Jean Poitras, "A Study of the Emergence of Cooperation in Mediation," *Negotiation Journal* 21 (2005), 281–300.
16. Jordi Agustí-Panareda, "Power Imbalances in Mediation: Questioning Some Common Assumptions," *Dispute Resolution Journal* 59 (2004), 24–31.
17. O. J. Coogler, *Structured Mediation in Divorce Settlement* (Lexington, MA: Lexington Books, 1978).
18. See, for example, Candice C. Carter, "Conflict Resolution at School: Building Compassionate Communities," *Social Alternatives* 21 (2002), 49–55; David W. Johnson and Roger T. Johnson, "Implementing the 'Teaching Students to Be Peacemakers Program,'" *Theory into Practice* 43 (2004), 68–79.

CHAPTER 12

Managing Conflict from a Theoretical Perspective

OBJECTIVES

At the end of this chapter, you should be able to:

- Explain the key concepts and assumptions that identify factors that play an important role in interpersonal conflict according to each theory.
- Explain key principles that describe how conflicts develop according to each theory.
- Identify the type of conflict explained by each theory.
- Show how one should manage or resolve interpersonal conflicts according to each theory.

KEY TERMS

anxiety
attribution error
attribution theory
blaming
comparison level (CL)
comparison level for alternatives (CL$_{alt}$)
displaced conflict
displacement

external attribution
false conflict
frustration
holistic
homeostasis
internal attribution
misplaced conflict
overblown conflict
psychodynamic theory

repression
skill
social exchange theory
system
systems theory
theory
uncertainty

In the first part of this textbook, our purpose was to provide you with skills you could start using immediately to manage the conflicts that you experience. But skills alone, without an understanding of their origin in theory, are sometimes underused or applied improperly. In this portion of the text, we apply to conflict situations various theories that social psychologists and communication researchers created to explain why people behave the way they do. A **theory** is a means of explaining how something works. The way we explain conflict determines how we interpret it and choose our responses. The focus of a theory's explanation directs attention to that part of the conflict and assigns causes at the point of its focus.

Theories allow us to carry skills from one situation to another and to apply them appropriately within situations; a **skill** is a behavior one learns, which means that the person can improve it. Theories allow us to understand what the appropriate time is.

There are several metaphors that can help explain the relationship between skills and theories. For example, having a toolbox does you no good unless you know what each tool is used for. Or, if you only know how to format a single-page document in using your computer's word processor, having many other programs available to you doesn't do you much good. Further, not everything can fit into the format you understand. Understanding a single instruction in a program (a skill) is not as helpful as understanding the entire program or an operating system (a theory).

Another analogy concerning the relationship of skills to theory has to do with color. Why do some colors work together and some don't? We have color theory, which says that complementary colors (across the color wheel) create excitement, analogous colors (alongside each other on the color wheel) create a restful feeling, and so on. How do you know what color to use when?

The point about theories is this: If we don't have a conflict communication theory, it is hard for us to repeat a successful conflict performance, because we don't know if the conditions are the same as they were before. Conversely, it is hard for us to avoid repeating a poor performance, because we don't necessarily know what we did wrong.

The key social psychological theories described in this chapter may be grouped as "intrapersonal" (psychodynamic, attribution, uncertainty) and "interpersonal" (social exchange and systems theories), depending on whether they take place within the individual or during interaction between people in an interpersonal relationship. Taken together, they clarify and explain the role of the individual and her or his perceptual processes, the nature of the relationship that binds the conflicting parties, and the structures that shape conflict behavior in a relationship. While the interpersonal theories are obviously relational in character, even the intrapersonal theories explain internal conflicts that affect interpersonal relationships. Each theory adds an additional set of factors to explain more precisely the causes and effects of interpersonal conflict.

Later, in Chapter 15, where we will consider protracted and entrenched conflict, we will look at two additional conflict theories—critical conflict theory and ripeness theory.[1] For this chapter, though, we will concentrate on those theories that best explain everyday conflicts.

We study these theories of everyday conflict because they call our attention to the key concepts, assumptions, and principles that lay the groundwork for developing techniques for effective management of conflict. You are expected to apply these theories to conflicts in your life, to identify the key theoretical principles that explain the conflicts, and to suggest how best to manage them.

INTRAPERSONAL THEORIES OF CONFLICT

Psychodynamic, attribution, and uncertainty conflict theories, generated by researchers in psychology and social psychology, have focused on individual cognitive processes, or what individuals bring to the interpersonal conflict situations and how that impacts the conflict process. The key concept that unifies these theories is their assumption that the way people act in conflict situations is due, in large part, to their individual dispositions and ways of thinking. These theories remind us that the individuals in a conflict play a large part in determining the direction that the conflict takes.

Psychodynamic Theory

Stemming from one of the most historically significant psychological theories, based on the work of Sigmund Freud and his followers, **psychodynamic theory** says that people experience conflict because of their intrapersonal (internal, psychological, emotional, mental) states. Displaced and misplaced conflict (where the conflict is acted out with the wrong person or over the wrong issue) and overblown conflict (where the conflict receives more attention than it really deserves) are the types of conflicts that are best explained by this theory. The following narrative illustrates a displaced conflict driven by psychodynamic tension.

> When I'm going to leave for an extended trip, I often wind up fighting with my husband before I go over some insignificant but overblown issue. This time, I was really aware of the tendency, and we had avoided any major blowups. It took a toll, though, in my response to a neighbor's irritating comments at the shared swimming pool. Normally I simply would have left the situation, but I wound up telling him off in no uncertain terms. I was really embarrassed that I blew up—not only was the issue simply not worth the anger I felt, but I didn't even know this person before and now I feel like I have to avoid him.

Freud's theory identifies frustration, tension, and anxiety as important to understanding and explaining the individual's state of mind that can lead to aggressive behavior and interpersonal conflict. Freud conceived of the mind as a body of psychic energy that is channeled into various activities. Not only is the psychic energy channeled, but it is channeled into appropriate or inappropriate places. For the person in the narrative above, the tension created by trying not to fight before leaving on a trip gets channeled onto a "safe person," a stranger. People often displace or misplace conflict when they think that dealing with the other person directly is not possible, they fear the other's reaction, or they believe it could make matters worse.

From a Freudian perspective, three aspects of the human mind affect the way in which frustration, or more generally, psychic energy, is released. The principal component of the mind is the *id*, the unconscious aspect that "contains everything that is inherited, present at birth, or fixed in the constitution."[2] The id contains the libido, the source of instinctual energy, which demands discharge through various channels. The id operates on the "pleasure principle," a tension-reduction process in which tension from a bodily need is translated into a psychological wish in order to reduce the tension. The id seeks pleasure and avoids pain; it seeks only to satisfy its needs without regard for the cost of doing so.

Opposing the id is what Freud called the *superego*, containing both the ego ideal and the conscience. The ego ideal is an internalized idea of what a person would like to be. The conscience contains morals and other judgments concerning correct and incorrect behavior. As a parent does, it tries to punish a person for "immoral" behavior and reward a person for "moral" behavior through feelings like guilt or pride.

Mediating between the id and the superego is the *ego*, governed by the "reality principle," which attempts to "postpone the discharge of energy until the actual object that will satisfy the need has been discovered or produced."³ The ego, in mediating between the id and the superego, plays a significant role in conflict situations—it tries to reconcile the desires of the id ("I want it all, and I want it right now") with the constraints of the superego ("Nice people don't throw temper tantrums"). The ego must constrain aggressive impulses and control the level of anxiety conflict creates.

Anxiety is a tension that occurs when people perceive danger in a situation. People can become anxious when they think that someone may interfere with their goals, when they fear their own impulses in a situation, or when they disapprove of their own actions. Psychodynamic theory explains how individuals respond to conflict situations, particularly in light of their anxieties.

Anxiety may lead us to suppressed issues. **Repression** is another defense mechanism that occurs when we try not to think about our situation. Scarlett O'Hara vocalized this process in *Gone with the Wind* when she would say, "I won't think about that today. I'll think about that tomorrow."

Repression can explain **misplaced conflicts,** which occur when people argue about issues other than the ones at the heart of the conflict. We engage in conflict with the right person, but the conflict occurs over the wrong issue. The following story, told by a wife about her marriage, is an example of misplaced conflict with serious implications for the relationship:

> We've been seeing a marriage counselor for several weeks now, and we deal with all sorts of issues like my husband's problem with the way I do the housework (even though I work full-time) and my concern that he doesn't put enough time and energy into his business. But I get the impression that we're just putting out little brush fires when the forest is burning down. The heat of the real conflict is so intense we keep going around it. I think the real problem is that he treats me more coldly and cruelly than he would treat a stranger. He never touches me or shows me any kind of affection.

Whereas displaced conflicts involve directing frustration toward a "safe" person, misplaced conflicts involve "safe" issues that people are more willing to talk about than the suppressed issues that underlie them.

In the preceding example, the husband's concern over the housework and the wife's concern about the effort put into the business are legitimate issues. The suppressed issues, however, are masked by these "safer" issues. The wife uses the housework as a weapon against a husband who emotionally abuses her: It bothers him to have the house messy, so she just cannot seem to get around to doing it. It helps that she works outside the home. She can legitimately say that there is not enough time to do everything. She does not really want to deal with his lack of respect, so talking about his lack of business efforts is a safer issue. Because they keep dealing with the small, visible conflicts instead of looking at the pattern of their conflict behavior, the small conflicts continue to multiply until one or the other leaves or until they learn how to deal with the conflicts. Deutsch argued that manifest or overt conflict is difficult, if not impossible, to resolve unless the underlying conflict has been dealt with in some way or unless the overt conflict is separated from the underlying conflict and treated in isolation.³

Because misplaced conflicts revolve around "safe" rather than suppressed issues, they are often difficult to diagnose. A conflict issue that comes up repeatedly may mask a deeper issue between those involved. However, you need to understand that, where conflicts are managed rather than resolved, the same issues may arise frequently with no other underlying meaning. For example, if you are a person of tidy habits rooming with a messy person, the issue of cleanliness is likely to arise often, but it probably does not mask a deeper issue other than the fact that you have different habits. Misplaced conflicts concern relational issues such as power sharing, expectations for behavior, respect, and means of showing affection. Because these issues are central to the way people relate to one another, people often find it easier to focus on visible issues, such as money or work habits, where any difference in action is observable.

Freud theorized that the ego experiences frustration when trying to constrain aggressive impulses. **Frustration** results from the internal battle between the id and superego that often erupts into conflict with others. Frustration can originate from many sources, for example, tension, stress, insecurity, anxiety, hostility, sexual urges, or depression.

Frustration can lead to **overblown conflict,** which we defined on page 123 as when one exaggerates a conflict concerning a relatively unimportant issue. The parties seem to invest far more emotion and energy than the situation deserves. This narrative illustrates an overblown conflict.

> I had been having a really bad day. I felt overburdened by homework and job responsibilities, and to top it off, I had a huge paper I was working on that was due in two days, which I had barely even started. Mary chose this particular time to enter the room and discuss the positioning of our bathroom towels on the rack. She seemed frustrated that the four of us, who were sharing the bathroom, had taken to haphazardly pushing and stuffing our towels through the narrow metal rods, thus having them all scrunched up together, which did not allow them to dry properly. I felt that this was such an inane discussion, I suddenly erupted and really told her off.

Although the towels represent a conflict issue the roommates should discuss rationally at some point, in this overblown conflict they have served the person trying to study as a way to release her frustration about her lack of progress. Overblown conflicts are often resolved when the person who has done the ranting and raving apologizes, usually making some excuse for the untoward behavior (e.g., "I was stressed out") that the target of the conflict accepts as a reasonable excuse.

The ego also deals with aggressive impulses by suppressing them or redirecting them through a process of **displacement,** which occurs when people take out their frustrations on those perceived as less dangerous to them rather than those persons who caused the original feelings. In displacement, the aggressive impulse is often redirected "toward a more vulnerable or socially acceptable target than the actual source of frustration. . . . Displacement is more likely when the true source of frustration is powerful or particularly valuable to the individual."[4]

Displaced conflict occurs when people direct a conflict toward the wrong person, avoiding a confrontation with the appropriate person.[5] This type of conflict almost always happens with people with whom we have an interpersonal relationship, and whom we think of as a "safe target" for our frustration. The person we avoid is someone we do not want to offend or provoke because that person has greater power (rank, physical strength, or nasty reputation). The common example of displaced conflict is Dan, who is angry at his boss but doesn't say anything to him, then comes home to his loving wife or children, whom he abuses with his anger.

A key point to remember about psychodynamic theory is that it explains those conflicts that, from the target's vantage point, often arise out of nowhere. The following narrative is an example of a displaced conflict due to internal frustration.

> I work in a retail store and I am often in charge of ringing people up at the register. I always make sure that when I ask for the next person in line that in fact the truly next person in line comes over or at least has a chance to. But when I asked for the next person in line, another lady who was not the next person in line came over. When I tried to get the proper person to come over, the woman that had come over started yelling at me. I calmly explained to her that it was part of my job to make sure that the next person in line had a fair chance to come over. She did not like this and went so far as to throw her credit card at me when paying. This made me absolutely furious and the worst part about it was there was nothing that I could say.
>
> So after I got off work I met my boyfriend at my house. Everything was going along smoothly until suddenly we got into a disagreement about whether we would go out that night or stay in. I was tired from working all day but he wanted to go out. Well I ended up blowing the whole situation out of proportion and I know that it was due to the tension I had held on to all day from the irate customer that I had dealt with earlier in the day.

This retail salesperson needs to learn how to deal more effectively with offensive customers so that she doesn't have so much pent-up frustration. Using some of the stress-reducing activities covered in Chapter 7 would probably help her quite a bit. Unfortunately, too many people do not do anything until after they have ruined one or more relationships with those who were the safe targets of their frustrations.

Attribution Theory

An attribution is an inference made about the causes of another's behavior. If I infer from your behavior that you are internally motivated, and I don't approve of what you did or said, I could say that you acted that way because you are evil, angry at me, anxious, unmotivated, depressed, or unintelligent. For example, I don't like the fact that you beat me at cards, so I call you a cheat (as though you are a bad person who intended to cheat me—all internal attributions).

If I approve of what you did or said, I might attribute the behavior to an external source such as a run of luck, God, your parents, and so on. For example, I might credit your spouse for your success at your job. Sillars argued that in a conflict situation, one makes conclusions about the other person's behavior and that those conclusions lead to theories to explain the conflict.[6] **Attribution theory** states that people act as they do in conflict situations *because of the inferences they make about others based on their behavior.* Attributions are internal, related to the person's general personality, or external, related to the other person's circumstances. Attribution theory also accounts for false conflicts, which are discussed in conjunction with uncertainty theory.

Sillars claimed attributions affect the way people define conflicts, interpret the other's behavior, and choose strategies to achieve their goals effectively within conflict

CHAPTER 12 Managing Conflict from a Theoretical Perspective   217

What kinds of attributions might be made about a person who dresses a dog in this manner?

situations. Furthermore, the process of making attributions about the other may discourage the selection of collaborative conflict strategies, because the process of attribution may shift the blame from oneself to the other. **Blaming** others is saying they are at fault. The act of blaming is a characteristic of negative conflict behaviors and is often associated with verbal and physical abuse, which increases the likelihood of escalating conflict.

People are most likely to perceive the other as aggressive and respond with anger and retribution when three conditions are met. First, the action the other person has taken is seen as a constraint to one's own alternatives or outcomes. Gabriel cannot act in the way he wishes because of Javier's actions. Second, the action taken by the other appears to have been done intentionally to do harm. Not only has Javier taken action that constrains Gabriel, but Javier appears to have done so in order to intentionally harm Gabriel. Third, the action taken by Javier is seen as abnormal or illegitimate. Gabriel sees no action on his part that might have provoked Javier into acting as he did. Anger or retribution is less likely on Gabriel's part if Javier is seen as having acted without choice and because forces moved him in the direction taken. Anger and retribution are more likely if Gabriel sees Javier's action as arbitrary or whimsical.

As you consider attribution theory, an important aspect to remember is that it explains retaliatory behavior. When we make **internal attributions** about another person (she wanted, he hates, she's stupid, he's evil, she's angry, etc.), it often results in name-calling (you cheat, idiot, lazy, good for nothing, etc.) and assigning blame (it's all your fault). Making **external attributions** for oneself is a way to avoid blame (it's my parents' fault that I am this way, I can't help that I didn't go to the right school) and to avoid giving credit to others where it is due (your spouse must have done it for you, you got the job because you graduated from the right school, you must have had connections, etc.).

Interestingly, we tend to make internal attributions to explain others' behavior when we don't like it and external attributions when we are impressed.[7] Meanwhile, we do the opposite for our own behavior. If I do something impressive, I like to take the credit for it (aren't I great!), but when it is nasty, I try to blame it on someone else (she made me do it). This is called the **attribution error.**

> The other night my three friends and I played a card game called spades. My partner and I were not doing as well as the other team. I figured that somehow they were giving each other some kind of signals; so I finally stopped the game and accused them of cheating us. One of them responded by saying, "We are winning simply because of the luck of the draw." But the conflict escalated into a yelling match. Luckily, someone suggested that we change partners, which solved the problem. We went back to playing cards, but I still ended up on the losing side.

One interesting study looked at the way attributions were made about the use of humor by participants in a conflict episode. When humor was attributed to internal motives (e.g., "that person just enjoys jokes"), it had a negative outcome on the conflict resolution, but when humor was attributed to an external motive (e.g., laughing at the situation), it had a more positive effect on conflict resolution.[8] In another study, Sillars and colleagues found that conflicting spouses saw their own messages in more favorable terms than their partner's.[9]

Uncertainty Theory

Uncertainty occurs at two levels. Conflict creates uncertainty within the relationship in which it occurs (e.g., romantic partners contemplate what happened and how they are supposed to relate to each other), and uncertainty also exists to different degrees within the particular conflict episode itself. **Uncertainty** in the conflict situation occurs when we have insufficient information to understand another's motives, goals, or behaviors or when we do not understand how another is responding to us.

Many events are capable of creating uncertainty in relationships: changes in the other person's behavior, the breaking of a confidence, a friend breaking off contact, a romantic partner going out with someone else. Interestingly, nearly all the events recalled by people as those causing uncertainty are classified as conflict episodes.[10] Most people cannot recall anything that might have been a clue to events causing uncertainty, or they can recognize clues only in retrospect. Uncertainty in a relationship does lead to increased communication with the other person, and when people communicate about events causing uncertainty, they are more satisfied. Those who do not talk about uncertainty-causing events generally express regret about avoiding the issue. As time passes, feelings about uncertainty-causing events become less negative.[11] Communication with the other, "doing" the conflict, is generally the best way to reduce uncertainty within a relationship. But there is a deeper level of uncertainty—that within the conflict itself.

Conflicts are inherently messy and filled with ambiguity. "The characteristic of conflict that is most difficult to capture in research is the chaos that pervades a heated argument or a long-simmering conflict."[12] There are three sources of ambiguity and disorder in conflict: the source of the conflict, the organizational complexity of conflict patterns, and the embeddedness of conflict in daily activities.

Issues in conflict are rarely singular or straightforward. Rational views of conflict assume that both people are able to identify the issue, develop straightforward goals about it, and move toward resolution through compromise or collaboration. However, the real case is that people may not share the same perception about the issue or may not agree on the conflict issue at all. They may think the conflict has arisen due to different causes; they may interpret the other's behavior differently than the other intends; and so on. Further, conflicts may exist simultaneously at different levels—superficial issues may also involve deeper relational implications. Mild conflicts generally reflect agreement concerning the deeper relational issues involved; in bitter and destructive conflicts, relational issues are entangled and difficult to resolve.

The complexity of conflict may also affect the level of ambiguity present. Whereas casual conversation is characterized by adherence to a set of cooperative principles, these principles are often violated in conflict when it is not in one's best interest to converse in a succinct, relevant, and orderly manner. In addition, patterns in conflict (beyond the broad stages of prelude, initiation, differentiation, and resolution) are difficult to identify. Most conversation shows a reciprocal pattern, in which message types are generally followed by similar types, but "conflicts often have a dynamic quality characterized by oscillation between aggression and withdrawal."[13] Further, participants in conflicts often introduce, drop, reintroduce, and expand topics in an unpredictable pattern, making it difficult for the other person to know where the conversation might lead.

A final source for the situations of uncertainty created by conflicts is the embeddedness of conflict in our everyday lives. They can occur anywhere, at any time. Often we may feel surprised by them. It's rare that we can make an appointment for a conflict!

When a person is in an uncertain relationship, they tend to "test the waters," so to speak, in order to reduce the uncertainty they feel. They are alert and observe the other person's behavior. They'll look for positive behaviors, but may overestimate the meaning of a negative behavior (e.g., she looks upset—she's probably thinking about breaking up with me). Indeed, in a situation of uncertainty, this overemphasis on the meaning of the behaviors the uncertain person observes makes it harder to reduce the uncertainty. This conflict narrative demonstrates how uncertainty makes interaction between both people difficult.

> After a terrible conflict in which I felt physically endangered, I asked my partner to move out. She promised to reform, but the difficulty is that she doesn't really think she did anything wrong. So she'll say things that indicate she doesn't trust me. In the meantime, I'm worried about her losing her temper again, and I'm watching all the time to see what's going to happen. It's pretty hard for both of us to simply relax and be around each other.

Uncertainty theory helps explain **false conflict**s, which occur when at least one person in an interdependent relationship thinks that there is a conflict but after talking to the other(s) involved, finds there is no conflict. This narrative demonstrates a false conflict.

> I was hanging curtains in my daughter's room, and it was pulling at the material, so I picked the kitten up and put it behind me without looking. I should have known better—there were objects all over the floor and apparently it landed on something the wrong way. I heard a

meow-spit-hiss, and turned around to see it favoring one leg. Horrified, I picked it up and rushed it to the vet to find that its leg was broken.

When I picked my daughter up from school, I tried to find some way to explain gently that it was my fault her kitten was injured. She simply looked at me and asked, "Is Sheba okay?" I replied that she was, although she would wear a cast for four weeks. My daughter said, "Well, accidents happen, Mom. You didn't mean to hurt her." I thought I would drive the car onto the sidewalk in amazement. I expected fireworks, and all that happened was a fizzle.

Because we may assume that we are in a conflict due to the limited knowledge we have, false conflicts are generally resolved with sufficient information. Asking, and being told, leads to resolution fairly easily. Other false conflicts have to do with what people think that the other person might have done before they get their facts straight. Conflicts concerning beliefs, facts, or perceptions generally arise from a lack of information or distorted information. Imagine thinking you are in conflict with someone only to find that you are not. This is one reason why we need to talk to the other party. Otherwise, we may fret for nothing.

People reduce uncertainty in conflict situations in one of three ways. First, they may choose to trust the other, although the ability to trust depends on past behaviors. Second, they may reduce uncertainty by taking the perspective of the other person. And third, they may reduce uncertainty by engaging in "imagined interactions," or thoughts about what they might say and what the other might do in a conflict situation.[14]

With the economy in such bad condition, people have been laid off from my work. We're all getting pretty paranoid around here, and it's hard not to read things into the messages we hear. I keep thinking about what I will say if I am laid off. I have all this stuff I'd really like to tell them about this crappy job. I think about it at night before I go to sleep and it actually makes me feel better.

RELATIONSHIP THEORIES OF CONFLICT

While the theories in the first section focused on the individual as a key element in conflict, this section considers theories that explain conflicts on the basis of the nature of the relationship between the people involved. The two dominant theories of this type are social exchange theory and systems theory.

Social Exchange Theory

Developed by Kelley and Thibault, **social exchange theory** states that people evaluate their interpersonal relationships in terms of their value, which is created by the costs and rewards associated with the relationship.[15] A person's feelings about a relationship, according to this theory, depend on assessments of the amount of effort put into the relationship (costs) compared to what is received as a result of the relationship (rewards). People assess the costs and rewards associated with their relationships through what is termed the comparison level (CL) and the comparison level for alternatives (CL_{alt}). People enter into conflict when they believe that the rewards they are receiving are too little in comparison with the costs they must pay in the relationship.

According to social exchange theory, people in relationships (interpersonal, group, or organizational) ask "What does the relationship have to offer me? How valuable is it? Am I better off with or without the other person?" Social exchange theory explains how people rate their relationships in terms of what they are giving and getting out of them. Rewards are resources of exchange (money, goods/property, love, sex, affection, companionship or shared time, status, services, information), while costs detract (pain/suffering, loneliness, abuse, loss of self-esteem, loss of resources of exchange, loss of investments). People make two comparisons (CL and CL_{alt}) to determine their level of relationship satisfaction and relationship commitment.

CL and CL_{alt} emphasize the role of relationship satisfaction and commitment in interpersonal conflict. The **comparison level (CL)** is a standard with which people determine how satisfactory or attractive a relationship is. This standard reflects what people think they deserve. If the rewards of a relationship compared to its cost fall above the CL, then a person considers the relationship satisfying; if the outcome falls below the CL, the person is probably dissatisfied with the relationship.[16] A person's CL is created by considering all the possible outcomes a relationship might have, either from direct experience in the relationship or by observation of other relationships.

For example, in an interpersonal relationship, a person might think that, although he or she has fun with another person, the aggravation of waiting for that person to show up on time is getting too costly. In this case, the individual's previous experience makes him expect the other to show on time. There is now a conflict, even if not expressed, between the person and the one he is tired of waiting for. There is a great deal we expect from new potential romantic partners and friends based on our previous experiences.

The **comparison level for alternatives (CL_{alt})** tends to be applied when a third party enters the picture. Third party intervention may lead a person to examine the current relationship and perceive inequity in it, in turn creating conflict. A person compares the rewards and costs of the present relationship with those of the alternative relationship, and if the current relationship's rewards exceed the alternative, they remain committed to it.

For example, a person in an interpersonal relationship may use a previous relationship as a comparison level, or they may look at others' relationships to compare them to their own. The possibility of opening a relationship with a new partner can change the value of the CL_{alt}. Likewise, in an organization, a person may compare their job requirements to someone in a similar situation to determine whether they are being paid fairly. Or, they might apply to other jobs and go on interviews to ensure that they really have the best working conditions they can get.

This narrative illustrates how a person begins to make changes in a relationship through a consideration of the rewards and costs.

> My mother graduated from high school early in order to marry my biological father and move with him to Germany, where he was stationed in the service. I was born a year later, and they divorced a few months after I was born. My mom then married Harry when I was about two. For the next fourteen years, I lived with my mom and Harry, seeing my dad on the weekends. I felt like I lived two separate lives. Home was where Mom and Harry were—in fact, I didn't call him my stepfather, I called him "Dad." My biological father didn't like that.
>
> My relationship with my biological father got worse over the years. I never enjoyed spending time with him and I even dreaded seeing him because he bad-mouthed my mom and Harry. My biological father resented the relationship I had with Harry and he kept trying

to make me think Harry was a bad guy. He would use gifts as a way of making me visit him. He bought me lots of toys, took me fun places, and as I got older the gifts got more expensive—a television, a stereo, the promise of a car. I accepted these gifts with a clear conscience because I figured he "owed" me for the miserable weekends I spent with him.

When I was sixteen, my biological father and I had a major confrontation over this pattern we had developed. I basically stood up to him and told him how I hated the way he bad-mouthed my mom and how I didn't want to spend any more time with him if he was going to be like that. My father comes from a culture where you don't argue with your parents, so when I stood up to him, he got upset and told me never to come back to his house. That was five years ago, and I have never spoken to him since that time.

The narrator in this conflict has a clear comparison level when she evaluates the relationship she has with her biological father. She has a good relationship with her stepfather, and wants only one family, not two. Her father appears satisfied with the relationship they had, but her dissatisfaction grows as the expensive gifts no longer are enough to make up for the unpleasantness of each weekend visit.

This conflict also illustrates the idea of CL_{alt}, which is the lowest level of outcomes a person may accept in a current relationship in light of available opportunities in other relationships. The more the outcomes in a relationship exceed the CL_{alt}, the more a person is committed to the current relationship, and the more dependent that person is on the relationship for psychological rewards. As time wears on, the rewards of the narrator's relationship with her father are too low for her to accept. The emotional cost of staying in the relationship is higher than the value of any gift her father can give her.

Social exchange theory assumes that people choose their behaviors due to self-interest and a desire to maximize rewards while minimizing costs. However, choices are made with respect to rules of fairness: People generally expect rewards proportionate to contributions they make to the relationship, based on their perceptions of the rewards and costs involved. So, even if a relationship is unsatisfactory at a particular point in time, if people think that it was a good relationship in the past and believe it might satisfy them in the future, they do not immediately abandon the relationship when problems arise.

From a social exchange point of view, conflict arises when one person in the relationship thinks that the outcomes are too low and perceives that the other may resist any attempt to raise the outcomes. This is precisely what happened in the narrative. It is possible that the narrator could have convinced her father that continuing to bad-mouth her mother (particularly 16 years after the divorce) was not appropriate. Such an outcome would have been the result of what social exchange theory terms *cooperative joint action*, where both people agree together to make changes in the relationship. Through independent action, the narrator could simply have continued her relationship with her biological father without expecting him to change, although this was unlikely as his behavior really bothered her. The actual outcome of the conflict was imposed joint action, where the narrator's father discontinued their relationship.

How people choose to alter their outcomes depends on the power held by each person in the relationship. Kelly and Thibault argued that the dependence of person A on person B constitutes person B's power, and vice versa. A person may have "fate control" over the other, the ability to affect the other's behavior regardless of what the other does, or may have "mutual fate control" over the other, the ability to make it desirable for the other to behave as the person wants.

Overall, social exchange theory leads to four insights about conflict behavior. First, the theory recognizes that people are often quite purposeful about the way they "do" conflict, calculating the costs of various options, and weighing those costs against the potential rewards the options might bring. This strategic calculation is illustrated by the following conflict account.

> For the last two years, the tasks associated with my job have increased until they are almost double what they were. There are two of us doing the same job, but the tasks were not distributed fairly between us. In addition, I had some extra duties that my colleague didn't have. My frustration was growing, but I knew I couldn't get a job anywhere else for the same amount of money I was making. On the other hand, my life was getting so overwhelming that I was beginning to think that maybe the money wasn't that good. I started looking at jobs similar to mine online. I thought my boss would see how the tasks were allocated, but he seemed oblivious. I also know that he really hates it when I point out stuff like this to him, so I was hesitant to go talk to him. I finally screwed up the courage, but all he said is that he would think about the allocation of tasks. I didn't feel confident about any change in the future, but two weeks later he announced a change that made it much fairer for the two of us.

The preceding account also illustrates a second concept emphasized by social exchange theory: the interdependence of those in the conflict. It is not possible, according to social exchange theory, to take steps to resolve a conflict without reactions from the other person involved.

The third social exchange theory concept is that conflict is a situation in which moves and countermoves take place. It helps us understand how people explain conflicts—when narrating a conflict episode, most people use a move–countermove format: He did this, so I did that, and so on.

The fourth concept of social exchange theory is that people in conflicts choose actions based not only on their particular outcomes but also on their cost for the relationship. People may deliberately avoid a conflict because the current costs of initiating one are too high. Conversely, they may engage in a conflict because the costs of not doing so are too high.

Although some people initially react to social exchange theory negatively, thinking it is wrong to use an economic model to explain relationships, social exchange theory does make sense. We don't like believing that we put more into a relationship than we receive. If we have hope of staying in the relationship, we work to increase our rewards relative to our costs. On the other hand, if the costs continue to rise without some increase in rewards, people tend to cycle out of the relationship—as they see conflict as creating too high a "cost" with respect to the "reward" they might receive, they do not communicate their concerns and eventually do not communicate at all.

Here is another example of a conflict that illustrates social exchange theory.

> Before college began, a high school friend and I had a great relationship. We would hang out all of the time together and knew all of each other's secrets. We promised that even though we'd be going away to different colleges, we'd always stay in touch and be the best of friends. After graduation, we both got absorbed in our own college life and lost our close ties. She eventually got bored with college and decided to take some "time off," while I remained in school where I am extremely busy with work, family issues, and my boyfriend.

Over the past three months, she has been trying to get me to come back home for a weekend and go out partying at the local bars with her. She won't give up and is very persistent that I spend more time with her, and she says that, after all of this time, I'm not living up to my promise. Recently we lost touch again when I was too involved with my local obligations to call her back or spend a weekend partying. When I finally did call her, she never returned my phone calls and I haven't heard from her since. I feel that she must have compared the lack of satisfaction of our present relationship to all the dissatisfaction she must be feeling and it is less satisfying than she expected. She had put a lot of time and effort into maintaining our present relationship, while I did not. She was clearly putting more into the relationship than she was receiving, and so she must have decided to end our relationship.

One idea we learn from social exchange theory is that we must work to make our partner happy, or other alternatives may appear more attractive and threaten our relationship. Investments of time and energy in a relationship increase partner satisfaction and commitment.

Systems Theory

Systems theory is best summarized by Ruben, who took issue with the idea of equating conflict with breakdowns. Rather, he argued, if human relationships are thought of as systems, communication, and therefore conflict, is not only inevitable but also continual.[17] Ruben's view of conflict within a system turns to an entirely different assumption from previous theories: Rather than being a disruption in the normal state of affairs, conflict is the normal state of affairs within any system. Conflict is necessary for the growth and adaptation of a system. Without conflict, a system faces the possibility of stagnation and decay. Conflict is the primary way in which a system adapts to the demands of its environment. According to this view, then, the major defining condition of conflict is the process of reducing alternatives as the system adapts to changes and demands in the environment.

Let's expand the idea of system. A **system** is a set of interrelated components acting together as a unit. A **holistic** perspective suggests that the unit (couple, family, team, organization, society, etc.) is key, not the individual. That is, while it helps to know what elements (people) are in a system (relationship), it is the system itself that is most important in helping us understand the behavior and conflicts within it. We know that people behave a certain way because they are married (marital system), because they are members of a family (family system),[18] because they are friends (friendship system), or members of a group or organization (organizational system). Because they are part of the system, they act accordingly. Thus, the interdependent relationship among the components (individuals) of the system is considered more important than the components themselves. As they say about systems, the "whole is greater than the sum of its parts."

A system also has some purpose—it is goal-directed and adapts to its environment through self-maintenance and regulation. **Homeostasis** means that the system maintains itself in pursuit of a goal. The goal in a marriage is to stay married—and it is much harder than it sounds! There are environmental changes that come in many forms: income reductions, in-law interference, job demands, and more. Conflict arises as these external factors make problematic keeping the relationship stable and growing.

From a practical point of view, conflict occurs within a relationship because a person in that relationship needs to adapt to demands of the other person or to demands in the environment surrounding the relationship. Here is an example of a conflict explained by systems theory, where the relationship (system) is in turmoil because of the inability of those in it to adapt to each other's demands and to the demands of the environment.

> Mike and Lori fight constantly. They dropped out of high school to get married very young and have a baby. Lori's parents were so much against the marriage that they cut off contact and support to the young couple. Mike has only one parent, his mother, who is living on welfare, is an alcoholic, and depends on Mike for some support. She wants to live with them, but Lori is against the idea. Mike lacks both an education and employment skills and continues to have trouble holding a job.
>
> Meanwhile, Lori claims that she is unemployable and wants to stay home to raise their daughter. Mike wants her to go back to school and get a job, while his mother could move in and take care of their daughter. During the first year, Mike felt that he had to locate and tear up all the credit cards in their home, because Lori was buying things for him, herself, and the baby, which he felt they couldn't afford. This is difficult because she keeps receiving new credit cards in the mail and tries to secretly use them. So, now they argue constantly over lack of money, his mother, her not working, credit cards, and his working off and on.

Perhaps the most important contribution of systems theory to theories of conflict and its management has been the idea that conflict is a normal part of interaction. Rather than seeing conflict as a disruption that occurs within an otherwise healthy and normally functioning relationship, systems theorists see conflict as an important part of a system that allows change and adaptation to various demands.

MANAGE IT

As we state at the beginning of this chapter, understanding theories can help us understand our conflicts better so that we can adapt to them more easily. Psychodynamic theory, for example, helps us understand that aggressive impulses result from internal conflict between the id and the superego, which produces frustration and tension. The internal conflict can arise from tension, stress, insecurity, anxiety, hostility, sexual urges, or depression. Psychodynamic theory explains displaced, misplaced, and overblown conflicts.

Attribution theory helps explain retaliatory behavior—we respond the way we do because we assume we understand why other people behave as they do. Making internal attributions for others often results in name-calling and assigning blame. We make external attributions for ourselves to avoid blame or to avoid giving credit to others. We tend to make internal attributions to explain other's behavior when we don't like it and external attributions when we do like what we see. Meanwhile, we do the opposite for our own behavior.

We can discuss uncertainty theory at two levels. Conflict creates uncertainty within the relationship in which it occurs, and uncertainty also exists to different degrees within the particular conflict. Uncertainty in the conflict situation occurs when we have insufficient information to understand another's motives, goals, or behaviors or when we do not understand another's behavior. Uncertainty theory helps explain false conflicts.

According to social exchange theory, partners determine the value of their relationships. Social exchange theory explains how people rate their relationships in terms of what they are giving and getting out of them. Partners make two comparisons to determine their level of

1. relationship satisfaction (based on previous experiences) and
2. relationship commitment (based on rewards/costs of alternatives).

Systems theory also deals with relationships. A system has some purpose—it is goal-directed and adapts to its environment—a type of self-maintenance or self-regulation. Thus the system maintains itself (homeostasis) in pursuit of a goal. Conflicts happen as people adjust to the demands of other people in the system or to the demands of the environment on the system itself.

Sometimes people will say that a theory sounds reasonable but doesn't work in practice. Good theories are those we can put to use. The theories presented in this chapter are part of a conflict manager's toolbox—they help to make sense of conflict behavior and guide us in the competent choice of conflict management strategies.

Think About It

1. Are there situations in your life where you are more likely to displace your anger or conflict with the other person than to deal with it directly? What characterizes those situations?
2. When have false attributions you have made about another exacerbated a conflict situation? Have there been times when making accurate attributions about the other has helped you?
3. What conflicts can you identify that were motivated by uncertainty? How could you have obtained more information before engaging in the conflict?
4. What conflicts can you identify that were motivated by a desire to increase your rewards or to decrease your costs in a relationship? Were you successful? Why or why not?
5. What conflicts can you identify that were motivated by systems theory principles? How best might you deal with such conflicts?

Apply It

1. This exercise is something you can start now and add to throughout the chapter. Take a piece of paper and draw two columns on it. In the left column, list your theoretical tools, starting with psychodynamic theory. In the right column, describe what your tool does in analyzing conflicts.
2. Add to the paper you started with Apply It #1. Write attribution theory in the left column, and explain how it helps you to analyze conflicts in the right column.
3. Add to the paper you started with Apply It #1. Write uncertainty theory in the left column, and explain how it helps you to analyze conflicts in the right column.
4. Add to the paper you started with Apply It #1. Write social exchange theory in the left column, and explain how it helps you to analyze conflicts in the right column.
5. Add to the paper you started with Apply It #1. Write systems theory in the left column, and explain how it helps you to analyze conflicts in the right column.

Work With It

1. Label the following statements by selecting either internal attributions (a) or external attributions (b). Check your answers on against those at the end of the footnotes.
   a. "He did this to me because he wants to get even."
   b. "She did this to me because she hates my guts."
   c. "He did poorly because his parents expect the worst from him, so he delivers accordingly."
   d. "He didn't show for the test because he is probably afraid he will fail."
   e. "He made the test too hard, so I flunked it."
   f. "Of course she didn't return the laptop. She is an idiot. What do you expect from an imbecile?"
   g. "They keep tearing up the parking lots and that is why I was late to class."
   h. "I've been in a slump, which is why I am not doing well these days."
   i. "She's immoral and only wants you for your money."
   j. "He treats you badly because you are so tall. He has a rotten attitude toward others taller than he is."
   k. "Luck is against me. Maybe next time I will get lucky."

2. Identify the theories that best explain the following conflicts. Check your answers against those at the end of the footnotes.

   a. Conflict situation: I blame my roommate for our current feud. All I can think about is getting even. Yesterday he took my car and returned it on empty. I thought I had plenty of gas so when I took off today I was shocked when I ran out on the way to classes. I had to walk into town and carry a can of gas back to the car three miles each way. I also missed my test. You want to know what makes me mad? I know that he had the money to buy gas, and he must have driven by at least three stations when going through town. He just wanted to get me into trouble with my professor and mess up my grades. He must hate my guts. I am going to retaliate. He has to meet an important study group tonight, and I am going to wait till he is ready to go to tell him he can't use my car. Let's see how he feels about flunking a test.
      1. Which conflict theory discussed in this chapter best explains this conflict?
      2. What is really the cause of the conflict?
      3. How could or should one resolve this conflict?

   b. Conflict situation: I am anxious before flying on a trip; so I become irritable and wind up fighting with my partner before I go over insignificant but overblown issues.
      1. Which conflict theory discussed in this chapter best explains this conflict?
      2. What is really the cause of the conflict?
      3. How could or should one resolve this conflict?

   c. Conflict situation: I am unhappy in my relationship because I have to do all the housework and my partner won't agree to do more. It seems unfair that I have to do more than my share. Why won't she help out?
      1. Which conflict theory discussed in this chapter best explains this conflict?
      2. What is really the cause of the conflict?
      3. How could or should one resolve this conflict?

NOTES

1. Toran Hansen, "Critical Conflict Resolution Theory and Practice," *Conflict Resolution Quarterly* 25 (2008), 403–427; Peter T. Coleman, Antony G. Hacking, Mark A. Stover, Beth Fisher-Yoshida, and Andrzej Nowak, "Reconstructing Ripeness I: A Study of Constructive Engagement in Protracted Social Conflicts," *Conflict Resolution Quarterly* 26 (2008), 3–42.
2. Calvin S. Hall, *A Primer of Freudian Psychology*, 2nd Ed. (New York: World, 1979), p. 28.
3. Ibid.
4. Ibid., p. 14.
5. Jeffrey W. Kassing and Rachel L. DiCioccio, "Testing a Workplace Experience Explanation of Displaced Dissent," *Communication Reports* 17 (2004), 114.
6. Alan L. Sillars, "Attributions and Communication in Roommate Conflicts," *Communication Monographs* 47 (1980), 180–200; Alan L. Sillars, "The Sequential and Distributional Structure of Conflict Interactions as a Function of Attributions Concerning the Locus of Responsibility and Stability of Conflicts," in Dan Nimmo (Ed.), *Communication Yearbook*, Vol. 4 (New Brunswick, NJ: Transaction Books, 1980), 217–235.
7. Stacy L. Young, "What the _____ Is Your Problem? Attribution Theory and Perceived Reasons for Profanity Usage during Conflict," *Communication Research Reports* 21 (2004), 338–347.
8. Amy M. Bippus, "Humor Motives, Qualities, and Reactions in Recalled Conflict Episodes," *Western Journal of Communication* 67 (2003), 413–426.
9. Alan Sillars, Linda J. Roberts, and Kenneth E. Leonard, "Cognition during Marital Conflict: The Relationship of Thought and Talk," *Journal of Social and Personal Relationships* 17 (2000) 479–502.
10. Sally Planalp and James M. Honeycutt, "Events that Increase Uncertainty in Personal Relationships," *Human Communication Research* 11 (1985), 593–604.
11. Sally Planalp, Diane K. Rutherford, and James M. Honeycutt, "Events that Increase Uncertainty in Personal Relationships II," *Human Communication Research* 14 (1988), 516–547.
12. Allan L. Sillars and Judith Weisberg, "Conflict as a Social Skill," in Michael E. Roloff and Gerald R. Miller (Eds.), *Interpersonal Processes: New Directions in Theory and Research* (Newbury Park, CA: Sage, 1987), p. 148.
13. Ibid., p. 153.
14. James M. Honeycutt, Kenneth S. Zagacki, and Renee Edwards, "Imagined Interaction and Interpersonal Communication," *Communication Reports* 3 (1990), 1–8.
15. John W. Thibault and Harold H. Kelley, *The Social Psychology of Groups* (New York: John Wiley, 1959); Harold H. Kelley and John W. Thibault, *Interpersonal Relations: A Theory of Interdependence* (New York: John Wiley & Sons, 1978).
16. Amy M. Bippus, Justin P. Boren, and Sabrina Worsham, "Social Exchange Orientation and Conflict Communication in Romantic Relationships," *Communication Research Reports* 25(3) (June 2008), 227–234.
17. Brent D. Ruben, "Communication and Conflict: A System-Theoretic Perspective," *Quarterly Journal of Speech* 64 (1978), 205–206.
18. Paul Schrodt, "Family Communication Schemata and the Circumplex Model of Family Functioning," *Western Journal of Communication* 69 (2005), 359–376.

CHAPTER 13

Managing Group Conflict

OBJECTIVES

At the end of this chapter, you should be able to:

- Describe the sources of conflict in groups.
- Describe the stages of development in a group.
- Explain how roles create conflict in groups.
- Explain how mismanaged conflict leads to poor group outcomes.
- List strategies you can use to manage conflict in groups.

KEY TERMS

Abilene Paradox
bias toward cooperation
formal role
forming
group/organizational conflicts
groupthink
grievance
identity conflict
informal role
information processing perspective
instrumental/task conflict
litigation
Lucifer Effect
norming
performing
process conflict
relationship conflict
role
storming
termination

It is really no surprise to discover that groups are a source of conflict in our lives. Throughout your time in school, you have probably participated in a number of group projects. Some went well, but others may have taxed all your reserves in your efforts to contribute to a quality group project because your work depended on cooperation with others. Conflict is inevitable.

These group conflicts in college may be viewed as a good training ground for the workplace. In fact, when you consider how much time you spend at your place of work, it should not surprise you that conflicts are inevitable. For many working people, more time is spent on the job than with loved ones. Bickering, arguments, and conflicts over the task and the relationships between work members can sap a group's energy and keep it from completing the task at hand. Prolonged, unresolved conflict may even have negative consequences for team members' health[1] and for individual, group, and organizational effectiveness.[2]

As a workplace group, coworkers become a network of relationships to be managed. As "teamwork in organizations is increasingly the norm,"[3] it is important to both understand the role of conflict in teams or groups and organizations and be prepared with different strategies to address it. As we begin, we want to point out that we are using the words *group* and *team* interchangeably.[4]

One of the assumptions we begin with is this: Because of the prevalence of work groups and teams in organizations, it is often difficult to distinguish between group and organizational conflict. They feed each other. What goes on in the overall organization affects the workgroups and teams, which in turn affect the performance of the organization.

Further, we want to distinguish the more common everyday group and organizational conflicts from the less common formal grievances and litigation. **Group/organizational conflicts meet** the definition of interpersonal conflict provided in Chapter 1, but the interdependence among the parties is organizational in nature because it involves workplace relationships (boss–employee, colleagues, department heads, employee–public, etc.). Workplace relationships are more or less mandatory relationships (if one wants a job and intends to keep it), and the conflicts of interest to us here involve a "mismatch in expectations of the proper course of action for an employee or group of employees."[5] Sometimes these conflicts rise to the level of formal **grievances** in the organization that must be resolved by third parties such as human resources specialists. **Litigation** may include both lawsuits and issues involving regulatory agencies that oversee an organization. Sadly, many organizations ignore group and organizational conflicts until they become formal grievances or even litigation, when they are forced to address them.

How do we avoid unproductive conflict while allowing healthy dissension? In this chapter, we will look at the causes of conflicts in groups, the functions of conflict in groups, outcomes of dysfunctional conflict in groups, and ways to respond to conflicts. We hope that this chapter will prepare you to be a more productive and less anxious member of group tasks. In addition, since some of the concepts in this chapter are also applicable to organizations, we will introduce them here referencing both contexts, and then spend Chapter 14 looking at conflicts particular to organizations.

THE NATURE OF CONFLICT IN GROUPS

In a team, or a group, members are dependent upon one another to complete the task. Personality clashes may fuel conflicts. Differences in goal seeking concerning the task may lead to conflict. Similarly, differences about the way to achieve the task may lead to conflict, and both kinds of differences have the potential to affect working relationships between team members.

As with interpersonal conflicts, we believe that team conflicts may not necessarily be overt, apparent, or open. Frequently, before a conflict is overtly expressed in a team, members are aware of the undercurrents and are already trying to predict the way in which the conflict will unfold so they can respond appropriately to it.

Types of Conflict

In Chapter 4, we introduced you to the types or goals in conflict that we should all focus on: instrumental, relational, identity, and process goals. Since many people differ in their goals or means to the same goal, most conflicts in groups can be broadly categorized into four types: instrumental/task-oriented conflict, relationship-oriented conflict, process-oriented conflict, and task-oriented conflict.[6] In this section, we will cover types of conflicts that occur both in groups and organizations.

While instrumental goals are set by the group in the form of mission statements, policies, and handbooks, or perhaps for school group projects by the requirements of an assignment, group members may have their own ideas of how best to go about getting a job done. **Instrumental/task conflict** occurs when there is disagreement between supervisors and subordinates or among members of a team over how to get a job done. When an organization or an instructor prescribes goals, positions, and tasks, there is usually some ambiguity associated with getting the job done. Frequently those setting goals are unclear about their expectations (because they are uncertain themselves) or inadvertently miscommunicate their expectations to subordinates. Similarly, employees or group members may not pay close enough attention or fail to understand the nature of the task. When others are involved, such as a team, they may disagree with one another over how best to do a task. This type of conflict may not be a problem in the long run. A moderate amount of instrumental/task-related conflict, while it may take precious time to resolve, may result in greater efficiencies and productivity in the long run.[7]

> I had just started working for a Fortune 500 Company, when I was told to plan and organize a weekend retreat for a department that excelled for the past year. I asked my boss for more details on such retreats and what resources I had available to make the arrangements. He said he could not give me any more information because he had never been on such a retreat himself. When I asked others I knew at work, they all said it was my responsibility (my problem). I contacted a person in human resources who informed me that this was the first such recognition retreat, so there was no precedent. I was really bummed and confused. I pulled myself together and over the next few days I devoted myself to the task, putting together a weekend I hoped the department members would find most memorable. I took several risks (on expenses, location, events). I was nervous the whole eventful weekend, running around and ensuring that all went as I hoped (I had to deal with a couple of major catastrophes). While everyone seemed to have a good time and thanked me at the end of the retreat, I was still unsure of my success. However, a few days later I received a call from the same person in human resources, and she asked me to write up a step-by-step description of how I planned and organized the event. She said it would serve as a model for future years. I asked her if she would put that in writing and add it to my personnel file, which she agreed to do.

Under some conditions, though, task conflict does decrease worker satisfaction and feelings of well-being. In private, profit-structured organizations, group conflict that persists over the best way to accomplish a task interferes with the feelings of its members. If conflicts persist even in the face of achieving goals, feelings of satisfaction and well-being are affected.[8]

Relationship goals in groups and organizations are formal and informal. The organization chart or "chain of command" depicts the formal links, showing who reports to whom. The informal links include some of the formal relationships but others it takes to "get a job done" as well as people one meets in the lunch room or at the water cooler. **Relationship conflict** is tied to concepts discussed in earlier chapters such as power, trust, supportiveness, competition, and rules that govern types of interpersonal relationships including those in task-oriented groups such as those found in the workplace. Under the best of circumstances, relational conflict may be a stimulus for critical thinking, disclosure, examination of motives, and an opportunity to understand another's viewpoint. Under most circumstances, though, relationship conflict is the prime culprit for stress among team members and loss of productivity within the team. The team's capacity for effectively and efficiently processing information is impacted as "members spend their energy focusing on the personal antagonisms rather than on the task."[9] In a study comparing private to public organizations, relationship conflict was found to negatively affect feelings of satisfaction and well-being in both types of organizations.[10]

Because one's identity in groups or the workplace is connected to that person's position in the group or organization, identity goals concern one's desires for status, prestige, and authority. Bosses or supervisors expect that their employees respect their role in the organization. At the same time, each worker also wants to be treated with respect and appreciated for the work she or he does as prerequisites for promotion to higher levels. "Worker of the month" is a coveted goal and its achievement is something an employee can be proud of. **Identity conflict** occurs when others treat a person contrary to the way that person sees himself or herself. Workers receiving high job evaluations have a right to be in shock when suddenly they are laid off. Students who believe they have performed well in a group assignment will be quite angry if they receive a poor grade. Bosses are usually unhappy when their workers go over their heads. Higher level supervisors are unhappy if they are not given larger, nicer offices and preferred parking spaces than employees at lower levels of the organization. Workers are unhappy with chief executives who make bad decisions for the organization because they are highly paid and expected to expertly manage day-to-day operations. Failure of people to live up to expectations associated with their position in the workplace usually results in conflict.

Instrumental tasks, working relationships, and individual identities do not occur in a vacuum. They are managed in a way that works toward the accomplishment of broader organizational missions and goals. Process goals refer to alternative ways to manage communication and conflict. As we noted in Chapter 4, some people prefer to manage others in more open, consensual, and fair way, while the others prefer to keep more to themselves, maintain control, and assert more authority. Still others seem more chaotic with no clear plan or set of expectations. Similarly, some organizations tolerate or advocate more autocratic styles, in which the supervisor makes the decisions with little or no input from employees. Other organizations promote or permit a more democratic style, where bosses consult with and utilize input from their workers. Such an organization may have a "suggestion/complaint box" and supervisors have an open-door policy. Finally, some organizations seem much more unstructured and disorganized with unclear channels of communication and divisions of responsibility. **Process conflict** has to do with disagreements over the management style that is typical of a particular organization. Parties do not always agree on their department or organization's process goals, resulting in conflicts.

One problem occurs when some important issues in one type of conflict are neglected in favor of less important issues of another type of conflict. For example, some positive effects of process conflict could be clarification of roles and responsibilities, consensus building regarding approach to the task, and equitable workloads for members. However, the parties may shift valuable time and effort to issues that are more relationship oriented. One young military officer will never forget his briefing of a commander in a military zone.

> I was in the middle of showing the displacement of units on the military map to show the Brigade Commander which lines of defense were in the greatest need of immediate reinforcements. He interrupted my briefing to say, "Lt. put your finger in your ear." I said, "excuse me"? "You heard me," he said. "Put your finger in your ear." I did as he said, and he responded, "See your sideburns are too long." I could not believe what I heard. Here I was trying to inform the person in charge of how to save lives and prevent disaster and he was more worried about the length of my sideburns. That was the last time I agreed to brief that commander and from then on I stayed as far away from him as I could.

When people fail to clarify differences over process issues, they may begin to experience negative emotions about them and personalize process issues into relationship issues.

The narrative below illustrates how process conflict may lead to frustration:

> I was sitting in a meeting being led by someone who has absolutely no idea how to do it. There was no agenda, no business to be conducted, and he kept rambling on and on about how we might do this, we might do that, yadda yadda yadda. He didn't actually ask for input. He just kept speculating. Finally, I had enough and said if he didn't know what he wanted the group to accomplish and we didn't know either there wasn't much point in being there.

The fact of the matter is that process conflicts should take precedence over other types of issues if an organization is to survive and prosper. Typically, writers have asserted that, while relationship and process conflict can be expected to have negative effects on team performance and satisfaction, task conflict should result in higher productivity in the long run. From this point of view, task conflict "prevents moving to premature consensus, and thus should enhance decision-making quality, individual creativity, and work-team effectiveness in general."[11] Moderate levels of task conflict alone (without relationship or process conflict) lead to the best productivity.[12]

The idea that moderate amounts of conflict may be beneficial is explained by an **information processing perspective.** This perspective assumes that conflict has a curvilinear relationship with "cognitive flexibility, creative thinking, and problem-solving abilities."[13] A curvilinear effect means that high and low levels of something do not impact the concept being discussed as much as moderate levels do. At low levels of conflict, groups may not experience enough stress to think actively, and in so doing may ignore important information. At high levels of conflict, groups are unable to process information well and so perform at lower levels. The authors state, "Compared to low levels of conflict, moderate levels arouse employees to consider and scrutinize the problem at hand, to generate ideas, and to select and implement adequate problem solutions."[14]

Groups that pay attention to task and process-related conflicts will be more productive than if they focus on relationship or identity conflicts.

What does this all mean to the competent conflict manager? For one, it is important to stay focused on process conflicts and to keep the other types of conflict at a minimum. Researchers conclude:

> . . . our findings go against the current thinking that task conflict is good for performance and that relationship conflict is worse than task conflict for performance; rather, they support the information processing perspective that suggest that whereas a little conflict may be beneficial, such positive effects quickly break down as conflict becomes more intense, cognitive load increases, information processing is impeded, and team performance suffers.[15]

It is apparent that if conflict in groups is to have any beneficial effect, it must be managed at its early stages using strategies appropriate to the type of conflict experienced. Conflict that is not managed quickly is a source of stress that can also make employees feel helpless[16] and may lead to emotional exhaustion, absenteeism, and turnover in organizations, particularly if employees feel as though they have no one they can turn to for help (such as an in-house mediator or ombudsperson) in resolving the conflict.[17]

Conflict as Group Developer

Whereas examining types of conflict leads us to ask what effect conflict has on things like job satisfaction and feelings of well-being, looking at conflict from a developmental perspective helps us see conflict as a "natural part of workgroup development."[18] Effective and productive groups experience clearly identifiable phases of development that are largely defined by the kind of conflict that happens within them and the way in which that conflict is handled. From this perspective, conflicts occur because of common challenges faced by workgroup members. Conflict is productive when it moves a group toward a higher level of functioning. Known as "forming, storming, norming, and performing,"[19] this maturation process is stimulated by both external (organizational task) and internal (dynamic group tensions) conflict. You have probably experienced these phases in a group that you have belonged to.

In the **forming** phase, a tremendous amount of unfamiliarity with who is in the group and what they bring to it creates some conflicts over expectations. Some authors refer to this as the dependency and inclusion stage, as much of the focus is on how people will be included in the group. As members become acquainted and test personal boundaries, the group's structure is very tentative and participants experience a great deal of dependence upon one another. Conflict in this stage forces members to define and develop roles and check personal assumptions about both team goals and personal responsibility. When this stage is accomplished successfully, members become more attracted to the group and develop a sense of loyalty to it; they will also have a good idea of how the group is structured.[20]

The next phase, **storming,** occurs as people begin to feel some identification with the group but don't really feel a sense of unity around its purpose. In many ways, group members are struggling with the idea of belonging and the desire to be independent; thus, this phase is also called counterdependency and flight. In the storming phase, group members may use conflict quite purposefully to help create a sense of their role in the group and to influence how the group will function. Successful management of this stage will increase trust among group members and a greater sense of their purpose.

As a group works through the conflicts of the storming phase and begins to fall into regular patterns of behavior, it reaches the **norming** phase. Also called the trust and structure stage, this phase allows group members to plan effectively for the work they will do. Spurred on by the need for quickly accomplishing a specific task or activity, the team members begin to accept both their own individual roles as well as the responsibilities of fellow participants. A sense of unity emerges as members begin to replicate functions and group norms become observable. Individuals may assert themselves more regularly and be recognized as a leader. In this phase, conflict serves to reiterate and strengthen a participant's chosen action and solidify her or his roles and responsibilities within the group. The norming phase allows a group to move into higher levels of productivity in the performing phase.

Finally, the group development process culminates in the team's awareness that they are focusing on the presenting problem. In this **performing** phase (work stage), conflict serves to focus individuals on accomplishing team goals and reaching consensus. At this point, there are clear expectations regarding problem-solving behaviors that are focused on goal attainment. Behaviors such as group interactions being focused on accomplishing the team's task, individuals consistently addressing potential solutions, and attainment of consensus confirm the team's arrival at becoming a highly productive and functional performing group.[21]

The final phase of group development is **termination,** either of the group or of particular group members. The group itself may end, the particular task may end, or some members will depart or be replaced by newcomers to the group.

During these intragroup processes, a group's development can be accelerated through conflict depending upon the group's capacity to remain focused on problem analyses, their establishment of goals, and their recognition of the positive and negative aspects of potential solutions.[22] Should groups lose their focus on outcomes, conflict may become unhealthy when it is avoided or perceived as an opportunity to beat up one's opponent.[23]

> At an institution where I once taught, four faculty decided to work together as a committee to bring in speakers from other campuses for the benefit of their academic department. At the first lecture attended by faculty and student majors, one of the four committee members got into an intellectual argument with the guest lecturer. To everyone's surprise, the committee member became hostile, standing, shaking his fist, and screaming at the guest lecturer, who became equally belligerent. The committee member suddenly made a final nasty comment and stormed out of the room, leaving everyone in a most uncomfortable position. Finally, one of the other committee members escorted the speaker out of the room and to his car. There were no more departmental events involving guest speakers after that.

Unless the group can effectively manage conflict, the sum of the conflicts may be greater than the group's capacity to be effective. Should the group not be able to appropriately handle conflict, outside guidance, training, or mediation may become necessary.

WHEN CONFLICT CREATES POOR OUTCOMES

A great deal of research has been conducted on the relationship of conflict to group outcomes. In this chapter, we look at four lines of research—conflict that arises from roles, mismanaged conflict (groupthink and the "Abilene Paradox"), and situational constraints that give rise to highly destructive behavior (the Lucifer Effect).

Role Conflict

As people join and form groups and organizations, they take on different roles. A **role** is not only a job assignment but the expected characteristics of the person who fills the role. Some roles are assigned, and some roles are assumed. Difficulties arise when people take their roles too seriously, don't perform their roles well, or find that they must play multiple roles that are mutually contradictory. Consider the narrative below and the conflicting roles involved in it:

> I have a conflict with a coworker that really stumps me. I am an analyst and she is a secretary for my boss. We tend to have a pretty flat organization and people don't tend to emphasize hierarchy much. Because of my experiences, I have a great deal of knowledge about all the office computer programs that we all use. I don't have a personal secretary (unlike others in my position) and I often think that it's (1) because I'm a woman and (2) I type faster and know more than most of the secretaries I could hire. Whenever my boss's secretary has a problem making a program work, she comes to me as though I'm some sort of super-secretary that everyone should be able to access. And because she does, others think they can as well, even my male colleagues whom I'm convinced pretend stupidity to get me to help them. Sometimes I'm in the middle of a very demanding task and the boss's secretary comes in to ask me something she could figure out for herself if she really tried. And I have to admit that her ingratiating manner really bothers me. Unfortunately, I feel as though if I were to say anything, I'd look like I was making myself out to be too important or too big for my britches.

From this narrative, we see that the person telling the story believes she should play a particular kind of role, given her position in the organization. Others, though, use the knowledge she has attained to define their approach to her. Despite her high position in the organization, coworkers tend to treat her as though she is still a secretary. This example also shows us that there are both formal roles that people play and informal roles.

A **formal role** arises out of a person's assigned position in a group or organization. The organizational chart or "chain of command" reflects these formal roles and prescribes who is supposed to report to whom. In a group, for example, there may be an assigned leader or convener for the group. In an organization, people have different positional roles such as secretary, executive, receptionist, marketer, manager, and so on. In addition to indicating one's place in the group or organization, formal roles have particular expectations associated with them. Role conflict may occur when people don't act in the way the role requires, or when people aren't treated in the way they believe the role deserves. In the narrative above, the person's formal role is analyst.

Informal roles in groups and organizations arise from the way in which people actually interact with one another. In any group or organization, those working together come to know which member can unclog the copier, explain a software program, finesse the arrangements for a social event, and so on. Such task competencies are not necessarily attached to formal roles. Again, in the narrative above, the narrator feels more valued for her informal role than her formal one, but lacks the skills to address the conflict.

As people act informally in groups and organizations, they can take on one of three types of informal roles: *task roles* that help the group or organization work toward expected outcomes, *maintenance roles* that facilitate communication and resolve conflict, or *disruptive roles* that keep the group from achieving its task. Task roles include giving and receiving information, helping information flow, clarifying ideas, keeping track of what the group has done, and playing devil's advocate (initiating appropriate conflict over tasks). Maintenance roles include supporting and encouraging others, helping relieve tensions in the group, and monitoring the feelings of the group. Disruptive roles are often the source of conflicts in groups and organizations, and include such things as being an isolate, demanding the center of attention, clowning around, being cynical about all the tasks the group takes on, and so forth.

Groupthink

Groupthink occurs when people are so committed to the group and its integrity as a cohesive unit that they fail to engage in conflict when they should. When a group is too cohesive and wants to maintain an image of being cohesive, members of the group censure themselves and do not speak up even when they believe the group is headed toward a bad decision. When people are "overly concerned with reaching agreement, avoiding conflict, and preserving friendly relations in the group,"[24] the result is often groupthink. Examples of groupthink at a national level include the political groups responsible for the bombing of Pearl Harbor, where warnings were ignored, the Bay of Pigs fiasco during John F. Kennedy's administration, Watergate during Richard Nixon's administration, and the invasion of Iraq during George W. Bush's administration.

Groupthink also occurs at the smaller group level, where members may decide on a course of action that doesn't work out for the group, as this student relates:

> We had this giant group project assigned by a pretty demanding teacher. He had given us clear instructions, but we had this person in our group who had taken a class from this instructor before and claimed that he knew what we needed to do to get a good grade. We weren't really convinced, but we liked this guy and figured he knew better than we did. We wound up doing terribly on the assignment.

The "Abilene Paradox"

Unlike the phenomenon of groupthink, which is the result of mismanaged conflict, Jerry Harvey believes that the "**Abilene Paradox**" results from mismanaged agreement.[25] That is, while people believe themselves to be in disagreement with others over the decision being made, they in fact do agree with others that the decision is wrong, but no one voices that opinion. An example of the Abilene Paradox in an interpersonal situation was relayed by this student:

> My friends and I had a great time at the beach and were trying to decide what to do next. The group of us settled on a movie, a new slasher flick that just had opened. I wasn't all that interested but wanted to continue having fun with the group, so I took off with two others in my car following those who had chosen the movie. On the way, I thought I would ask one of my passengers what they thought of going to that particular movie. He wasn't interested like I thought he was, and then I had the courage to say I didn't want to see it either. The other passenger then chimed in that she didn't want to see it either. We realized that none of us wanted to see it, so we called the others and told them we were going to go to a bar instead.

The Abilene Paradox occurs because people experience anxiety over choosing a particular course of action, fear being separated from the group, have negative fantasies about what might happen if they do speak up, and are unwilling to take the consequences of what might happen if they do. In the above example, once one was brave enough to speak his mind, the others quickly decided against the idea, breaking the Abilene Paradox. The paradox can be recognized from these conditions:

1. Those involved agree privately about the nature of the problem but don't actually say anything. In the example above, the three who went to a bar agreed that seeing the new slasher flick was a bad idea but didn't say anything.
2. Those involved also agree privately on what the solution would be but don't realize they are in agreement. Apparently some of the friends were thinking that they didn't really want to see that movie.
3. With nothing said, the group goes along with what they think the consensus is and generally wind up doing something they don't want to do. Only when someone speaks out, then others may openly voice their opinions.

   Similar to the chilling effect as described in Chapter 2, the Abilene Paradox reminds us that good conflict management is necessary for groups to function well. Lencioni argues that a fear of conflict is one of the five major dysfunctions of a team;[26] the Abilene paradox is evidence of that dysfunction.

The "Lucifer Effect"

The *Lucifer Effect* is a term coined by Philip Zimbardo, who conducted the now-famous Stanford Prison studies, where students randomly assigned to roles of prisoner or guard took their roles so seriously that negative consequences occurred and the experiment had to be shut down earlier than planned. The **Lucifer Effect** is applied to situations where groups come to commit great harms due to the release of situational constraints that would otherwise keep them from behaving in such manner.[27] We include it here as an example of conflict in groups because, largely, this effect occurs where people fail to resolve issues by avoiding conflict. In a sense, it is a perversion of groupthink, where the failure to engage in conflict results in consequences that are dreadful in nature.

What leads to the Lucifer Effect and how can it be combated? The effect occurs when the right combination of circumstances in a group cause group members to act in ways contrary to their personal beliefs and values. In essence, the circumstances of the situation become more powerful than the people within it. These circumstances include the rules that govern the situation, the roles that people play, and the ways in which roles relate to one another. Let's look at each of these things.

We have previously discussed the importance of rules, which tell people what to expect and how to act in particular situations. When people are in a group or organization for a long period of time, rules may come to have "an arbitrary life of their own and the force of legal authority even when they are no longer relevant, are vague, or change with the whims of the enforcers."[28] For example, you may be in a group or organization that when you question why something is done a particular way, you are told that is just the way it is or that is the way we always do it. Thus, the first aspect of the circumstance that leads to Lucifer Effect is when rules are unquestioned, and people obey them without thinking.

A second aspect of the situation that leads to the Lucifer Effect is the role that a person enacts in the situation. When a person cannot separate himself or herself from the role that is expected, there can be negative outcomes. For example, if you are in a subordinate role in a group or organization, you may not feel it is your place to bring up negative aspects of a decision being made. Your decision not to engage in a conflict in this case may lead to serious consequences.

The final aspect of the situation that leads to the Lucifer Effect is the way in which roles relate to one another. You can't be a subordinate unless someone is over you and vice versa. When the roles that people play become entwined to the point that they no longer think about what they are doing or what others expect of them, the Lucifer Effect becomes possible.

Essentially, the Lucifer Effect is a condition that occurs when people do not stop and think about what is happening and engage in conflict when they realize they are veering off into dangerous territory. The Lucifer Effect is a reminder of the importance of engaging in a moderate amount of task conflict and a sufficient amount of process conflict to ensure that we know what we are doing and where we are going in a group. As Zimbardo notes:

> We all want to believe in our inner power, our sense of personal agency, to resist situational forces . . . For some that belief is valid . . . For many, that belief in personal power to resist powerful situational and systemic forces is a little more than a reassuring illusion of invulnerability. Paradoxically, maintaining that illusion only serves to make one more vulnerable to manipulation by failing to be sufficiently vigilant against attempts of undesired influence subtly practiced on them.[29]

STRATEGIES TO RESOLVE CONFLICT

By far the largest amount of research on group and organizational conflict takes a "styles and strategies" approach to explaining conflict. This approach emphasizes that people may have a predisposition to use a particular conflict style that results in a corresponding strategy and has focused on the relative effectiveness of each style.[30]

While a number of different authors have described various strategies for engaging in conflict, the three described by Putnam and Wilson (1982) are most often used in describing conflict experienced by groups in organizations.[31] We have discussed these strategies in Chapter 3. *Contending,* previously referred to as competition, is the attempt to impose one's will on the other. A second means is *collaborating*, which involves working with each other to find mutually acceptable outcomes. The third strategy is *avoiding* the conflict by ignoring it or working around it. Each of these strategies has an important place in team conflict and development. A fourth strategy, *compromising*, or trying to find a least objectionable alternative, may also be of occasional use, although its distinctiveness as a separate strategy has been debated. Finally, one may also use an *accommodating* strategy, which involves sacrificing one's own interests in order to maintain harmony in the group. While this strategy has been identified as an option, in its use it will resemble avoiding so closely that an observer would be hard-pressed to tell the difference.

The strategy one should employ to effectively manage conflict depends on the type of conflict experienced. It also requires that we have a **bias toward cooperation** as we deal with conflicts in groups. Thus, we would argue, first of all, that a contending strategy constitutes an inappropriate response to conflict within a group. Unless a person is convinced, and has the force of evidence to support his or her conviction, that the group's direction is not only wrong but also harmful, contending is a strategy best left unused.

If contention is out of the picture as a possibility, we are left with avoiding, accommodating, collaborating, and compromising as our alternatives. The preponderance of evidence suggests that task and process conflicts are productively confronted in their early stages through collaborating and compromising strategies. This is a logical conclusion: Since task and process conflicts have the potential to clarify issues and processes, it is most effective to deal with those conflicts early in a direct way so that information-processing activities are activated, resulting in team creativity, innovation, and productivity.

A conflict manager may need to avoid some conflicts, such as relationship-oriented issues. One might think that it makes sense to openly confront all issues facing the team, but research says otherwise. Recall that "relationship conflicts concern insights and information that are unrelated to the task, involve negative emotions and threaten one's personal identity and feelings of self-worth."[32] Trying to deal with such issues may actually escalate their intensity rather than resolve them. In the case of relationship-oriented conflict, maintaining ambiguity through avoidance may allow the issue to simply resolve itself over time. De Dreu and Van Vianen's research concluded that using avoiding responses to relationship-oriented conflicts resulted in higher levels of team performance, whereas the use of contending or collaborating responses lowered team performance overall. The authors concluded that avoiding responses might be better for two reasons:

- The first is that relationship conflict is difficult to settle to mutual satisfaction... Thus, being cooperative and understanding in the case of relationship conflict is unlikely to solve the problem, and make it instead loom bigger and intractable....
- The second explanation is that collaborating and contending responses direct team members away from their tasks and instead focus them (even more) on their interpersonal relations. As a result, team members do not invest their time and energy in teamwork, and team functioning and effectiveness suffers...[33]

Overall, then, the successful handling of conflict in groups requires a great deal from conflict managers. First, it requires that we develop a habit of cooperation and act in ways that build group cohesiveness, because it is clear that groups that trust one another handle conflict in more productive terms. Second, it seems a good idea to avoid, at least initially, relationship-oriented conflicts, because they have the potential of being resolved over time as team members come to know one another better. Finally, it is best to approach process- and task-related conflicts in an expedient manner, favoring collaborating strategies as a way to explore alternatives for future behavior.

MANAGE IT

Although conflict in groups and organizations has the potential to slow productivity and negatively impact job satisfaction, the fact is that it does occur. Ultimately, whether the presence of conflict in groups and organizations becomes productive or destructive, improves functioning or derails the group or organization from its task depends upon team members' response to it.

You learned in this chapter that conflict in groups is a variation on conflict between two people. There are more parties involved, but generally speaking, conflicts occur over the goals that people bring to the situation. Instrumental/task goal conflicts concern the best way to accomplish the group's assignment. Relationship goals are related to what group members want in power, trust, supportiveness, competition, and rules that govern types of interpersonal relationships within the group. Identity goal refers to the way that person wants to see himself or herself. Process goals concern the way group members want to interact together. Research from the information-processing perspective indicates that focusing on process goals is most effective for a group.

Group development proceeds through stages or phases. In the forming phase, a tremendous amount of unfamiliarity with who is in the group and what they bring to it creates some conflicts over expectations. The next phase, storming occurs as people begin to feel some identification with the group but don't really feel a sense of unity around its purpose. In the norming phases, a sense of unity emerges as members begin to replicate functions and group norms become observable. In the performing phase, conflict serves to focus individuals on accomplishing team goals and reaching consensus. At this point, there are clear expectations regarding problem-solving behaviors that are focused on goal attainment. The final phase of group development is termination, either of the group or of particular group members. The group itself may end, the particular task may end, or some members will depart or be replaced by newcomers to the group. Unless the team can effectively manage conflict in all phases, the sum of the conflicts may be greater than the team's capacity to be effective. Should the team not be able to appropriately handle conflict, outside guidance, training, or mediation may become necessary.

In this chapter, we looked at four lines of research—conflict that arises from roles, mismanaged conflict (groupthink and the "Abilene Paradox"), and situational constraints that give rise to highly destructive behavior (the Lucifer Effect). In many ways, conflicts over roles and people's inability to be flexible within the roles they play resulted in negative outcomes for groups characterized by groupthink, Abilene, and Lucifer.

Finally we discussed the various strategies people may use to manage conflicts in groups. These include avoiding, accommodating, compromising, contending, and collaborating. For some issues, especially those involved in relationship and identity, avoidance and/or accommodation can be a good way to manage the conflict, as groups that develop over time also develop an understanding for those kinds of differences. However, we recommend a bias toward cooperation as we deal with conflicts in groups. In Chapter 14, we build on the various concepts of conflict introduced in this chapter and then discuss some specific kinds of conflicts that are present in organizations.

Think About It

1. When have you seen task-related conflict contribute to productivity in a group or organization? When has it been unproductive?
2. Have you used an avoiding strategy in the past with a group and found that things did work out over time?
3. What kind of roles do you play in groups? Are you comfortable with those roles?
4. When have you seen groupthink, the "Abilene Paradox," or the "Lucifer Effect" take place in a group? What conditions gave rise to them?

Apply It

1. Think back to one of your experiences in a group. Describe the experience and show how your group went through the five stages of group development.
2. Give an example of an instrumental/task conflict, a process conflict, a relationship conflict, and an identity conflict in a group or organization.
3. Using the example you identified in Think about It, or a new example, analyze a situation in which groupthink, the "Abilene Paradox," or the "Lucifer Effect" took place. Who was involved? What roles did each person play? What was the situation? How did it come to be dysfunctional?
4. Recall a group conflict in which you have been involved. List the five strategies for dealing with a group conflict and show how each of them might have been used to manage the conflict.

Work With It

1. Read the following case study. Imagine that you are a human resources officer to whom this person is relaying the information. How would you advise this person to operate more effectively in his or her group given the information you have learned in this chapter?

   When I began working at my new job a little over 18 months ago I found that I always had to prove myself to my coworkers. Where I work, we often work as a team to get the job done. Perhaps it was my coworkers' way of "testing" me, but whatever the reason I found it frustrating. Even my good ideas would be brushed off simply because I was the "new guy." After awhile I stopped arguing and took my ideas straight to our boss. The team got really upset over that. Now we aren't working together at all.

   a. What kind of conflicts did this person encounter?
   b. What stage of development is this group?
   c. How have roles created conflict in this group?
   d. What strategies from this chapter did she use to address the conflicts that arose?
   e. What strategies from this chapter might have produced better outcomes?

2. Read the following case and answer the questions following it.

   A few years ago my position at work changed, and I suddenly became responsible for the nursing and ancillary staff on the unit. I had worked with some of these nurses as equals and I was now playing a supervisory role; suddenly my friends were now my subordinates. Deciding how to deal with the various conflicts were quiet challenging at first. One of my greatest challenges was trying to make the monthly staffing schedule. The problem was that everyone wanted specific time off, which would sometimes mean that most of the staff would request to be off on a particular day. Since we were already short staffed it was impossible to give everyone what they wanted and as such it was up to me to decide how it was going to be done in a way that would ensure we had enough staff to provide quality patient care, and at the same time not alienate the staff.

   a. What kind of conflicts did this person encounter?
   b. What stage of development is this group?
   c. How have roles created conflict in this group?
   d. What strategies from this chapter did she use to address the conflicts that arose?
   e. What strategies from this chapter might have produced better outcomes?

NOTES

1. Carsten K. W. De Dreu, Dirk van Dierendonck, and Maria T. M. Dijkstra, "Conflict at Work and Individual Well-Being," *International Journal of Conflict Management* 15 (2004), 6–26; Maria T. M. Dijkstra, Dirk van Dierendonck, Arne Evers, and Carsten K. W. De Dreu, "Conflict and Well-Being at Work: The Moderating Role of Personality," *Journal of Managerial Psychology* 20 (2005), 87–104.

2. Carsten K. W. De Dreu, Arne Evers, Bianca Beersma, Esther S. Kluwer, and Aukje Nauta, "A Theory-Based Measure of Conflict Management Strategies in the Workplace," *Journal of Organizational Behavior* 22 (2001), 645, 645–668.

3. Carsten K. W. De Dreu and Laurie R. Weingart, "Task versus Relationship Conflict, Team Performance, and Team Member Satisfaction: A Meta-Analysis," *Journal of Applied Psychology* 88 (2003), 741.

4. Generally, people in academe write about groups, and people in business write about teams, but there

is not enough difference in the way they are discussed to try to maintain a distinction here. Portions of this chapter are adapted from Frank Berry and Ruth Anna Abigail, "Cooperation in Conflict: The Key to Effective Teaming," in David McIntire (Ed.), *Teamwork: Making the Dream Work* (Indianapolis, IN: Precedent Press, 2007).

5. David B. Lipsky and Ronald L. Seeber, "Managing Organizational Conflicts," in John G. Oetzel and Stella Ting-Toomey (Eds.), *The Sage Handbook of Conflict Communication: Integrating Theory, Research, and Practice* (Thousand Oaks, CA: Sage Publications, 2006), p. 362.

6. Karen A. Jehn, "A Qualitative Analysis of Conflict Types and Dimensions in Organizational Groups," *Administrative Science Quarterly* 42 (1997), 530–557; A. M. Passos and A. Caetano, "Exploring the Effects of Intragroup Conflict and Past Performance Feedback on Team Effectiveness," *Journal of Managerial Psychology* 20 (2005), 231–244.

7. Carsten K. W. De Dreu, "When Too Little or Too Much Hurts: Evidence for a Curvilinear Relationship between Task Conflict and Innovation in Teams," *Journal of Management* 32 (2006), 83–107.

8. José M. Guerra, Inés Martinez, Lourdes Munduate, and Francisco J. Medina, "A Contingency Perspective on the Study of Consequences of Conflict Types: The Role of Organizational Culture," *European Journal of Work and Organizational Psychology* 14 (2005), 157–176.

9. Tony L. Simons and Randall S. Peterson, "Task Conflict and Relationship Conflict in Top Management Teams: The Pivotal Role of Intragroup Trust," *Journal of Applied Psychology* 85 (2000), 102–111.

10. Guerra, Martinez, Munduate, and Medina, "A Contingency Perspective on the Study of Consequences of Conflict Types."

11. C. K. W. De Dreu, and Bianca Beersma, "Conflict in Organizations: Beyond Effectiveness and Performance," *European Journal of Work and Organizational Psychology* 14 (2005), 109, 105–117.

12. Karen A. Jehn and E. Mannix, "The Dynamic Nature of Conflict: A Longitudinal Study of Intragroup Conflict and Group Performance," *Academy of Management Journal* 44 (2001), 238–251.

13. De Dreu and Beersma, "Conflict in Organizations," p. 108.

14. Ibid., p. 108.

15. De Dreu and Weingart, "Task versus Relationship Conflict, Team Performance, and Team Member Satisfaction," p. 746.

16. Maria T. M. Dijkstra, Dirk van Dierendonck, and Arne Evers, "Responding to Conflict at Work and Individual Well-Being: The Mediating Role of Flight Behaviour and Feelings of Helplessness," *European Journal of Work and Organizational Psychology* 14 (2005), 119–135.

17. Ellen Giebels and Onne Janssen, "Conflict Stress and Reduced Well-Being at Work: The Buffering Effect of Third Party Help," *European Journal of Work and Organizational Psychology* 14 (2005), 137–155.

18. Marshall Scott Poole and Johny T. Garner, "Perspectives on Workgroup Conflict and Communication," in John G. Oetzel and Stella Ting-Toomey (Eds.), *The Sage Handbook of Conflict Communication: Integrating Theory, Research, and Practice* (Thousand Oaks, CA: Sage Publications, 2006), p. 269.

19. B. Tuckman, "Developmental Sequences in Small Groups," *Psychological Bulletin* 63 (1965), 384–399.

20. Poole and Garner, "Perspectives on Workgroup Conflict and Communication."

21. Ricky Griffin, *Management,* 8th Ed. (Boston, MA: Houghton Mifflin Company, 2005).

22. Passos and Caetano, "Exploring the Effects of Intragroup Conflict and Past Performance Feedback on Team Effectiveness," 2005.

23. D. Levi, *Group Dynamics for Teams* (Thousand Oaks, CA: Sage Publications, 2001)

24. J. Dan Rothwell, *In Mixed Company*, 7th Ed. (Boston, MA: Wadsworth, 2010), p. 231.

25. Jerry B. Harvey, *The Abilene Paradox and Other Meditations on Management* (San Francisco, CA: Jossey-Bass, 1988).

26. Patrick Lencioni, *The Five Dysfunctions of a Team* (San Francisco, CA: Jossey Bass, 2002).

27. Philip Zimbardo, *The Lucifer Effect* (New York: Random House, 2007).

28. Ibid.

29. Ibid., p. 180.

30. Anne Maydan Nicotera and Laura Kathleen Dorsey, "Individual and Interactive Processes in Organizational Conflict," in John G. Oetzel and Stella Ting-Toomey (Eds.), *The Sage Handbook of Conflict Communication: Integrating Theory, Research, and Practice* (Thousand Oaks, CA: Sage Publications, 2006), p. 298.

31. Linda L. Putnam and C. E. Wilson, "Communicative Strategies in Organizational Conflicts: Reliability and Validity of a Measurement Scale," in Michael Burgoon (Ed.), *Communication Yearbook*, Vol. 6 (Beverly Hills, CA: Sage, 1982).

32. De Dreu and Van Vianen, p. 310.

33. Ibid., p. 322.

CHAPTER 14

Managing Organizational Conflict

OBJECTIVES

At the end of this chapter, you should be able to:

- Describe the sources of conflict in organizations.
- List strategies you can use to manage conflict in organizations.
- Describe diversity-based conflict.
- List strategies you can use to manage diversity-based conflict.
- Describe work–life conflict.
- List strategies to manage work–life conflict.
- Describe workplace bullying.
- List strategies you can use to combat bullying in the workplace.

KEY TERMS

bullying
civility
collective voice
diversity-based conflict
exodus
psychological detachment
retaliation
reverse discourse
subversive (dis)obedience
work–life conflict
workplace conflict

This chapter focuses more on issues that give rise to conflict in organizations, more commonly referred to as the **workplace conflict.** Of course, in the workplace, organizational dynamics may be similar on a smaller scale in a group, so much of what we have to say about organizational conflict can also apply to task-oriented groups.

Mismanaged conflict in organizations can result in lowered productivity, less creativity, and less innovation. Prolonged, unresolved conflict may even have negative consequences for team members' health.[1] According to De Dreu:

> The effectiveness of individual employees, teams, and entire organizations depends on how they manage interpersonal conflict at work . . . Managers spend an average of 20 per cent of their time managing conflict . . . , and evidence suggests that conflict and conflict management at work substantially influences individual, group and organizational effectiveness.[2]

In this chapter, then, we describe three important organizational phenomena: conflict arising from diversity, work–life conflict, and the prevalence of workplace bullying. We also introduce the concept of civility as an important conflict management tool.

ORGANIZATIONAL DIVERSITY AND CONFLICT

Perhaps the greatest cause of conflicts in organizations arises from our differences. **Diversity-based conflict** occurs when our personal characteristics, such as our identification with cultural, ethnic, and racial groups, are the source of the conflict. As the working world becomes more diverse, it is inevitable that different values, beliefs, and practices will come into conflict with one another. Whether or not the results of this kind of conflict are productive depends on a number of factors. The research in this area has produced contradictory findings. On the one hand, conflict from perceived differences between group members may result in negative effects; on the other hand, those differences may enhance the information and perspectives available to group members.[3]

Differences may arise from two basic sources: social category characteristics (age, ethnicity, gender, etc.) and informational characteristics (work experience, education, values, beliefs, etc.). Conflicts arising from social category characteristics may be tied to perceptions of an in-group and an out-group, us versus them.[4] Further, it is possible that, since it is one person's perception that indicates the presence of a conflict, those who are members of minority groups are more likely to perceive a conflict than those in the dominant group. Dominant group members may be so accustomed to taking their view for granted that they "sometimes fail to realize their own prejudices. Modern racists, for example, do not recognize themselves as racist despite their capacity for holding subtly racist attitudes."[5] Two such conflicts about taken-for-granted assumptions are related below:

> Monday was my birthday and my supervisor invited me to have lunch. I was upset with her at first because she did not ask me but simply told me the date we were going out, the time that I should meet her, and where we would be eating. I felt that she was forcing me to do something and not taking my interest into consideration.

> Our office has a habit of going out to lunch once a month. Although not everyone can attend, we try to make it local and get as many people to go as possible. There is an understanding that we will pick restaurants that appeal to the range of people's eating habits—some of us are on diets, and a couple of us are vegetarians. When it was one man's turn to pick, he did his typical "white male, I'm privileged, you're invisible" routine and chose a BBQ place that doesn't even serve vegetables and covers fatty pieces of meat with sauce. Needless to say, we had a poor turnout on that one, but he couldn't understand why.

Of course, eating preferences are not the only way personal characteristics lead to diversity-based conflict in the organization. We subtly make judgments about the other person's gender, race, social standing, and so on, whether or not we meet them face to face. As we do so, our own gender, race, and so on become important to the interaction with other. The problem is that we are often unable to see what we do.[6] When conflicts over such characteristics are covert rather than overt, it is hard to know how to manage the conflict.

Informational characteristics also create conflict in ways we are often unable to see. While a group is more likely to be productive and have a variety of resources at its disposal where there is a high level of informational diversity, those invisible characteristics may lead to conflict that is difficult to manage. For example, a person who has studied communication might have very different expectations about the way instructions are relayed than someone with a technical background. As the narrative below indicates, we need to work hard to understand where the conflict is coming from in order to manage it correctly:

> I sometimes have to work with this particular woman in our organization. She really drives me crazy, because we will try to accomplish some task, and then a day or two after I think it's been taken care of, she'll shoot an email that starts off, "I've been thinking . . . " I dread those. It means we're not done yet, because she outranks me and can keep me returning to something that feels pretty finished to me.

Differences due to diversity often manifest themselves in intractable conflict, so we expand on strategies for managing such conflicts in Chapter 15. For now, though, we suggest the following for dealing with conflicts that arise from issues of diversity.

To begin with, while it risks stating the obvious, we would caution you to be willing to accept that you may be wrong. Rather than engaging in conversation with the readiness to refute all the other has to say, be willing to listen to the other. Listening does not imply agreement, after all. It simply implies respect and regard for the other as a human being.

Second, we would ask you to remember that not only are your experiences unique, but so are the experiences of others. You cannot presume to understand what another person has lived, felt, or seen. Honoring the stories of others, understanding that each person carries with them a narrative important to them, is probably the most effective way to manage conflicts due to diversity.

Civility as a Response

An important means of responding to conflicts across all contexts, but particularly organizational ones, is the habit of civility. Civility is not to be confused with simple etiquette or communication rituals. **Civility** is constituted by an attitude of respect toward others manifested in our behavior toward them; that respect is not predicated on how we feel about them in particular. Gonthier defines civility as "being mindful of the dignity of the other person in your sphere at all times."[7]

Is civility really a problem for us? The answer, unfortunately, is yes. One needs only to drive on an interstate, stand in a long line, deal with a government agency, or listen to people in a shopping mall to realize that civility is lacking in our society. The use of profanity is at an all-time high; according to a recent radio station's *"Guess What?"* game, the average American curses 70–80 times a day. Incivility is no stranger to the workplace, either. As Sutton points out, "many workplaces are plagued by 'interpersonal moves' that leave people feeling threatened and demeaned, which are often directed by more powerful people at less powerful people."[8] Sometimes, incivility becomes so intense that it is better characterized as bullying, a set of behaviors we discuss later in this chapter.

Carter's seminal work on *Civility* provides a perspective on why we have become so uncivil toward one another. He traces the historical development of books of etiquette, developed to help people get along in close quarters. Some of the earliest American writings on civility were proposed as guidelines to help people get along on railway cars, where they were thrown together with strangers for long periods of time. The early writings were reminders to passengers that they were not alone on the train. They were in the company of others who would be affected by untoward behavior. As Carter points out, in many ways, we have become unaware of the fact that we are not solitary passengers through life. The relative isolation of our lives today, whether in our cars, our homes, and our communities, often leads us to act in ways that are rude to others.

Carter also indicates that attitudes and behaviors constitute civility, but he takes the idea a bit farther. Civility, Carter argues, "is the sum of the many sacrifices we are called to make for the sake of living together."[9] These sacrifices may include giving up the need to be right or the need to be heard in order to attain a greater good for the organization as a whole. This does not mean we suppress needed and helpful conflict, but that we stop and think about whether speaking up really is necessary for the good of all. Carter argues that "a nation where everyone agrees is not a nation of civility but a nation withered of diversity. . . . When we are civil, we are not pretending to like those we actually despise; we are not pretending to hold any attitude toward them, except that we accept and value them as every bit our equals. . ."[10] In other words, how we treat others should be independent of what we think of them. Sometimes, it takes a while for people to catch on to this notion, as the narrative below indicates:

> I have to work with someone who has been a thorn in my side for a long time. We have been on the opposite sides of most issues, and he has done some things that would get him fired anywhere else. To my dismay, I found that I would have to attend the same conference as he and be in his company for a week! I was not happy about it, and spent some time bad-mouthing him to one of my colleagues who was also attending the conference. He finally told me that if I was going to continue like that for the week, he was going to ask for hazardous duty pay when we returned. I realized at that moment that I was turning into the kind of jerk I thought the other person was. I decided to try something different. I was nice to him the whole conference. I'm not going to tell you that I like him any better now, but being civil did have its own rewards. I wasn't anxious; I wasn't irritated; I was just polite. The colleague who formerly had said he wanted hazardous duty pay was amazed.

Given the importance of civility, what are the behaviors a person should adopt that reflect it? To begin with, civility is a way of being attentive, acknowledging others, thinking the best of others, listening, being inclusive, speaking kindly, accepting others, respecting their boundaries, accepting personal responsibility, and apologizing when necessary.[11] Troester and Mester offer five specific rules for civil language at work:

1. The best words to choose when caught in an unexpected, emotional-charged situation are no words at all.
2. Use words respectful of the specific listener to whom they are addressed.
3. Respect the reality of the situation by choosing temperate and accurate, not inflammatory, words when describing or commenting on ideas, issues, or persons.
4. Use objective, nondiscriminatory language that respects the uniqueness of all individuals.
5. Respect your listeners by using clean language all the time on the job.[12]

We close with some of the principles that Carter lays out in his book, as they provide the most wide-ranging set of assumptions that can help us to engage in civil behavior.

As we discussed previously, the decision to be civil to others should not depend on whether we like them. Further, since civility is seen as sometimes sacrificing one's own wishes, that sacrifice must be extended to strangers as well as people we know. Civility is both a commitment not to do others harm but a commitment to do good for others. When we disagree, civility requires that we be honest about our differences and do our best to manage them rather than suppressing them or ignoring them. Finally, as Carter argues, civility requires that we come into the presence of others with a sense of awe and gratitude, rather than a sense of duty and obligation.

Civility is an important skill in our conflict management toolbox. Along with the strategies covered later that can be used to respond to bullies, and the methods of response to intractable conflicts that we discuss in Chapter 15, we believe civility should be the primary skill people learn in order to function more effectively inside and outside the workplace.

WORK–LIFE CONFLICT

A common source of conflicts in organizations concerns **work–life conflict,** which arises from keeping a balance between one's personal life and the demands of work. As more women have entered the workforce, questions of child and family care become more evident, and not simply for women in cases where men are the primary caregivers. Further, workers in the United States work longer hours and more weeks per year than any other industrialized nation. We are the only first world country with no guarantee of a vacation. Especially for the working poor, work–life conflict reaches critical levels when attending to one's personal life may result in lost income.

Work–life conflict isn't limited to one socioeconomic class. For example, technology such as wireless phones carried by practically everyone including those in managerial positions has created a sense of always being on call. We expect that people are immediately available and get frustrated when we are unable to get a speedy answer to a question we have. We may find ourselves trying to do more than one task at one time because of such devices—answering e-mails while in a meeting, and checking e-mail in the evening while watching television.[13] Even train engineers have had accidents while texting, which raises the question of whether we can effectively do more than one task at a time. In fact, the availability of such technology actually slows down decision making in an organization rather than speeding it up, because those at higher levels expect to be consulted since their availability can be taken for granted. Decisions that really don't require consultation wind up getting it anyway.

Work–life conflict is not necessarily limited to those with families, because single persons or couples without children also expect to have a personal life outside of work. There are three different kinds of conflict that can arise from the interference of work and life demands: conflicts due to time limitations, conflicts due to interference between roles at work and roles at home, and conflicts that arise when behaviors appropriate to one role carry over to another where they are not appropriate. We will look at each of these in turn.

Clearly, the easiest conflict to identify and probably the hardest one to address is the limitation of time. When a person has multiple roles, the hours required by each role added together may overwhelm that person. Sometimes a second role is demanded by the organization itself, as this narrative indicates:

> I work for a religiously oriented organization. Not only am I expected to put in my 40-plus hours a week, but I am also expected to be an active member of my church. That means not only am I expected to attend services each week (in some ways, creating a longer work week), but I am expected to take part in the activities of the church and contribute my time and energies to a number of programs. That means if I have other personal interests and want to participate in other family activities, they have to take second place to this expectation my organization has of me. It's hard to find enough hours in the week to have interests besides work and church.

The second type of work–life conflict occurs when a work role interferes in some way with a role outside of work. For example, one role a person is playing (e.g., work) may create a great deal of pressure, which makes the person difficult to live with at home.

> I am a financial consultant, who manages the investments of many well off corporate executives. When the markets are up, I get invited to parties and golf outings, meet other prospective clients, and receive many pats on the back. However, when the markets are way down, I feel like I am really under the gun. My clients act as though I am to blame for losses in their portfolios. They accuse me of mismanaging their money and want to withdraw all their investments at the worst time. I try to reason with them, and some understand that financial markets are naturally volatile, but others call me at all hours day and night to rake me over the coals or to get me to calm them down. With the recent down market, I haven't slept well in weeks, not eaten well, and am not feeling well.

And as this person relates:

> As a human resources specialist, I deal with conflicts all day long. I listen to people. I try to hear their stories. I try to help them work out their problems. By the time I get home, I do not want to hear one word about something that may be wrong. When I leave work, I have had it with people's problems and just want to be left alone. It's not a good way to respond to my family at home, but I am exhausted.

A final contributing factor to work–life conflict concerns inappropriate behaviors. When a person is used to giving orders at work, it may be hard to turn that off when he or she comes home. Likewise, a person who is nurturing at home may be expected to be so at work as well, leading to compassion fatigue. Problems arise when a person is unable to adjust from one setting to the other.

> One of the difficulties with being a teacher is that I often respond to questions at home the same way I would in the classroom—by explaining a concept and checking for understanding. It worked okay when my kids were young because they thought I knew everything anyway. By the time they were teenagers, though, it was apparent from the eye-rolling and their impatience with the way I answered even a simple question that it wasn't effective.

Organizations and workers can lessen the impact of work–life conflict. For example, "Flex-account policies" offer employees options depending on their work–life circumstances. Some need more flexibility in working hours, vacation times, child care, maternity leave, and elder care. What works well for me might not work for you and vice versa. Such policies help reduce work–life conflict. Unfortunately, not everyone supports flex-account policies.

Some managers resort to the "fair but consistent" approach (deciding that everyone should be treated alike—claiming that is the only "fair" way to make decisions—denying flexibility to everyone).

Supportive coworker relationships may also help reduce work–life conflict. "Talking with coworkers about family and personal life has been shown to lead to greater work satisfaction and higher work functioning as well as higher satisfaction with family activities."[14] Likewise, one can talk with family and friends about problems at work. However, you may recall, back in Chapter 8 on "Managing Anger," we cautioned frustrated individuals from venting their anger on others rather than the problem person. While we recommended using the constructive confrontation steps in Chapter 2 to work through conflicts with the person responsible for them, we also realize that not all people in the workplace or at home respond well to assertiveness. We recommend that you start out trying to be assertive, but if this backfires, then you can temporarily resort to accommodation and avoidance. In such cases, you may benefit by talking with coworkers about marital problems at home or venting to family and friends about problem people at work.

Overall, work–life conflict is a serious issue for organizations and the employees who work within them. Balancing demands, having sufficient rest and "down time," and setting reasonable boundaries on what organizations demand will continue to be challenges for us.

WORKPLACE BULLYING

From the Playground to the Boardroom

While workplace bullying is not a new phenomenon, the study of it is fairly recent. According to a recent study, "Workplace bullying behavior is a noteworthy and prevalent issue in organizations around the world (e.g., Denmark, Sweden, Norway, Finland, Ireland, UK, Korea, Japan, Germany, Italy, Australia, New Zealand, Mexico, US, and other countries),"[15] and almost 80 percent of workers report having witnessed or experienced bullying.[16]

Bullying is "a frequent, enduring abusive interaction distinguished by targets'—bullied workers'—inability to defend themselves."[17] Bullying is behavior far more serious than general unpleasantness or single-issue conflict. It is distinguished by "four specific features: intensity, repetition, duration, and power disparity."[18] It is meant to control or harm others through insults, gossip, criticism, ridicule, and other verbally aggressive behaviors. Bullying is a pattern of abuse that persists; it is estimated that "... the average duration for US workers is 18–20 months."[19] One of the difficulties organizations have in dealing with workplace bullying is that there are no legal remedies for it as there are for sexual harassment or racial discrimination in the workplace; there is simply no law against being a jerk.[20]

> Bullying behavior is manipulative, divisive and vindictive and can be expressed aggressively, passively or with a mixture of both behaviors. This blend of passive-aggressive behavior is common. People on the receiving end not only feel bullied but are confused by the mixed messages. Employees on the receiving end feel diminished—neither respected nor valued. The only way in which people who resort to bullying can feel better about themselves is to hurt others, putting them down and humiliating them.[21]

The effects of bullying on the target can range from mental stress through physical illness. The longer or the more a person is bullied the more the individual is harmed physically, mentally, and emotionally. Victims often report headaches, body aches, anxiety and panic attacks, sleeplessness, self-medication, overeating or undereating. They also often dread or fear going to work. They frequently are afraid their complaints about the bullying will not be heard or will make it worse. For their own protection, victims often isolate themselves.[22] When people are bullied, they may feel shame at being so vulnerable, and in turn create negative self-talk that essentially revictimizes them.[23] "Victims of bullying may even show symptoms of post-traumatic stress disorder (PTSD) . . . "[24]

Unfortunately, one response of those who are bullied is to try to bully back. Those who experience verbal aggression are likely to respond with it in kind. However, counterattack is generally unsuccessful and may even worsen the bullying taking place. As the authors noted,

> Targets who successfully coped with bullying . . . [counterattacked] less often and sought to avoid further escalation. In contrast, the less successful targets contributed to the escalation of bullying by their own aggressive counterattacks and "fight for justice."[25]

Generally, those who bully perceive themselves to have more power than those who are bullied, although that power may not be derived from a formal position. Bullying by someone above the target's formal position is most frequent (superior to subordinate), followed by horizontal bullying (peer to peer), and upwards bullying. This student relates an example of superior–subordinate bullying:

> While serving in the Coast Guard, I had a supervisor who only knew one way to communicate with his co-workers—he was always the boss. He demanded everything he wanted and most of his co-workers felt bullied in the workplace. Instead of using language that would encourage co-workers to work harder, he chose to demean people and challenge them with personal attacks. We later learned that he took the assignment in our office not because he wanted to but because he knew it would help him get promoted to the next rank. He did not care about being fair to the employees he was working with.

Upwards bullying, while not common, may occur where employees see the supervisor as weak and ineffective. It is often the result of employees believing that the manager-as-victim is responsible for stress-causing factors in the organizational environment. Bullying may be one way that staff members express dissatisfaction with the weak leadership style of the manager. Upward bullying also often follows organizational change or a change in leadership.[26]

> Whenever, one of my employees, Michael, is upset with policies or programs that are communicated from above, he rushes into my office, shuts the door, paces back and forth, and with red face and bulging eyes makes demands that will satisfy some need that has been sitting on a back burner until this ripe moment. I am a woman, and I am terrified of Michael and fear that he may lose control completely, so I find myself always agreeing with him right away and giving him what he wants. To me this is taking the "squeaky wheel" idea to the extreme by forcing the weak into submission. I tolerate his abusive

behavior because I don't want to ask for help from my boss for fear that she will think I am incompetent. Unlike me, she is a large woman and is known for her menacing and dominating management style.

The effects of bullying are not limited to the victim. Witnesses to bullying often suffer from decreased creativity and mental performance.[27] Those who witness someone being bullied are more likely to perceive their organization in a negative manner than those who do not.[28] When a group is aware that one of its members is being bullied, relationships among group members may be affected. Other group members may fear to intercede lest they become the bully's target. Further, prolonged exposure to bullying behaviors may desensitize members to it and lead them to eventually engage in it themselves.[29]

Does a particular type of person engage in bullying? Early work in the area identified dispositional hostility, a lack of self-control, a history of enacting aggression, positive attitudes toward revenge, and substance and/or alcohol abuse as predictors of workplace aggression.[30] There is some evidence that a person likely to bully is also likely to act in a discriminatory manner toward groups other than his or her own. Additionally, trait anger, verbal aggressiveness, and ethnic/racial superiority are associated with bullying. Further, a person less able to take the perspective of another is more likely to bully others as well.[31] Men appear to be more likely to bully than women, at least in those who have been studied, although typically men bully men and women bully women. In addition, large organizations that are male dominated tend to have more bullying in them than other types of organizations.[32]

If a particular type of person is likely to bully, is there a corresponding target profile? One study found that about a third of those who were bullied tended to be "more anxious and neurotic and less agreeable, conscientious and extravert than non-victims,"[33] while the rest had no characteristics that distinguished them from people who weren't bullied. The danger, of course, in even trying to determine whether there is a particular target profile is that it runs the risk of blaming the victim rather than preventing the negative behavior in the first place.

Managing Bullies

What is the most effective way to combat workplace bullying? In the absence of organizational systems that keep it in check, targets of bullying have several other ways of responding. The research discussed above indicates that counterattack is not effective. We believe that civility may be an effective response to bullying, but it is difficult to employ. In addition to civility, other strategies have been discovered.

Lutgen-Sandvik's research found that there were a variety of ways that people found to combat bullying.[34] First, a strategy that may be more empowering for the target is **reverse discourse,** which encompasses several tactics of responding to the bully through communicative means. One means is simply turning an insult around and treating it as though it is a compliment—"yes, I'm a troublemaker." Other communicative strategies include the use of lawyers, outside experts, or oversight agencies to help in bringing a halt to the bullying. The target may also file a formal or informal grievance against the bully. The target may document all interactions with the bully so that he or she can accumulate a large body of evidence before engaging in a formal complaint. A person may confront a bully by using the confrontational ritual presented in Chapter 2, which seems on the surface as the most positive approach. As teachers and researchers of communication, we (the authors) believe in trying communication first, but unfortunately, we have found that it does not always work as we hoped. At least we can say we tried. Don't be surprised if bullies are resistant to change and often fail to respond productively to what you think, feel, or want. One mark of a bully is a person who wants to control, dominate, and abuse others.

A second means of coping with bullying is **subversive (dis)obedience,** which falls under the category of passive-aggressive behavior we discussed in Chapter 3, where the target changes his or her work output or communication patterns in ways that disadvantage the bully. For example, the target of a bully may increase his or her work for a while and then let it drop off, making it difficult for the bully to predict workflow. The target may also work-to-the-rule, doing exactly what is required or the minimum required of the bully. A worker can insist that a particular job takes a particular amount of time to process, even though it could be done more quickly. As this person writes in his narrative:

> I was in a meeting with my boss and tried to say something when he told me to shut up. Not only did he say it to me once, he actually said it to me three times, even though I was trying to explain something really important to me. I was pretty steamed at him. I thought it was degrading and parental. I decided that two could play that game. For nearly three weeks, I gave him no information and initiated no communication with him. He had to ask for everything. He never apologized, but I felt better.

A person may also engage in **retaliation,** which includes hostile gossip and/or fantasies for physically harming or killing the bully. Using these options a person uses the system in order to create problems for the bully or to have others take action against the abusive person. Subversive (dis)obedience also encompasses the creation of distance between oneself and the bully, physically if possible but also by limiting communication options.

Realize for your own protection that there is a fine line between the aggressive behavior taken by a target of bullying and a problematic employee. Deciding on your own that a supervisor is "out to get you" does not mean that your retaliatory behavior is justified. The abusive supervisor must in fact truly be a bully. Others must agree with you that the problem supervisor has a history of engaging in clearly inappropriate tactics, including picking on weaker people, and menacing, threatening, and offending them. Bullies cannot hide; they stand out clearly and are usually a problem for everyone including their own bosses.

A third means of coping is through **psychological detachment,** or creating a sense of being away from work. Psychological detachment reduces the effect a bully has, as well as providing for better leisure time away from work. It is largely achieved through self-talk, reminding yourself to leave work and the bully at the office. In the office, it is the equivalent of taking a mental vacation. For instance, if you can imagine the bully in a ridiculous situation, or envision something funny happening, your stress level comes down. Be aware, though, that thoughts of revenge increase stress levels.[35]

A more positive approach to dealing with bullying is **collective voice,** when employees talk amongst themselves about their experiences and what they can do about them. The important aspect of collective voice is that it helps the bullied victim realize that he or she is not alone and that what he or she is experiencing is real. Collective voice results in people agreeing to protect each other and even start recording and reporting the bullying. However, some bullies may respond by increased harassment of individuals when they are not gathered as a group with the goal of forcing them to quit one by one. Knowing this, some find the workplace terrifying.

Finally, one last way to deal with a bully is **exodus.** This works especially well when one is only in a temporary situation. A person can quit, make a threat to quit, put in for a transfer, or aid others in quitting. This response is found in the following narrative:

> One of my jobs getting through school was at a fast-food restaurant. The night manager with whom I worked was a royal bully. She found fault with everything, called people stupid, and told them to do work over just to please her. One night, I had as much as I could take. I was working the window, she was cooking, and the person backing me up was not good at making change. So when the night manager insulted me, I simply quit. There were cars lined up around the building to place orders, but I had enough.

When we have recommended quitting, others tell us that they can't for some financial reason or other. In such cases, we suggest that they view their work situation as temporary and plan ways to transfer or find a better place to work at some clearly defined time in the future, such as graduation, marriage, pregnancy, separation from a spouse, or repayment of debt. We recognize that we all have to put up with bad work situations from time to time, but we do not want them to last longer than absolutely necessary.

MANAGE IT

The fact that we spend a third of our waking hours in organizations make it important for us to understand and manage conflict within them. We defined conflict earlier in this textbook but we need to emphasize here that the interdependence among the parties is organizational in nature because it involves workplace relationships (boss–employee, colleagues, department heads, employee–public, etc.) and organizational rules of conduct. Although conflict in organizations has the potential to slow productivity and negatively impact job satisfaction, the effective management of such conflict may enhance worker productivity and job satisfaction or at least reduce its harmful effects. Ultimately, whether the presence of conflict in organizations becomes productive or destructive, improves functioning or derails the organization from its task depends upon team members' response to it.

In this chapter, then, we address the sources of these everyday conflicts in organizations and discuss various means to manage them. We also discuss three important organizational phenomena: diversity-based conflict, work–life conflict, and the prevalence of workplace bullying.

For conflicts resulting from diversity in the workplace, we need to be more in tune with cultural differences and how they may be accommodated in the workplace. We need to embrace civility. As for work–life imbalances over the long run, we must strive for relieving hyperstress by balancing demands, having sufficient rest and "down time," and asserting ourselves when negotiating with our supervisors reasonable boundaries on what they can demand of our time and energy. For dealing with bullies in the workplace, a person may use a variety of communicative means, such as turning an insult around and treating it as though it is a compliment; solicit the help of lawyers, outside experts, human resources, or oversight agencies; file a formal or informal grievance against the bully; document all interactions with the bully to accumulate a large body of evidence; and/or confront a bully by using the confrontational ritual, but be prepared for failure because bullies are resistant to change and often fail to respond productively to what we think, feel, or want. Remember our warning that one mark of a bully is a person who wants to control, dominate, and abuse others.

In the event that communication with a bully does not bring about desirable results, there are other options. A person may engage in passive-aggressive behavior like subversive (dis)obedience, by changing his or her work output or communication patterns in ways that disadvantage the bully. A person may rally others at work in an effort to "gang up" on the bully, although the bully may retaliate and pick on lone individuals when others are not there to protect them. As a last resort, a person can quit her or his job or put in for a transfer.

Our approach in this chapter is to encourage you to carefully analyze an organizational conflict so that you apply the appropriate response to it. Effective conflict management also includes awareness of options that exist in every situation. All too often we respond to problematic situations by habit rather than make a more effective and appropriate response.

Think About It

1. Where have you seen issues related to diverse members become a conflict in the workplace?
2. Do you agree that people in the United States are less civil to one another than they were in the past? Is it possible today to adopt the principles of civility? What reservations do you have with respect to them?
3. How do you try to balance your work and personal life? How do you avoid or minimize conflicts between them?
4. Have you ever been the victim of a workplace bully or witnessed bullying? How did you and others respond to it? Were your efforts effective?

Apply It

1. Consider a situation in which you experienced a conflict based on diversity issues. What was it about? How did you manage the conflict? List the principles of civility that would be most useful in dealing with such a conflict.
2. Return to the situation you identified for Think about It, or consider a new situation. List five different strategies you could use to deal with a workplace bully in that kind of situation.

Work With It

1. Imagine you are in charge of creating a new program for employees at your place of business. Based on your reading of this chapter, create a list of principles for working together that you would teach to incoming employees.
2. Read the following case study and answer the questions following it.

> In the last six months our department has seen a lot of change from new staff members, people leaving, and changes in production and structure taking place in a very short period of time. One very important piece of our department left us in three months ago to move onto another organization. Since his departure, we have watched his area take a nose dive in morale and teamwork.
>
> The problem is between two individuals who are fighting to be top dog. They each think that they should be able to run the facility and tell the other one what to do and how to do it. When one thinks the other isn't doing what he is supposed to, she will do it for them and then tell the acting supervisor "he was supposed to do it, but I did it for him." They each are trying to get to the top of the ladder but the rest of us are just not sure what ladder they are trying to climb considering there is no ladder in that particular area. Their positions are equal and although they do have different responsibilities each day, these responsibilities were created for each of them so we can allow for the area to run smoothly each day.
>
> These two individuals will argue about every little thing possible including not breaking down boxes for the bailer, not slicing the ham the way the other likes it, or not making the marinara sauce the way the other likes it. Once the arguing escalates, it turns into verbal aggression. Their verbal aggression has included name-calling or yelling about what the other does not do to help out or how they deal with new student interns verses those who have been around for a while.
>
> It all came out in the open when both employees blew up and created a scene in front of a small group of student interns. Both employees were sent home for the remainder of the day to cool off and were asked to come back to work the next day afternoon so that they could sit down and talk with their supervisor and one other management team member. All the different types of conflict were brought to the table including the way they speak to each other and how it reflects on the department and how it affects the students and other employees that they work with each day. The managers explained to them that there was no reason to compete for the top, tell on each other, or be aggressive because it did not change the situation that was taking place.
>
> They also asked each person to share what their goals were by working in this department and for their future. Each employee was given a duty list that needs to be followed each day without issue and any issues that did arise must be logged in a book and also explained to the manager. They were also given each a new project that they could take ownership of. This summer they will share their projects with the rest of the department and, if approved, the projects will be implemented.

1. In the above case study, what kinds of strategies were used to manage the conflict between these two workers?
2. Do you think they were effective?
3. How might you have managed the conflict differently?

NOTES

1. Carsten K. W. De Dreu, Dirk van Dierendonck, and Maria T. M. Dijkstra, "Conflict at Work and Individual Well-Being," *International Journal of Conflict Management* 15 (2004), 6–26; Maria T. M. Dijkstra, Dirk van Dierendonck, Arne Evers, and Carsten K. W. De Dreu, "Conflict and

Well-Being at Work: The Moderating Role of Personality," *Journal of Managerial Psychology* 20 (2005), 87–104.
2. Carsten K. W. De Dreu, Arne Evers, Bianca Beersma, Esther S. Kluwer, and Aukje Nauta, "A Theory-Based Measure of Conflict Management Strategies in the Workplace," *Journal of Organizational Behavior* 22 (2001), 645, 645–668.
3. Karen A. Jehn, Katerina Bezrukova, and Sherry Thatcher, "Conflict, Diversity, and Faultlines in Workgroups," in Carsten K. W. De Dreu and Michele J. Gelfand (Eds.), *The Psychology of Conflict and Conflict Management in Organizations* (New York: Lawrence Erlbaum Associates, 2008).
4. Kristin Smith-Crowe, Arthur P. Brief, and Elizabeth E. Umphress, "On the Outside Looking In: Window Shopping for Insights into Diversity-Driven Conflict," in Carsten K. W. De Dreu and Michele J. Gelfand (Eds.), *The Psychology of Conflict and Conflict Management in Organizations* (New York: Lawrence Erlbaum Associates, 2008).
5. Ibid., pp. 416–417.
6. Cecilia L. Ridgeway, "Framed before We Know It: How Gender Shapes Social Relations," *Gender and Society* 23 (2009), 145–160.
7. Giovinella Gonthier, *Rude Awakenings: Overcoming the Civility Crisis in the Workplace* (Chicago, IL: Dearborn Publishing, 2002), p. xiii.
8. Robert I. Sutton, *The No Asshole Rule* (New York: Warner Business Books, 2007), p. 20.
9. Steven Carter, *Civility* (New York: Harper Perennial, 1998), p. 11
10. Ibid., p. 23.
11. P. M. Forni, *Choosing Civility: The Twenty-Five Rules of Considerate Conduct* (New York: St. Martin's Griffin, 2002).
12. Rod L. Troester and Cathy Sargent Mester, *Civility in Business and Professional Communication* (New York: Peter Lang Publishing, 2007), pp. 78–85.
13. Ronald J. Burke argues that such technology reinforces the value of "workaholism" in the organization by rewarding those who are constantly on call. Ronald J. Burke, "Workaholism in Organizations: The Role of Organizational Values," *Personnel Review* 30 (2001), 637–645.
14. Erika L. Kirby, Stacey M. Wieland, and M. Chad McBride, "Work Life Conflict," in John G. Oetzel and Stella Ting-Toomey (Eds.), *The Sage Handbook of Conflict Communication: Integrating Theory, Research, and Practice* (Thousand Oaks, CA: Sage Publications, 2006), p. 333.
15. Joyce Heames and Mike Harvey, "Workplace Bullying: A Cross-Level Assessment," *Management Decision* 44 (2006), 1214, 1214–1230.
16. Pamela Lutgen-Sandvik, "Take this Job and . . . : Quitting and Other Forms of Resistance to Workplace Bullying," *Communication Monographs* 73 (2006), 407, 406–433.
17. Lutgen-Sandvik, "Take this Job and . . . ," p. 407.
18. Pamela Lutgen-Sandvik, Sarah J. Tracy, and Jess K. Alberts, "Burned by Bullying in the American Workplace: Prevalence, Perception, Degree and Impact," *Journal of Management Studies* 44 (2007), 841, 837–863.
19. Lutgen-Sandvik, "Take this Job and . . . ," p. 408.
20. Helen LaVan and Wm. Marty Martin, "Bullying in the U.S. Workplace: Normative and Process-Oriented Ethical Approaches," *Journal of Business Ethics* 83 (2008), 147–165.
21. Anni Townend, "Viewpoint: Identifying and Managing Bullying in the Workplace," *Human Resource Management* 16 (2008), 3, 3–5.
22. Anni Townend, "Understanding and Addressing Bullying in the Workplace," *Industrial and Commercial Training* 40 (2008), 270, 270–273; see also Lutgen-Sandvik, Tracy and Alberts, "Burned by Bullying in the American Workplace."
23. Dianne M. Felblinger, "Incivility and Bullying in the Workplace and Nurses' Shame Responses," *JOGNN* 37 (2008), 234–242.
24. Lars Glasø, Stig Berge Matthiesen, Morten Birkeland Nielsen, and Ståle Einarsen, "Do Targets of Workplace Bullying Portray a General Victim Personality Profile?" *Scandinavian Journal of Psychology* 48 (2007), 317, 313–319.
25. Raymond T. Lee and Cé leste M. Brotheridge, "When Prey Turns Predatory: Workplace Bullying as a Predictor of Counteraggression/Bullying, Coping, and Well-Being," *European Journal of Work and Organizational Psychology* 15 (2006), 371, 352–377.
26. Sara Branch, Sheryl Ramsay, and Michelle Barker, "Managers in the Firing Line: Contributing Factors to Workplace Bullying by Staff—An Interview Study," *Journal of Management & Organization* 13 (2007), 264–281.
27. C. Porath and A. Erez, "Overlooked but not Untouched: How Rudeness Reduces Onlookers' Performance on Routine and Creative Tasks," *Organizational Behavior and Human Decision Process* 109 (2009), 29–444.
28. Lutgen-Sandvik, Tracy, and Alberts, "Burned by Bullying in the American Workplace."
29. Heames and Harvey, "Workplace Bullying."
30. Jana L. Raver and Julian Barling, "Workplace Aggression and Conflict: Constructs, Commonalities, and Challenges for Future Inquiry," in Carsten K. W. De Dreu and Michele J. Gelfand (Eds.), *The*

Psychology of Conflict and Conflict Management in Organizations (New York: Lawrence Erlbaum Associates, 2008), p. 219.
31. Irina Sumajin Parkins, Harold D. Fishbein, and P. Neal Ritchey, "The Influence of Personality on Workplace Bullying and Discrimination," *Journal of Applied Social Psychology* 36 (2006), 2554–2577.
32. Margaretha Strandmark and Lillemor R.-M. Hallberg, "The Origin of Workplace Bullying: Experiences from the Perspective of Bully Victims in the Public Service Sector," *Journal of Nursing Management* 15 (2007), 332–341.
33. Glasø, Matthiesen, Nielsen, and Einarsen, "Do Targets of Workplace Bullying Portray a General Victim Personality Profile?" p. 317.
34. Lutgen-Sandvik, op. cit.
35. Bernardo Moreno-Jiménez, Alfredo Rodriguez-Muñoz, Juan Carlos Pastor, Ana Isabel Sanz-Vergel, and Eva Garrosa, "The Moderating Effects of Psychological Detachment and Thoughts of Revenge in Workplace Bullying," *Personality and Individual Differences* 46 (2009), 359–364.

CHAPTER 15

Managing Social Conflict

OBJECTIVES

At the end of this chapter, you will be able to

- Define social conflict.
- Explain why social conflicts are often intractable.
- Explain an intractable issue using critical theory.
- Explain an intractable issue using ripeness theory.
- Explain the difference between nationalism and patriotism.
- Describe the ways in which people distance themselves from others.
- Explain the concept of embrace.

KEY TERMS

critical theory	intractable conflicts	patriotism
colonize	intractable issue	pluralism
embrace	moral issue	praxis
exploitation	mutually enticing opportunity	ripeness
demonize	mutually hurting stalemate	romanticize
generalize	nationalism	silence
group-based hatred	nonviolent communication	trivialize
homogenize	oppression	vaporize
injustice	Other	worldview

In Chapters 1 through 4, we focused on conflicts that could be cleared up by communication. As soon as people assert themselves, confront the issue and other person, they often find that they can come to agreement. In Chapter 5, we explored conflicts that were more complicated because they dealt with tangible issues, resources that are often scarce, so more than communication was required to deal with the conflict. By using techniques learned from the field of negotiation, we offered ways to think more creatively and expand the range of options for resolving such conflicts.

In this chapter, we emphasize yet another type of issue that cannot be resolved by communication and negotiation techniques because they involve different and conflicting value systems. We call these intractable issues. What makes the intractable issues different from other issues? An **intractable issue** becomes part of an interpersonal conflict situation when those involved not only fail to agree on their goals, or see their activities as incompatible, or feel as though relational rules have been broken, but, when those involved become so entrenched in the discussion of who is right and who is wrong, they are unable to get past the issue. While those involved may have started the conflict by trying to persuade each other to their point of view, the conflict begins to repeat itself over and over as those involved fail to change the other and thus begin to see the other as someone who is unable to understand reason. In a sense, an **intractable conflict** transcends the people involved because it is a clash of their social or cultural, religious or political, and economic philosophies. In everyday encounters, these conflicts are represented by conflicting parties from different cultures, races, ethnic, religious, or political groups.

American society, and indeed most of the world today, faces problems created by pluralism. The **pluralism** we must learn to live with is "the socio-cultural reality of discrepant worldviews, ideologies, and moral frameworks, existing side by side."[1] If we are to live in peace with others who are different from us, it is absolutely essential to learn how to manage the intractable issues that arise from such deep differences.

This living side by side with people we characterize as **Other**, or as strange and different from ourselves, has provided fertile ground for the establishment of intractable issues. Also referred to as social conflicts, societal conflicts, and moral conflicts, we prefer the term **intractable issues** and distinguish them as those fueled by distrust and dislike of other groups due to differences in attitudes, values and beliefs.

UNDERSTANDING INTRACTABLE ISSUES

What happens when representatives of conflicting value systems try to resolve their differences? In the field of communication, much of the early work on intractable issues was conducted using the term **moral issue,** referring to those conflicts that arose out of opposing views of right and wrong. Because of the inability of participants to agree on how to resolve their differences, intractable issues are persistent: They "fuel themselves and are therefore self-sustaining. Often the original issue becomes superfluous . . . Participants in a moral conflict tend to treat each other as mad, bad, sick, or stupid, and they experience a crisis of rationality, feeling that they cannot reason with people 'like that.' "[2] An example of this inability to communicate is found in the abortion controversy. A person who believes that a woman has the right to control her body finds no common ground with a person who believes that a fetus is an unborn human being with rights independent of its mother.

Intractable conflicts often take on a pattern that is something other than what any of the participants wanted or expected. Each side is hard-pressed to understand why its best efforts to communicate are not understood by the other side. What makes perfectly good sense to one person may be totally ridiculous to another when each is viewed within his or her values. As each party in the conflict is unable to understand, hear, or agree with what the other has to say, or disregards the arguments of the other, the conflict becomes more entrenched. The pattern of discourse in a conflict involving an intractable issue moves from persuasion to schism. Each side initially believes the other capable of understanding if it hears both sides. However, after getting nowhere, it treats the other side as crazy and unworthy of communication. When conflicts become entrenched, participants on one side have nothing to say to those on the other side and that is when they start labeling the other as subhuman, perverts, and infidels.[3]

As the conflict becomes more deep-rooted, the discourse in the conflict becomes more simplified and shallow. It no longer reflects the richness of reasoning that first characterized the conflict; instead, slogans and simple answers substitute for arguments and reasoning as each side despairs of winning the other to its way of thinking. When a person on one side in the intractable conflict addresses those who think like him or her, discourse continues to be eloquent and elaborated; in addressing outsiders, discourse becomes simplified and defensive. As discourse fails, violence becomes more likely; "as a response to moral conflict, force becomes a self-sealing pattern. Each side views the other as aggressor or oppressor, and violence is viewed as necessary for self-protection."[4] An example of a conflict that is already entrenched is found in this narrative:

> I was listening two family members argue about the topic of abortion. The first said she believed in the right to choose. The second got so mad that he said "that's what all liberal dogs believe." At this point I stepped in and said "Just because you do not agree with her views does not mean you should call her or liberals 'dogs.' " Next, he said "how about pigs, then, is that better? Whose side are you on? I thought you were against abortion!" I responded that I am against abortion, but I respect and understand her view. She has been a social worker for over thirty years and has seen a girl as young as 11 who was raped by a family member (father). As a result the girl became pregnant, so do you believe they should now force an 11 year old who did not make a choice to have sex in the first place to give birth to her own biological sibling? She strongly believes that this would further mentally and physically damage this young victim of domestic sexual abuse. I told him he was dehumanizing her and others whom he may not fully understand because of their views.

Intractable issues are fueled by many variables in the context surrounding them. The media may help inflame conflicts. Polarizing talk that asserts only two sides in the debate fuels intractable issues. Creation of an out-group, and dehumanization of the out-group, is especially provocative. Personal attacks rather than focus on issues, violence, and calls for sacrifice may also fuel intractable issues.

The characteristics of intractable issues are:

1. In terms of actors, intractable issues involve states or other actors with a long sense of historical grievance, and a strong desire to redress or avenge these.
2. In terms of duration, intractable issues take place over a long period of time.
3. Intractable issues involve intangibles such as identity, sovereignty, or values and beliefs.
4. In terms of relationships, intractable issues involve polarized perceptions of hostility and enmity, and behavior that is violent and destructive.
5. In terms of geopolitics, intractable issues usually take place where buffer states exist between major power blocks or civilizations.

6. In terms of management, intractable issues resist many conflict management efforts and have a history of failed peacemaking efforts.[5]

Because of the nature of intractable issues, people often try to avoid topics that are likely to escalate, as this person notes:

> Participating in the discussions of morality is often not first choice for most people, including me. I like to think/act respectful of everyone's opinion, and for this I have been told that I lack conviction. Our ability to think and express ourselves is a double-edged sword; we have morals that differ based on our religion, culture, and family and yet we are part of one world. What is most mind-boggling for me is that if we live in a country where we have freedom of religion, why is it then that we do not have freedom of morality? Is it fair to say that what is right for some is not right for all?

Sometimes, those involved in intractable issues may have the opportunity to simply ignore one another, engaging in **silence** as a way of dealing with the conflict. Silence, however, cannot bring understanding or reconciliation to an intractable issue. Morgan and Olsen argue, "So long as dialogue in a community is perceived as dangerous, the community will forgo again and again the opportunity to learn from one another and to heal the differences and relational fractures that quietly separate them.[6]

In other cases we can agree to disagree. We can grant each other our views without them affecting us emotionally or intellectually. This approach works when we can accept the other but continue to think and believe as we do. This often happens in families or among friends. But what if the intractable issue is such that it presents a real problem for the parties? Some intractable issues cannot be ignored, accepted, or tolerated.

Problematic intractable issues that exist at the societal level are often driven by group-based hatred. **Group-based hatred** is orientated toward a particular goal; those who hold it want to hurt, relocate, or even eliminate the out-group. Group-based hatred fuels the notion that the in-group is right, good, and holy and the out-group is wrong, bad, and evil. As Halparin notes:

> Hatred is a powerful, extreme, and persistent emotion that rejects the group toward which it is directed in a generalized and totalistic fashion. Group-based hatred is provoked in consequence to recurrent offenses committed against the individual or his or her group. These offenses are perceived as intentional, unjust, threatening the person or his or her group, and of a nature with which in practice the individual has difficulty coping.[7]

Intractable conflicts often revolve around these type of issues:[8]

- One person or group seeks to deny another person or group their sense of self, or denies the legitimacy of the other's group identity. For example, in most parts of the United States, a gay couple cannot marry. And even if they can marry, they still are not allowed spousal benefits such as tax benefits, health care proxy, and so on.
- One person or group seeks to deny another person or group such fundamental needs as security or the ability to pursue one's own goals. For example, the homeless are often told to leave public parks if they try to sleep during the day. At night, there are few places for them to sleep, and if they create places for themselves, those places are often destroyed when

discovered by authorities. Another example is when abortion protestors block the entrance of clinics, making it difficult for women to enter.
- One person or group seeks to put themselves ahead of others in the social, political, or economic structure. For example, commentators on both sides of the political spectrum often deride and denounce those holding political views different from themselves. They reflect no appreciation for others' desire and ability to hold different positions.
- One group seeks to control resources in a win–lose conflict where no expansion of the resources is possible. The ongoing conflict between Israel and Palestine over occupation of territory is an example of this intractable issue.

The narrative below gives an example of how intractable issues that are global in nature filter down to interpersonal relationships.

> For me, one of the most memorable experiences I had as a first-year student at a large public university was developing friendships with people who were not likely welcome at my parents home. While I was Protestant, my best friend was Catholic, and we sat up many nights discussing the nature of God, Heaven, and Hell, from our respective viewpoints. We both seemed open minded at the time, willing to hear each other out, and learn from one another. Another of my classmates was from Switzerland and another from Jordan. My Swiss friend was predictably neutral on his attitudes about the United States, while my friend from Jordan was critical of America's role in the Middle East. I learned from them that other views existed on the actions America has taken in the world at large. I have continued my friendship with the Catholic and Swiss citizen although I lost track of my friend from Jordan. Somehow we were able to address issues and remain friends because we were open to each other's views.

This narrative suggests that two common intractable issues, one political/economic philosophy and the other religious beliefs, may be managed in a way that does not do damage to the relationships. What is the nature of these intractable issues and how can they be managed in conflict situations?

In order to better understand the nature of more problematic intractable issues, we offer an example of intractable issues: those fueled by patriotism and nationalism.

Patriotism and Nationalism

Few would argue that the character of communication in the United States has not changed since 9/11. For the first time since World War II, the United States was attacked on its own ground, by terrorists who hated the United States. Since that time, there has been a rising level of nationalism that characterizes questioning actions taken by the United States as unpatriotic and unsupportive of our armed forces. Although one of the founding fathers, Thomas Jefferson, claimed, "Dissent is the highest form of patriotism," such an ideal has been largely lost with the rise of neoconservatism in the years since 9/11.

This rising nationalism of the United States and the way in which ideas were expressed during the Bush administration made for some unhappy leaders in the rest of the world. Hugo Chavez, president of Venezuela, characterized President Bush as the devil himself. In his speech to the UN General Assembly on September 20, 2006, he said:

> Yesterday, ladies and gentlemen, from this rostrum, the president of the United States, the gentleman to whom I refer as the devil, came here, talking as if he owned the world. Truly. As the owner of the world.
>
> I think we could call a psychiatrist to analyze yesterday's statement made by the president of the United States. As the spokesman of imperialism, he came to share his nostrums, to try to preserve the current pattern of domination, exploitation and pillage of the peoples of the world. . . . the American empire is doing all it can to consolidate its system of domination. And we cannot allow them to do that. We cannot allow world dictatorship to be consolidated.

Such extreme communication is at the heart of an intractable issue. But the criticism of Bush's form of patriotism did come from within the United States as well. As many neoconservative writers began to claim that what was good for America was good for the rest of the world, one author went so far as to compare Bush's form of patriotism to fascism. She claimed "at the heart of fascism is a . . . nationalism that identifies the nation with all that is good—not just for the individual but for the world and all humanity."[9]

We are not arguing that patriotism is bad. We are saying that nationalism can fuel intractable issues. **Patriotism** is "love for one's country as it is and a willingness to defend it against foreign aggression."[10] **Nationalism,** on the other hand, is a "love of one's nation as it will be once it has exterminated all its enemies, become totally unified, and achieved its grand purpose of world-historical destiny."[11] A nationalist not only wants world dominance, but believes that his or her nation is the only one suited to such dominance and that dominance will benefit others. When a person is attacked for criticizing the decisions made by his or her government, it is a good sign that nationalism, rather than patriotism, is dominating the conversation.

You may argue that you can ignore one's nationalism and patriotism—they fuel conflicts at a level where you don't need to operate. Think, however, of the way you talk to people who make different political choices from you, as the person in this narrative:

> I'm not sure how my sister and I grew up in the same family, because we are totally different politically. My sister is a Republican. I'm not always a Democrat; sometimes I register Independent or Green. She is completely a party-line person. There's no one in any other party worth her trouble, and she will vote for a Republican over a Democrat even if she doesn't like the candidate. All during the Bush administration she expressed her admiration for many decisions that I felt were wrong. When I told her I was supporting Barak Obama for president, she asked me how I could support a Black Muslim who hated America. That was when I just said we ought to avoid talking about politics with one another as we weren't likely to come to any mutual understanding.

Republicans and democrats or conservatives and liberals alike need to try to comprehend each other's political or economic view rather than view each other in terms of generalizations about "what the Republicans and conservatives think" or "what Democrats and liberals hold true." This will perhaps demand more of those in power because their view becomes the dominate one until an election changes who is in power. Of course, each political or economic group must also explain their views in a way that does not show disrespect to the other group.

We hope that you believe with us that our nation is best served by the presence of all the voices within it. Voices that suppress dissent and do not allow for the healthy exchange of ideas are those that create and perpetuate intractable issues. As one student wrote:

> It occurred to me that as we become a smaller world, we are "rubbing up against" people of many different cultures and backgrounds and the dissonance created has increased tremendously. The fallback reaction of self-justifying our own beliefs is not a solution. I think one of the reasons that I dread the upcoming political season is because we do not get to hear the underlying beliefs of either group. Instead, the name-calling rhetoric has taken center stage and no one winds up a winner. Ironically, it is the Christians who have gotten the worst reputation for being self-righteous, unwilling to hear other viewpoints, and in general, seen as ignorant fools. I do not have to accept others' beliefs as my own; however, I do have to accept their right to have those beliefs. By practicing the methods of civility and nonviolent communication, I would have the opportunity to gain a greater understanding of why other people believe what they believe, and also the opportunity to explain my own value system as well.

THEORIES OF SOCIAL CONFLICT

Two recent theories have been proposed to account for the way intractable issues are managed by the parties engaged in them. Critical theory helps both participants and consultants understand the dynamics of the conflict situation, while ripeness theory accounts for the timing of a solution to an intractable issue.

Critical Theory

Critical theory is a complex approach to understanding situations, which analyzes power relations between the participants in an effort to uncover oppression, exploitation, and injustice.[12] Practitioners of critical theory are oriented toward social justice outcomes, changing situations that cause people to live in dehumanizing ways. As this definition is rather complex, let's take it apart and examine each of the terms.

At the core of critical theory is the assumption that the distribution of power in a society creates and perpetuates instances of oppression and injustice in societies. **Oppression** characterizes human relations where one group or set of groups are able to dominate and exploit another group or set of groups. **Exploitation** may be economic, physical, or psychological in nature. **Injustice** occurs where such patterns of exploitation are perpetuated and controlled through dominant social classes and may include exploitative wage labor, poverty, homelessness, and lack of access to adequate education or health care.

In order to understand patterns of domination and oppression, critical theory analyzes power relationships between groups. This can be a difficult task, as power is not always expressed overtly. Dominant groups may use their power to restrict access to information or resources without making it seem as though they are the ones doing the restriction. Unlike a mediator, who tries to be as neutral as possible in helping others to manage a conflict, a critical theorist takes the approach that social actions cannot be neutral. In fact, if a practitioner attempts to be neutral, he or she might actually wind up supporting the status quo that continues in oppression. Critical theorists often align themselves with the less powerful party in order to teach them how to change their society.

The primary method of critical theory is **praxis,** which

> ... is the reciprocal, dynamic, and reflexive relationship that practitioners engage in when their theorizing about societal oppression informs their actions taken to challenge that oppression, and vice versa ... *Praxis* also puts the scholar or practitioner in a position of continuous reflection, questioning the theory-action relationship in order to continuously revise his or her approach. A *praxis* orientation is inherently future-oriented and hopeful, with scholar-practitioners creating new visions for societal relationships in overcoming societal domination, which in turn are an impetus for further societal analysis and action.[13]

A person involved as a critical theorist has to know a great deal about his or her worldview and what is valued within that worldview. Without that knowledge, one runs the risk that personally held values and beliefs may actually subvert the process of getting those in an intractable issue to find new ways of acting together.

So, how might one approach an intractable issue from critical theory assumptions? First, the conflict mediator will examine his or her own assumptions about the conflict. Where do his or her sympathies lie? How do his or her values impact the way the conflict is viewed.

Second, the conflict mediator will look for ways in which people are allowed access to the expression of their ideas on the conflict. Is one group allowed better access than the other? Does one group have more resources than the other? Does one group have more right to define the conflict than the other group? One author argues that media coverage of crowds demonstrating with respect to a particular issue often can frame public reaction to them:

> ... studies of press accounts likewise point to an association between the political position of the commentator and the type of language used to describe crowd events ... those critical of crowd participants' motives are more likely to describe an event in negative terms (e.g. "riot") rather than neutrally (e.g. "demonstration") or positively (e.g. "people power"). The delegitimizing functions of such negative language and explanations are obvious. If the crowd is pathologized and criminalized, then its behaviour is not meaningful. There can therefore be no rational dialogue with it. Since the crowd is not part of the democratic process, it is legitimate and even necessary to suppress it with the full force of the state.[14]

Finally, the conflict mediator needs to use many of the communication, mediation, and negotiation skills from our earlier chapters to analyze the problem; however, recognizing that a solution may be a long time in coming.

Ripeness Theory

In addition to critical theory, ripeness theory is a means of accounting for and addressing intractable issues.[15] As reflects its name, this theory focuses on ripeness, which is a condition that is linked to one side's decision to negotiate with the other in a conflict. Proponents of this theory argue that when conflict participants realize that the path they are following produces pain, they will begin to seek ways to reduce that pain. If a less painful alternative is found for them, the parties will want to seek out that alternative. **Ripeness** occurs when participants in a conflict realize that they are involved in a **mutually hurting stalemate** (neither can get the advantage, and all actions hurt both self and other) and recognize a **mutually enticing opportunity** (both may gain without giving away something of value). "Thus, ripeness is based on two core motives: pain and opportunities to escape from pain."[16]

Some people have argued that a limitation of ripeness theory is that it assumes rationality. Some people may be so committed to their cause that pain, suffering, and sacrifice mean nothing as long as the cause is advanced. Further, the theory assumes that both parties have to be ripe at the same time, and that ripeness is an either/or means of orientation toward a conflict rather than a more of/less than means of approaching the conflict. Despite these shortcomings in the theory, practitioners can work toward the management of conflict by doing the following:

1. Look for factors that might strengthen positive attitudes toward alternatives to the conflict. For example, help the participants see alternatives as less costly and painful.
2. Emphasize the factors that create pain for the participants in the current situation. Help the participants understand that continuing with the status quo will continue to increase pain and suffering for them.
3. Look for factors that can tip the participants toward ripeness by making destructive conflict less attractive and peace more so.

WAYS OF APPROACHING "THE OTHER"

Both critical theory and ripeness theory suggest some skills and strategies for dealing with an intractable issue. We believe that at the heart of any success in ameliorating an intractable issue is the ability to approach someone who is *other*—different—in ways that are honoring to that person and in using communication that is nonviolent in nature.

Let's start with the ways of dealing with otherness that people sometimes engage in due to fear and misunderstanding of their differences. Each of these ways increases our separation from others.[17]

First, we sometimes **demonize** the other, by treating him, her, or the group as someone to be feared and eliminated if possible. Think, for a moment, of the way in which Americans talk about terrorists. Are terrorists people with ideas? With wants and desires? With any kind of agenda to be heard? It is unlikely that you will hear such sentiments.

A second means of increasing separation is to **romanticize** the other by considering the other as far superior to ourselves. One student took issue with the romanticizing of former criminals:

> I am always amazed when people celebrate dirt bags like Stanley "Tookie" Wilson because they turned their life around and spoke out against those who still do the same horrific things they did. Or when they write a book like *Monster* or *Always Running* and are celebrated for these "masterpieces" and their support of community values.

The Western world has a long history of engaging in the third means of separation. For centuries, the British Empire, France, Spain, and, later, the United States engaged in colonization. When we **colonize** others, we treat them as inferior, worthy of pity (perhaps) but more likely contempt. Proponents of slavery in the United States often argued that it was beneficial for African Americans because they couldn't take care of themselves. Entire native civilizations in Asia, Africa, and North and South America were decimated by those who colonized them.

The fourth means of separation is to **generalize** the other, treating people as nonindividuals. When we say things that reflect knowledge of a group rather than knowledge of an individual, we are generalizing. For example, any time we respond to another person solely on the basis of his or her apparent ethnicity, we are engaging in generalization.

Two ways of treating the other that enhances separation are at opposite ends of the spectrum. At the one end, we may **trivialize** the other—by ignoring what makes the other disturbingly different; at the other, we may **homogenize** the other—claiming there really is no difference between them and ourselves. Both refuse to see the other as an individual.

Finally, perhaps the most disturbing way people create separation is to **vaporize** the other—refusing to acknowledge the presence of the other at all. We do that when we walk down a street and ignore those who might hand us a leaflet or ask us for money. Sometimes we do this because we're in a hurry. It still renders the other invisible. As Sutton notes, though, "The difference between how a person treats the powerless versus the powerful is as good a measure of human character as I know."[18]

If we are to deal effectively with intractable issues and those with whom we are in conflict, we must find a way to diminish the separation between ourselves and others. We must see them as individuals, and much like the steps in forgiveness, we must not only see them as "like ourselves" but see ourselves as "like them" without denying the differences that do exist. Cameron argues that this may be accomplished through

> . . . curiosity about the other person and their perspective. Curiosity and a sense of commonality also characterize sympathy; what takes empathy beyond sympathy is a third factor—the "imagining and seeking to understand the perspective of another person" even when that perspective may be distasteful or lead to "emotional ambivalence."[19]

Miroslav Volf, a native of Bosnia who is intimately acquainted with the level of conflict there, takes this perspective seeking even farther. Noting that so many conflicts have identity issues at the heart of them, he argues that we must be willing to embrace the other. He asks, "What kind of self do I need to be to live in harmony with others?" where harmony is defined as more than simply getting along. To live in harmony with others is to live in an attitude of embrace. He defines **embrace** as

> . . . *the will to give ourselves to others and "welcome" them, to readjust our identities to make space for them . . . prior to any judgment about others, except that of identifying them in their humanity.* The *will to embrace* precedes any "truth" about others and any construction of their "justice." This will is absolutely indiscriminate and strictly immutable; it transcends the moral mapping of the social world into "good" and "evil."[20]

You may find such an attitude toward others hard to adopt. Clearly, it is something to be worked toward rather than a change that can be employed overnight. But then, all of the skills involved in conflict are difficult. Even the authors, who have been teaching and writing on this subject for many years, sometimes slip up and do a conflict quite poorly. We would argue, though, that to the extent that we can suspend our judgment of others and welcome them into our world, without denying the existence or legitimacy of theirs, we will be able to alleviate some of the effects of intractable issues.

Managing Conflict through Nonviolent Communication

In addition to the way in which we view the other, our language must reflect a desire to welcome the other and engage in communication. Nonviolent language goes beyond the notion of civility discussed in Chapter 14, in that it takes seriously the notion that words shape our worlds, and to use violent language is a means of committing violence against others. According to Rosenberg, **nonviolent communication** makes observations, states needs, and makes requests, not demands. In that sense, it is akin to the S-TLC system we introduced you to in Chapter 4. But nonviolent communication is driven by both thinking and language, with an intention to "create the quality of connection with other people and oneself that allows compassionate giving to take place. In this sense it is a spiritual practice: All actions are taken for the sole purpose of willingly contributing to the well-being of others and ourselves."[21] Rosenberg argues that people who employ nonviolent communication are concerned with two questions: What is alive in me and you? What can we do to make life more wonderful?

How do we use nonviolent communication? To begin with, we reject the use of force in our communication; threats, for example, have no place in nonviolent communication. We try to avoid judgments of the other as a person. We try to observe without evaluating. We take responsibility for our feelings and make requests that allow the other to say no to us. We bring genuine presence to our listening to another person, and we develop empathy that allows us to be vulnerable to the other. We express anger appropriately.

Finally, we realize that even in giving a compliment, we may make a judgment. If someone has done something good for us, we tend to say something like "you're a nice person for doing that." Although the statement is positive, it is still a judgment. Rosenberg argues that the most effective compliments are those where we identify:

1. the actions that have contributed to our well-being;
2. the particular needs of ours that have been fulfilled; and
3. the pleasureful feelings engendered by the fulfillment of those needs.[22]

Sometimes, a simple "thank you" does all of the above. But people are more likely to appreciate our appreciation more when we are specific about what we value.

UNDERSTANDING YOUR WORLDVIEW

In this final section, we introduce you to the notion of worldview as a means of determining your own attitudes toward a number of issues that are potentially intractable and problematic. Acute awareness of one's own beliefs and values is the first step in understanding and embracing others.

What is a **worldview**? It is a composite of all the values, beliefs, and attitudes you hold toward the world, which assists you both in describing what you see and in prescribing what you should do. Worldviews provide such assumptions about people as "people are basically good" as opposed to "people are basically rotten," as well as helping us sort out our attitudes toward large social issues such as homosexuality, the role of the church in politics, and the appropriate response of a nation toward terrorism.

Components of a Worldview

What is *your* worldview? Worldviews generally contain, either implicitly or explicitly, the answers to these questions:[23]

1. What is a human being? Where do we come from? How are humans different from or similar to other living creatures?
2. What is the ultimate reality? Is it a supernatural being?
3. What happens to people at death?
4. What is right with our society? Another way of thinking about this is to ask "what is the good?"
5. What is wrong with our society? Another way of thinking about this is to ask "what is evil?"
6. What should we be striving to do in this lifetime?
7. What are your responsibilities in the various roles you play? For example, what is your role as a human being on this planet, as a citizen of your nation, as a member of your community, as a member of your family, as a friend, an employee, and so on?

One of the difficulties with identifying the cluster of beliefs, values, and attitudes that we hold as important is that we are rarely aware of them until they are challenged. Our worldview has a "taken for granted" aspect to it. We assume others believe as we do. But that is not the case. As Hollinger notes, we do take for granted the fact that we live side by side with other races, nationalities, ethnic groups, and cultures. But unlike a century ago when we could assume that most others thought as we did (or agreed to live according to our rules because our group was dominant), this is not the case today.

> We not only rub elbows with people who are culturally and ethnically different from ourselves, but more significantly people (many of the same culture and ethnicity) who have varying perspectives regarding reality, moral frameworks, and the nature of a good society. They put their worlds together in significantly different ways from each other. In pluralistic societies humans live, work, and attempt civic responsibilities with people whose fundamental outlook on reality is at odds with their own.[24]

The Importance of a Worldview

Worldviews drive our behavior. Because of their take-for-granted nature, they underlie most intractable issues and drive them by blinding the participants to seeing the world in an alternative way. One author argues that it was the difference in worldviews and the inability of the participants to understand those differences that led to the deaths of nine people at Waco when the Brnach Davidians engaged in a standoff with the FBI.[25]

You can see how differing worldviews can create intractable issues between individuals who believe that they must convert others to their way of thinking. Consider the two sets of abbreviated answers to some of the worldview questions in the example below:

Question	Person One	Person Two
What is a human being?	A human being is a divinely created organism reflecting the image of God.	A human being is a highly evolved animal.
What is the ultimate reality?	God is the holder of all time and purpose.	The universe is moving toward a state of disorder.
What happens to people at death?	They live eternally, either with or without God.	They die. Their bodies return to the earth.
What is the good?	Serving God's purpose.	Making a good living for oneself.
What is evil?	Failing to do God's will.	Treating oneself and others badly.

Now, consider all the ways in which difficult, worldview-based conflicts play out in American politics alone: Is the religious affiliation of the president relevant? Should we allow abortion and stem cell research? Is the death penalty an appropriate response to crime? How should we deal with issues of addiction? Should homosexuals have the same marriage rights as heterosexuals? How should we respond to poverty and to the homeless? What role should the government play in the care and protection of its citizens? Is health care a right? The list is endless. As we try to live together in a world that is increasingly pluralistic in its worldviews, somehow answers to these questions must be forged in a way that neither denies nor magnifies the differences inherent in our worldviews.

MANAGE IT

In this chapter, we emphasized a type of issue that cannot be resolved by communication and negotiation techniques alone because it involves a clash of different and conflicting value systems. We called these intractable issues.

What makes the intractable issues different from other issues? An intractable issue becomes part of an interpersonal conflict situation when those involved become too entrenched in the discussion of who is right and who is wrong. While those involved may have started the conflict by trying to persuade each other to their point of view, the conflict begins to repeat itself. In a sense, an intractable issue transcends the people involved because it is a clash of their social or cultural, religious or political, and economic philosophies.

What happens when representatives of conflicting value systems try to resolve their differences? Because of the inability of participants to agree on how to resolve their differences, each party is hard-pressed to understand why its best efforts to communicate are not understood by the other side.

As the conflict becomes more entrenched, slogans and simple answers substitute for arguments and reasoning as each side despairs of winning the other to its way of thinking. Actions toward one another may become more violent and turn into a self-sealing pattern. In order to better understand the nature of more problematic intractable issues, we offered an example involving patriotism and nationalism.

Two recent theories have been proposed to account for the way intractable issues are managed by the parties engaged in them. Critical theory analyzes power relations between the participants in an effort to uncover oppression, exploitation, and injustice. In order to understand patterns of domination and oppression, critical theory analyzes power relationships between groups, based on praxis, which examines ways in which people are allowed access to the expression of their ideas during a conflict.

While critical theory examines the distribution of power in a society, ripeness theory focuses on the alternatives confronting conflicting parties. Proponents of ripeness theory argue that if conflicting parties realize that the path they are following produces pain, they will begin to seek ways to reduce that pain. If a less painful alternative is found for them, the parties will want to seek out that alternative. Ripeness occurs when participants in a conflict realize that they are involved in a mutually hurting stalemate and recognize a mutually enticing opportunity.

Both critical theory and ripeness theory suggest some skills and strategies for dealing with an intractable issue. We believe that at the heart of any success in ameliorating an intractable issue is the ability to approach another who is different in ways that are honoring to that person and in using communication that is nonviolent in nature.

However, in an effort to separate ourselves from others, untrained conflicting parties try to demonize, romanticize, colonize, generalize, or vaporize the other. If we are to deal effectively with intractable issues and those with whom we are in conflict, we must find a way to diminish the separation between them and us. We must see them as individuals, and much like the steps in forgiveness, we must not only see them as "like ourselves" but see ourselves as "like them" without denying the differences that do exist. In addition to the way in which we view the other, our language must reflect a desire to welcome the other and engage in nonviolent communication by rejecting the use of force, avoiding judgments of the other as a person, taking responsibility for our feelings and making requests that allow the other to say no to us, bringing genuine presence to our listening to another person, and developing empathy in a way that allows us to be vulnerable to the other. Finally we need to express anger appropriately.

As a means of determining your own attitudes toward a number of issues that are potentially intractable and problematic, we ended this chapter by introducing you to the notion of a worldview, which is a composite of all the values, beliefs, and attitudes you hold toward the world. Our worldview has a "taken for granted" aspect to it. We assume others believe as we do. But that is not the case because we live side by side with other races, nationalities, ethnic groups, and cultures. As we try to live together in a world that is increasingly pluralistic in its worldviews, we must work together to forge answers to the most pressing social, political, and economic problems in a way that neither denies nor magnifies the differences inherent in our worldviews.

Think About It

1. On what issues are you likely to find yourself embroiled in an intractable issue? What happens when you argue with people who believe they have absolute Truth and will not even listen to what you have to say? How can you learn to listen to the other side of issues that are very important to you?
2. Have you heard the term *worldview* before? In what context? Does it seem like a useful concept to you? Why or why not?
3. What is the place (if any) of faith (of any kind) in politics? What are the advantages of a faith-based government? The disadvantages?
4. How has the world changed for you since 9/11? How do you see the impact of that event on life in general? What would you like to see happen?
5. Is the idea of nonviolence in words and action workable? Why or why not?

Apply It

1. Watch television for an hour, paying close attention to the commercials. Alternatively, go through an advertisement-heavy magazine such as *Vogue*. What are the values being sold to the viewer or reader? Are these good values? Why or why not? How do they reflect a worldview?
2. Look up information about one of these intractable geopolitical issues: Sudan, Israel, Ireland, Guatemala, or another of your choice. Try to summarize the positions of the major parties to the conflict. How would you use critical theory or ripeness theory to advise those in the conflict?
3. Look at Web sites associated with secular humanism (e.g., *Free Inquiry* magazine at http://www.secularhumanism.org/index.php?section=fi&page=index) and evangelical Christianity (e.g., *Reasons to Believe* at http://www.reasons.org/). How does each side characterize itself? How does each side characterize the other? What would you do if you were the mediator between these two positions?
4. For one day, listen closely to what you and others say in conversation. How do you use words that are essentially violent (e.g., jokingly saying, "I'm going to smack you if you don't stop") or nonviolent? What would it take to change your language habits? Will it really change anything at all?

Work With It

1. Create a worldview map
    Create a "map" of your worldview by considering your answers to the following questions. Put the answers on one page, if possible, so that you can see how they correspond to one another. Are there inconsistencies in what you believe and think? Where are they? How do you reconcile them to one another?

    Worldview Questions:
    a. What is a human being? Where do we come from?
    b. What is the ultimate reality? Is it a supernatural being?

c. What happens to people at death?
d. What is right with our society? Why do you think that is? Another way of thinking about this is to ask, "What is the good?"
e. What is wrong with our society? Why do you think that is? Another way of thinking about this is to ask, "What is evil?"
f. What should we be striving to do in this lifetime?
g. What are your responsibilities in the various roles you play?
- As a human being?
- As a citizen of this country?
- As an inhabitant of earth?
- As a family member?
- As a friend?
- As an employee?
- As a student?

2. Morality and Reality

   Read the case study below and answer the questions that follow it.

When I was a sophomore in college, I got pregnant and had an abortion. It was soon after *Roe* vs. *Wade* had been decided. I went to Planned Parenthood, and when I blurted out that I wanted an abortion, no one tried to dissuade me or offer me any alternatives. I felt trapped. I didn't know that there were places I could go and have the baby and give it up for adoption. All I could think of was my high school friend who had to drop out of school when she got pregnant and carried the baby to term. I didn't want to do that. So I had the abortion. It was probably the most horrifying experience of my life. I know that some women have abortions and never feel any qualms about it. I went under the anesthetic screaming and came out weeping. It took a long time for me to forgive myself for what I had done. I felt I had taken the coward's way out of my situation. I'm married and have children and I love them to death, but I still think about that one baby and who it might have been. Well, one of my employees came to me and told me she had to have some time off. She hadn't been with us very long and I asked her if it could wait until Easter because we'd be closed. She said no, that it couldn't. I asked her if something was wrong and she just said that she had to have time off. She looked nervous and upset, and it seemed like she wanted to talk to me but was afraid, so I just asked her point blank, "Are you pregnant?" At first she looked away and said she didn't want to talk about it, and then she burst into tears and said, "How did you know?" Having been down that road myself, it wasn't all that hard for me to figure out.

I talked to her and she said she was scheduled to have an abortion. I asked her if that's what she really wanted to do, and she said she thought it was all she could do. I'm not a person who would ever work to outlaw abortion because I don't think that really addresses the real issue, which is keeping people from getting pregnant to begin with. But I knew that I wanted to save her baby if I could, and I thought if she just knew that there were people who would support her and that there were alternatives that maybe she wouldn't have the abortion. We took off from work and talked all afternoon. I told her about my experiences, and why I wanted so much for her not to make the same mistake I made. I took her to my doctor and paid for the examination, because all she had taken was a urine test, and she hadn't had a physical exam yet. We went to a pregnancy counseling center where she saw *The Silent Scream*. That was probably a bit heavy-handed, but I really believe that abortion is murder and if you're going to do it, you ought to do it with your eyes open. We talked; she talked to friends. As she was wavering in her decision, she confided to me that she didn't want to have an abortion but that she was afraid to tell her parents about her problem. She was afraid they'd disown her.

She delayed the abortion a week, and during that time I found five couples who were interested in being prospective parents. None of them knew who she was, but I told her about them. There were two families who volunteered to have her stay with them during her

(Continued)

pregnancy. One family offered to help her with her medical bills. I lined up all these people willing to help her, hoping to make her see that she wouldn't have to deal with the problem alone. Unfortunately, what mattered to her was whether she had support at least from the baby's father or from her parents. The father had taken off for parts unknown after urging her to have an abortion. She still hadn't told her parents and was afraid if she did she would lose them too.

Questions to address:
a. What is the moral issue in this case study?
b. Did both people act in ways that honored the other's point of view?
c. How would you have responded if you were the employer? The employee? Why?

NOTES

1. Dennis Hollinger, "Pluralism and Christian Ethics: Responding to the Options," *Christian Scholar's Review* 30 (2000), 165, 163–183.
2. Sally A. Freeman, Stephen W. Littlejohn, and Barnett W. Pearce, "Communication and Moral Conflict," *Western Journal of Communication* 56 (1992), 315.
3. W. Barnett Pearce, "Keynote Address: Communication Theory," Institute for Faculty Development: Communication Theory and Research, Hope College, Holland, Michigan, July 1992.
4. Freeman, Littlejohn, and Pearce, "Communication and Moral Conflict," p. 319.
5. Jacob Bercovitch, "Characteristics of Intractable issues," in Guy Burgess and Heidi Burgess (Eds.), *Beyond Intractability* [electronic book] (Boulder, CO: Conflict Research Consortium, University of Colorado) Posted: October 2003; http://www.beyondintractability.org/essay/Characteristics_IC/ (accessed May 27, 2009).
6. Julie W. Morgan and Richard K. Olsen, "Discursive Taboo in Community Discourse: Communication Competence and Biblical Wisdom," *Christian Scholar's Review* 38 (2009), 346, 341–358.
7. Eran Halperin, "Group-Based Hatred in Intractable issue in Israel," *Journal of Conflict Resolution* 52 (2008), 718, 713–736.
8. Conflict Research Consortium, University of Colorado, Boulder, Problem List 2: Core Conflict Problems, http://www.colorado.edu/conflict/peace/!core_problems.htm (accessed May 27, 2009).
9. Shadia B. Drury, "Fascism American Style," *Free Inquiry* (April/May, 2009), pp. 26, 26–27.
10. Ibid., p. 27.
11. Ibid.
12. Toran Hansen, "Critical Conflict Resolution Theory and Practice," *Conflict Resolution Quarterly* 25 (2008), 403–427.
13. Ibid., p. 409.
14. John Drury, " 'When the Mobs are Looking for Witches to Burn, Nobody's Safe': Talking about the Reactionary Crowd," *Discourse and Society* 13 (2002), 42, 41–73.
15. Peter T. Coleman, Antony G. Hacking, Mark A. Stover, Beth Fisher-Yoshida, and Andrzej Nowak, "Reconstructing Ripeness I: A Study of Constructive Engagement in Protracted Social Conflicts," *Conflict Resolution Quarterly* 26 (2008), 3–42.
16. Ibid., p. 5.
17. Robert J. Schreiter, *Reconciliation* (Maryknoll, NY: Orbis Books, 2003), pp. 42–53.
18. Robert I. Sutton, *The No Asshole Rule* (New York: Warner Business Books, 2007), p. 25.
19. Lynne J. Cameron, "Patterns of Metaphor Use in Reconciliation Talk," *Discourse and Society* 18 (2007), 199, 197–222.
20. Miroslav Volf, *Exclusion and Embrace* (Nashville, TN: Abingdon Press), p. 29. (italics in original).
21. Marshall B. Rosenberg, *Speak Peace in a World of Conflict* (Encinitas, CA: PuddleDancer Press, 2005), p. 16.
22. Marshall B. Rosenberg, *Nonviolent Communication: A Language of Life*, 2nd Ed. (Encinitas, CA: PuddleDancer Press, 2005), p. 186.
23. Adapted from James W. Sire, *The Universe Next Door*, 4th Ed. (Downer's Grove, IL: IVP Academic, 2004); James W. Sire, *Naming the Elephant* (Downer's Grove, IL: IVP Academic, 2004); and James H. Olthuis, "On Worldviews," *Christian Scholar's Review* 14 (1985), 153–164.
24. Hollinger, "Pluralism and Christian Ethics," p. 164.
25. Robert R. Agne, "Reframing Practices in Moral Conflict: Interaction Problems in the Negotiation Standoff at Waco," *Discourse and Society* 18 (2007), 549–578.

CHAPTER 16

Creativity and the Ideal Conflict Manager

OBJECTIVES

At the end of this chapter, you should be able to:

- Explain what it means to take a creative approach to resolving conflicts.
- Apply at least two different creative methods to the analysis of a particular conflict you are experiencing.
- Explain the principles of effective conflict management to another person.
- Apply the principles of effective conflict management to a particular conflict you are experiencing.

KEY TERMS

attention point
creativity
entry point
lateral thinking
mind mapping
reversal
six hats
trained incapacities
vertical thinking
visual journal

Emilé Chartier, a French philosopher, once said, *Nothing is more dangerous than an idea when it is the only one we have.* We might add that there is nothing like discovering a better idea! Unfortunately, too many conflicts turn sour because the conflicting parties do not take the time and effort to find a more mutually satisfying resolution.

How do we come up with these better ideas? In Chapter 5, we explained several ways to generate more options in a negotiation. If the conflicting parties are willing to devote the time and energy, shifting from interests to positions, brainstorming, and bridging may result in a new solution to the problem that neither party envisioned prior to the conflict. In this final chapter, we want to take the idea of generating more and better resolutions by focusing on creativity and exploring the important role it can play in the effective management of conflicts that you experience. We'll provide you with a brief overview of the concept, discuss its importance, and then show you several ways you can incorporate creative problem solving into your conflict management activities. Afterward, we'll take a broader, more encompassing view of conflict management and summarize most of what you have learned as 18 key conflict management principles or skills. After reading this chapter, we hope that you can engage in effective communication and more effectively manage conflicts in a variety of interpersonal situations.

CREATIVITY AS IT RELATES TO CONFLICT

What is creativity? Creativity is not the same as intelligence—creative people need not have high IQs and vice versa.[1] **Creativity** is a process of making sense of some problem in a new way.[2] Most authors identify four stages of the creative process:

- The preparation stage includes all your previous learning as well as any information you gather to address the problem at hand.
- The incubation stage is a period of thinking about the problem—giving it time to take shape and form.
- The illumination stage occurs when a particular idea finally appears in response to the problem.
- The verification stage allows you to test whether the creative response you have come upon will truly work.

Traits of Creative People

One of the most stunning findings in all the work on creativity is this: There are not a lot of innate differences between people who are creative and people who are not. Runco argues that everyone has creative potential, in that everyone is capable of transforming the physical world through their interpretations and that everyone has the ability to decide when those interpretations are useful or not.[3] Crosby puts it this way:

> A major reason for overlooking the importance of creativity is a misunderstanding of the nature of this basic resource. It is often thought of as a rather exclusive province of the "boffin," arising from unusual intelligence and intensive training, or as a peculiar knack possessed by a few colourful (sic) personalities in business.[4]

Many people erroneously think of creativity as present in only a few people. However, all of us are capable of cultivating creativity and applying creative methods to our lives. In fact, it comes down to this: People who are creative think they are; people who aren't creative think they're not. Think you're not creative? There are four habits that you can cultivate your natural ability to be creative.[5]

- *Courage* allows us to take the risk of failing. We don't necessarily expect to get the right answer the first time.
- *Expressiveness* leads us to be ourselves and not fear what others may think of us.
- *Humor* permits us to put incongruous *ideas* together and see new relationships between them.
- *Intuition* involves having faith in what you think is a good idea and how you feel about your ideas. Intuition is a part of our personalities—some of us listen to our "inner voices" more than other people do.

As teachers we have met many students who "knew the right answer" to a question in class but were afraid to voice it. Sometimes students will copy down something they suspect is not true but lack confidence in their ability to challenge what they hear. Becoming more creative means listening to your intuition more closely.

Why Is Creativity Important?

Perhaps the most important reason creativity is important is a self-serving one: You are more likely to develop mutually satisfying outcomes in conflict situations when you and the other party approach your conflicts creatively. The use of creative methods in problem solving is also associated with higher levels of health: People who have more chances to utilize creative problem solving in their jobs are physically younger than their years would suggest.[6]

Even more significantly, writers are identifying creativity as the only way to solve problems that face us as people, as nations, and as the world.[7] Colvin goes so far as to predict that:

> Creativity and innovation may even be the key to the future economic prosperity of America and other developed countries . . . .for three hundred years the source of economic dominance has clearly been leadership in science and technology . . . . this era may be ending. Technology will become commoditized by China and India, they say, being dispersed and adopted almost instantly after it's created. Economic value will arise instead from the powers of the right brain—creativity, imagination, empathy, aesthetics.[8]

Colvin's assertion is underscored by Murnighan and Mowen, who examined high-stakes decisions that people in organizations make. They suggest seven parameters that help ensure that decisions will be sound:

- Search for the threats and opportunities in the decision.
- Find the cause of the situation.
- Evaluate the risks of the situation.
- Apply intuition and emotion.
- Take different perspectives.
- Consider the time frame for making the decision.
- Solve the problem.

Most of those steps involve applying creative methods to the problem solving. In addition, the authors suggest that people who make good decision share some characteristics:

- Each experience allows them to gain knowledge—they learn from both their successes and their mistakes.
- Fun is part of the decision-making process, as well as risk taking.
- They know when to ask others for help.
- Once a decision has been reached, they implement it without second-guessing themselves.[9]

Misassumptions Preventing Creativity

With the explosion of books on creativity, there are many lists of reasons why people tell themselves they can't be creative. As we pointed out before, a primary reason people don't behave creatively is because they don't think they're creative. Beyond that, though, there are other reasons that prevent people from taking chances with ideas. While some of these may not seem application to the creative management of conflict situations, most are. According to Crosby, these factors arise from society and educational processes. They are

- success orientation, due to a fear of failure;
- peer pressure and conformity is valued;
- sanctions against critical exploration—too much curiosity is felt to be disruptive and is discouraged;
- overemphasis on sex roles—some attitudes and behaviors are reserved for one sex only;
- equation of divergent behavior with "abnormality" in its popular sense—a throwback to the genius/madness equation;
- work/play dichotomy—work is a burden; play is an end in itself, unrelated to work.[10]

CAN WE LEARN TO BE CREATIVE?

Generally speaking, the answer is yes, although it is quite easy for the training to fade if not supported by others important to the one trained (e.g., teachers, supervisors, etc.) or if the training is too domain specific. For example, if you are trained to solve a particular kind of puzzle (spatial, verbal, or mathematical), it is unlikely that your training in one type of puzzle will carry over to the other kind.[11] On the other hand, few of us are called upon to solve spatial, verbal, and mathematical problems of the type used in this research. Training has also been demonstrated as effective for small group brainstorming, with those trained generating a larger number of ideas overall and more creative ideas than groups that were not trained.[12] Creativity training is most effective when people receive training that can be applied across a number of problem-generating situations.[13] The techniques we will discuss later in the chapter are of that nature. Most important to becoming more creative is the decision to do so; however, as Robert Sternberg says: "Deciding for creativity does not guarantee that creativity will emerge, but without the decision, it certainly will not."[14]

BARRIERS TO CREATIVITY

Perhaps the most significant factor that stuns our creativity happens when the skills that we have learned to do blind us from new and insightful ways of thinking—our trained incapacities. In this sense, it is our talents that blind us to other solutions.

We could more easily think about our problematic situations if it were not for our trained incapacities. What are they? A **trained incapacity** occurs when a person's abilities and talents actually limit the person's thinking. Because the behavior has become generally beneficial (in nonconflict situations), the person expects it to work in all situations but sometimes the ability may interfere with creativity. Four such trained incapacities are task oriented/goal centeredness, redefinition, critical thinking, and using standards.

On the one hand, being a *task-oriented and goal-centered leader* is generally viewed as a positive trait in American mainstream culture: People identify the end point they hope to reach and then push and pull others to get there as quickly and efficiently as possible. In many cases, the outcome is necessary or beneficial. However, sometimes it is not. For example, a task leader may push an idea through a group process, not giving the members adequate time to reflect on all its implications, which may result in a poorly thought-out outcome. This task-oriented, goal-centered approach can function as a trained incapacity, when people are so eager to achieve the end point that they do not adequately think about all the implications of what they are doing.

If you are task oriented and goal centered, you need to realize that your approach may have some limitations. You want to stop occasionally to ask if everyone is "on board" or feeling rushed. You might plan in some time for reflection. "Let us not make a decision today but sleep on it and meet again tomorrow. Let's take time to try to think of alternatives, imagine the possible outcomes of our decision, and determine whether we can live with this decision."

It is similar for *redefinition,* which we often believe is a useful skill especially for third parties who are helping others settle their conflicts. Redefinition is the ability to restate an idea in a way that provides for more beneficial treatment such as when conflicting parties stop defining the conflict in their own terms and start defining it in terms of mutuality. However, people may agree to an idea that simply "sounds good" without fully understanding what it means or entails. "I like what you said initially, but it was only later on that I discovered that I would be affected for the worse."

Of course we can look at something from different vantage points. If we think of something in a more positive light, are we sure it has the positive features we think it has? What might we be overlooking? What are the chances that we might be worse off with our decision?

As a third trained incapacity, *critical thinking* is the ability to evaluate and challenge an idea that other people take for granted. Critical thinking may generate new ideas and insights and enable a more complete discussion of an issue. However, critical thinking can also stifle the introduction of new ideas or issues, leading to situations in which individuals fear voicing their own opinions and ideas for fear of rejection. When critical thinking is seen as attacking others' ideas, they may no longer want to participate in the discussion.

We must recognize some limitations to creative thinking. Beware of fault finding and too much criticism of others and their ideas. We all need to "cut one another some slack" in life, or a relationship becomes too stressful. Some people think they are always right, know what's best for others, and think their ideas are always better than others. They may have some good ideas, but there are times they are wrong and should have the stomach to admit it. It would also help to withhold your opinions until after you have heard from the others so as not to stifle their creative efforts.

A final kind of trained incapacity is the use of *objective standards,* which are often useful as guidelines for decision making and interaction but become a problem when parties in the conflict believe there is one right answer and refuse to compromise that position. "I know that we men usually open doors for women, but there I was with my coffee mug in one hand my books in the other, and this woman just stood there like I was supposed to drop everything to open the door for her." Her adherence to an objective standard (when men and women arrive at the door at the same time, men open the door women go through first) prevented her from opening the door for him in this instance when his hands were full.

Objective standards work best when everyone agrees to them. Is it OK if we draw straws? Ask if others agree to the objective standard before simply imposing it. Let us now turn our attention how to think differently than we usually do in a conflict situation.

CREATIVITY AS THINKING DIFFERENTLY

To approach problems creatively, we often have to think of them differently. One way to do this is to start asking questions that we don't normally ask. For example, we can ask "what if" in silly ways. "How would I respond if the other person were the president of the United States?" "How would I respond if the other were a gorilla?" "What would I do if I knew I only had 10 days to live?" The point is to ask questions that may not even be related to the conflict in order to think about it differently.

> I was very upset with how my boss assigned my work schedule. I was about to barge into his office and let off some steam. However, I decided to think instead that the boss was a Martian with antenna sticking out of its head. This alien visitor cannot understand what it is to be a human being. It can't even understand English very well. So I really had to rethink what I was going to say and do. I figured the boss couldn't do anything about the schedule now that it was published. I decided that it was best to just let the boss know that I would have preferred a different work schedule and wished I'd be consulted more in the future, but I didn't make a scene about it.

Second, we can imagine how others might handle the conflict. How would your sister, brother, mother, father, aunt, uncle, or friend handle it? How would the other person handle it? Finally, we can imagine we're the conflict itself—how would you want to be handled if you were actually the conflict? Although a little silly, these methods can lead us to new ways of thinking. As one writer says:

> I have a good friend, Jack, who teaches in the philosophy department. In the past I have shared my writing projects with him because I value his feedback. He always looks at the paper from a macro view, and comments on my overall logic and organization. So now, after I finish writing a paper, I consciously ask myself, what would Jack say about my paper. I immediately look at the organization of the paper, especially focusing on the overall logic. Do I move clearly from problem to solution? Do my examples and date prove the points I am making? Are my generalizations in need of toning down? It amazes me how I suddenly now see problems in my paper that Jack would have later pointed out to me. I don't normally think like my friend, but I know him well enough that I can look at my paper from his point of view and realize errors in my thinking.

To take the idea of thinking differently further, de Bono has identified two ways of thinking differently, "vertical and lateral."[15] In **vertical thinking**, we move through a series of steps, making sure that one is completed before the next one is started. If we were to take a vertical thinking approach to the process of conflict (see Chapter 2), we would analyze everything about the prelude before thinking about the triggering event, everything about the triggering event before the initiation, and everything about each of the other steps before moving on to the next. The danger inherent in vertical thinking is that, if we believe we have drawn all the right conclusions as we go along, the final conclusion is inevitable. We won't reconsider how we got there.

Lateral thinking "is concerned with restructuring ... patterns (insights) and provoking new ones (creativity)."[16] If we utilize the lateral thinking approach to brainstorming (see Chapter 5), we would permit every group member's contribution regardless of how ridiculous it might seem. Whereas in vertical thinking we search for the "right" pattern, in lateral thinking we search for all the patterns we can see. Lateral thinking does not require that we be right; it only requires that we consider a number of different options. Sometimes a bad idea causes one to think of a much better one, or causes one to see ways to combine bad and good ideas into a superior one.

Some of techniques proposed by de Bono have become standard in communication textbooks—such as fractionation, which you were introduced to in Chapter 5. Three will be mentioned here.

One means of lateral thinking is **reversal**, or working backwards from the goal or end result. What would it take to get there? What would it take to get to some intermediate point? What would it take to get to the next step. For example, what do we teachers of conflict management hope students will learn at the end of studying a unit or chapter? Once that is known, what readings, exercises, and activities would contribute to that result? Thinking this way helps us to see some of the precipitating factors we might not have seen before.

A second means of lateral thinking is changing the choice of entry point and attention area. Whereas the **entry point** is the part of the problem or situation that is first examined, the **attention point** is the part of the problem that is then focused on. For example, you realize that your romantic partner or roommate or friend isn't speaking to you without considering why. We would call this the entry part of the problem because this is the first time you realized that there is a problem of some kind. Back in Chapter 2, we identified the "initiation stage" of the conflict process as the point at which one lets the other know that a conflict exists. At this point, one may not remember or realize that something he or she did or forgot to do may have "triggered" the conflict. However, once the offended or upset person pointed out that the other did something that offended or upset him or her, our perspective of the conflict takes a dramatic shift. The conflict trigger now becomes the attention point because it was the cause of the problem or conflict. The trigger is something the offended or upset person is unlikely to quickly get over, so the issues linger on for that person. The other may have to admit some wrongdoing, offer restitution, or make an apology, so the triggering event may linger for that person as well. This is why we call this the attention point, which differs from the entry point of the conflict.

Suppose I realize that you are not speaking to me (entry point). When asked, you say it is because I didn't call when you thought I should (attention point). Whereas normally a lot of the conflict would now center around the fact that my not calling you upset you, we might suggest that you consider (1) Why were you so upset or offended when I didn't call (focus more on the entry point)? (2) Why did I forget to call (focus more on the attention point)? These questions create different views of the conflict for resolving it.

The final method created by de Bono—the Six Hats approach—requires one to ask questions from different vantage points. In so doing, it pulls together a variety of ways to more creatively manage conflicts in one's life. The various hats and their questions are:

White Hat—calls for information known or needed. Using the white hat approach, you would list everything you know about the conflict—who is involved, why they are involved, what the issues are, when the conflict started, and so on.

Red Hat—signifies feelings, hunches, and intuition. Using the red hat approach, you would list the feelings you have about the conflict. What do you think is going on that might not be evident?

Yellow Hat—symbolizes values and beliefs. From this perspective, you want to think about whether the solution you're seeking is consistent with the person you believe yourself to be. Is it something that can work for you? Is it something you can live with? Is it something you can be proud of?

Black Hat—stands for a contrarian judgment, the devil's advocate. Now you focus why something may not work or why it could go wrong. The black hat approach is to be a pessimist. When everything is going well, what might you be overlooking that could go wrong?

Green Hat—focuses on creativity: unforeseen possibilities, imaginative alternatives, and new ideas. The green hat asks for different ways of looking at the problem. This is the lateral thinking approach.

Blue Hat—takes a macro approach to managing the thinking process. Using a blue hat perspective is a way of keeping yourself honest in the whole process. Have you really thought of all the angles? Are there other ways of achieving the same goal? Is the goal worthwhile?

While the hats appear as a list, you are free to begin with any one of them: There is no a right or wrong way to start. You can also go back and forth among the various hats.

Essentially, lateral thinking is a way of turning problems on their sides or upside down in order to think about them and see them in a new way. Such thinking can be helpful in moving us toward resolution of a conflict we are facing.

CREATIVITY AS SEEING DIFFERENTLY

While learning to think differently is something that most people can learn to do with ease, learning to *see* differently requires a bit more practice. Often, people resist these methods because they do not seem practical or logical. But learning to employ these methods can open an number of creative avenues to those who use them.

Mind Mapping

Some methods in creative thinking are visual in nature, "right-brain" approaches to analysis using colors and images instead of logical relationships between words. One of the foremost is called **mind mapping.** Similar to brainstorming and fractionation, mind mapping uses ideas to generate others. By looking at them together and linking them, you can often think of a better way to deal with a problem than you would have otherwise. This method has become a great tool for encouraging creativity, brainstorming, and learning. Mind mapping is a process that was popularized by Tony Buzan; it was actually first created to help people take notes more effectively. Since that time, several computer programs have been created to help people make mind maps.

Unlike outlining, which presumes a linear relationship between elements of a problem, and which also requires that we know how those elements are related before starting, mind mapping does not require a starting point. For example, we encourage our students to think about conflicts in terms of steps beginning with prelude and ending in resolution (see Chapter 2). Sometimes, though, it's really hard to figure out where a conflict has begun or why the other is upset or offended. Useful for identifying issues, the mapping technique helps us analyze conflicts. Mind mapping has several loose rules:

- There is always a central image or graphic representation of a problem, which is always placed in the center (of the page).
- Ideas flow freely—there is no censorship.
- Only one or two words are used as labels to represent key ideas.
- Color is important to the map—it gives emphasis to different ideas.
- Lines (solid/dotted) are used to make connections between ideas.[17]

To make a mind map, you should have a large piece of unlined paper and something to write with. You can make your map smaller and without color, but colors help you start to see relationships between concepts. Start in the middle of the paper and write down what you think the conflict is about (using 1–2 words as a label). Now, write down everything about the conflict that comes to your mind (again using 1–2 words as labels). Write quickly and don't restrict your thinking. The first step is getting everything on paper.

Once you have your thoughts down, start making connections. Draw colored lines between concepts that seem related. Use those colors to help make sense of the conflict. Identify ideas that are related. At this point, it helps to ask a few questions:

What were you thinking when you started? Is it still the same?
When you see the whole picture, how is your thinking affected?
What unexpected ideas or relationships among them emerged?
Are there any parts out of balance?
Do you need to fill anything else in?[18]

Figure 16.1 illustrates a simplified, finished map. A complete map would have subbranches for each topic that derives from the center of the map. We have limited the detail here to two of the six branches.

For this person, the problem concerned time management and her family. Having just started a master's degree program, being married, having four children, and holding a full-time job was beginning to look too difficult to manage. By mind mapping she saw more clearly the various issues and how they were related to one another. A lot of the conflict management will have to come from balancing the various demands and getting others to help in addressing them.

Once the working mother identified the conflict issues, she was in a better position to prioritize them: What is the most important issue here? What issues exceed her ability to control them? For this person, family emerges as most important—giving them enough time and energy and making sure they know that they are her top priority.

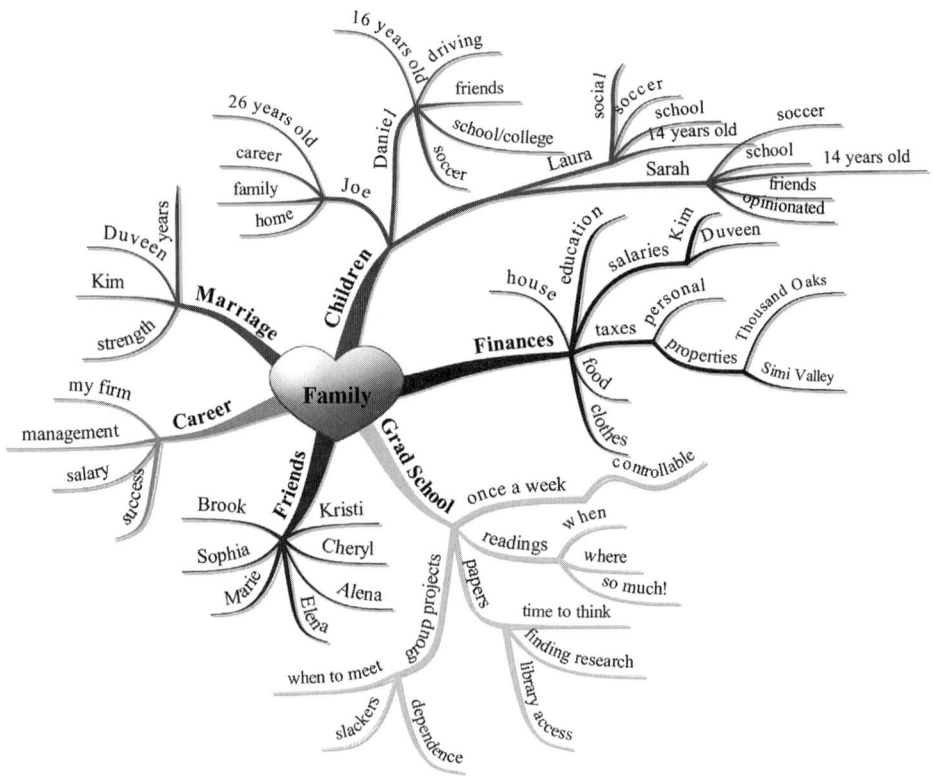

FIGURE 16.1

The mind-mapping technique shows how many issues are really present in a conflict and how they affect each other, at least from one person's point of view. It can also be used like a diary, for self-analysis, to prepare for teaching and presentations, and for management of tasks.[19]

Visual Journaling

Visual journaling is a fairly recent phenomenon, with ties to scrapbooking and collage. It is a way of making sense of things without using large amounts of text. Generally, it puts incongruent images together and looks for patterns and possibilities among them. Just as a journal is a written record of what we experience, a **visual journal** is an image-filled response to events that are happening in your life.[20] Since a visual journal is indeed a picture, the best way to understand it is to examine two examples.

In the photo given in p. 287, the person who made the journal was experiencing a conflict in her dating relationship. She was finding that her boyfriend was rather controlling and she felt as though too often she was losing a part of what she valued in herself. In the photo given in p. 288, the person was dealing with a situation where she felt that she was hearing too much information about a negative situation that she could not control. As you can see, visual journaling is a sort of self-talk, much like a written journal is.

CHAPTER 16 Creativity and the Ideal Conflict Manager   287

"How Far" by Ania Mulka.

To use this technique effectively, you must first realize that it is guided by the process of creativity—preparation, incubation, illumination, and verification. To prepare, you need to first put aside any idea that you are going to create "art." You may in fact create it, but it is safer to begin by thinking that you are simply going to explore ideas. Second, have many more images at hand than you think you will need. You can use all kinds of found images, such as those in old magazines, or what you download from the Internet. It helps to have five or six different types of magazines that you can mutilate. Cut both images and interesting text and don't worry about always cutting neatly or in a square. Cut around objects that you find interesting.

Incubate your ideas by placing images in different places on the page. Put more on the page than you intend to use. Don't think about what you are using; simply reach for images as you feel led to them. Look at them upside down. Rearrange them at least three times. When you are satisfied, glue them in place.

Next, seek illumination by studying the array of images and text you have chosen. What is it saying about the conflict? What is it saying about your feelings? Finally, verify your conclusions by showing the journal to a trusted friend. Ask that person what they see in it. They may help you see the conflict even more differently than you thought.

Visual journaling can be a great way to work through problems when we simply have no words to describe them. When our emotions threaten to overcome us, images can help us focus so that words might come later.

"Hear no Evil" by Ania Mulka.

I create art to help me understand problems in my own life as well as to help unblock my writing. One of the questions I found that really opened up some possibilities was a simple one that occurred in the middle of a piece of art—"Where would I be without my fear?" Answering that question helped me later on.

We're not suggesting that everyone start creating art (but it wouldn't hurt if we did); we are suggesting moving beyond the obvious to deal with conflicts in new ways that might ultimately be more fruitful.

We, the authors, have attempted to blend together tried and true techniques for managing conflict with some new and different ideas of our own. To ensure that you are not lost in the details of any one chapter, we conclude this chapter with a summary of the main principles that should guide you as you manage your conflicts.

PRINCIPLES OF EFFECTIVE CONFLICT MANAGEMENT

We believe the following principles describe an "ideal conflict manager." As you read through these principles, think about how you will make these principles an enduring part of your communication toolbox.

1. *The effective conflict manager does not view conflict negatively but rather sees opportunities for personal and relationship growth in conflict situations.*

The most important step in managing conflict is to adopt a mind-set that embraces conflict as an opportunity while recognizing the risks involved in it. Your other skills in conflict depend on your ability to transform how you think about conflict in general. Cloke remarks:

> We can all recognize that in order to resolve our conflicts we have to move towards them, which is inherently dangerous because it can cause them to escalate. It is somewhat more difficult for us to grasp that our conflicts are laden with information that is essential for our growth, learning, intimacy, and change, that they present us with multiple openings for transformation and unique opportunities to let go of old patterns.[21]

This mind-set recognizes the importance of personal responsibility for one's actions and encourages flexibility in oneself and in others within the conflict situation. The mind-set also recognizes that communication works no miracles but that it usually helps when managing many of our conflicts. Most important, this mind-set rejects easy solutions and recognizes the complexity of conflict situations and their outcomes.

The conflict art in the photo below illustrates the "ideal conflict manager" mind-set. It recognizes the inherent danger in conflict—there may be some thorns involved, and

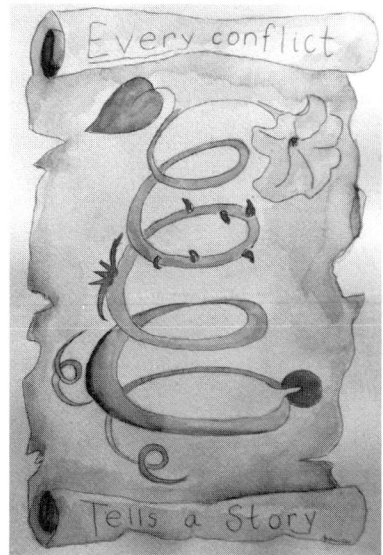

This watercolor painting by Lynn Palmer titled Every Conflict Tells a Story *reflects a healthy view of conflict. There may be some painful spots involved, and there may even be places where the conflict is derailed or stalled, but overall, conflict yields positive results.*

there are places where a person can get trapped. At the same time, it demonstrates the positive outcomes that can arise from conflict handled well.

2. *The effective conflict manager understands the nature of interpersonal conflict.*

Truly competent conflict managers view interpersonal conflict as a problematic situation with the following four unique characteristics: The conflicting parties are interdependent; perceive that they seek incompatible goals or outcomes; or they favor incompatible means to the same ends; the perceived incompatibility has the potential to adversely affect the relationship if not addressed; and there is a sense of urgency about the need to resolve the difference.

> Sometimes I think conflict is like leftovers you forget about in your refrigerator. If you don't eat them or throw them away, they start growing things all on their own. And the longer you put off cleaning them out, the worse it is to take care of them. No matter how well I cook, there are always leftovers to contend with. No matter how well I am getting along with other people, there will always be tensions to resolve.

By viewing conflict this way, we quickly realize that conflict is inevitable because as relationships become closer, more personal, and more interdependent, we find that more conflicts occur, trivial (minor) complaints become more significant, and feelings become more intense.

3. *The effective conflict manager takes a transactional approach to communication and conflict.*

A competent conflict manager prefers the transactional model of communication over the linear model, focusing on communication as a transactional process by which people make or create meaning together. Such an approach recognizes that communication (and by extension, conflict) isn't something we do "to" one another, but something we do "with" one another (like teamwork or like a dance).

The advantage of the transactional model is that we recognize the importance of both people's behavior in the conflict situation. One person acting "competently" in a conflict situation, using good communication skills, usually cannot bring the conflict to a successful resolution. It takes two people to make the conflict, and it takes two people to manage or resolve it.

> One of the things I did following my husband's request for a divorce was to look over my prayer journals from the years preceding it. Over and over I prayed that God would make me a better wife, more understanding, and so on. But it didn't matter how good or understanding I was when my husband wasn't willing to change or meet me even part of the way. I tried and tried and tried, but it took two. I couldn't do it alone.

4. *The effective conflict manager views conflict as a process*

Competent conflict managers know the five stages of constructive, successful conflict: the prelude to conflict, the triggering event, the initiation phase, the differentiation phase, and the resolution phase. They know that the prelude to conflict sets the stage by identifying the people, place, and time of your conflict; that the triggering event functions as a stimulus often leading to the initiation of your conflict; that the initiation phase is the response to a triggering event; that the differentiation phase is the ongoing interaction pattern; that the resolution phase is the mutually satisfactory agreement or outcome and requires a follow up.

Competent conflict managers can explain how avoidance, chilling effect, and competition conflict cycles are spin-offs at one stage or another of the constructive, successful conflict process. The conflict avoidance cycle is characteristic of a relationship between people whose first impulse is to avoid initiating conflict or to quickly withdraw when conflicts arise. The chilling effect conflict cycle may have a stage one prelude (e.g., one or more of the participants has reason to fear the reaction on the other person based on a past history of abuse during conflict), followed by a stage two triggering event (e.g., one partner does something that upsets the other), but like the conflict avoidance cycle instead of progressing to stage three initiation, the offended individual does not initiate the conflict because he or she fears the outcome. The competitive conflict escalation cycle may have a stage one prelude (e.g., one or more of the participants has a past history of poorly managing conflicts), followed by a stage two triggering event (e.g., one partner forgets an important date), moves through stage three initiation, but gets mired down in stage four differentiation, instead of progressing to the fifth and final stage resolution.

The key to effective conflict management is an understanding of both what gives rise to conflict (what we have termed the prelude to conflict) and what occurs at different stages in the process of conflict. The way we view our relationship with the other person, our past successes and failures in enacting conflict with the other, how we identify an issue, how we assign blame, and how we voice our complaint affect the pattern of interaction. Somewhere in the maze of options, including avoidance, chilling, and competitive cycles is potentially productive conflict behavior. Similarly, in each stage of productive conflict, there are opportunities to spin off into the avoidance, chilling effect, and competitive cycles. As with the destructive cycles, productive conflict behavior stems from attitudes about conflict and from what is assumed true.

When we see conflict as something that is a normal part of relationships, when we are willing to listen and assert ourselves, when we are realistic about our expectations for the outcome of the conflict, we are less likely to get locked into destructive conflict cycles. Becoming aware of behavior and ways of thinking about conflict can help us; the more aware we are of behaviors at each stage of a conflict, the more successful we are in dealing with the conflicts in our lives.

5. *The effective conflict manager recognizes the role of choice in conflict situations.*

While we think conflict is inevitable, the competent conflict manager does not think that interpersonal violence or verbal aggression is a natural outcome of conflict. Violence is a choice we make or reject. By realizing that we have options in a conflict situation and by learning nonviolent solutions to problems, setting an example in our daily lives, and raising our children to resolve interpersonal conflicts peacefully, we are helping to reduce a serious social problem.

Effective conflict management can change potentially destructive conflict into productive conflict, containing expansion of the issues, number of people involved, costs to the participants, and intensity of negative feelings. Effective conflict management can attenuate the desire to hurt the other person and to get even for past wrongs and move us away from reliance on overt power and manipulative techniques. It features an awareness of options in conflict situations. Along with these characteristics, a productive view of conflict situations includes flexibility and a belief that all conflicting parties can achieve their important goals.

Probably the most important factor that affects your ability to put the advice in this book into effect is to remember that you always have choices in conflict situations. Even when you believe that everything is happening too fast or that you must deal with problems that arise suddenly, you still have choices as to how you act or react with respect to the other person.

6. *The effective conflict manager knows when to use the appropriate communication option in a conflict situation.*

What are the three factors you should consider when choosing among the four conflict communication options? You should point out that effective communicators are frequently assertive, sometimes nonassertive, or rarely aggressive depending on the occasion/time/location, the other person, and their own needs. If you understand the communication considerations described in this chapter, you are in a better position to decide when it is appropriate to use one type of conflict communication behavior or another.

In a conflict situation, your first response is not necessarily the best one. Slow down, think about the situation, and then respond to the other, using the skills discussed here. Learn from your mistakes, don't let them get you down, and move on. The only way to develop conflict skills is to use them in conflict situations.

In conflict situations, competent communication behavior occurs when people have the knowledge to behave skillfully, are able to apply that knowledge in a particular situation, and are able to repeat their performance in similar situations. Competent conflict behavior is a matter of learning skills of analysis and skills of communication and then applying them in conflict situations. One success does not mean you have achieved competency any more than one failure means that you may not achieve it.

7. *The effective conflict manager knows how to collaborate.*

Competent conflict managers know the advantages of employing a collaborative strategy so that it produces less personal and relationship stress and the most personal and relationship growth. You may recall that the five conflict management strategies are *avoiding, accommodating, competing, compromising,* and *collaborating.* The two basic dimensions underlying the five strategies are concern for self (or for one's personal goal) and concern for others (or for the relationship).

When collaborating, you clarify perspectives, focus on a goal of mutual satisfaction, but remain flexible in the means to achieve that goal, and work together to develop a mutually acceptable outcome. To collaborate effectively, you need to include your interests, feelings, and needs. Then you need to listen to her or his interests, feelings, and needs, to see if you can support them in future interaction. Finally, you need to see if the other is willing to collaborate and invest the time and effort to develop understandings that are mutually advantageous or does the other prefer to avoid, accommodate, compromise, or compete.

Hopefully, you use interpersonal communication skills that are associated with collaborative or integrative strategies. You are analytic, conciliatory, and problem solving in focus; attempt to clarify the issues and facilitate mutual resolution of the problem; describe behavior; disclose feelings; ask for disclosure from the other person; ask for criticism from the other person; qualify the nature of the problem; support the disclosures or observations the other person has made; and accept responsibility for each one's part in the conflict.

We also learned that conflicting parties may find it useful to think of their positions as end points on a continuum with many intermediate views. Another technique for generating mutual understanding involves reordering the partners' views on the matter at hand, or helping the other person to see that he or she might define the problem differently than his or her first impression of it.

8. *The effective conflict manager employs the S-TLC system.*

As a competent conflict manager, you know that we need to stop, think, listen, and communicate (the S-TLC system) with the other person. Stopping gives you time to think and avoid a knee-jerk reaction. Thinking about the conflict means that you bring your skills of analysis to the situation. Moreover, by following these four steps, one can often resolve interpersonal conflicts through basic communication skills.

"Stop" means that we don't react blindly to the other person. When you realize that a conflict exists, begin by saying, "STOP!" Don't become so upset that you start to lose control of yourself. Instead, try to calm down and cool off. Try to use the suggestions for taking a "time out" to control your mental faculties. When we take time out, we can then consider our options in a conflict situation and try to exercise them rationally.

Taking a time out gives you time to "get your act together." Think means we analyze the situation to try to know what is really happening within it and the range of possibilities. At an elementary level, try not to take the conflict personally. At a more advanced level, think about changing the other, the situation, or yourself. Think about your goals, wants, and needs and those of your partner. Again, use the techniques recommended above for analyzing the conflict situation. Consider the outcomes of different reactions to the situation. Think both about the problem and about your relationship with the other person. Avoid jumping to conclusions. In both your personal and professional life, taking time to analyze can make the difference between a competent and incompetent response to a conflict situation.

> While the time to fully understand all the driving forces of a challenge is a luxury few can afford in a competitive business environment, acting precipitously with inadequate diagnosis and insight is an even more costly indulgence.[22]

Go lightly on yourself and on the other person. Don't make mountains out of molehills. If possible, find some humor in the situation. Remember to take the conflict a step at a time. Try to think optimistically and tell yourself that you can handle the situation.

Listening means that we consider the other person's opinion important, and that we try to hear and understand it before we make a point of saying what's on our mind. We understand the tendency of most people to defend themselves the moment they hear criticism, rather than really listening to what the other person is saying. Point out that as important as what we say in a conflict is the ability to truly hear what the other person is saying.

You know that you have communication options when in a conflict situation. When communicating nonassertively (communication apprehension), you can avoid a conflict altogether or accommodate (by simply giving in) to the desires of the other person. When choosing a competing conflict style, you may communicate aggressively or passive aggressively. You communicate aggressively when you force your will (i.e., wants, needs, or desires) on another person in a way that violates socially acceptable standards. You can also choose to communicate in passive-aggressive manner by imposing your will on others through the use of verbal and/or nonverbal acts that appear to avoid an open conflict or accommodate to the desires of others, but in actuality are carried out with the intention of inflicting physical and/or psychological pain, injury, or suffering. While it would seem that aggressive communication behavior is seldom, if ever, warranted except in situations of self-defense, passive-aggressive behavior is not recommended, except if confronting the other may result in physical harm to you. Finally, you can choose the compromising (where you only get some of what you want) or collaborating conflicts styles (where you get and the other get what you want) and communicate assertively by speaking up for your interests, concerns, or rights in a way that does not interfere with the interests or infringes on the basic communication rights of others.

9. *The effective conflict manager knows how to appropriately confront others.*

Confrontation is a conflict process in which the parties call attention to problems or issues and express their feelings, beliefs, and wants to one another. There are six steps to confronting interpersonal problems. They are:

- Preparation: Identify your problem/needs/issues.
- Telling the person "we need to talk."
- Interpersonal confrontation: Talk to the other person about your problem.
- Consider your partner's point of view: Listen, empathize, and respond with understanding.
- Resolve the problem: Make a mutually satisfying agreement.
- Follow up on the solution: Set a time limit for reevaluation.

10. *The effective conflict manager knows how to effectively word an "I-statement."*

Competent conflict managers know that assertive behavior is characterized by personalized communication—language using "I" statements (i.e., I think, I feel) versus "you" or depersonalized statements (i.e., you always, most people think). They can list the four parts of an effective I-statement, which are an effective way to take responsibility for yourself and assert yourself if they take the following form: "I feel . . . (feeling statement) when I . . . (problematic behavior statement) because I (consequences statement) . . . I'd like (goals statement) . . . " By asserting yourself in this way, you provide much needed information, demonstrate honesty, and reduce defensiveness in others.

You need to consider your partner's point of view during a conflict. Don't forget the role of active listening, other orientation, rephrasing, and sensitivity.

Because people are responsible for what they do and how they feel in conflict situations, we are competent to the extent that we take responsibility for how we feel and act. However, instead of owning what they say and how they feel, people often tend to express themselves in impersonal or generalized language. Another common type of responsibility avoidance is the use of "you-language." We often resort to blaming the other person for our behavior and feelings, but again we need to tell the truth, strive for accuracy, and take responsibility for our words and actions.

11. *The effective conflict manager knows when and how to incorporate negotiation principles and techniques.*

Competent conflict managers know that when tangible resources are scarce, conflicts involving them take more than basic interpersonal communication skills to resolve; they require more advanced problem-solving or negotiation techniques. Competent conflict managers know that negotiation works best when the parties trust each other and the situation is one where mutually satisfactory outcomes are possible, even though the parties may not know that at the outset.

Competent conflict managers adhere to the four principles of negotiation. In bargaining situations, people often confuse the problem at hand with the people involved. Keeping these elements of the situation separated helps you to focus on issues rather than on personalities. In addition, you should focus on the interests of the people involved rather than on their articulated positions. By focusing on interests, you may find areas of overlap, which is likely to happen if you focus just on the people's positions. When looking for areas of overlap, brainstorm many options, some of which may allow both parties to gain from the situation. Many situations that appear initially as win–lose are eventually resolved in a win–win fashion. We recommend that negotiators try to agree ahead of time on objective criteria that may facilitate mutually satisfactory outcomes.

Competent conflict managers can explain how one converts a potentially competitive negotiation into a cooperative one. You can recall the following:

- Seeking commonalties
- Talking cooperation
- Consulting before acting
- Communicating frequently
- Controlling the process, not the outcomes
- Thinking positively
- Considering your BATNA
- Engaging in fractionation

12. *The effective conflict manager strives to create and maintain a favorable communication environment.*

Competent conflict managers can explain the role played by the climate in conflict situations. On the one hand, an imbalance of power, distrust, and defensive behavior create a harmful conflict environment, where mutually satisfactory outcomes are unlikely. On the other hand, equity, trust, and supportive behavior create a nurturing conflict environment that is more likely to produce mutually satisfactory outcomes.

Communicators who create nurturing climates are more likely to create mutually satisfying outcomes because they participate in the decisions, agreements, solutions to problems, and resolution of conflicts that affect them. If we feel safe enough to assert our interests, needs, and goals, listen to the expression of others, and cooperate in the process of achieving an understanding, the more likely we can cooperate and collaborate.

13. *The effective conflict manager avoids letting stress and anger gain control over her or his communication behavior in conflict situations.*

   Competent conflict managers can identify the sources of stress in their lives, and they can deal constructively with them. They remember many of the suggestions from Chapter 9 on how to better manage the stresses in their lives.

   Competent conflict managers know when they are starting to get angry and how to control it by taking a "time out," by engaging in relaxation exercises, by engaging in helpful self-talk, and by "finding the fear" that manifests itself as anger. We are going to feel both stress and anger. They are unavoidable. What we do with each, though, is within our control. We can learn to rid ourselves of thoughts that contribute to stress and to control anger.

14. *The effective conflict manager knows the role of positive face, autonomous face, and face saving in conflict.*

   People are motivated to create and maintain favorable impressions of themselves. Not only are people striving to present and save face, this motivation may also generate or exacerbate conflict situations because the introduction of face issues into a conflict can escalate the severity of the conflict, making it difficult for people to resolve the original issue. A person's positive face is supported when others appear to value what the person values, or express admiration for the person, or show acceptance of the person as a competent individual. Autonomous face is the desire people have for freedom from constraints and impositions. When others respect a person's independence, the person's autonomous face is supported. The desires for positive and autonomous face, under the best of circumstances, can create a dilemma. One may communicate support of another's positive face by expressing admiration for that person, spending time with that person, and so on but, by doing so, can encroach on the person's autonomy. So supporting a person's positive and autonomous face requires a balance under the best of circumstances.

   You can use general and specific techniques to support another's face in conflict situations. In general, people want others to like them, respect, encourage, consult, include, appreciate, and reward them. They want others to ask them, greet them warmly, help them when needed, and make them feel safe. We can also support others in a more specific way. To do this, you need to determine what traits or characteristics the other perceives in himself or herself and point out the ones you have in common or are capable of supporting.

15. *The effective conflict manager knows when and how to forgive and perhaps reconcile.*

   Forgiveness is a cognitive process that consists of letting go of feelings of revenge and desires to retaliate. Even though you have not forgotten the relational transgression, you can let go of feelings of anger, resentment, and revenge. In many ways, forgiveness is the opposite of revenge. Revenge is based on the notion of "an eye for an eye." One wants to follow evil with more evil. Forgiveness is a process that starts with anger over a transgression and moves toward transforming the meaning of the event. Cognitively, forgiveness is characterized by a reduced focus on the other person and the transgression as a defining event in one's life (in nonforgiveness, one might obsess over the source of hurt), affirmation of the other as an individual, lack of desire for revenge, and a rejection of the role of victim. It is the ability to move beyond victimization or the feeling of being a victim that leads to a state of forgiveness. The affective dimensions of forgiveness include the presence of positive feelings and absence of negative feelings toward the other. Forgiveness is defined behaviorally as movement toward reconciliation rather than avoiding the other or withdrawing and giving up a grudge against the other.

While forgiveness refers to how we manage our negative and positive feelings, reconciliation is a behavior process in which we take actions to restore a relationship or create a new one. Once you have forgiven the other for the relational transgression, you do not have to reconcile unless it is to your advantage to do so. You may wish to forgive at a distance and not communicate your forgiveness to the transgressor, or you may decide that you wish to reestablish a relationship or create a new one, so you chose to reconcile. Through the processes of forgiveness and reconciliation, we can forge new relationships or repair former ones and move forward by letting go of the past. Of all the skills in conflict, the ability to put the conflict into perspective and move forward is one of the most important for our well-being.

Like the ability to analyze conflicts and the ability to effectively communicate feelings and desires, the effective use of forgiveness and reconciliation strategies to cope with difficult conflicts is a skill we can learn. The process of forgiveness and reconciliation works like a self-fulfilling prophecy. We tell each other that the act is forgiven, which allows us to act without reference to the offense; in turn, we feel better about our relationship with one another and can talk about our relationship without reference to the offense; so in turn we tell each other that all is forgiven. We call this a "forgiveness–reconciliation loop."

What specific steps should you take to forgive others following conflict interaction?

- First, sometimes, the transgressor explains her or his offensive behavior and offers an apology (optional).
- Second, when this occurs, the offended person either accepts the account and apology and/or simply decides on one's own that it is no longer in her or his best interest to harbor feelings of anger, resentment, and revenge (even in the absence of an explanation and apology).
- Third, the offended person actually lets go of any feelings of anger, resentment, and revenge.
- Fourth, if reconciliation is desired, the offended person must communicate her or his forgiveness to the transgressor, or if reconciliation is not necessary, the offended person may forgive without engaging in communication with the transgressor (optional).

16. *The effective conflict manager knows how to mediate conflicts as a neutral third party.*

A dispute is a conflict that has reached a point where the parties are unable to resolve the issues by themselves (necessitating the intervention of a third party) because there is a breakdown in communication and normal relations are unlikely until the dispute is resolved. Unlike other forms of dispute resolution such as conciliation, ombudsperson, arbitration, and adjudication/litigation, mediation differs in that a neutral third party facilitates communication between the conflicting parties so that they may work out their own agreement.

As facilitators, mediators know how to create a supportive and constructive environment to encourage the disputants to communicate, cooperate, and work out their own mutually satisfying solution. Mediators are neutral and unbiased, have no decision-making power with respect to the outcome of the mediation, must maintain confidentiality, also communicate with competence themselves, and encourage cooperation and discourage competition between the parties. Mediators are also "communication rule enforcers" because they announce and enforce communication rules. Rules are obligations (they tell us what we must say or do, such as "agreeing to confidentiality") and prohibitions (they tell us what we better not say in certain situations, such as "no name-calling").

Once the parties realize that they cannot resolve the dispute without help, the mediation steps are as follows:

a. One or both disputants seek mediation, or mediators talk them into it (the intake process).
b. The mediators bring the disputants together and make an opening statement.
c. Following the mediators' opening statement, they ask each person to take a few minutes to describe the dispute from his or her point of view without interruption.
d. The mediators find common ground on which to build agreement.
e. The mediators write up the final agreement.
f. The mediators end the mediation.

17. *The effective conflict manager knows how to formulate a mutually satisfactory agreement.*

When drafting the agreement, the mediators need to employ the following format and say, "X agrees to this . . . Y agrees to that . . . " The mediators attempt to keep the agreement simple. They use clear, specific details (spelling out who, what, where, when, how). It helps to think of the agreement as a list of behavioral commitments because it enumerates the specific observable actions each party needs to take to fulfill the agreement. In developing the agreement, the mediators should strive for balance or "something for everyone." The agreement also needs to address questions of feasibility and practicality because the parties should find the agreement workable as mutually acceptable. Finally, the culminating step occurs when the mediators ask both parties to sign the agreement.

18. *The effective conflict manager knows how to think outside the box to derive creative resolutions to conflicts.*

Creativity can be learned but it means listening to your intuition more closely. However, two barriers prevent us from responding creatively to the conflicts we experience. One of those is where the skills that we have learned to do blind us from new and insightful ways of thinking—our trained incapacities—such as task-oriented and goal-centered leader, redefinition, critical thinking, objective standards. The other barrier that keeps us from responding to conflict creatively is not knowing how to think differently when in a conflict situation. One way to think differently is to ask questions that we don't normally ask. Second, we can imagine how others might handle the conflict. Third, you can try thinking vertically so as you move through a series of steps; you make sure that one is completed before the next one is started. Fourth, you can think laterally, which is a way of turning problems on their sides or upside down in order to think about them and see them in a new way. One means of lateral thinking is reversal, or working backwards from the goal or end result. Thinking this way helps us to see some of the precipitating factors we might not have seen before. Other approaches to creative thinking are more visual. Mind-mapping, six hats, and visual journaling are "right-brain" approaches to analysis using colors and images instead of logical relationships between words.

MANAGE IT

In this chapter, we overviewed creativity, discussed its importance, and then showed you ways to incorporate creative problem solving into your conflict management activities. Creativity occurs when a person makes new and insightful connections between what he or she knows, the problem at hand, and possible solutions to that problem. It is important to realize that there are not a lot of innate differences between people who are creative and people who are not; creativity can be learned but it means listening to your intuition more closely.

Can we learn to be creative? The answer is "yes," but there are two barriers that prevent us from responding creatively to the conflicts we experience. One of those is where the skills that we have learned to do blind us from new and insightful ways of thinking—our trained incapacities—such as task-oriented and goal-centered leader, redefinition, critical thinking, objective standards. Each of these skills may lead to positive outcomes, but they may also blind us to new ways of thinking about solving problems.

The other barrier that keeps us from responding to conflict creatively is not knowing how to think differently when in a conflict situation. One way to think differently is to ask questions that we don't normally ask. Second, we can imagine how others might handle the conflict. Third, you can try thinking vertically so as you move through a series of steps, you make sure that one is completed before the next one is started. Fourth, you can think laterally, which is a way of turning problems on their sides or upside down in order to think about them and see them in a new way. One means of lateral thinking is reversal, or working backwards from the goal or end result. Thinking this way helps us to see some of the precipitating factors we might not have seen before.

Other approaches to creative thinking are more visual. Mind-mapping, six hats, and visual journaling are "right-brain" approaches to analysis using colors and images instead of logical relationships between words. To raise you to the level of a macro conflict manager, we concluded this chapter with a summary of the main principles that should guide you as you manage your conflicts.

The 18 key conflict management principles are as follows: The effective conflict manager,

1. Does not view conflict negatively, but rather sees opportunities for personal and relationship growth in conflict situations.
2. Understands the nature of interpersonal conflict.
3. Takes a transactional approach to communication and conflict.
4. Views conflict as a process.
5. Recognizes the role of choice in conflict situations.

6. Knows when to use the appropriate communication option in a conflict situation.
7. Knows how to collaborate.
8. Employs the S-TLC system.
9. Knows how to appropriately confront others.
10. Knows how to effectively word an "I-statement."
11. Knows when and how to incorporate negotiation principles and techniques.
12. Strives to create and maintain a favorable communication environment.
13. Avoids letting stress and anger gain control over her or his communication behavior in conflict situations.
14. Knows the role of positive face, autonomous face, and face saving in conflict.
15. Knows *when and how* to forgive and reconcile.
16. Knows how to mediate conflicts as a neutral third party.
17. Knows how to formulate a mutually satisfactory agreement.
18. Knows how to think outside the box to derive creative resolutions to conflicts.

Think About It

1. What training have you had in creativity in the past? What did you learn here that was different?
2. How would you explain the importance of creativity in conflict management to another person?
3. Why do you think people have such negative views of conflict? Do you think that as people know more about conflict, they fear it less? Why or why not?
4. What do you think you can do to help the people in your life learn to deal with conflict more effectively?
5. If you had a chance to talk to a student who was planning on taking a class in conflict management, what would you tell that person to expect? What are the benefits of taking such a class? What are the disadvantages?

Apply It

1. Use the mind-mapping technique method to analyze a conflict you have experienced recently. After you are done, write the answers to the five review questions: What were you thinking when you started? Is it still the same? When you see the whole picture, how is your thinking affected? What was surprising? Are there any parts out of balance? Do you need to fill anything else in?
2. Use the six-hats problem-solving method to analyze a conflict you have experienced recently. Be sure to write the names of each hat and the conclusion that perspective brings to you.

Work With It

1. In the following case studies, how might you use the ideas in this chapter to produce a creative and more insightful resolution to the conflict.

   ### Case Study 1

   An interesting situation is occurring with another tenant and my roommate and me in our apartment building. We have assigned parking spaces, and the tenant that parks next to my roommate has a tendency to pull his car in and park it in half of her space. She has asked him to move over because she has trouble opening her car door. He becomes upset because his car is soaked by the sprinklers located on the other side of it. Two nights ago when we came home, he was over his line and into our space. My roommate parked very close to his car because she thought it might make him realize how close he was parking. However, he got angry and left a nasty note on her windshield. Both parties are not happy. I see the situation as petty, and I think that the neighbors need to work out some kind of agreement instead of exchanging unpleasant words or nasty notes.

   a. What trained incapacities might exist in this example?
   b. How might you think differently in this situation? Ask unusual questions, imagine how someone you know might view the situation, and/or try thinking laterally.
   c. How might you apply visual methods of creative thinking: mind mapping, six hats, and visual journaling.
   d. Using any or all of the above methods, describe a creative approach that produced a preferable, constructive solution to the problem that was different from initial attempts to resolve the conflict.

   ### Case Study 2

   My husband and I went out for an early dinner at a nice restaurant. The restaurant was practically empty, but we were seated next to a table that had a recently stained cover. The table had been cleared but had not been reset for dinner. My husband, who once worked as a server in a five-star restaurant, was horrified that the cloth was there—he felt that it should have been removed immediately even if the table wasn't set. He told the person who seated us that it was disgraceful, he told our server, and when the manager came over to ask if she could be of help, he told her. He was not appeased by their report that the busboy had not come in and it would be taken care of when he arrived. And no one was taking his "hint," if you could call it that, that the cloth simply be removed regardless of whether the table would be immediately reset. The manager finally took it off but I could tell she was completely exasperated by his disgust at the tablecloth. Even after it was removed he kept saying that being forceful was the only way to get things done, and he was convinced he was right because everyone gave in to his demand. I was so embarrassed by his behavior that I left the waitress a *very* good tip.

   a. What trained incapacities might exist in this example?
   b. How might you think differently in this situation? Ask unusual questions, imagine how someone you know might view the situation, and try thinking laterally.
   c. How might you apply visual methods of creative thinking: Mind mapping, six hats, and visual journaling.
   d. Using any or all of the above methods, describe a creative approach that produced a preferable, constructive solution to the problem that was different from initial attempts to resolve the conflict.

NOTES

1. Howard Gardner, *Creating Minds* (New York: Basic Books, 1993).
2. Robert Weisberg, *Creativity: Genius and Other Myths* (New York: W. H. Freeman and Company, 1986).
3. Mark A. Runco, "Everyone Has Creative Potential," in Robert J. Sternberg, Elena L. Grigorenko, and Jerome L. Singer (Eds.), *Creativity: From Potential to Realization* (Washington, DC: American Psychological Association, 2004).
4. Andrew Crosby, *Creativity and Performance in Industrial Organization* (London: Tavistock Publications, 1968), p. xii.
5. Joyce Wycoff, *Mindmapping: Your Personal Guide to Exploring Creativity and Problem Solving* (New York: Berkeley Books, 1991), pp. 26–27.
6. John Mirowsky and Catherine E. Ross, "Creative Work and Health," *Journal of Health and Social Behavior* 48 (2007), 385–403.
7. See, for example, S. Ramachander, *Creativity @ Work* (New Delhi: Response Books, 2006).
8. Geoff Colvin, *Talent Is Overrated* (New York: Portfolio Books, 2008), pp. 147–148.
9. Keith Murnighan and John C. Mowen, *The Art of High Stakes Decision Making: Tough Calls in a Speed Driven World* (New York: John Wiley and Sons, 2002).
10. Crosby, *Creativity and Performance in Industrial Organization*, p. 116.
11. Gayle T. Dow and Richard E. Mayer, "Teaching Students to Solve Insight Problems: Evidence for Domain Specificity in Creativity Training," *Creativity Research Journal* 16 (2004), 389–402.
12. Jonali Baruah and Paul B. Paulus, "Effects of Training on Idea Generation in Groups," *Small Group Research* 39 (2008), 523–541.
13. Ginamarie Scott, Lyle E. Leritz, and Michael D. Mumford, "The Effectiveness of Creativity Training: A Quantitative Review," *Creativity Research Journal* 16 (2004), 361–388.
14. Robert J. Sternberg, "Creativity as a Decision," *American Psychologist* 57 (2002), 376.
15. Edward de Bono, *Lateral Thinking: Creativity Step by Step* (New York: Harper and Row, 1970).
16. Ibid., p. 14.
17. Wycoff, *Mindmapping*, p. 43.
18. Nancy Margulies with Nusa Maal, *Mapping Inner Space* (Chicago, IL: Zephyr Press, 2002), p. 26.
19. Tony Buzan with Barry Buzan, *The Mind Map Book* (New York: Plume Books, 1993).
20. Some good references are Sharon Soneff, *Art Journals and Creative Healing* (Beverly, MA: Quarry Books, 2008) and Kelly Rae Roberts, *Taking Flight* (Cincinnati, OH: North Light Books, 2008).
21. Kenneth Cloke, *Mediating Dangerously* (San Francisco, CA: Jossey-Bass, 2001), pp. 3–4.
22. "How IBM Boss Embraced His Dilemmas," *Strategic Direction* 20 (2004), p. 17.

Index

ABC approach, 131
Abilene Paradox, 238
Accommodation
    as communication option, 48
Accounts, 165
Acknowledgment, 165, 167
Adjudication, 195
Aggressive communication,
Alternative dispute resolution
    (ADR), 195
Analyzing conflicts, 70–73
    mind-mapping as a means, 284–286
    specific questions for, 71
    visual journaling as a
        means, 286–288
Anger
    and anger controllers, 146
    and anger-ins, 143
    and anger-outs, 145
    control of, 147–148
    defined, 140
    experiencing, 142–143
    expressing effectively, 149–151
    responding to, 151–152
    as secondary emotion, 148–149
    ventilation approach, 144
Anxiety, 214
Apologies, 167
Arbitration, 195
Argument, 32
Aspiration point, 88
Assertive communication, 53
Attention point, 283
Attribution
    error, 218
    internal vs. external, 217
    theory, 216–220
Autonomous (negative) face, 159
Avoidance
    as a communication option, 48
    as a conflict cycle, 27–29

Bargaining range, 88
BATNA, 89
Behavioral commitments, 205
Bias toward cooperation, 240
Blaming, 217
Brainstorming, 91

Bullying
    defined, 251
    managing, 253–255

Caucus, 203
Chilling effect, 29–30
Civility, 247–249
Climate
    competitive, 110
    defensive vs. supportive, 113–115
    defined, 103
    nurturing vs. harmful, 103
Collaboration
    as a conflict strategy, 57–60
    as a preferred strategy, 57–58
    phases of, 58–60
Collective voice, 254
Common ground, commonalities, 95, 203–205
Communication
    apprehension of, 48
    choosing best option for, 62–64
    considerations, 54
    defined, 290
    linear model of, 10
    rights, 54
    transactional model of, 11
Communication options
    aggressive communication, 51–53
        nonverbal aggression (physical
            violence), 52–53
        verbal aggression, 52
    assertive communication, 53
        avoiding early compromise, 56–57
        collaborating, 56–57
        compromising, 56
        enacting collaboration, 58–60
    passive-aggressive communication, 49–51
    nonassertive communication, 47
        avoiding, 48
        accommodating, 49
Communication orientations
    defined, 44
    other-oriented, 45–49
    relationship-oriented, 53–62
    self-oriented, 49–53

Communication rules enforcers, 199–200
Common ground, 203–205
Comparison level, 221
Compensation, 93
Competition, as a conflict strategy. *See*
    Aggressive communication
Competitive escalation cycle, 30–32
    escalation factors, 34
Compromise, as a conflict strategy, 56
Concessions, in bargaining, 95
Concessions, in impression
    management, 167
Conciliation, 198
Conflict
    climate, 103
    cycle. *See* Cycles of conflict
    defined, 4–5
    destructive, 12
    as a fact of life, 6
    management, defined, 8
    management vs. resolution, 8
    metaphors, 14
    process view, 9–11, 21–22
    productive, 12
    theory. *See* Theories of conflict
    viewed negatively, 13–14
    viewed positively, 14–15
Conflict issues
    behavioral, 86
    defined, 85
    intangible, 85
    normative/relational, 86
    about personality, 85
    tangible, 86–89
Conflict messages
    consequences statements, 77
    feeling/needs statements, 77
    goal statements, 77
    I-statements, 75
    personalized communication, 76
    problematic behavior statements, 77
    you-statements, 76
Conflict process
    controlling the process, 96
    differentiation, 23
    initiation, 23
    prelude, 23

INDEX

Conflict process (*Continued*)
   resolution, 24
   triggering event, 23
Conflict proneness, 126–127
Confrontation
   defined, 34
   steps in, 35
Confrontation avoidance cycle, 27–29
Consequences statement, 77
Consulting, in negotiation, 96
Core relational rules, 164
Corrective facework, 164
Cost-cutting, 92
Creativity
   barriers to, 280–282
   defined, 278
   importance, 279
   learning, 280
   misassumptions about, 280
   as seeing differently, 284–288
   as thinking differently, 282–284
   traits of creative people, 278–279
Cycles of conflict
   confrontation avoidance cycle, 27–29
   chilling effect, 29–30
   competitive conflict escalation cycle, 30–32
   defined, 22–25
   schismogenesis, 26
   successful conflict cycle, 22
   undesired repetitive pattern (URP), 26
   violence cycle, 32–34

Deception, 175–176
Defense mechanisms, 214
Defensiveness, vs. supportiveness, 113–114
Describing the dispute, 202–203
Destructive conflict, 12
Differentiation phase, 23
Disclaimers, 162
Displaced conflict, 213–216
Dispute, 195
Distress, 125
Distrust, 111
Diversity-based conflict, 246

Effective Conflict Management Principles, 288–299
Ego, 214
Emotional residues, 5, 176
Entry point, 283
Equifinality, 91

Eustress, 122
Excuses, 166
Exodus, 255
Exploitation, 266

Face
   autonomous (negative) face, 159
   corrective facework, 164
   defined, 216–217
   facework, 161
   impression management, 157
   positive face, 159
   preventive facework, 161–163
   repair rituals, 164–168
   supportive facework, 163–164
Facebook, 169–170
False conflict, 216, 219–220
Feeling/needs statements, 77
Forgiveness
   advantages of, 178–179
   defined, 176
   distinct from reconciliation, 177, 183
   levels of, 180–181
   and moving beyond victimization, 187
   revenge, 177
   seeking, 188
   unforgiveness, 177
Forming, 235
Fractionation, 97, 204
Framing, 204
Frustration, 215

Goal-centeredness, 281
Goals, 72
Goal-statement, 108
Grievances, 230
Group conflict strategies, 240–241
Group and organizational conflicts, 230
Group-based hatred, 263
Groups, stages of
   forming, 235
   norming, 235
   performing, 235
   storming, 235
   termination, 235
Groupthink, 237–238
Gunny-sacking, 77

Healthy trust, 112
Helping orientation, 176
Holistic perspective, 224
Homeostasis, 224

Hyperstress, 103
Hypostress, 102

Id, 213
Ideal conflict manager, 288
Identity conflict, 232
Identity goals, 72
Imagined interactions, 35
Impression management, 164
   in mediated communication, 169–170
Incompatible goals, vs. means, 5
Inevitability of conflict, 7
Information processing perspective, 233
Information reception apprehension, 38
Injustice, 266
Initiation phase, 23
Instrumental conflict, 231
Instrumental goals, 72
Intake, 200
Intangible issues, 85
Interdependence, 4–5
Interests, vs. positions, 92
Interpersonal conflicts, 4
Interpersonal violence, 8, 140
Intractable issue, 261
   characteristics of, 262–263
   typical issues, 263–264
Issues. *See* Conflict issues
I-statements, 74–79

Justifications, 166

Language of cooperation, 96
Latent conflict. *See* Prelude to conflict
Lateral thinking, 283
Lies, *See* Deception
Linear model of communication, 10
Listening, 73–74
Litigation, 230
Lucifer effect, 231

Mediation, 195
   common ground, 203–205
   describing the dispute, 202–203
   ending the mediation, 206–207
   final agreement, 205–206
   formal vs. informal, 196–197
   intake, 200
   opening statement, 201
Mediators
   communication rules enforcer, 199–200
   role, 197–199

Meta-conflict perspective, 9
Metaphors, for conflict, 14
Mind-mapping, 284–286
Minimax principle, 88
Misplaced conflict, 213–215
Mixed motives, 112
Moral issue, 261
Mutually enticing opportunity, 267
Mutually hurting stalemate, 267

Nationalism, 265
Negative face. *See* Autonomous face
Negative view of conflict, 13–14
Negotiation
    aspiration point, 88
    bargaining range, 88
    BATNA, 89
    competitive, 90
    cooperative, 90
    defined, 88
    minimax, 88
    resistance point, 88
    separating people from the problem, 95
    status quo, 88
Neutral speech, 106
Nonassertive communication, 47–49
Nonverbal aggression, 52–53
Nonviolent communication, 270
Norming, 235

Objective criteria in negotiation, 98
Objective standards as trained incapacity, 281
Offending situation, 165
Ombudsperson, 195
Opening statement, 201
Oppression, 266
Other, approaches to
    colonize, 268
    demonize, 268
    embrace, 269
    generalize, 269
    homogenize, 269
    romanticize, 268
    trivialize, 269
    vaporize, 269
Other, the, 261
Outcomes, 12–13, 45
Overblown conflicts, 123, 215

Passive-aggressive communication, 49–51
Pathological trust. *See* Unhealthy trust

Patterns and cycles in conflict. *See* Cycles of conflict
Patriotism, 265
Personalized communication, 76
Personal stress, 57
Phases of conflict. *See* Conflict process
Physical aggression, 32, 52–53
Pluralism, 261
Positions, vs. interests, 92
Positive face, 159
Positive view of conflict, 14–15
Power
    abuse, 104
    defined, 104
    sharing, 107
Powerful, vs. powerless speech, 106
Praxis, 267
Prelude to conflict, 23
Prioritizing, 94
Prisoner's Dilemma, 112
Preventive facework, 161–163
Problematic behavior statement, 77
Problematic situations, 4
Process, 21
Process conflict, 232
Process goals, 72
Process view of conflict, 21
Productive conflict, 12
Psychodynamic theory, 213–216
Psychological detachment, 254

Reconciliation
    as self-fulfilling prophecy, 185–186
    defined, 177
    distinct from forgiveness, 177, 183
    levels of, 182–183
    steps toward, 183–187
Redefinition, 281
Reframing, 204
Relational conflict, 232
Relational goals, 72
Relational stress, 58
Relational transgressions, 175
Remedy, 165
Repair rituals, 164–168
Repression, 214
Reproach, 165
Resistance point, 88
Resolution phase, 24
Responsibility for behavior, 76
Retaliation, 254
Revenge, 177, 254
Reversal, 283
Reverse discourse, 253
Rights, 54

Ripeness, 267
Role
    conflict, 236
    defined, 236–237
    formal vs. informal, 237
Rules, 199

Schismogenesis, 26
Scarce resources, 87
Secondary emotion, 148–149
Seeking commonalities, 95
Self-fulfilling prophecy, 186
Self-talk
    defined, 35
    effect on stress, 133–135
Sense of urgency, 5
Silence, 263
Situation, 4
Six Hats, 283–285
Skill, 212
Social exchange theory, 220–224
Social network sites, 169–170
S-TLC, 69
    communicating, 74–79
    listening, 73–74
    stopping, 70
    thinking, 70–73
Storming, 235
Strategies
    accommodation, 49
    avoidance, 48–49
    avoiding early compromise, 56–576
    backstabbing, 49
    compromise, 56
    collaborative, 56
    competitive, 51 53
    defined, 45
    forcing, 51
    sabotage, 50
Stress
    ABC approach, 131–133
    and conflict proneness, 126–127
    defined, 121
    distress, 125
    eustress, 122
    hyperstress, 102–103
    hypostress, 102
    impact on conflict, 203–204
    managing, 124–125
    personal, 57
    relational, 58
    self-talk and, 133–135
    stressors, 130
Subversive (dis)obedience, 254
Successful conflict cycle, 22

Superego, 213
Supportive facework, 163–164
Supportiveness, vs. defensiveness, 113–114
Systems theory, 224–225

Tangible issues, 86
Termination, 235
Theories of conflict
    attribution, 216–218
    critical, 266–267
    psychodynamic, 213–216
    ripeness, 267–268
    social exchange, 220–224
    systems, 224–225
    uncertainty, 218–220
Theory, 211
Thinking positively, 96
Third-party intervention. *See* Mediation
Threats and promises, 105
Thromise, 105
Trained incapacities, 280–282
Transactional model of communication, 11
Transforming meaning, 176–177
Triggering events, 23
Trust, 111
Truth bias, 175
Types of conflict. *See also* Conflict issues, Physical aggression, Verbal aggression
    displaced, 213–216
    false, 216, 219–220
    misplaced, 213–215
    overblown, 213, 215

Uncertainty theory, 218–220. *See also* Theories of conflict
Undesired repetitive pattern (URP), 26
Unhealthy trust, 111
Unforgiveness, 177

Venting, ventilation approach, 144–145
Verbal aggression, 32, 52, *See also* Aggressive communication
Vertical thinking, 282
Victimization, 187
Violence, 52–53
Violence cycle, 32–34
Visual journaling, 286–288

Work-life conflict, 249–251
Workplace bullying, 251–255
Workplace conflict, 245
Worldview, 270
    components of, 271
    importance of, 271